ETHNIC LOS ANGELES

ETHNIC LOS ANGELES

ROGER WALDINGER *and* MEHDI BOZORGMEHR

Editors

RUSSELL SAGE FOUNDATION *New York*

The Russell Sage Foundation

The Russell Sage Foundation, one of the oldest of America's general purpose foundations, was established in 1907 by Mrs. Margaret Olivia Sage for "the improvement of social and living conditions in the United States." The Foundation seeks to fulfill this mandate by fostering the development and dissemination of knowledge about the country's political, social, and economic problems. While the Foundation endeavors to assure the accuracy and objectivity of each book it publishes, the conclusions and interpretations in Russell Sage Foundation publications are those of the authors and not of the Foundation, its Trustees, or its staff. Publication by Russell Sage, therefore, does not imply Foundation endorsement.

Library of Congress Cataloging-in-Publication Data

Ethnic Los Angeles / edited by Roger Waldinger and Mehdi Bozorgmehr.
     p.   cm.
    Includes bibliographical references and index.
    ISBN 0-87154-901-8 (cloth : alk. paper) ISBN 0-87154-902-6 (pbk.)
    1. Ethnology—California—Los   Angeles. 2. Immigrants—California—Los Angeles. 3. Pluralism   (Social   sciences)—California—LosAngeles. 4. Los Angeles (Calif.)—Ethnic   relations. 5. Los   Angeles (Calif.)—Race   relations. 6. Los Angeles (Calif.)—Population.
    I. Waldinger, Roger David. II. Bozorgmehr, Mehdi.
    F869.L89A1   1996b
    305.8'00979494—dc20
                  96-20380
                  CIP

Text design by John Johnston.

RUSSELL SAGE FOUNDATION
112 East 64th Street, New York, New York 10021
10 9 8 7 6 5 4 3 2

For Mimi—R.W.
For R.W. and M.K.—M.B.

Contents

III
MAJOR ETHNIC GROUPS

IV
CONCLUSION

Acknowledgments

FINISHING A BOOK generates many pleasures—not least of which is the chance to thank publicly everyone who made this venture possible. At the top of our list stand the organizations that supported this project: the Russell Sage Foundation and the Andrew Mellon Foundation. An equal measure of appreciation goes to the John Randolph Haynes and Dora Haynes Foundation, which funded Roger Waldinger's "Immigrants and the Los Angeles Economy," the fruits of which are largely, though not entirely, reported in this book. We are especially grateful to the foundation officers—Eric Wanner at Russell Sage, Harriet Zuckerman and Stephanie Bell-Rose at Mellon, and Diane Cornwell at Haynes—who saw merit in our plans to study Los Angeles and its ethnic transformation.

Since this book is the product of one of America's great public universities—UCLA—we also wish to thank the people of California: their investment in public higher education propelled UCLA's rise to excellence and their continuing support has been particularly meaningful during the past several years, when the state weathered hard times. The university has further benefited from the generosity of far-sighted and public-minded individuals: we take particular pleasure in acknowledging Ralph and Goldy Lewis, whose gift to UCLA established the Lewis Center for Regional Policy Studies, which in turn has provided our institutional home. We are also indebted to assistance from UCLA's Institute of American Cultures, which provided a small grant that proved invaluable in bringing this project to closure.

Our friends, colleagues, and students deserve equal thanks. Allen Scott and Alejandro Portes encouraged us to pursue this project when it was still in its infant and unfunded stage, and their confidence did much to spur us along. Georges Sabagh was a constant source of sage advice. Vanessa Dingley, who ran the Lewis Center during most of this project's life, heroically managed the complicated financial and administrative sides of our project, while also maintaining a pleasant working environment. Thanks also to Margaret Johnson, who capably took over from Vanessa during the project's waning days. Elisabeth Stephenson and Martin Pawlocki, data archivists at the UCLA Institute for Social Science Research, provided access to data and assistance in using the complex census data files.

We also wish to thank Ali Modarres and Steve Gold, who are contributors to this volume in all but name. Ali designed and produced the original maps that appear in chapter 5 and in chapters 9 through 14. Steve provided the photographs that grace the opening of each part of the book. We are grateful to them for their meticulous work and their good visual sense.

We consider ourselves especially fortunate to have enlisted the help of a particularly talented group of students. Top billing for research assistance goes to Claudia Der-Martirosian and Michael Lichter, whose work in preparing tabulations from the censuses for most of the chapters in this volume went far beyond the call of duty. We extend further thanks to Nelson Lim, who prepared most of our graphs and tables, adding much order and clarity in the process; to Richard Adams, then a post-doctoral fellow at UCLA, who worked with Nelson in preparing the indexes of residential segregation from the 1980 and 1990 censuses; and to Richard Bernard, who worked with the historical censuses reported in chapter 2. Deborah Ho, an outstanding UCLA undergraduate, did a superb job preparing the manuscript, while also helping us to sort out many details. We also express our gratitude to Judy Iriye, a recent Harvard graduate with roots in the Los Angeles region, who made herself available during our last revision, and to Rena Hasenfeld, who provided much needed assistance in editorial fine-tuning.

The choice of reviewers engaged by the Russell Sage Foundation turned out to be a stroke of particular good luck: Janet Abu-Lughod and John Mollenkopf wrote extensive, searching comments on the entire project as well as the individual chapters. Their reactions did much to improve the manuscript, though undoubtedly, their expectations will not be fully met. Steve Gold, David Heer, and Pyong Gap Min were kind enough to comment on individual chapters.

Additional thanks go to the editors associated with Russell Sage, especially Lisa Nachtigall and David Haproff, directors of publications during this project's life, and also Rozlyn Coleman. We send a special note of appreciation to Nina Gunzenhauser, whose copyediting of our large manuscript remains the most meticulous we have ever seen. John Johnson, who has been responsible for text design, did a painstaking job in preparing graphics.

Our last words are directed to our co-authors, who not only lent their interest and enthusiasm to this project, but graciously put up with our numerous requests for revisions. Their colleagueship and continuing friendship are greatly appreciated.

Roger Waldinger
Mehdi Bozorgmehr

Contributors

Roger Waldinger is Professor of Sociology and Director of the Lewis Center for Regional Policy Studies, University of California, Los Angeles.

Mehdi Bozorgmehr is Assistant Professor of Sociology, City College, City University of New York.

Lucie Cheng is Professor of Sociology, University of California, Los Angeles.

William A. V. Clark is Professor of Geography and Chair of the Department of Geography, University of California, Los Angeles.

Claudia Der-Martirosian is completing her doctoral work in sociology at the University of California, Los Angeles.

David M. Grant is a graduate student in the Department of Sociology and a Research Fellow at the Center for the Study of Urban Poverty at the University of California, Los Angeles.

Angela D. James is Assistant Professor of Sociology and a Research Associate of the Population Research Laboratory at the University of Southern California.

John H. M. Laslett is Professor of History, University of California, Los Angeles.

Michael Lichter is a doctoral candidate in sociology at the University of California, Los Angeles.

Ivan Light is Professor of Sociology, University of California, Los Angeles.

David E. Lopez is Associate Professor of Sociology and Chair of the Latin American Studies Program, University of California, Los Angeles.

Melvin L. Oliver is on leave from his position as Professor of Sociology, University of California, Los Angeles, currently serving as Vice-President of Programs for Communities, Families, and Livelihoods, the Ford Foundation.

Paul Ong is Chair of Urban Planning and affiliated faculty of Asian American Studies, University of California, Los Angeles.

Vilma Ortiz is Associate Professor of Sociology, University of California, Los Angeles.

Eric Popkin is a graduate student in the Department of Sociology, University of California, Los Angeles.

Elizabeth Roach is a graduate student in the Department of Sociology, at the University of California, Los Angeles.

Georges Sabagh is Professor Emeritus of Sociology, University of California, Los Angeles.

Allen J. Scott is Professor of Geography and Associate Dean of the School of Public Policy, University of California, Los Angeles.

Edward Telles is Associate Professor of Sociology, University of California, Los Angeles.

Abel Valenzuela, Jr., is Assistant Professor in the Department of Urban Planning and the Caesar Chavez Center, University of California, Los Angeles.

Philip Q. Yang is Assistant Professor in the Department of Ethnic Studies, California Polytechnic State University, San Luis Obispo.

PART

I

INTRODUCTION

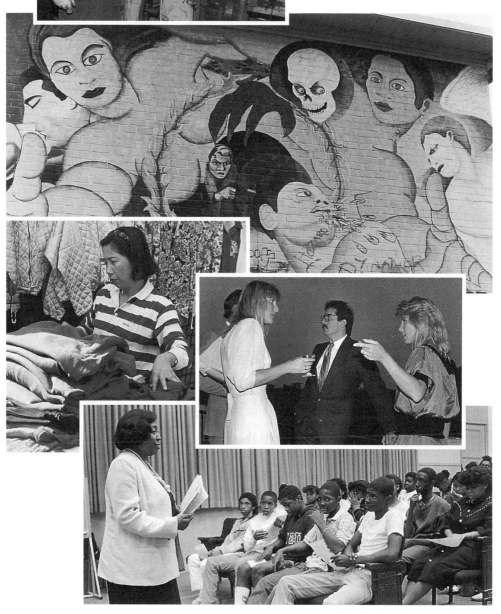

(See photo captions on next page)

The Making of a Multicultural Metropolis

Roger Waldinger and Mehdi Bozorgmehr

THE HISTORY of the Los Angeles region took a new turn on April 29, 1992. On that afternoon, nine jurors—all white, all residing in a white suburban enclave just outside Los Angeles County—acquitted four white officers of the Los Angeles Police Department who had been accused of using excessive force against black motorist Rodney King. Police violence against L.A.'s black and Latino populations was nothing new, but in this case, the beating had been videotaped and then broadcast to the region's teeming millions time and again. Within hours of the jury's action, violent protest engulfed the city's historically African American South Central district; it then quickly spread throughout the region. As the whole world watched, Los Angeles burned.

Was it a riot, as the forces of law and order charged, or a rebellion, as some leaders and spokespersons of L.A.'s Latino and African American communities maintained? Continuing controversy makes it hard to label the events of those days and nights of spring 1992. But what happened then told Angelenos—and everyone else interested in the City of Angels and its environs—that something new, different, and hard to comprehend was occurring under the Southern California sun.

In a sense, the events of April 1992 encapsulated L.A.'s transformation into a few tension-packed days. The African Americans among whom the initial outbursts occurred were quickly joined by their neighbors, who turned out to be new immigrants, mainly from Central America and Mexico. The rioters directed their fury against the local storeowners and landlords, an ethnically diverse group among whom Korean immigrants loomed particularly large. Unlike the Watts riot of 1965, which had remained confined to a fairly narrow area deep in the South Central ghetto, the disturbances of 1992 spread throughout the Southland, as the locals call it. Beverly Hills, Long Beach, Pomona, and even the San Fernando Valley—the very apotheosis of white suburban living circa 1965—saw considerable violence. Meanwhile, Boyle Heights and East Los Angeles, the region's longest-established Mexican American barrio, remained eerily quiet. Witnessing the spectacle on their television sets were the region's Anglos, a diminishing population, many of whom, like the jurors whose decision unleashed the violence, had fled multicultural Los Angeles County for the more homogeneous areas on the region's periphery.[1]

As turmoil exploded among the palm trees, the Los Angeles that the nation had known and fantasized about for most of the twentieth century slipped decisively into the past. Ironically, this Los Angeles of old had always been a different kind of metropolis. Unlike New York, that archrival on the East Coast with its densely packed, polyglot, contentious urbanites, Los Angeles was more a slice of white bread, a settlement of Protestant midwesterners transplanted to an irrigated arcadia on the Pacific shores. Of course, Eden was never quite so blandly homogeneous as white Angelenos imagined. The Spanish had come here first, and though the Hispanic presence waxed and waned over the years, the Mexican-origin population never went away. African Americans found their way to Los Angeles as well, in numbers that grew rapidly in the three decades after 1940. And many Chinese and even more Japanese also made L.A. their home.

But in 1970, the typical Angeleno could be forgiven for looking around and seeing an incredibly dynamic region that was expanding yet ethnically looked much the same as it had for the past seven decades. A mere twenty years later, the images of stores being plundered and houses set afire made it clear that the Southland of old was no more. L.A.'s sudden, profound ethnic transformation is unquestioned; the problem, rather, is how to understand the changes so tightly telescoped into the past two decades. The region's self-invented past and equally distorted self-image clearly get in the way. So too does the unhealthy miasma of anxiety and apprehension released by the severe, unexpected economic decline of recent years. Further complicating the task is the region's aura as the province of fabulists and mythmakers, a setting appropriate for movies and mystery novels—not social science.

But Los Angeles and its people deserve a closer, searching look. California has been a trendsetter for the nation for the past several decades. And nowhere can one detect the shape of emerging America better than in L.A., where newcomers to the United States have transformed the country's second largest metropolis in complex ways and have set the region on a new course sure to be followed by other urban areas.

This volume of scholarly essays sets fears and myths aside to describe the new Los Angeles of the late twentieth century and to explain the scope, characteristics, and consequences of the region's ethnic transition. We tell this story in numbers, using the wealth of information contained in the U.S. population censuses of 1970, 1980, and 1990 to portray the region's ethnic mix in all its complexities. We have organized this volume into four parts. The first part, consisting of the remainder of this introductory essay and a historical chapter that takes the reader from 1900 to 1970, sets the stage for what will follow. Part 2 examines the implications of the region's recent ethnic shifts for the jobs its residents hold, the neighborhoods in which they live, the languages they speak, and the incomes they earn. Part 3 focuses on the new ethnic mosaic itself, with chapters on each of the region's major ethnic groups. The last part sums up the volume's lessons and peers into the future to see where ethnic Los Angeles might be heading.

THE REGION IN BRIEF

There are many L.A.'s: the once-glamorous, now-tawdry Hollywood; Huntington Beach and other affluent areas along the coast; hard-pressed South Central with its old, deteriorating bungalows and dilapidated apartments resembling motels; Moreno Valley and other instant suburbs that have popped up from farmland and desert on the region's periphery. These and all the other L.A.'s fall within the compass of this book. For our purposes, Los Angeles means a five-county region with Los Angeles County at its core, surrounded by Orange, San Bernardino, Riverside, and Ventura counties. Unless otherwise noted in the text, the words *Los Angeles* or *L.A.* or *Greater Los Angeles* will always refer to the Los Angeles region as defined here (figure 1.1).[2]

The Los Angeles region extends over a vast area encompassing 33,210 square miles. With this expanse, the region surpasses all the nation's other major metropolitan areas: It is almost twice as large as the New York and San Francisco metropolitan areas (18,134 and 19,085 square miles, respectively), over twice the size of Chicago and Philadelphia (14,553 and 13,844 square miles, respectively), and four times larger than Miami (8,167 square miles), that other newly minted capital of immigrant America. In this land of freeways, driving distances best communicate the region's urban sprawl: 129 miles separate coastal Ventura on the west from San Bernardino on the hot, arid east, while the affluent seaside enclave of Laguna Beach lies 119 miles south of scorching Lancaster, swollen by Angelenos in search of the affordable suburban dream, which these days usually comes at the expense of a hundred-mile round trip to jobs in the San Fernando Valley. Encompassing beaches, mountains, and deserts, the region varies widely in landscape and climate. On a typical summer day, the temperature ranges from highs in the mid-seventies at the beaches to the mid-nineties in the valleys

FIGURE 1.1 | Los Angeles Region

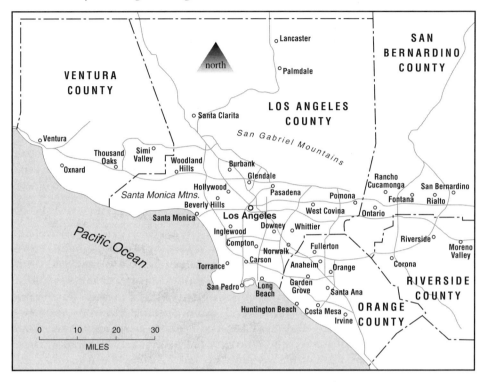

and the low hundreds in the deserts. As long as they forget about their congested freeways, Angelenos can brag that they can swim in the ocean and ski in the mountains on the same day.

Writing about an earlier Los Angeles, the historian Robert Fogelson called L.A. the "fragmented metropolis," a characterization that has proved ever more appropriate as the population has exploded, taking over farmland, desert, and coastal wetlands alike.[3] At the region's epicenter lies the city of Los Angeles, the lineal descendant of *el pueblo de Nuestra Senora la Reina de Los Angeles de Porciuncula,* founded by the Spanish in 1781. Somnolent up until the mid-1850s, the city of Los Angeles then grew rapidly, spreading its tentacles west to the Pacific, south to the harbor in San Pedro, and north to the San Fernando Valley, in the most fabulous land grab of all. But for all practical purposes, the expansion of the city's boundaries came to a halt by the mid-1930s.[4] Thereafter, a profusion of new, smaller cities popped up throughout L.A. County as the population grew and newcomers filled in the once-agricultural land. By the 1960s, the population had spread past the Los Angeles County lines, converting the farms and ranches that occupied the outlying counties into tract developments of unvarying appearance. Initially, the peripheral suburban areas served as bedroom communities for workers commuting to jobs in Los Angeles; by the 1980s, however, analysts detected an "exopolis," a set of new "edge cities" made up of the high technology clusters, office centers, and retail emporia scattered throughout the region's periphery.[5] The economic bust of the 1990s suggests that the region's heyday probably belongs to the past. Even in the doldrums, however, L.A.'s tendency to diffuse toward its outer rings remains in full swing. As this book goes to press, the remaining farms and wetlands in Ventura and Orange counties are succumbing to the developers' bulldozers.

For most of the twentieth century, the Los Angeles region has been home to a fabulous job machine. To be sure, the 1910s and 1920s did not see the region's economy diversify quite as quickly or as extensively as its leaders in real estate and commerce had wished. But the heavy industrial base that developers and business interests so coveted arrived in the 1930s, in the form of branch plants of the tire, steel, and auto giants of the time. The advent of the Second World War then unleashed a fury of growth and, more importantly, transplanted the nascent aerospace industry from the East to the West Coast. The Cold War did the rest, thanks to the robust growth of Southern California's high technology complex, which belonged almost entirely to the Department of Defense.[6] Though natural resources, tourism, and Hollywood—"*the* industry" in local parlance—helped, the region's emergence as the nation's premier concentration of manufacturing jobs accounts for its history of stupendous growth.

A new pattern emerged in the late 1970s and 1980s. On the growth side, the Reagan-era defense build-up kept the high-tech complex alive and well up until the late 1980s. The climate of easy money and the region's attraction to foreign—especially Japanese—capital made for an extraordinary burst of office development. As in other metropolitan areas, the service and finance sectors enjoyed the greatest growth. For a while, Los Angeles—home base to the junk-bond king Michael Milken and the savings and loan financier, Charles Keating, then headquartered in Orange County, later housed in jail—seemed poised to emerge as an international finance complex, smaller than but still rivaling New York. Not all the region's sectors, however, enjoyed equally favorable times: The older, high-paying manufacturing base in non-defense-related durables had begun to erode in the 1970s, and by the early 1990s had been reduced to a fraction of its former self. To some extent, expansion in the region's labor-intensive sectors took up the slack, but these rapidly expanding jobs paid miserably low wages.

Located on the West Coast, far from the nation's historic population concentrations in the East and Midwest, Los Angeles has always depended on long-distance migration for its growth; thanks to its economic dynamism, the region has enjoyed a steady stream of new arrivals. At the turn of the century, the city of Los Angeles was a modest urban concentration of just over 100,000. It then exploded, gaining another 2.2 million residents by 1930. The depression slowed its growth, but the region's demographic expansion took off again with the advent of the Second World War and the years of postwar prosperity. By 1960, Los Angeles County boasted a population of 6 million, making it the second largest metropolis, after New York. Unlike other major urban centers, Los Angeles then kept on expanding, spilling over its historic boundaries as its population burgeoned. As of 1990, the five-county region was home to 14.5 million people—still smaller than the New York region but launched on a growth curve that should leave the Big Apple behind within the next decade or two.

For most of its modern existence, Los Angeles attracted newcomers who were mainly white and native-born. In 1920, just before the close of the last great immigration wave, only 17 percent of Angelenos had been born abroad, as compared with 35 percent of their contemporaries in New York.[7] Despite the region's proximity to Mexico and the ebb and flow of Mexican migration over the years between 1920 and 1965, immigrant Los Angeles remained relatively inconspicuous. More important than any immigrant influx during these years was the large-scale arrival of African Americans, attracted by the region's relatively hospitable race-relations climate and its burgeoning economy.

And then it all changed. What had been a small community of Mexican-born Angelenos—not quite 2 percent of the region's 7.6 million residents as of 1960—suddenly found its numbers growing, and by leaps and bounds. The 1990 census counted 3.7 million Angelenos of Mexican origin, of whom 46 percent had been born abroad. Of course, Mexicans were by no means the only group of foreign newcomers to converge on Los Angeles in massive numbers. Other countries lying south of the border—Guatemala and El Salvador, in particular—sent sizable groups of immigrants to L.A., and Asia emerged as a major sending area as well. In 1990, immigrants made up 27 percent of the region's population and 33 percent of all those living in Los Angeles County.

Other, related demographic trends produced the multicultural, multi-ethnic Los Angeles of today. Not only did the region lose its attraction for the type of native white migrant who used to gravitate west, but its Anglo population steadily deserted Southern California for greener—or perhaps whiter—pastures elsewhere. Since the immigrants were also younger than the natives and their fertility rates were higher, Californians were increasingly likely to be the offspring of the foreign-born. As of 1990, Los Angeles became a region without any ethnic majority, though Hispanics seem likely to hit the halfway mark within the foreseeable future. Since the arrival of foreign-born newcomers lies behind L.A.'s extraordinary ethnic transformation, it is to immigration and the immigrants that we now turn our attention.

THE NEW IMMIGRATION

Unlike New York, Los Angeles is new to its present-day role as an immigrant mecca. While the comparatively late advent of immigration is not a uniquely Los Angeles phenomenon, L.A. has experienced immigration differently from almost all other major urban regions. This section briefly describes the characteristics of the new immigration to the United States and then focuses on those immigrants moving to Los Angeles.

The New Immigration to the United States

Passage of the Hart-Celler Act in 1965 provides the conventional date for the onset of the new immigration to the United States. The 1965 reform transformed the immigration system with a few bold strokes. First, it abolished the old country-of-origins quotas, which allotted small quotas to southern and eastern Europe and still smaller—almost prohibitively small—quotas to Asia. Second, it established two principal criteria for admission to the United States: family ties to citizens or permanent residents or possession of scarce and needed skills. Third, it increased the total numbers of immigrants to be admitted to the United States.[8]

The system established by the 1965 reforms essentially remains in place to this day, despite constant debate and continuous overhauling. But the Hart-Celler Act spawned changes that were entirely different from its advocates' plans. The reformers thought that the new act would keep immigration to modest proportions. But for various reasons the numbers quickly spiraled; 7.3 million new immigrants arrived in the United States during the 1980s, an influx second only to the peak of 8.8 million newcomers recorded during the first decade of the twentieth century. To be sure, at 8 percent, the immigrants constituted a far more modest share of the nation's population in 1990 than was true in 1910, when fifteen of every hundred Americans were foreign-born. Still, the 1990 level represented a substantial increase over the 5 percent level recorded when the foreign-born share of the U.S. population hit its historic nadir in 1970.

A second unexpected twist concerned the act's beneficiaries. The 1965 legislation was principally targeted at eastern and southern Europeans, the groups hardest hit by the nativist legislation of the 1920s. By the 1960s, however, workers from Italy or Yugoslavia had fallen out of the orbit of trans-Atlantic migration. Instead, the newcomers who took advantage of the newly liberalized system came from Asia, Latin America, and countries of the Caribbean.

What no one expected in 1965 was the burgeoning of Asian immigration. The reforms tilted the new system toward immigrants with kinship ties to permanent residents or citizens. There had been very little Asian immigration in the previous fifty years; how, then, could Asian newcomers find settlers with whom to seek reunification? The answer is that kinship connections were helpful but not essential. The 1965 reforms also created opportunities for immigrants whose skills—as engineers, doctors, nurses, pharmacists—were in short supply. Along with students already living in the United States, who enjoyed easy access to American employers, these professionals made up the first wave of new Asian immigrants, in turn creating the basis for the kinship migration of less-well-educated relatives. The system was sufficiently flexible for longer-established groups, like the Chinese, to renew migration streams while also allowing entirely new groups—most notably Koreans and Asian Indians—to put a nucleus in place and then quickly expand.[9]

Political developments added momentum to the migrant flow across the Pacific. Though the 1965 act allowed for a relatively limited influx of refugees, carefully defined to give preference to those fleeing Communist regimes, unexpected pressures repeatedly forced the United States to expand greatly its admission of refugees. The collapse of the U.S.-supported regime in South Vietnam, followed by Communist takeovers in Cambodia and Laos, triggered a sudden, massive outflow of refugees, many of whom settled on the West Coast. The first wave of exiles from the Southeast Asian elite was followed by a larger, more heterogeneous group of refugees in search of sanctuary and a new home in the United States. Thus, the original core of high-skilled immigrants from Asia rapidly grew. By the 1980s, Asia emerged as the number two source area of the foreign-born, accounting for 37 percent of all the newcomers who moved to the United States during the 1980s.[10]

Asian immigrants passed through the front door opened by the 1965 reforms in a variety of ways. Mexicans and later on Central Americans were more likely to come through the back door of unauthorized migration. The immediate roots of Mexican unauthorized migration lie further back, in the Bracero Program begun during the Second World War to eliminate shortages of agricultural workers. Ostensibly, the Bracero Program was destined for a short existence, and the workers it imported were supposed to head back to Mexico after a short stint of temporary labor in the United States. But the influence of agribusiness kept the Bracero Program alive until 1963, and with time, an increasing number of migrants dropped out of the bracero stream, heading for better jobs in Los Angeles, San Francisco, and other urban areas. By 1964, when Congress abolished the program, networks between the United States and sending villages throughout Mexico's central plateau were already in place, providing all the information and connections needed to keep the migrants coming, whether or not they had legal documents in hand.[11]

Once the former braceros abandoned the farm labor stream, the institutional mechanisms of the 1965 act facilitated their passage to legal status. Marriage to a citizen or a legal resident, a change in the legal status of one's sibling, assistance from an employer eager to retain a skilled and valued hand—any one of these was enough to bring about the eventual transformation of yesterday's undocumented worker into today's legal immigrant. Since the newly minted legal immigrant could then bring over those immediate relatives still lingering in Mexico, albeit with some delay, the official statistics show a steadily expanding stream of legal migration from Mexico.

While Mexicans were drawn by the inducements of American employers, the Salvadorans and Guatemalans who headed for the U.S. border in increasing numbers in the late 1970s and afterwards were responding to different factors. Like the Vietnamese, Cambodians, and Laotians, the Central Americans were escaping political unrest, but unlike their Asian counterparts, the Central Americans had the bad fortune to be fleeing right-wing regimes propped up with U.S. government support. Hence, these newcomers mainly moved across the border as unauthorized migrants. As chapter 10 on Central Americans describes, court battles forced the U.S. government to grant some of these refugees temporary asylum in the late 1980s, though the number benefiting from this status has dwindled over the years, and at present the asylum itself seems doomed.

Just how many newcomers have arrived without authorization has long been a matter of dispute; wildly disparate estimates and guesstimates—ranging from 2 to 12 million—are stock-in-trade in the debate. Recently, demographers have settled on a methodology for "counting the uncountable," which has yielded estimates on which most immigration researchers can agree. This methodology suggests an undocumented population of about 2 to 4 million residing in the United States as of 1980, of whom over half had come from Mexico.[12]

Doing something about undocumented immigration has dominated immigration policy debates ever since enactment of the Hart-Celler Act; with the passage of the Immigration Reform and Control Act of 1986, known as IRCA, Congress attempted to close the back door and control this unauthorized flow. IRCA had three major provisions: a so-called general amnesty for undocumented immigrants who had resided continuously in the United States since January 1, 1982; a second, "special agricultural workers" program, inserted at the behest of agricultural interests and with the help of California's then-Senator Pete Wilson, for agricultural workers who had been in the United States for a minimum of ninety days in the year preceding May 1986; and sanctions against the employers of illegal immigrants. In IRCA, undocumented immigrants found at best a "cautious welcome," as Susan Gonzalez Baker concluded, with countless bureaucratic hurdles and anxiety-provoking administrative rules obstructing their path to amnesty.[13] As of 1992, 1.76 million persons had applied for IRCA's general amnesty, alongside approximately 1.3 million persons who used the special agricultural worker option, a program widely known for its openness to fraud and abuse.

As expected, amnesty did diminish the pool of undocumented immigrants. Although Congress designed sanctions, and more stringent border controls were adopted to curb future undocumented flows, these efforts ultimately failed to stem the flow. Unauthorized migration clearly persists, contributing a net increment of 300,000 undocumented entrants each year.[14] The best estimates suggest that the total number of undocumented residents grew by over 50 percent between 1980 and 1992, even though more than 3 million persons had passed from illegal to legal status as a result of IRCA.[15]

Given the many circumstances of migration, it should be no surprise that the newcomers of the post-1965 years are an extraordinarily diverse lot. Though some experts have looked at the educational characteristics of the foreign-born to conclude that the "quality" of America's immigrant streams has gone down,[16] the extraordinary educational differences *among* various immigrant groups suggest that skill levels have gone up *and* down. Highly educated professionals and managers dominate some streams, most notably those from the Middle East, from Africa, and from South and Southeast Asia; among many of these groups, median levels of schooling leave America's native white workers far behind. Manual workers with little schooling predominate among other groups—Mexicans are the most conspicuous example—and the contribution of low-skilled workers to America's immigrant pool has risen substantially in recent years. Those populations with refugee origins tend to be internally diverse, with highly educated immigrants characteristic of the early wave and less-educated newcomers common among those who emigrate in later years. Thus, national origins and skills are inextricably intertwined, a fact of considerable importance for newcomers to Los Angeles and their fate.

Los Angeles and Its Immigrants

Immigrants to the United States have always been urban-bound. While one is tempted to argue that the situation is no different today, the urban attraction is in some sense greater than ever before. In 1910, when immigration from Europe hit its peak, the five largest U.S. cities contained just over a quarter of the nation's 13.5 million foreign-born residents. By 1990, when a different set topped the list of the largest metropolitan regions, just over half the country's immigrants lived in these five largest urban places. Of course, the United States is a more urban society than it was eighty years ago. But relative to total population, the five largest urban places of 1990 are comparable to the five largest cities of 1910 in their share of the foreign-born. Still, geographical concentration remains the salient trait of contemporary immigration.

Comparing Los Angeles with the major immigrant metropoles of the past and present puts the distinctive features of today's immigrant L.A. into relief. Contemporary Los Angeles is home to a far larger share of today's foreign-born population than the immigrant New York of old. Large as it is, Los Angeles contains roughly the same portion of the nation's *total* population as did New York in the early 1900s. Consequently, immigrants are far more overrepresented in the Los Angeles of the 1990s than they were in the New York of the 1910s (see figure 1.2).

FIGURE 1.2 | **Urban Immigrant Concentration, 1910 and 1990**

A. 1910: Five Largest Cities, Share of U.S. Total and Foreign-Born Population

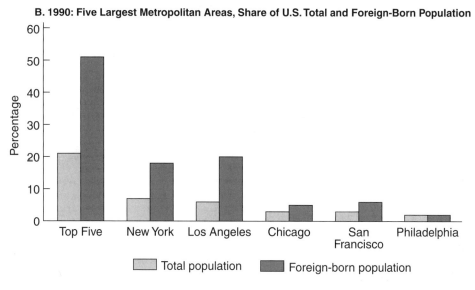

B. 1990: Five Largest Metropolitan Areas, Share of U.S. Total and Foreign-Born Population

In terms of immigrant density, the Los Angeles region, with 27 percent of its population foreign-born, does not quite compare with turn-of-the-century New York, 40 percent of whose residents had been born overseas. But as we reduce the geographical scale, going first to Los Angeles County, at 33 percent foreign-born, and then the city of Los Angeles, at 37 percent foreign-born, the resemblance to the older immigrant pattern becomes increasingly clear. Since 1990 already lies several years in the past, one can be sure that L.A.'s immigrant density has increased in recent years, moving the city closer to the type of immigrant city that seemed to belong to the dim past.

Impressive in these retrospective comparisons, contemporary Los Angeles also stands out from today's other major immigrant areas in more ways than one. In 1990, Los Angeles was home to 3.9 million immigrants, 400,000 more than New York, which stood in second place. In foreign-born proportion, its population outranked that of almost every other major U.S. city by a good degree; only much-smaller Miami, where 34 percent of the region's population comes from abroad, pulls ahead of L.A. on this count. L.A. also exceeded the others as a magnet for the very recently arrived; the immigrant wave of the 1980s made up 13 percent of the region's population, as opposed to 4 percent for the United States as a whole.

The advent of immigrant density also took place more suddenly in Los Angeles than almost anywhere else, Miami excepted. As we have already noted, the region's population leaped from 8 to 27 percent immigrant between 1960 and 1990, adding 3.3 million foreign-born residents in the process. By contrast, the other major metro areas had long served as entries for the foreign-born; hence, the new, post-1965 arrivals replaced an aging, dwindling mass left over from the earlier European immigrations.

In a sense, the key to understanding immigrant L.A. is the border and its proximity to the City of Angels. In 1990, more than half of L.A.'s post-65 adult immigrants came from three countries alone—Mexico, El Salvador, and Guatemala—with Mexico accounting for the great bulk of this group (see figure 1.3). Since many of these newcomers, as we have noted, entered the United States through the back door, L.A.'s role as the principal magnet for migrants from Mexico and Central America meant that it attracted far more than its share of unauthorized immigrants. The Los Angeles region accounted for a third of all the undocumented immigrants estimated during the 1980 census and roughly the same proportion of the population who obtained amnesty under IRCA. Despite the large number of amnesty applications, which temporarily diminished the number of unauthorized immigrants living in Los Angeles, the undocumented population continued to grow in the late 1980s and early 1990s.

Elsewhere, immigrant origins are far more scrambled. New York's new immigrant population, for example, is extraordinarily diverse. Dominicans constituted the single largest group counted in the 1990 census, and they

FIGURE 1.3 | 1990 Foreign-Born Population, by National Origin and Decade of Immigration

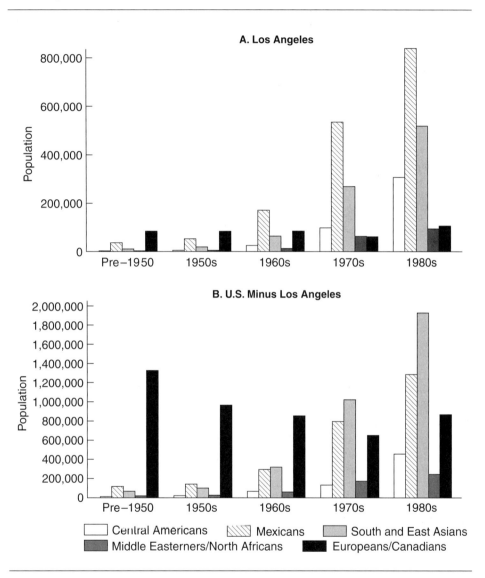

accounted for just over 13 percent of the new immigrant arrivals. Chinese were the next largest, with 9.7 percent of new arrivals, followed by Jamaicans, with just over 6 percent; no other foreign country accounts for more than 5 percent of the new immigrant arrivals. Although other immigrant cities are less diverse than New York, none approaches the Mexican/Central American dominance characteristic of L.A., Miami excepted. In this respect, the top immigrant cities more closely resemble the pattern for the United States as a whole, where Mexico, El Salvador, and Guatemala account for 25 percent of the foreign-born total.

Attractive as it may be for Mexicans and Central Americans drawn by the lure of *el norte,* Los Angeles also exerts its magnetic pull on Asia, the principal—though by no means unique—source of its high-skilled foreign-born arrivals. Starting from a relatively small base in 1970, the Asian population skyrocketed; as immigrants from China, the Philippines, Korea, Vietnam, and India (in that order) poured into the region, Asians emerged as L.A.'s third largest group, outnumbering the previously established African American population. The newcomers transformed Los Angeles into the capital of contemporary Asian America, pushing it well beyond the other major Asian American centers of New York, San Francisco–Oakland, and Honolulu. With the exception of the Vietnamese and the much less numerous Cambodians and Hmong, the new Asians became a source of extraordinarily high-skilled labor, importing schooling levels that left natives far behind as well as other endowments like capital and entrepreneurial talents that gave them a competitive edge.

Although they were the largest group, the Asians were not the only group of middle-class immigrants to gravitate toward L.A. New arrivals from the Middle East, many of them professionals and/or entrepreneurs, also converged on Los Angeles, yielding the largest regional concentration of Middle Easterners in the entire United States.

The newcomers to L.A. come from all walks of life, but the very distinctive national origins of L.A.'s immigrants means that its foreign-born mix is characterized not by diversity but by socioeconomic polarization. Elsewhere in the United States, as figure 1.4 shows, the educational profile of the foreign-born tilts toward the better educated; college graduates are as common among immigrants as among the native-born. In Los Angeles, immigrant ranks are weighted down by the prevalence of newcomers with little or no schooling, a reflection of the size and skill characteristics of the region's large Mexican and Central American populations.

Thus, the making of immigrant Los Angeles is the convergence of two broadly different types of migration streams. The combination of high- and low-skilled immigrants alters the conventional story of immigrant adaptation, as we shall now see.

ASSIMILATION AND ITS PROSPECTS

At the top of the immigration research agenda stands the question of how the newcomers change after they have arrived. The conventional wisdom,

FIGURE 1.4 | Years of Education Completed, Foreign-Born Population 18 Years and Older, 1990

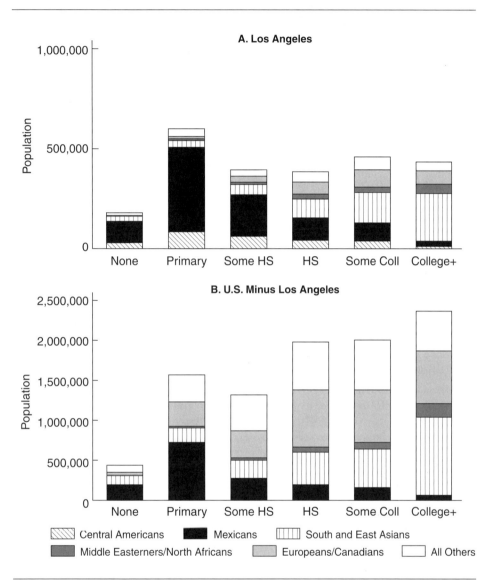

both academic and popular, says that immigrants *should* change by entering the American mainstream. The concept of assimilation stands as a shorthand for this point of view.

The traditional paradigm of ethnic assimilation began with two crucial assumptions: first, that immigrants arrived as "ethnics," and second, that they started at the bottom and gradually moved up. From these premises it followed that groups were most distinctive at the point of their entry into American society. Over time, the immigrants and their children would advance up the pecking order, narrowing the economic gap. Economic progress would yield cultural convergence; the newcomers and their offspring would give up their old country identities and cultural orientations as they increasingly resembled other Americans.[17]

Although it retains its defenders, assimilation theory no longer shapes the direction of current immigration research. The best-developed line of attack contends that the assimilation model works much better for some groups than for others. "Straight-line" theory does seem to fit the trajectory of European origin groups.[18] For Americans of European ancestry, nowhere has assimilation worked better than in Los Angeles. As chapter 14 shows, ethnicity among the region's whites appears to have melted under the California sun. Few traces of earlier differences persist; most have been lost in extensive mixing among whites of various ethnic backgrounds.

In general, the historical experience of immigrants of non-European origin requires a different approach. In straight-line theory, ethnic disadvantages ease and then gradually fade with the passage of time. But trends have followed a different path among the groups of non-European origin. In some cases—for example, Mexican Americans—time has worked less effectively, as chapter 9 will show. In part, the Mexican American lag reflects persistently lower skills, but it also results from an opportunity structure that rewards Mexican Americans less well than native whites. The Asian American experience in Los Angeles comes closer to the assimilation model of gradual convergence with native whites, but its historical background is one of much greater and more persistent disadvantage. And though the relatively small population of native-born Asians (mainly Chinese and Japanese) generally does very well, chapter 11 suggests that Asian Americans are not sharing the same rewards as their native white counterparts.

The latest wave of immigration to the United States confronts the assimilation framework with an additional, indeed thornier set of problems. The classic assimilation trajectory projects great initial difference that then narrows over time. That assumption made good sense at the turn of the century, when immigrants were a relatively homogeneous population narrowly concentrated at the bottom of the occupational scale. At the time, domestic servants and general laborers dominated the ranks of immigrants; one could assume that newcomers were similarly low-skilled and therefore entered at the bottom.[19]

But the immigrant situation at the end of the twentieth century looks very different because of the social and economic diversity among the newcomers who move to Los Angeles. A good number of the highly skilled, often college-educated immigrants who have made L.A. their home begin, not at the bottom but in the middle class or beyond, as will be recounted in chapter 11, on Asians, and chapter 12, on Middle Easterners. Though ethnic studies usually focus on the downtrodden, the hidden story of today's immigration is the large number of newcomers who find themselves in a far more elevated status. In contemporary Los Angeles, such coveted occupations as medicine, dentistry, and various engineering and computer specialties have become immigrant niches. When else do we find a parallel in American ethnic history?

This starting point reverses the tenets of assimilation theory, since now the newcomers often start out close to parity with native whites, if not actually ahead. Consider the transformation of Beverly Hills, known globally for its movie stars but locally for its more recent evolution as the capital of the Iranian exile elite.[20] A still-better case is that of Monterey Park, a small city just east of downtown Los Angeles, which emerged in the late 1980s as the nation's first suburban Chinatown, thanks in part to the marketing efforts of a clever Chinese real estate developer who sold affluent Taiwanese on the idea of moving to the "Asian Beverly Hills." The ethnographer John Horton reported that

> in this middle-class suburb . . . [a]n elderly white resident expressed a frequently heard complaint: "Before, immigrants were poor. They lived in their own neighborhoods and moved into ours after they learned English, got a good job, and became accustomed to our ways. Today, the Chinese come right in with their money and their ways. We are the aliens."[21]

While Monterey Park's sudden evolution seemed unusual to its established native white residents, it marked the beginning of a trend. Today, Monterey Park is just one piece in a growing belt of Asian middle-class suburbs in the western parts of Los Angeles County.

Many immigrants leap right into the middle class, not only because they import skills or capital but also because of their premigration exposure to American culture and American styles of living and making money. Part of the story involves the relentless spread of the mass media and the globalization of American culture; acculturation now begins before the newcomers ever move to the United States. But some newcomers are likely to arrive more acculturated than the rest, as chapter 5, on language, shows. Filipinos and Indians, for example, grow up in English-proficient environments. Others—Iranians, Israelis, Taiwanese, and Koreans—have moved through school systems in their home countries that gravitate toward the U.S. orbit. Many come to the L.A. region as students, motivated by the dream of returning home with a prestigious U.S. degree; years later, they discover that they have stayed for the duration. Still other immigrants, most notably the Taiwanese, come as entrepreneurs, extending transoceanic business networks. What- ever the precise nexus connecting the region to the home societies from which its immigrants come, that linkage makes today's newcomers more "American" right from the start than were their predecessors of a century ago.

That the region's well-to-do immigrants begin with advantages does not mean that they compete on equal terrain. Middle-class Iranians, Koreans, and Chinese do better than the average white Angeleno, but they do not surpass their similarly educated white counterparts. The same proficiencies and skills yield better rewards for whites than for immigrants, as we shall see in the chapters on Middle Easterners and Asians. Consequently, the de- bate over immigrants' progress runs into complexities foreign to the sim- pler assimilation framework. Yes, the high-skilled immigrants are doing well, the argument goes, but having run into a glass ceiling, they do not do as well as they *should*. It is not clear what normative expectations inform that "should"; is it reasonable to anticipate that the foreign-born—as op- posed to their children—will ever catch up with comparably schooled na- tives? Would such a forecast be in line with the historical record? However one answers these questions, the controversies engulfing the concept of "model minority"—dissected in chapter 11—illustrate the difficulties in ana- lyzing the adaptation of the region's more successful newcomers.

As for those immigrants who start out at the other end of the skill spec- trum, many of L.A.'s newcomers seem to resemble their turn-of-the-century counterparts; at first glance, the ex-*campesinos* from Mexico or El Salvador can be seen as the functional equivalents of the Slovaks, Poles, or Italians of yesteryear. But a closer look induces caution. If assimilation theory as- sumed a gap between natives and low-skilled newcomers, the disparity be- tween "Anglos"—regional parlance for whites—and Mexican or Central American immigrants has grown to a yawning divide. Historians, for exam- ple, point to contrasting literacy rates as an indicator of skill differences at the turn of the century; in 1910, 61 percent of Italian immigrants aged ten or over were literate, as opposed to 95 percent of comparable native white descendants of native-born parents.[22] However dramatic this contrast may seem to historians, it pales alongside the disparities that we find in contem- porary L.A. Take the case of completion of primary education. It was virtu- ally universal in 1990 among native whites, but among the region's immi- grant Latinos, one out of ten adults had no formal schooling at all, and an additional four out of ten had advanced no further than the eighth grade. One might argue that these initial deficits can and will be overcome with time. But the evidence that will unfold in the chapters to come presents a different, more somber picture. Latino immigrants have become more, not less, likely to live and work in environments that have grown increasingly segregated from whites. Relative to earlier arrivals, the most recently arrived newcomers are lagging ever farther behind Anglos. And the transformations in the region's economy—the burgeoning of its low-wage sector, the attenuation of its high-wage manufacturing core, the expansion of its knowledge-intensive industries—create structural obstacles to moving beyond the initial low-level placements that the immigrants have achieved.

To all this we should factor in a final trait that sets today's immigration apart from earlier immigration histories—and from the intellectual attempts to understand those experiences. In a sense, the assimilation paradigm derives from the historically specific circumstances under which newcomers from Europe moved to and settled down in the United States. Whereas the immigrant waves from the Old World did bring extraordinarily large numbers of people to the U.S. shores, they lasted for limited periods of time. Immigration from northern and western Europe, for example, reached its peak before 1880 and then went into eclipse, in part because accelerated industrialization in the Old World kept would-be emigrants at home. The large-scale exodus from southern and eastern Europe similarly lasted for about forty years; in this case, the triumph of U.S. nativism, not home-country development, stopped the immigrant flows.

But the cessation of immigration, not its causes, is what counts for patterns of ethnic adaptation. Once the flow of newcomers stopped, old-country influences declined. As the immigrant presence weakened and diminished, the second generation moved to center stage, shifting out of the jobs, neighborhoods, and cultural institutions that the foreign-born had established. The assimilation paradigm tells the story of this particular sequence of generational succession.

That pattern stands at some remove from the contemporary scene. While contemporary immigration from Latin America and Asia is adding to a long-established population base, by their numbers the newcomers' overshadow the smaller second- and third-generation components. Mexicans and Asians are fragmented populations, made up of recent immigrants commingled with the descendants of earlier waves (see figure 1.5B). Fragmentation is particularly characteristic of Los Angeles, home to foreign-born populations that are proportionately larger than elsewhere in the United States (see figure 1.5A).

More important still is the fact that the large foreign-born population is newly arrived. Angelenos of Mexican birth constitute the longest-established, best-settled of the region's newcomer groups. But even among the Mexican-born, half came to the United States between 1980 and 1990. Other immigrant groups are equally, if not more heavily, tilted toward the recently arrived; 53 percent of the region's Middle Easterners, 59 percent of its Asians, and 70 percent of its Central Americans moved to the United States during the 1980s.

The prevalence of recent arrivals means that for many if not most of

FIGURE 1.5 | **Distribution of Generations in Major Ethnic Groups, 18 Years and Older, 1990**

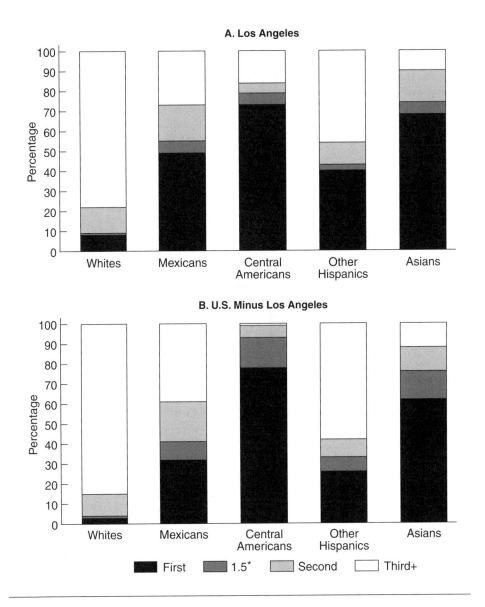

*Immigrated at age 10 or younger

the region's immigrants the process of assimilation has only begun. And the future holds more of the same. With immigration on the upswing, the "foreign-ness" of L.A.'s newcomer population will surely grow. Granted, time will push longer-established immigrants in the direction of assimilation and acculturation. But any continuing influx of large newcomer cohorts will certainly slow that process, and not just by maintaining an active link to the culture and language of the immigrants' home country. Growing numbers of immigrants will retard the process of diffusion out of established residential and occupational enclaves. They are also likely to yield changes in the behavior of native-born Angelenos, who have already begun to leave the region and whose continued exodus will produce lower rather than higher levels of ethnic mixing.

A future of continuing high levels of immigration also complicates the analytic tasks. Generation provides the master concept in the analysis of assimilation; with each succeeding generation the descendants of the immigrants move further and further away from the values, orientations, and identities of their ancestral forebears.[23] While native-born Mexicans, Chinese, and Japanese have moved down the road toward assimilation, as subsequent chapters will show, one must be wary about extrapolating from these experiences the prospects for the children or grandchildren of today's immigrants. As of this writing, Mexican, Chinese, and Japanese American adults still include the offspring of an earlier, much smaller immigration. Most importantly, they came of age at a time when the foreign-born presence did not loom so large and the region's economy was strong—conditions unlikely to hold for the children of today's immigrants.

In a sense, the analyst suffers the problems of the still photographer trying to capture a moving target. As we shall see in chapter 4, on residential change, the data show that the region's neighborhoods have greatly changed. Twenty years ago, Angelenos lived with people of their own ethnic kind; today, they live with neighbors of increasingly diverse origins. But is today's diversity a stable arrangement, or is it simply a stage in the evolution of a new type of homogeneity, in which most residents will be foreign-born? The answer lies largely in the size and attributes of tomorrow's immigration, characteristics that cannot be accurately predicted.

Of course, the prospects for ethnic Los Angeles do not hinge on the immigrants alone. Just how the newcomers change will depend a good deal on whether they succeed in moving ahead. But optimism about immigrants' progress is tempered by concern over the structural shifts under way in the region and in American cities at large. While immigrants join a much larger group of Angelenos imperiled by the urban economic transformations of the late twentieth century, their advent complicates the adjustments to the challenges of the 1990s.

ETHNICITY AND OPPORTUNITY IN LOS ANGELES

If L.A.'s transformation from Iowa-on-the-Pacific to a multicultural metropolis has been more rapid than similar transitions in other urban areas, the scope and direction of change remain roughly the same. Like other metropolitan areas, L.A. now has a "majority minority" population, along with an economy that increasingly tilts toward higher-level service-sector jobs. Hence, the question of how L.A.'s population base fits into its evolving economy ranks high on the research agenda.

For the first half of this century, the nation's large urban areas worked as staging grounds for the integration of unskilled newcomer groups. Not only did cities have large concentrations of low-skilled jobs, but they had an industrial structure that allowed for upward movement based on the gradual acquisition of skills on the job. Low-skilled migrants could get jobs and slowly start the climb up the occupational ladder; with modest effort their children could count on surpassing the attainments of their parents.

But an influential set of writings, associated with such well-known researchers as William J. Wilson and John Kasarda, tells us that this scenario no longer holds. According to these authors, the postindustrial transformation of late-twentieth-century America has robbed urban areas of their absorptive capacity. Changes in technology and communications, argues John Kasarda, decimated the "traditional goods-processing industries that once constituted the economic backbone of cities, and provided entry level employment for lesser skilled African Americans." In return for the eroding factory sector, cities have gained a new economy dominated by "knowledge-intensive white-collar service industries that typically required education beyond high school and therefore precluded most poorly employed inner city minorities from obtaining employment.[24] Thus, on the demand side, the "very jobs that in the past attracted and socially upgraded waves of disadvantaged persons . . . were disappearing"; on the supply side, the number of "minority residents who lack the education for employment in the new information processing industries [was] increasing."[25] In part, the burgeoning ranks of low-skilled workers reflected the advent of African American baby boomers; in part, it resulted from the renewal of mass immigration and the arrival of poorly schooled newcomers. But whatever the precise source of demographic change, it boded ill for urban America and its future.

While this perspective has been enormously influential and has provided the underpinnings for the "underclass debate," it sheds little light on Los Angeles and its ethnic groups. From an empirical standpoint, the basic facts about the area's population and economic changes do not fit with the tenets of the skills-mismatch hypothesis just outlined. To begin with, the story of industrial decline—whether of light manufacturing in New York and Philadelphia or of the auto and steel industries in the cities of the Great Lakes—has no ready parallel in Los Angeles. As chapter 8 shows, employment in L.A.'s goods-producing sector has followed an upward course for most of the postwar period. Admittedly, Los Angeles can now boast a "rust-belt" of its own, thanks to the demise of its auto and auto-related branch plants and the more recent erosion of its aerospace and defense sector. But manufacturing decline has come rather late in the day, and more importantly, the industries that have suffered the recent declines never provided much employment shelter to L.A.'s minorities.

A second problem concerns the interactions between supply and demand. The mismatch hypothesis began as an account of the economic problems of black men, and it is in that context that it has remained most compelling. In Los Angeles, as in other cities, the economic position of African American men has indeed changed for the worse; an increasing proportion of the region's black males are either out of work or have dropped out of the labor force entirely. But as will be seen in chapter 13, African Americans in Los Angeles are far better schooled than the recently arrived but more commonly employed immigrants from Mexico and Central America. The region's abundance of goods-producing jobs suggests that manufacturing decline is the wrong culprit for the deteriorating fortunes of less-educated black men. And black males enjoyed only limited success in gaining access to the factory sector in the first place, so they stood less exposed than others to the dislocation associated with any industrial decline.

Of course, as immigration has made urban populations increasingly diverse, the mismatch hypothesis has been recast; in this updated incarnation, the population mismatched with the urban economy is now an undifferentiated aggregate of everyone classified by the government as nonwhite. In this form, the mismatch hypothesis is fundamentally at odds with the immigrant phenomenon that has so dramatically transformed L.A. If indeed the region's employers are hiring none but the highly educated, why has the region emerged as the choice immigrant destination, particularly for newcomers with the lowest skills?

An oft-cited answer, and one more in keeping with the region's specific experience, suggests that immigration is part of a fundamental process of urban economic restructuring, in which the growth of services breeds a demand for both high- *and* low-skilled labor while increasingly excluding workers with middle-level qualifications. In this view, the postindustrial transformation of American cities yields service industries with a bifurcated job structure, offering both high wages and stable employment for highly educated workers and low wages and unstable employment for less-skilled workers displaced from manufacturing. The result is an increasingly high level of inequality. Job arrangements in the service sector also lack well-developed internal labor markets, with the result that low-skilled workers, whether new entrants to the labor market or displaced workers from manufacturing industries, have few opportunities for upward mobility.

Restructuring, so the argument goes, works in dynamic relationship with immigration. By creating jobs for people with low skills, it also creates the demand for workers willing to work at low-status, low-paying jobs. While such low-wage jobs are increasingly found in the advanced services, the simultaneous proliferation of high-paid service workers adds further to the demand for immigrant workers. Once in place, the immigrants provide a cheap, easily managed labor force that can bolster the declining goods-producing sector and help revive sagging urban economies.[26] Thus, unlike the mismatch hypothesis, the restructuring hypothesis tells us that urban areas retain abundant, perhaps even increasing numbers of easy-entry jobs. The downside of the restructured metropolis is not the paucity of starting places, as in the mismatch view, but rather the absence of better jobs or developed mobility paths that would let the newcomers get ahead.

Even skeptics will admit that the restructuring hypothesis enjoys at least some validity when applied to Los Angeles. As we have noted, Los Angeles has become a favored place for the lowest-skilled among the nation's new arrivals. The region's massive absorption of immigrants has paralleled an equally great shift in its industrial structure: Low-wage, immigrant-dominated manufacturing industries have flourished, continuing to do well even in recessionary years, while high-wage, high-value-added manufacturing has foundered in a twenty-year-long state of decline. But there is more to this story, as chapter 8 shows; a new cultural division of labor is emerging, along with a widening high-wage/low-wage gap, and Hispanic immigrants are increasingly split off from the rest of the manufacturing work force in a tier of poorly paid jobs. Evidence of the linkage between restructuring and immigration need not be limited to manufacturing. Chapter 10, on Central Americans, for example, underlines the centrality of low-level service work for this recently arrived population; among Guatemalans and Salvadorans, one of every four works as a private servant, janitor, maid, or cook. For some groups, the immigrant job ceiling also appears to be very low—indeed, getting lower over time. Chapter 9 shows that the wage gap between Mexican immigrants and native whites has increased over time. The emergence of an hourglass economy may also provide the best explanation for the limited occupational attainments of the region's native-born Mexican Americans, a population that will expand rapidly in the very near future.

While it is a useful guide to the impact of changes in opportunity structures, the restructuring hypothesis is nonetheless incomplete. It offers a more plausible explanation of the immigrant convergence on L.A. than the mismatch hypothesis, but it treats the foreign-born as an undifferentiated mass, whereas the newcomers are highly diverse, not just in original characteristics but in the social and economic experiences they undergo once in L.A. How immigrants do is influenced by the endowments they bring with them, and here the fact that Los Angeles has been the destination for a large group of highly skilled, sometimes affluent professionals and entrepreneurs is an especially important consideration. An adequate analysis must deal with the emergence of a large, diversified immigrant middle class, the growth of a variety of ethnic economies, as well as the expansion of the immigrant working class and a burgeoning lower class, with foreign- and native-born components.

More importantly, the restructuring hypothesis neglects the economic problems of blacks. As an explanatory framework, it shares the deficiencies of the mismatch approach, starting from the premise that workers are matched to jobs on the basis of skill. This assumption begs the question of why so many low-level jobs go to the newest arrivals from abroad and not to African Americans. And it forecloses the possibility of labor-market com-petition—between immigrants and various native groups and among differ-ent immigrant groups themselves.

In the end, both mismatch and restructuring approaches tell a story of impersonal structures inexorably working on an inert urban mass. In our view, by contrast, the historical transformations of L.A.'s economy yield a set of parameters for adaptation within which groups might follow a variety of possible paths. Seen in this light, the ethnic division of labor in L.A.'s economy represents a social arrangement, responding to broader economic forces but shaped by the various groups that make and maintain the struc-tures of the region's economy.

As we have seen, L.A.'s ethnic groups differ from the outset. But they also vary in the historical context of incorporation, a point that directs our attention to the interaction between structures and groups. Because ethnic incorporation is a social process, seemingly similar groups get sorted into different positions. The contrast between Mexican and Central American immigrants nicely illustrates the point. As groups, both tend to cluster at the bottom tier of the region's economy, but not necessarily in the same positions. Domestic service, for example, which counts as a sector of high Central American concentration, employs a relatively low proportion of Mexicans, whereas agriculture, which still ranks high in the Mexican pro-file, has absorbed few Central Americans.

In the aggregate, individual cases of clustering yield distinctive occupa-tional or industrial patterns. These patterns are measured with the index of dissimilarity (D), which reveals, for example, the percentage of Central Americans who would have to change jobs in order to have the same occu-pational distribution as Mexicans. While detailed discussion of the many sets of Ds will have to await the individual chapters, the reader can count on a wealth of evidence pointing to the central role of ethnicity in the or-dering of L.A.'s economy. Clear lines of ethnic demarcation show up not just among lower-skilled groups like Mexicans or Central Americans but among groups that are more likely to work in upper-tier positions—for example, the variety of Middle Easterners discussed in chapter 12. And in some cases, the economic disparities among groups conventionally gathered under the same ethnic rubric are large enough to bring the category itself into question, a theme that emerges from chapter 11, on Asians.

Ethnic economic distinctiveness often reflects the development of an ethnic niche, an occupational or industrial specialization in which a group is overrepresented by at least 50 percent. Ethnic networks sort workers among jobs, with the result that groups move into distinctive places in the labor market and then maintain those concentrations over time, albeit at varying rates of persistence.[27] The burgeoning of L.A.'s ethnic economies exemplifies this process, which we can trace through the development of initial specializations and then the diffusion of ethnic entrepreneurs into related occupations and trades. Chapter 7, on self-employment, illuminates the economic singularities in this classic ethnic niche. Not all groups move into entrepreneurship at equal rates; consider the contrast between Mexicans, among whom roughly seven out of every hundred men are self-employed, and Iranians, among whom one of every three men is working on his own account. Sorting also occurs among the most entrepreneurially active groups; the Chinese, for example, have carved out a niche in high-tech and advanced services, such as engineering services and data processing, while the Koreans concentrate in traditional middleman minority lines.

Business represents one classic ethnic niche, public employment another. In Los Angeles, as in most other American cities, the search for opportunity and mobility has taken African Americans deeply into the public sector. As chapter 13 shows, the black experience in government illustrates both the tendency toward concentration and its consequences: Just six government functions, each providing wages well above the region's average, employ 13 percent of the region's black work force.

In the conventional wisdom, convergence in niches is a transitory experience, limited to the first generation and then abandoned as later generations move up and diffuse through the occupational structure. Even the first generation is likely to spill over beyond the boundaries of the niche, since few economic specializations seem large enough to absorb a continuing influx of new arrivals.

But in Los Angeles, as in other metropolitan areas, ethnic concentration turns out to be an enduring element of the economic scene. Ethnic carrying capacity naturally differs from one industry or occupation to another; still, many of the groups studied in this book concentrate in some relatively small set of specializations. Nor does clustering inevitably diminish over time; the African American convergence on government employment has increased substantially in recent decades. The public sector seems a likely destination point for second-generation Mexicans as well as for Asians, who have already established notable concentrations in a variety of government functions. And the group most concentrated of all turns out to be L.A.'s U.S.-born Jews, who have clustered in a particularly favorable set of postindustrial niches, as chapter 14 will show.

If ethnic ties pull one group of categorically distinctive workers into a set of occupations or industries, they may also lead to crowding, as the newest arrivals cluster in the very same activities that engage more established workers. Indeed, the prevalence of intragroup job competition seems to be the one point of consensus in the massive econometric literature on the subject, a finding consistent with the description in chapter 9 of the deteriorating economic prospects of Mexican immigrants. Conversely, ethnic sorting could also bar the route to others, in which case L.A.'s massive immigrant population might have gained jobs that would otherwise have gone to the region's native-born, an argument developed by several authors in this book, most notably Paul Ong and Abel Valenzuela. But one could also imagine a scenario in which ethnic networks bring in a new group of low-ranked outsiders, enabling a previously established group to jump up the ladder; it is precisely this pattern that appears to characterize the interaction between Latina immigrants and black women workers.

In the end, events on both supply and demand sides have probably reduced the region's ability both to absorb newcomers and to propel its residents up the occupational ladder; in this respect, the turn-of-the-century urban pattern seems unlikely to recur in late-twentieth-century Los Angeles. But if changes in demography and economy have limited the possibilities for some portion of L.A.'s myriad ethnic groups, they have not done so in the deterministic way that the literature often suggests. Since ethnicity turns out to be crucial in understanding who gets which jobs in L.A.'s economy and why, we can count on diverging ethnic fates as the region's cultural division of labor evolves.

ABOUT THIS BOOK: ORGANIZATION, CONCEPTS, AND MEASURES

A few words are needed to explain how this book is organized and to provide a brief, nontechnical overview of some of the recurrent themes and measures. Harold Rosenberg once described New York intellectuals as a "herd of independent minds," and some such combination of intellectual autonomy and collectivity applies to the authors who have written this book. While the authors here all thought and studied at the same institution (the University of California at Los Angeles) and frequently exchanged ideas and papers as this project evolved, the book should not be read as a group statement. Rather, it is a collection of closely related but still independently authored papers, which do not necessarily adhere to a single line. Similarly, the reader should be warned that the introductory and concluding chapters do not so much represent the collective wisdom of the group as express the views of the editors (first Roger Waldinger and Mehdi Bozorgmehr jointly, and later Waldinger alone) and their understandings of the lessons to be distilled both from the chapters in the book and from the data on which those chapters are based.

All the authors agree, however, that Los Angeles is in the throes of an unprecedented ethnic transformation, largely brought about by immigration, with enduring consequences for all aspects of the region's life. We also agree that the job of understanding the ethnic changes underway in Los Angeles is fundamentally a comparative enterprise, in which the relevant contrasts are both external and internal, involving, on the one hand, whites—the socially, if not numerically, dominant group—and, on the other, any of the various subgroups that get lumped together under the conventional ethnic labels.

These essays also share an assumption about what the word *ethnic* denotes when attached to the name of a place, as in *Ethnic Los Angeles*. For our purposes, *ethnic* is an adjective that refers to the culture, language, history, or religion of a category of people. By contrast, when linked to the noun *group,* the word *ethnic* implies that members have some awareness of their distinctive cultural characteristics and historical experiences and that they share a sense of attachment to or identification with the group.[28] In this book, we begin with the understanding that what is ethnic about Los Angeles is the proliferation of people sharing common historical experiences and linked through a set of connections that promote regular patterns of interaction. Consequently, we focus on the subcultural dimensions of ethnicity—that is to say, the social structures that bind an ethnic group, attaching members to one another and either circumscribing or promoting their interactions with outsiders. These social structures consist, broadly speaking, of two parts: (1) the networks around which ethnic communities are arranged, and (2) the interlacing of those networks with positions in the economy and space.

Seen from this perspective, the social structures that bind an ethnic group are in part a matter of choice, in part a matter of constraint. It follows, therefore, that race is a special case of the broader ethnic phenomenon, in which the degree of separation from others is mainly, if not entirely, imposed by outsiders; members of a racial group may wish to work or live together or marry one another but have few options to do otherwise if they so prefer. In this sense, Irving Kristol's famous article "The Negro of Today Is Like the Immigrant of Yesterday"[29] got the issue right, although the interpretation was largely, if not completely, wrong. As their subtitles indicate, the chapters on the population of Mexican origin and on Central Americans suggest that today's newcomers might be headed toward a dead end, a trajectory quite different from that followed by their predecessors, and one that would move these groups closer to a situation of a racial kind.

By contrast, the chapter on African Americans, emphasizing the development of *two* black L.A.s that differ considerably in their options for work and residence, argues that at least some component of this population is moving to a situation of a more conventional ethnic kind.

Our approach also implies that the relevant categories are not given but constructed. Ethnic groups are made by insiders interacting with outsiders under conditions not of their own making. Here, we are engaged in a simpler, though certainly debatable, enterprise of applying labels for the purposes of comparing and contrasting. We make no claim that our labels reflect the ways in which the various peoples of Los Angeles see themselves; we do believe that our categories are sensible, given the work we have set out to do and the danger of proliferating groups into an intractable number. Of course, we are not free to combine people into groups as we choose; given our reliance on census data, we have to work with the various ethnic categories developed by the Census Bureau over the past decades. These categories have their virtues, most notably a growing accuracy in identifying persons who might be members of minority groups. They also have their faults, including the tendencies to pigeonhole people into groups that make no sense, as when persons originating from any part of Asia that lies west of Pakistan get turned into whites, and to deny ethnic categories the fluidity they possess. Readers interested in details about census definitions and how they are used to create the groups we examine are urged to consult the technical appendix to this book.

We have organized the book to take two passes at the region's changing ethnic configuration. The first, consisting of a series of thematic essays, surveys a set of topics holistically, seeking to understand the pattern of social and economic changes among many, if not all, of the region's major groups. In the second pass, we look at the major groups one by one. While the authors do not march in lockstep fashion with one another, our focus on the social structures of ethnicity has led us to cover a series of recurring topics in roughly similar ways, allowing readers to attempt their own comparisons. Here, of course, the potential for comparison is constrained by our own assessment of which groups deserve special scrutiny and how those groups should be defined. Considerations of numbers, relevance, and the space available in this book dictated our choice: Seeking to focus on the most important groups, with importance usually defined in terms of size, we have devoted individual chapters to the Mexican-origin population, to Central Americans, to Asians, to Middle Easterners, to African Americans, and to Anglos and white ethnics. Mexicans make up the largest of the region's immigrant groups; they are dominant among Latinos, who in turn rank second, after whites, among the region's ethnoracial groups (see chapter 3, figure 3.3). Since the Mexican-origin population is also split, roughly in half, between native- and foreign-born components, and since native/foreign differences are considerable and command our attention, it seemed appropriate to devote a separate chapter to Central Americans, a recent, rapidly growing, and immigrant-dominated group. Asians rank third among the region's ethnic groups, albeit as an extraordinarily varied collection differing by nationality and birthplace, of whom only the Chinese exceed the Salvadorans in numbers. African Americans fall into fourth place among the region's major groups; the Middle Easterners are the last. Although a hodgepodge of different nationality and ethnic groups, the Middle Easterners possess a basic social and economic commonality, and their immigration has given Los Angeles the largest Middle Eastern concentration in the United States. In view of the historic importance of ethnic differences among whites, we have devoted a final chapter to a comparison of subgroups within the region's European-origin population.

The group chapters use a series of common indicators designed to examine the social structure of L.A.'s ethnic groups in terms of specialization and rank. These indicators are described briefly in the paragraphs that follow; further detail and clarification are provided in the technical appendix to this book.

Specialization refers to the horizontal dimension of ethnic social structure; here, the emphasis is on the boundaries that distinguish one group from another. One convenient way of thinking about ethnic distinctiveness is to begin with those boundaries that lie closest to the self and then move outwards. In a recurrent note of discontent, our authors complain that the census tells us nothing about ethnic self-concept or identity. It does, however, provide information on the ethnic structures of a reasonably intimate relationship, namely marriage, and our first indicator is the traditional measure of ethnic in- and out-marriage or intermarriage. For example, a raw in-marriage rate tells us that 24 percent of Russian-ancestry women aged 25–34 years are married to comparably aged Russian-ancestry men. While informative, this raw rate tells us much less than the whole story, since the Russian-ancestry population is small, and Russian-ancestry men are a relatively rare element in the pool of marriageable men and therefore available in limited supply. To compensate for this problem, we also calculate the *odds ratio* of in- to out-marriages, which, after adjusting for differences in group size, shows that Russian-ancestry women are thirty-eight times more likely than other women to marry Russian-ancestry men. By contrast, in-marriage rates are identical among comparable English-ancestry women, but since the English-ancestry population is so much larger, English-ancestry women are only six times more likely than other women to marry English-ancestry men.

Since personal relationships often arise in a local context, residential patterns constitute another component of the horizontal dimension of ethnic social structures.[30] We are interested both in differences in the distribution of groups over space and in the way in which those distributions affect the types of in- and out-group contacts available within neighborhood settings. The *exposure index* (P*) measures how likely members of a *subject group* (for example, Salvadorans) are to be exposed either to members of a *target group* (let us say, Mexicans) or to their own group. This measure is dyadic and ranges between zero (no likelihood of contact) and one (certainty of contact). P* is also an asymmetric measure, since differences in the relative size of groups affect the likelihood of contact. For example, the Salvadorans, a small group, tend to have frequent exposure to Mexicans, yielding a relatively high score of .36 on P*; Mexicans, a very large group, have relatively little likelihood of contact with Salvadorans, which produces the very low P* score of .03.

The *index of dissimilarity* (D) is like the exposure index in that it ranges between 0 and 1, but it measures the degree of difference between the distributions of two groups. As of 1990, the index of residential dissimilarity in the Mexican/Salvadoran case stood at .54, indicating that the residential patterns of these two groups overlap to a considerable extent, despite the differences in contact probabilities. More precisely, D tells us that 54 percent of the region's Mexican population would have to move to have the same distribution as the region's Salvadoran population. Unlike P*, D is a symmetric measure; consequently, full integration of the region's Mexican and Salvadoran residents would require 54 percent of the region's Salvadoran population to move.

We also use the index of dissimilarity (D) to describe the ethnic division of labor, the way in which groups are sorted among occupations and industries. The same interpretation that is used for residential dissimilarity applies when D is used to describe the degree of difference between occupational or industrial distributions. The *ethnic niche* is the concept that we apply to identify the distinctive occupational or industrial clusters that groups develop. For the purposes of this book, a niche is an occupation or an industry in which a group is overrepresented by at least 50 percent. For example, blacks constitute 6.6 percent of all employed persons in the region but 12 percent of all janitors; dividing the black share of janitors (.12) by the black share of total employment (.06) yields an index of representation of 1.8, which makes janitors a black occupational niche.

One could argue that the ethnic division of labor involves issues of rank more than specialization. Indeed, the traditional approaches to the adaptation of ethnic groups assumed that segregation in the labor market was a transitory phenomenon, associated with initial disadvantage and transcended as groups moved ahead and diffused throughout the economy. Since we make no such assumption, contending instead that ethnic niches may be either temporary or durable and that ethnic group mobility may take the form of either diffusion or persistent concentration, we think of the ethnic division of labor as pertaining to the horizontal dimension of ethnic social structures. Nonetheless, ethnic niches clearly differ in the quality of the jobs they contain, and we use several straightforward indicators to show how one group's niches compare with another's.

The vertical dimension of ethnic social structures concerns the degree of ethnic inequality; in pursuing this issue, we repeatedly ask how well the various groups of ethnic outsiders are doing relative to the region's dominant ethnic group, native whites. For the most part, those comparisons use simple descriptive statistics that require no further elaboration. But efforts to measure ethnic economic disparities often involve a two-part question: First, we want to know how much of the difference is due to the fact that a given group has not yet caught up to native whites on some crucial ingredient to economic success, such as education. Second, we want to know how the disparity might change if there were no background differences among persons of the same gender, so that the average Mexican American male, for example, had the same education as the average native white male. To answer these questions, we first look at *raw earnings* among persons with at least $1,000 of earnings in the year prior to the census and then compute their *adjusted earnings,* assuming that members of a group had the same background characteristics as native whites of the same gender.

Not all the group chapters use all these indicators, since their authors have quite rightly varied in their decisions as to which aspects of ethnic social structure deserve greater emphasis. Still, there is sufficient uniformity for the reader to make an informed judgment about the shape of ethnic differences in contemporary Los Angeles. We invite the reader to do so and then see how this assessment compares with our own appraisal, which appears in the concluding chapter to this book.

Notes to Chapter 1

1. For an assessment of the civil unrest of 1992 and its implications, see the essays in Mark Baldassare, ed., *The Los Angeles Riots: Lessons for the Urban Future* (Boulder, Colo.: Westview, 1994).

2. This definition is identical to the Census Bureau's definition of the Los Angeles Standard Consolidated Statistical Area.

3. Robert M. Fogelson, *The Fragmented Metropolis: Los Angeles, 1850–1930,* 2nd ed., (Berkeley: University of California Press, 1993).

4. Major annexations ceased after 1927. Though many smaller additions were subsequently made, almost all involved relatively small parcels, varying from less than one acre to one hundred acres. As the population mushroomed, the city also experienced numerous secession efforts, generally unsuccessful, with the great exception of West Hollywood, which became a separate municipality during the 1980s. See Winston W. Crouch and Beatrice Dinerman, *Southern California: A Study in Development of Government for a Metropolitan Area* (Berkeley: University of California Press, 1963), chapter 6.

5. Edward Soja, "Los Angeles, 1965–1992: From Restructuring-Generated Crisis to Crisis-Generated Restructuring," in Allen Scott and Edward Soja, eds., *The City: Los Angeles and Urban Theory at the End of the Twentieth Century* (Berkeley: University of California Press, forthcoming); Joel Garreau, *Edge City: Life on the New Frontier* (New York: Doubleday, 1991); Rob Kling, Spencer Olin, and Mark Poster, *Postsuburban California: The Transformation of Orange County since World War II* (Berkeley: University of California Press, 1991), chapter 1.

6. Allen J. Scott, *Technopolis: High-Technology Industry and Regional Development in Southern California* (Berkeley: University of California Press, 1993), 13–14.

7. The data for Los Angeles apply to the region; in Los Angeles County, the foreign-born share of the population was half a percent higher.

8. David Reimers, *Still the Golden Door: The Third World Comes to America* (New York: Columbia University Press, 1985).

9. The same trajectory was followed by other groups—various Middle Easterners and Africans—with the result that the immigrant population diversified to groups that had never previously made the United States their home.

10. Calculated from *1991 Statistical Yearbook of the Immigration and Naturalization Service* (Washington, D.C.: Government Printing Office, 1992).

11. Ernesto Galarza, *Merchants of Labor: The Mexican Bracero Story* (Santa Barbara, Calif.: McNally and Loftin, 1964); Douglas Massey, et. al., *Return to Aztlan* (Berkeley: University of California Press, 1988).

12. Robert Warren and Jeffrey Passel, "A Count of the Uncountable: Estimates of Undocumented Aliens Counted in the 1980 United States Census," *Demography* 24 (1987): 375–93.

13. Susan Gonzalez Baker, *The Cautious Welcome: The Legalization Programs of the Immigration Reform and Control Act* (Santa Monica, Calif.: Rand Corporation, 1990).

14. Barry Edmonston and Jeffrey Passel, "The Future Immigrant Population of the United States," in Edmonston and Passel, eds., *Immigration and Ethnicity: The Integration of America's Newest Arrivals* (Washington, D.C.: The Urban Institute, 1994), chapter 11.

15. Robert Warren, *Estimates of the Unauthorized Immigration Population Residing in the United States, by Country of Origin and State of Residence: October 1994* (Immigration and Naturalization Service Statistics Division, 1994), 30.

16. See George J. Borjas, *Friends or Strangers* (New York: Basic, 1990). Borjas argues that educational levels among immigrants have declined over the past several decades.

17. Milton Gordon, *Assimilation in American Life* (New York: Oxford University Press, 1964); Nathan Glazer and Daniel P. Moynihan, *Beyond the Melting Pot* (Cambridge: MIT Press, 1969).

18. Herbert J. Gans, "Second-Generation Decline: Scenarios for the Economic and Ethnic Futures of the Post-1965 American Immigrants," *Ethnic and Racial Studies* 15 (1992): 173–92.

19. Richard Easterlin, "Immigration: Social and Economic Characteristics," in S. Thernstrom, ed., *Harvard Encyclopedia of American Ethnic Groups* (Cambridge: Harvard University Press, 1980).

20. Ron Kelley, "Wealth and Illusions of Wealth in the Los Angeles Iranian Community," in Ron Kelley, Jonathan Friedlander, and Anita Colby, eds., *Irangeles: Iranians in Los Angeles* (Berkeley: University of California Press, 1993), 247–73.

21. John Horton, *The Politics of Diversity: Immigration, Resistance, and Change in Monterey Park, California* (Philadelphia: Temple University Press, 1995), 20–21.

22. Calculated from Susan Cotts Watkins, ed., *After Ellis Island: Newcomers and Natives in the 1910 Census* (New York: Russell Sage Foundation Press, 1994), 376.

23. Richard Alba, *Ethnic Identity* (New Haven: Yale University Press, 1990).

24. John Kasarda, "Cities as Places Where People Live and Work: Urban Change and Neighborhood Distress," in Henry Cisneros, *Interwoven Destinies: Cities and the Nation* (New York: Norton, 1993), 82. The article we are citing here provides a particularly succinct and clear expression of Kasarda's views, which he has elaborated in many publications over the past fifteen years or so. For other examples, see his "Entry-Level Jobs, Mobility, and Urban Minority Employment," *Urban Affairs Quarterly* 19 (1984): 21–40; "Jobs, Mismatches, and Emerging Urban Mismatches," in M.G.H. Geary and L. Lynn, eds., *Urban Change and Poverty* (Washington, D.C.: National Academy Press, 1988, 148–98; "Structural Factors Affecting the Location and Timing of Urban Underclass Growth," *Urban Geography* 11 (1990): 234–64. William J. Wilson, a still more prominent mismatch proponent, liberally cites Kasarda's findings and endorses his views, in his influential book, *The Truly Disadvantaged* (Chicago: University of Chicago Press, 1987).

25. Kasarda, "Cities as Places," 83.

26. Saskia Sassen, *The Mobility of Capital and Labor* (New York: Cambridge University Press, 1988); *The Global City: New York, London, Tokyo* (Princeton: Princeton University Press, 1992); Bennett Harrison and Barry Bluestone, *The Great U-Turn* (New York: Basic Books, 1988).

27. Though using the term "special niches," Stanley Lieberson similarly argues that "most racial and ethnic groups tend to develop concentrations in certain jobs which either reflect some distinctive cultural characteristics, special skills initially held by some members, or the opportunity structures at the time of their arrival" (*A Piece of the Pie* [Berkeley: University of California Press, 1980], 379). He then notes that "such specialties can only absorb a small part of a group's total work force when its population grows rapidly or is a substantial proportion of the total population"—a contention not supported by the evidence in this book. For a formulation analogous to ours, see Suzanne Model, "The Ethnic Niche and the Structure of Opportunity: Immigrants and Minorities in New York City," in Michael Katz, ed., *The Historical Origins of the Underclass* (New York: Princeton University Press, 1993). Model operationalizes a niche as a "job" in which the "percentage of workers who are group members is at least one and a half times greater than the group's percentage in the labor force" (164). For a further discussion of the ethnic niche and its consequences, see Roger Wal-

dinger, *Still the Promised City? New Immigrants and African-Americans in Post-Industrial New York,* (Cambridge: Harvard University Press, 1996).

28. William Petersen, "Concepts of Ethnicity," in S. Thernstrom, ed., *Harvard Encyclopedia of American Ethnic Groups* (Cambridge: Harvard University Press, 1980).

29. Irving Kristol, "The Negro of Today Is Like the Immigrant of Yesterday," in Peter I. Rose, ed., *Nation of Nations: The Ethnic Experience and the Racial Crisis* (New York: Random House, 1972); Kristol's essay originally appeared in the *New York Times Magazine* in 1966.

30. We recognize that there is also a hierarchical dimension to the diffusion of groups across space, since localities differ widely in the amenities and resources they provide.

Historical Perspectives: Immigration and the Rise of a Distinctive Urban Region, 1900–1970

John H. M. Laslett

IN LESS THAN a hundred years Los Angeles was transformed from a small, largely Hispanic backwater into a huge multicultural metropolitan region. Focusing on the period between 1900 and 1970, this chapter is intended to explore modern Los Angeles' cultural and economic roots, to disentangle its ethnic and racial complexity, and to provide the reader with a historical understanding of the structural changes that occurred as the city grew.

By 1970, Los Angeles was on the brink of becoming America's second largest and most prosperous conurbation and aspiring to be a world city to which others would look as a successful example of multicultural diversity. But that image hid a darker side. By this time, for reasons which we shall explore, L.A. appeared to be just as culturally fragmented as—if not more so than—any other major American city. It possessed an accumulation of ethnic, racial, and class tensions that belied its public image and was forcing it to come to terms with the painful legacy of a segregated and stratified past. Two serious race riots, one in 1965 and the other in 1992, have shown that the city still has not resolved these issues; some even doubt that it can.[1]

This chapter attempts to couple the story of the arrival and subsequent history of several of the city's most important ethnic and racial communities with a description of the spatial and economic factors that both shaped and interacted with the city's ethnoracial order. Lack of space precludes a detailed account of all the racial and immigrant groups who settled in Los Angeles during this period or an extensive analysis of the internal life of their communities. Because the Koreans, the Filipinos, and the

Pacific Islanders who today play such a prominent part in the city's life did not arrive in large numbers until after 1970, little will be said about them here; they will be discussed in chapter 11.

In ethnoracial terms, this account begins with an examination of the early status of the indigenous Mexican community (that is, those born in California) and its relations with incoming Anglos and blacks. Chinese immigrants, as well as first-generation Japanese *(issei)*, had little contact with Anglo Americans at the turn of the century, so they are treated as separate groups. A description of the arrival of small groups of "new European immigrants" in downtown Los Angeles in the late nineteenth century leads into a discussion of the cultural conflict that developed during and after the First World War between the hundreds of thousands of socially conservative Anglo Americans who migrated to Southern California from the Midwest, on the one hand, and African Americans, other Angelenos of color, and Jews, on the other.

The argument here is that it was the class and cultural gap that opened up in the 1920s between the Protestant midwesterners and newcomers of color, as well as Catholics and Jews, that largely determined the uneasy set of racial and ethnic relations between Anglos and others that persists in Los Angeles to this day. Attention will also be paid to the cultural implications of the city's peculiar structure as an urban agglomeration and to the ethnically distinct ranches and farms that existed inside the city limits up to the Second World War.

Geographically, the focus will first be upon the twenty-eight square miles of the city's original downtown. Attention will then be given to the suburban islands of middle-class Anglo Americans that developed before and after the First World War outside the original Plaza area but still within the boundaries of the present-day city of Los Angeles. These suburban islands are contrasted with the ethnically discrete agricultural zones that filled up the broad interstices between them until the 1950s.

After the rapid industrialization of the 1930s and 1940s, L.A.'s residential neighborhoods spilled out still farther across Southern California's coastal plain. In recent years, they have spread into Los Angeles, Orange, and several other counties. Instead of simply linking the new suburban islands that had emerged after the Second World War, however, the new areas that attached themselves to the built-up portions of Southern California in the 1970s and 1980s evolved into a new urban form. Today, Los Angeles taken as a whole is no longer a city in the conventional sense at all. Instead, it has become a metropolitan region of multiple centers connected by freeways. Los Angeles' early building blocks—city, suburb, and agricultural zone—have amalgamated into one vast urban agglomeration.[2] Since the last of these developmental stages took place mostly after 1970, however, little attention will be devoted to it here.

ETHNIC MIXING IN EARLY DOWNTOWN, 1900–1940

Despite the land booms of the 1880s, in 1900 business and ethnic life in Los Angeles was still largely confined to the tiny original downtown area (see figure 2.1). Social and economic life revolved around the original Plaza and its daily market or around the nearby cluster of Mexican stores, hostelries, blacksmiths, and harness-making shops, which coexisted uneasily with recently constructed modern office buildings. The Anglo Americans who lived here nicknamed the Plaza neighborhood "Sonoratown," for a group of Mexican miners who had settled there after being forced to leave the Sierra goldfields three hundred miles to the north.[3] Other incoming Anglos, even more contemptuous in their recently won political dominance, called the neighborhood "Los Diablos," in reference to the "social banditry" practiced by those Mexican immigrants and longtime residents who resented the ethnic slurs, land grabs, and other forms of injustice practiced upon them by vigilantes and by competing Anglo businessmen.[4]

The outstanding social fact of the early downtown era, however, which lasted from 1880 until the 1920s, was not social conflict and ethnic segregation but rather racial mixing and relative tolerance. Admittedly Chinatown, which had been founded in the late 1860s in the area around First and Main streets, was cut off from social and business interaction with the other parts of downtown. But along the edge of the Los Angeles River, behind the Plaza, many other ethnic groups lived side by side. Near the Plaza area, for example, was the city's largest Russian colony, consisting of several hundred émigré members of the Molokan religious faith.[5] During the 1880s, nearby Boyle Heights became the center of a large, flourishing Jewish community, its focal point Brooklyn Avenue. Mixed in along the downtown streets were Italian groceries, African American blacksmith shops, Irish saloons, and German *Turnvereine* (gymnastics clubs). One commentator, noting several German breweries in the emerging Little Tokyo district, said that the area should have been called Little Berlin instead, because Germans "were the largest single nationality in the district."[6]

Scattered widely among these small clusters of Europeans, Asians, and blacks, the native Mexicans were divided into distinct economic groups. Those original *Californios,* who had settled in the Plaza area during the Spanish and Mexican periods and had not lost their land to the incoming Anglos, became small ranchers and tradesmen in the neighborhoods near downtown. On the other hand, some of the early waves of poor Mexican peasants, miners, and railroad workers, who had migrated north from Mexico in the late nineteenth century to escape Porfirio Diaz's repressive regime, became artisans and skilled workers, particularly in the furniture, garment, and building trades.

But in the early twentieth century, most poor Mexican immigrants to

FIGURE 2.1 | **Territorial Expansion of the City of Los Angeles, 1880–1930**

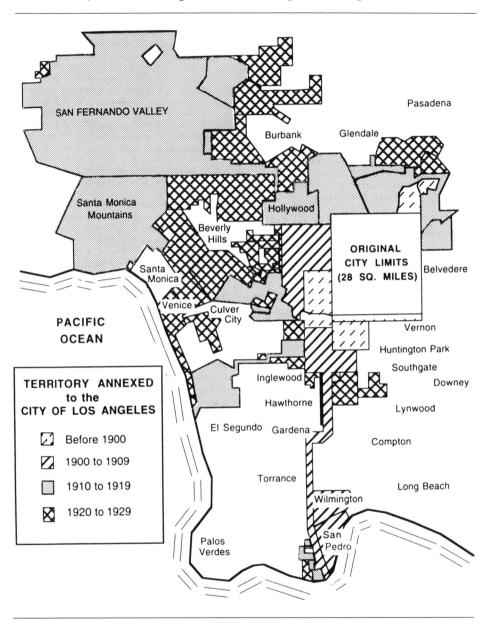

Source: George J. Sanchez, *Becoming Mexican-American: Ethnicity, Culture and Identity in Chicano Los Angeles, 1900–1945* (New York: Oxford University Press, 1993), 89.

Los Angeles (who at first came in at a rate of no more than a few hundred per year) either became construction workers or toiled as farm laborers and seasonal harvesters in the rural areas between downtown and the outlying suburbs. Despite these class distinctions, no clearly defined or segregated Mexican barrio existed in East Los Angeles at this time. Figure 2.2 shows just how widely spread the Mexicans remained throughout the downtown area right up until the 1920s. One local bureaucrat proclaimed in 1912, "There is no spot which we can call 'Mexican Villa' or 'Little Mexico.' "[7]

The growing number of Japanese immigrants—who with a population of 4,238 by 1910 outnumbered several European ethnic groups—also fared relatively well during this period. Like the Chinese, the Japanese suffered from the stigma of the "yellow peril," a stigma made worse by the cutting off of Japanese immigration in 1907, the Alien Land Acts of 1913 and 1920, and the denial of citizenship that resulted from the immigration act of 1924. But in the early 1900s most of the Japanese in downtown Los Angeles were the owners of small businesses, employing fellow immigrants as workers. Few *issei* at this time were employed by non-Japanese.[8]

A group that was somewhat better off in Los Angeles than in the South or in most eastern cities at this time was the African Americans. The superior attraction of Los Angeles as a destination for migrating blacks is reflected in the 1910 census, which shows that 83 percent of all black Angelenos had migrated from elsewhere, compared with only 59 percent of all whites. Migrating blacks also preferred to settle in Los Angeles rather than in Oakland or San Francisco in this period. Hence the numbers of African Americans scattered about in the downtown area, as well as in places like South Pasadena, rose from 2,131 in 1900 to 15,579 in 1910, when blacks made up about 3 percent of the city's total population. In 1913, W. E. B. DuBois proclaimed to a largely black crowd at Temple Auditorium on behalf of the NAACP, "Out here in this matchless Southern California there would seem to be no limit to your opportunities, your possibilities."[9]

The period from 1900 to 1920 was labeled the golden age of black Los Angeles for several reasons. One was easier access to housing and land. The 1910 census revealed that 36 percent of blacks in L.A. owned their own houses, compared with 2.4 percent in New York City and 11 percent in New Orleans. Another factor was the relatively high proportion of incoming blacks who secured jobs as teachers, tradesmen, and pharmacists or who worked as fairly high-status sleeping car porters for the Southern Pacific Railroad. While newspaper advertisements often exaggerated the employment opportunities open to blacks, most of whom worked as domestics or unskilled laborers just as they did elsewhere, the local African American press was quick to jump on evidence of growing black entrepreneurship in L.A.[10]

The centerpiece of the African American community in the downtown area was Central Avenue. By 1915, "the Avenue" was the main thoroughfare

FIGURE 2.2 | Areas of Mexican Residence in Downtown Los Angeles, 1880–1920

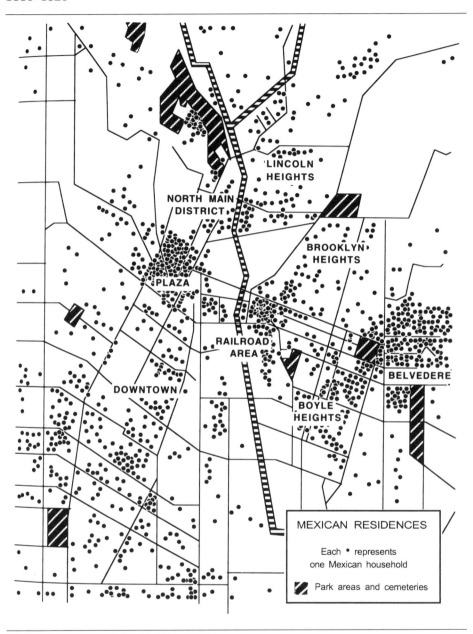

Source: George J. Sanchez, *Becoming Mexican-American: Ethnicity, Culture and Identity in Chicano Los Angeles, 1900–1945* (New York: Oxford University Press, 1993), 73.

of black Los Angeles; its focal point was 9th and Central, later moving south to 12th and Central. Some even thought of Central Avenue as a miniature Harlem, where musicians and literati took the pulse of the community by day and read poems and performed jazz at night. Others proudly noted the offices of black physicians and businessmen. More thoughtful commentators, however, also pointed to the overcrowded homes and apartments to the north and south of the area, as well as to the poverty of migrants recently arrived from the South, which testified to the color line and to the fact that by 1917 racially exclusive housing covenants, intended to confine blacks, Mexicans, and other people of color to limited areas, were beginning to spring up in the western and southern parts of the city. This move toward segregation also affected public education among both Mexicans and blacks. For example, a 1926 survey showed that six out of ten public schools in the emerging Mexican area of Belvedere were more than 90 percent Hispanic.[11] For all its ethnic intermingling, the downtown era in Los Angeles was far from racially harmonious.

Table 2.1 provides a picture of ethnic and racial Los Angeles as it grew between 1870 and 1920. By 1919, both city and county were about to experience the greatest and most rapid expansion that any American metropolis has ever known. L.A. County's population grew from 936,000 in 1920 to 2,208,000 in 1930.[12] The fact that the incoming, mostly native-born Anglo American population did its best to separate itself off from *all* downtown immigrants and ethnics by settling on the west side or leapfrogging south to Long Beach or farther west to Santa Monica was another sign that the so-called era of good feelings—which had never really encompassed Mexicans and Asians—was rapidly passing.

Table 2.1 reveals some of the other special features that distinguished L.A.'s immigrant population from that of most eastern cities in this period. The outstanding fact was the rare *combination* of Mexicans, African Americans, Europeans, and Asians that made up the city's population in this period as well as later on. Although there were a number of Chinese in New York and a few Mexicans in Chicago and Detroit, no other U.S. city possessed quite the same ethnic mix as Los Angeles did at this time. By contrast, L.A. had almost half as many Hispanics as European-born immigrants, as well as substantial groups of Asians and African Americans.

Table 2.1 also shows the somewhat peculiar configuration of the Anglo American community in Los Angeles in the early years of the century. The small number of Irish-born immigrants in the city differentiated L.A. in important ways from cities like Boston and Chicago, not least in its political life. There were no true political machines in Los Angeles comparable to those in the East. And unlike eastern industrial cities like Pittsburgh, Los Angeles in 1920 had a population of "old European immigrants" from Great Britain, Germany, and France that outnumbered the 117,706 "new immigrants" from southern and eastern Europe—specifically, from Italy and

TABLE 2.1 | African Americans and Foreign-Born by Selected Country of Origin, Los Angeles County, 1870–1920

	Mexico[1]	Great Britain	Ireland	France	Germany	Russia	Italy	China	Japan	African American
1870	1,886	113	471	317	635	48	60	233	N/A	149
1880	1,721	843	725	603	1,075	69	249	1,144	N/A	870
1890	493	2,198	1,322	724	2,767	73	447	1,831	40	1,202
1900	817	3,746	1,720	993	4,023	293	763	1,885	152	2,419
1910	5,632	9,584	3,878	1,916	9,604	4,758	3,802	1,481	3,931	6,821
1920	21,653	14,287	4,932	2,685	10,563	9,775	7,931	1,792	8,536	8,841

SOURCE: William S. Rossiter, *Increase in Population in the United States, 1870–1920, Census Monograph*, No. 3 (Washington: GPO, 1922), 243–49, 281–82.
1. It is hard to explain the reasons behind the drop in the number of Mexicans in 1890 and 1900 because the U.S.–Mexican border was extremely porous at the time, and as a result these numbers are estimated.

Russia. By this time, virtually all these older European immigrants had become either tradesmen or middle-class professionals.[13]

RED CARS, AUTOMOBILES, AND THE
RISE OF SUBURBAN ISLANDS, 1910–1930

Before the turn of the century, few native-born whites migrating across America chose to come to Los Angeles. Early train travel from the East was arduous and expensive, municipal water and other amenities were rarely available outside of downtown Los Angeles, and the appeal of alternative western destinations like Denver or San Francisco was greater. But after the mini-booms of 1904–06 and 1910–13, newspaper advertising and propaganda efforts that had been conducted by real estate companies and by Los Angeles boosters in the East finally began to pay off. They were assisted by several adventitious events: the discovery of oil near downtown by Edward Doheny in 1892, the completion of the Owens River Aqueduct to the San Fernando Valley by the engineer William Mulholland in 1913, and the creation of the Pacific Electric interurban system by Henry E. Huntington between 1902 and 1911.

The discovery of oil in the 1890s brought a series of spectacular oil booms to the area, culminating in the opening of the giant Signal Hill oilfield south of downtown, which turned San Pedro from a quaint multi-ethnic fishing village of Japanese, Italians, Portuguese, and Croatians into the world's largest oil port. The aqueduct led to rapid real estate development. It brought adequate supplies of water not just to the San Fernando Valley but to millions of acres of land throughout the Los Angeles basin as a whole. The result, before and after the First World War, was one of the largest, most profitable, and most sustained land booms in American history. The rise in values in a boomtown like Glendale, for example, where land sold for $2.50 an acre in 1906 and for $1,500 a lot in 1908, was created by the magic of promotion and the availability of water.

Little of this growth would have been possible without the last of the adventitious developments noted above, the creation of the famed Red Car system, formally known as the Pacific Electric Railway Corporation, which was completed in 1911. But it was the growing availability of the automobile before and after the First World War that did more than anything else to consolidate and fill out the new system of suburban islands. Expanding the electric railway's radial lines of settlement, the automobile increased accessibility to new real estate sections that had been bypassed by the railroad. It served locations far from the Red Car railway stations, and it opened up foothills in the Santa Monica and San Gabriel mountains that had hitherto been inaccessible.[14]

The establishment of these suburban islands separates Los Angeles' postwar development from the period before 1917. These suburban entities must, in turn, be distinguished from the small cities outside L.A. proper that have been mentioned. Whereas places like Long Beach and Glendale had by this time acquired their own businesses and downtowns, as well as a separate sense of identity, the new suburban islands were at first little more than isolated housing tracts that sprang up at the end of one or another of the Red Car system's newly established lines. Not until in the 1930s did most of them develop a full range of their own services.

Some of the Anglos who rushed in to fill up Southern California's new suburban islands in the 1910s and 1920s were first- or second-generation European immigrants from downtown who had benefited from the city's growing prosperity and could now afford to move out to Long Beach or Santa Monica to take advantage of bigger lots and an ocean view. But a great many were Anglo newcomers who migrated to Los Angeles in this period, especially from the rural states of the American Midwest (see table 2.2). The number of migrants from Illinois between 1920 and 1930, for example, jumped from 38,064 to 72,933. Many of these midwesterners, according to one observer, were "retired farmers, grocers, Ford agents, hardware merchants, and shoe merchants. . . . Toil broken and bleached out . . . they flocked to Los Angeles, fugitives from the simple inexorable justice of life, from hard labor and drudgery, from [the] cold winters and blistering summers of the prairies."[15]

The suburban islands these midwesterners flocked to—many of which, like Glendale, subsequently became independent municipalities—were not unique to Los Angeles. Highland Park in Detroit and River Oaks in Houston, for example, were also legally independent suburbs completely surrounded by large cities.[16] What distinguished L.A.'s suburban islands and added to the city's unique ethnic and racial character was the economic importance of the agricultural zones that surrounded and enveloped the islands, especially in the San Gabriel and San Fernando valleys. These zones were not, for the most part, residual areas of subsistence agriculture left over from the Spanish/Mexican period. They were modern, labor-intensive "factories in the fields" that employed migrant Mexican workers who usually harvested or canned a single crop. These crops included both soft and citrus fruits, as well as a wide range of vegetables.[17]

Not all these interstitial agricultural zones were single-crop producers. Some contained hay or cattle spreads or were broken up into small but productive truck farms, often run (but not usually owned) by skilled Japanese American farmers, who in turn employed Mexican and other migrant laborers. But beginning with the 27,000-acre Newhall-Saugus ranch, set up in 1883, by the time of the First World War a whole series of large citrus ranches, usually owned by Anglos, had been established in both Los Angeles and Orange counties. Smaller versions of them were also set up in many of the rural gaps between Santa Monica, Pasadena, and Los Angeles itself.

TABLE 2.2 | Native-Born Population of Los Angeles County, by Selected State of Birth, 1880–1940

	Mass.	New York	Penn.	Ohio	Indiana	Missouri	Illinois	Minnesota	Wisconsin	Michigan	Iowa	Virginia
1880	424	1,413	534	815	600	905	853	N/A	N/A	857	523	N/A
1890	960	2,938	1,489	2,559	1,320	N/A	2,607	493	709	1,985	1,652	345
1900	1,691	5,537	3,225	5,237	2,903	3,501	14,114	1,204	1,759	7,944	3,501	573
1910	5,033	16,469	11,761	17,107	10,709	16,319	21,713	3,946	5,667	13,657	11,706	1,665
1920	7,873	26,958	19,457	27,511	17,329	24,104	38,064	8,252	10,716	25,830	19,968	2,734
1930	15,316	49,337	36,638	42,212	29,344	49,590	72,933	24,333	21,958	27,419	41,352	4,580
1940	13,419	51,082	43,401	48,911	38,302	52,700	84,903	23,819	28,222	32,064	40,916	3,219

SOURCE: Fogelson, *Fragmented Metropolis*, 82; *Sixteenth Census of the United States, Characteristics of the Population*, Vol. 2. (Washington: GPO, 1943), 631–33.

Until 1940 these agricultural zones provided Los Angeles County with its most important source of wealth.[18]

By 1930 it was estimated that 16,000 foreign-born Mexicans lived in Los Angeles County. Most of the males (and some of the females) divided their work time between rural and urban *colonias,* or communities. In the summer, they picked, chopped, and canned a sequence of crops in the agricultural zones. In the winter, they worked in construction, on the railroads, or in urban laboring jobs. Most of their wives and daughters, by contrast, stayed in the city year round, toiling at low-wage jobs as domestics or in the garment industries. By 1920, not only a dual labor market but also a deep cultural gap had developed between these Mexican American workers and their Anglo counterparts in the suburbs and wealthier parts of downtown.[19]

The white European or native-born migrants who sought to control Los Angeles in the 1910s and 1920s were very different from the Mexicans, Asians, and blacks alongside whom they now lived. Coming for the most part from farms or small midwestern towns, they brought with them the individualistic, Protestant, and pietistic values of small-town life. These values were antithetical both to the lifestyles and to the Catholic faith of the Mexicans, the Irish, and the eastern European immigrants, as well as to the Buddhist values of the Japanese. The Anglo-Saxon newcomers, suspicious of large cities by tradition, also objected to the overcrowding of the urban ghettos in which people of color resided in the eastern and southern parts of Los Angeles. Seeking to protect themselves from contact with allegedly inferior cultures, the white midwesterners moved away from downtown to the suburban islands when they could, setting up geographical barriers between themselves and all people of color. In the period between 1910 and 1930 the social reformers among them, drawing on one of the more ambiguous sides of the Progressive tradition, also sought to "Americanize" these supposedly inferior peoples in the name of modern education, sanitation, and domestic economy. In 1913, Governor Hiram Johnson, riding into office on the flood tide of urban reform, established the Commission of Immigration and Housing, which was the main instrument of attempted Americanization during the next decade.[20]

Since significant numbers of poor peasant families from the rural areas of Mexico had begun to show up in the immigration lists, it was to them that the reformers turned their primary attention. At first Mexican men were considered the most suitable targets for this Americanizing thrust. The idea was to teach them thrift, sobriety, and promptness at work, as well as respect for their wives and employers. But soon the reformers found it better to focus their efforts on African American and Mexican women and children rather than on their husbands and fathers, who moved frequently for their jobs. Progressive thought taught that women were the true bearers of civilized values in any case. In addition to teaching the English language, therefore, Anglo reformers sought to maintain the structure of the Mexican family while transforming its dietary, sanitary, and childbearing habits. Birth control was pushed, both to limit the size of the immigrant family and to enable black and Mexican women to work outside the home in the domestic, restaurant, and garment trades.[21] The Anglo-run public school system also became a vehicle for these Americanization schemes. In an effort to achieve social conformity, schoolteachers concentrated their efforts on raising the sporting activities, the domestic habits, and the language skills—not only of Mexicans but also of Asians and Eastern Europeans—to the prevailing middle-class standards of Anglo-Saxon propriety.[22]

Socialization into the American language and allegedly superior white values was thought to increase social stability among the immigrant communities, as well as to boost the self-confidence of African American and Mexican children so that they could more readily climb the social ladder. But these Americanization efforts, along with the natural tendency of American-born children to challenge the values of their immigrant parents, sometimes led to painful cultural clashes between the generations, especially where dating patterns and intermarriage were concerned.[23]

Some Mexicans and African Americans, as well as a few eastern European families, responded positively to the Progressives' well-intentioned but condescending reform efforts. However, they could not help but see the glaring contradiction between these humane ideals and the growing tendency of the Anglo American population to restrict immigrant access to equal housing, schools, and jobs through zoning restrictions, racist legislation, and biased court rulings.

It is important to note that people of color were not the only ones to suffer from cultural prejudice during the 1910s and 1920s. Jewish migrants from East Coast cities did so, too. As we saw earlier, in the 1880s Boyle Heights had become a thriving center of Jewish culture. But when second-generation Jewish businessmen from downtown sought to better themselves by buying houses and businesses on the west side of Los Angeles, they initially ran into the same kind of racial slurs and zoning restrictions that Asians, blacks, and Mexicans did. During the 1920s, in particular, the message of hate that the Ku Klux Klan brought to the West Coast was directed against Jews almost as much as it was against immigrants of color. But Jewish immigrants had two advantages. One was a familiarity with European traditions of education, which enabled them to benefit disproportionately from the city's burgeoning high schools and colleges. The other was the important role they came to play in Los Angeles' most glamorous industry, Hollywood.

The first of these two advantages enabled a minority of established Jews to mount the ladder of social mobility fairly rapidly during this period, as they did in a number of eastern cities. Many of their recently arrived

compatriots, meanwhile, remained employed in the downtown garment industry and other skilled trades.[24] The prominent role that Jews came to play
in the film industry—after an influx of talent and capital from New York—
also gave some of them sufficient prestige and financial resources to overcome the worst excesses of anti-Semitism. Hence, as the first wave of urban
renewal in the teens and twenties demolished old downtown neighborhoods
to make way for new commercial offices and city buildings, many second-
generation Jewish immigrants moved their families out of downtown Los
Angeles to the Fairfax District and Pico Boulevard neighborhoods on the
city's recently established west side. Later on, some of these same Jews, although still restricted from moving into the richest Anglo areas, located
farther afield in the San Fernando Valley.[25]

The Jewish movement to the west side in the 1920s reflected a more
general tendency among white Europeans to move from Los Angeles' small
downtown to the northern, western, and southern edges of the city. This
process was both a means of dispersal, to relieve congestion in the urban
core, and a step in upward mobility. The same procedure rarely applied to
either Mexicans or blacks and only somewhat more often to Asians. An
exception here can be seen in the Japanese market gardens, such as the
ones at Sawtelle and Olympic, which were set up on the west side to serve a
growing Anglo clientele.[26] Most of the Mexican immigrants, as opposed to
seasonal migrants from Mexico, settled alongside their California-born
counterparts in places like Belvedere, Elysian Park, and Boyle Heights.[27]
Their lower socioeconomic status, as well as Los Angeles' increasingly ubiq-
uitous restrictive zoning laws, prevented them from moving to the west side.
Class and racial factors were now beginning to intertwine in the creation of
a fragmented metropolis.

Already in 1912, the African Americans of Los Angeles, like blacks in
other cities, had found special reasons to feel angry. In that year, they were
confronted with the so-called "Shenk Rule," enacted by city attorney John
Shenk, which permitted saloons to charge blacks more than whites for a
glass of beer. Both Mexicans and blacks were even more angered in 1929
when the California Supreme Court upheld a restrictive covenant to "keep
West Slauson Avenue white," by declaring that restrictions preventing families of color from buying houses in white areas on the west side of the city
were valid.[28] Resultant overcrowding began for the first time to push Mexicans into the East Los Angeles barrio and African Americans into South
Central. According to George Sanchez, "Class-stratified Los Angeles exhib-
ited a rigid separation between its core and eastern regions and the rest of
the city."[29] A growing consciousness of this double standard helped to set
the stage for sporadic movements of both ethnic- and class-based protest,
which grew more intense as the twentieth century wore on.

BUILDING THE INDUSTRIAL CITY, 1930–1945

Before either the ethnic- or the class-based side of these protest movements (or an interweaving of the two) could gain any real momentum, however, Los Angeles had to develop both an industrial base and a more clearly differentiated working class. By eastern standards, in 1930 both were still conspicuously lacking. It is true that by the end of the First World War the city possessed a large construction industry, a number of garment and furniture-making factories, and a rapidly growing movie industry. Most of these jobs, except for those in Hollywood, were located downtown. The extended city also laid claim to a developing harbor system in Long Beach and San Pedro that employed a high-wage caste of white engineers and craftsmen mixed with a low-wage caste of Mexican, Croatian, and Japanese roustabouts. The city also possessed an exploding oil industry to the north of Long Beach in Signal Hill and elsewhere, which was similarly stratified in terms of ethnic employment.[30] But in the late 1920s, L.A. County's economy was still heavily dependent on the large output of agricultural produce grown in the rural zones between the suburban islands. Compared with cities like Pittsburgh and Chicago, Los Angeles still had very little heavy industry in this period.

L.A.'s industrial backwardness would now be eliminated. Attracted by cheap oil, a growing consumer market, and an abundant supply of non-union labor, several major eastern and midwestern steel, auto, and rubber producers decided to set up branches out west. Because it was an open-shop town, Los Angeles was their main choice, rather than San Francisco. In 1935, Ford Motor Company built a large assembly plant in Pico Rivera, while keeping its central manufacturing base in Dearborn, Michigan. In 1936, General Motors followed suit. It constructed a three-million-dollar assembly plant in South Gate to compete with Ford. Chrysler had done the same thing in 1931, and Studebaker in 1935. By 1940, these four automobile companies had invested $16 million in South Central Los Angeles. Rubber, the major ancillary to auto production, followed suit. Goodrich, Goodyear, and Firestone built major plants in South Gate, Lynwood, and Pico Rivera during the course of the 1930s. By 1936, the auto and rubber industries employed more than 40,000 men. Many other spin-off trades, from glassmaking to plastics and engineering, grew up alongside. Unbeknownst to most of its wealthy suburban residents on the west side, by 1939 Los Angeles had become second only to Detroit in auto assembly and to Akron, Ohio in tire and rubber production.[31]

But the most spectacular modern industrial growth took place in the shipping and aircraft industries, particularly during the Second World War. The major advantage of Southern California for airplane manufacturers, as for moviemakers, was the climate. The sunshine not only allowed outdoor filming but permitted uninterrupted aircraft testing all year round. Flat terrain for experimental flights and landings, coupled with proximity to the Second World War battlefields of the Pacific, also helped. In quick order the small aircraft plants that had been established for civilian production in the 1920s were expanded and converted to produce fighters and bombers. These plants were scattered throughout the periphery of the conurbation, not in South Central Los Angeles. The main aircraft companies were Lockheed in Burbank, Douglas in Santa Monica, and North American in Inglewood. Liberty ships were also built in Long Beach. By 1943, these shipping and aircraft plants employed a total of 147,422 men and women.[32] This dispersal of industrial development helped bring industry to the urban periphery, but it also increased the fragmentation of Los Angeles' working class, rendering it more difficult for the newly established Congress of Industrial Organizations (CIO) to organize the industry into trade unions.[33]

The accompanying expansion of industrial jobs, both in the southern part of the city of Los Angeles and at its western and northern edges, was almost as remarkable as the development of the suburban islands that surrounded them. The most spectacular growth years were between 1942 and 1945, when the nation was engaged in total war. The number of wage and salaried workers in Southern California rose from 812,000 in 1939 to 1,402,000 in 1943, a gain of almost 70 percent, nearly double the national rate. In Los Angeles County, into which the new industrial plants soon spilled, employment grew from approximately 900,000 in March 1940 to 1,450,000 by October 1943, an increase of over 60 percent.[34] By 1945, the state of California, which had formerly been very largely agricultural, ranked among the ten leading industrial states in America. For Los Angeles and its immigrants, a new metamorphosis had begun.

Who got the new industrial jobs of the 1930s and 1940s? The short answer is mostly native-born white males, although a significant number of white women and a few Asian and African American women moved into the shipping and aircraft industries during the Second World War. By 1943, this number had reached 113,000, which amounted to the second largest conglomeration of female wartime employees in the United States.[35] The long-range answer is more complicated. Some minorities trying to secure high-wage jobs in the auto, munitions, and shipbuilding industries in the southern and eastern parts of Los Angeles were excluded while others were not. The phenomenon rendered the region's ethnoracial hierarchy more complex. Besides whites, the group benefiting most from industrialization, albeit after a struggle, were the African Americans.

Why didn't other minority groups fare as well as blacks? Let us look first at employment patterns among Asian Americans, a population that was diversified by a small influx of Filipinos and Koreans in the 1930s and 1940s. This group came in at the bottom of the list for industrial employment. Those jobs proved off-limits to the Japanese for two obvious reasons.

First, most of the Japanese were still employed in small family businesses, such as truck farming and fishing, or they were serving the white community in a quite different sector of the economy and in quite different parts of the city. Second, the few Japanese Americans who remained in Los Angeles after the bombing of Pearl Harbor in December 1941 and the mass evacuation that took place a year later were by definition suspect. The same was not true of the Chinese or Koreans; since China was a wartime ally, these two groups underwent something of a rehabilitation during this period, although they lost it again when the Communists came to power on the Chinese mainland in 1949. But at the outset of the war, most Chinese were still occupied in low-wage service jobs far from the industrial sectors of the city or, like the Japanese and the Koreans, were self-employed, either in Chinatown or elsewhere in ethnically specific occupations.[36] Therefore, few of them took industrial jobs.

While some Mexicans, both native-born and immigrant, secured employment in the Los Angeles steel, auto, and rubber industries during and after the Second World War, in addition to racism they faced a logistical problem. In 1940, most Mexicans still lived in Central and East Los Angeles, which were several miles away from the burgeoning industrial neighborhoods of Maywood, Pico Rivera, South Gate, and Vernon. Mexicans could not purchase homes in these cities because of the racially exclusive housing covenants. One scholar has even argued that the supposedly benign Home Owners Loan Corporation of the New Deal period was manipulated by Los Angeles realtors and bankers to initiate the practice of "red lining." By denying home loans to people of color, banks made it very difficult for minorities to secure accommodations in L.A.'s new industrial zones.[37] Thus, when the war came along, very few Mexican Americans were in a position to apply for high-skill, high-wage jobs in the shipbuilding, aircraft, or munitions industries located far from Central and East L.A., even if they had not been excluded on racial grounds. The wartime records of the Fair Employment Practices Commission show that Mexican Americans faced discrimination in all but the lowest-paid jobs.[38] Those who did travel to the industrial cities on the Red Cars secured employment only in unskilled tasks like laboring and hauling.

It seemed at first as though blacks, like Mexicans, would also be prevented by geography and racial barriers from gaining a foothold in Los Angeles' heavy industry in this period. In the 1930s and 1940s there was certainly no shortage of African Americans looking for industrial jobs; in the 1930s, the city's black population rose from 38,894 to 63,774. Most of these new migrants came from rural southern states like Alabama and Tennessee.[39] But it was in the spring of 1942, when the wartime shortage of labor became chronic, that the largest migration of poor rural blacks began. At first these newcomers, like their predecessors, tended to settle in the downtown and Central Avenue areas. But these neighborhoods, like the East

L.A. barrio, were now becoming painfully overcrowded. Instead, African American would-be industrial workers sought to move into Watts, which was closer to the cities where the new industrial jobs lay.

Already in the 1930s a few blacks had tried to move into the Watts neighborhood, but the white citizens in the area, as they had done with the Mexicans, refused to permit African Americans to break down the restrictive zoning laws by settling there. As employment opportunities opened up during the Second World War, however, the more persistent blacks managed to settle on land that most white residents considered undesirable. Racial tensions continued to mount. The matter moved toward some kind of legal resolution in 1944 when the Laws, a black family, moved into a racially restricted site on the Good Year Tract, at 92nd Street in Watts. The Laws family received an eviction notice but decided to fight it in the courts. A legal defense fund was started by black activist Charlotta Bass, who was editor of the *California Eagle*. The NAACP and the black churches, especially the First American Methodist Episcopal and the Second Baptist, also raised funds to support the cause. In 1948, after several years of litigation, the Supreme Court finally found in favor of the Laws family, thereby striking down all racially motivated real estate covenants as illegal.[40]

This legal decision did not fully solve the problem, of course. At that time, social pressures, intimidation, and the refusal of banks to lend money meant that the great majority of both African American and Mexican American residents of Los Angeles remained trapped in the ghetto. Real estate covenants were not dealt with effectively until the Open Housing Act of 1968. Meanwhile, during the Second World War most black applicants for industrial jobs had to content themselves with commuting by Red Car to the auto, rubber, steel, and munitions plants on the city's south side. Most of their wives and daughters continued to work in low-paying jobs as domestics, in unskilled labor, or in the garment industry.[41]

But residential segregation was not the only problem. During the early part of the Second World War, most shipbuilding and defense firms refused to hire incoming Mexicans and blacks, despite the chronic labor shortage. The situation became so bad that President Franklin Roosevelt, responding to a threatened protest march on Washington by CIO leader A. Philip Randolph, issued Executive Order 8802, on June 21, 1941. This order forbade discrimination in the employment of workers in defense industries or government "because of race, creed, color or national origin."[42] President Roosevelt also set up the Fair Employment Practices Commission to enforce the order. The FEPC had little actual power, but after numerous public hearings and continued protests by the NAACP and other African American community groups, the situation at last began to change. By December 1944, blacks, who made up only 6.5 percent of the total population of Los Angeles, had 14 percent of all shipyard jobs.[43] Their representation in aircraft plants was significantly lower, but it nevertheless gave a minority of them access for the first time to well-paying semiskilled if not skilled jobs.

The difficulties that both blacks and Mexican Americans experienced in their efforts to secure industrial jobs during the Second World War were symptomatic of a more general increase in racial tensions during this period, as whites struggled to confine people of color to unskilled jobs, segregated schools and swimming pools, and certain well-defined parts of the city. The prejudice against poor white dust-bowl migrants coming in from Oklahoma and Arkansas at this time showed that the social tensions generated by the war were not caused solely by race.[44] Behind these racial tensions lay the more fundamental class and cultural clash examined earlier in this chapter between the values of large numbers of small-town, Protestant midwesterners, on the one hand, and working people who sought to benefit from the rapid process of industrialization, on the other. Nevertheless, racism had a lot to do with it. During the depression of the 1930s, for example, thousands of Mexican migrant workers—along with quite a few native Californians of Mexican descent—had suffered the humiliation of being deported back to Mexico from Los Angeles as a means of getting them off the relief rolls.[45]

Ironically, as labor shortages intensified after Pearl Harbor in December 1941 and thousands of Angelenos went off to war, the clamor to bring cheap labor into the Los Angeles basin resumed. The revolving door was opened once more, and migrant Mexican workers were brought back in to work the land under the Bracero Program, described in chapter 1. Despite an agreement between the Mexican and U.S. governments providing that these farm workers would be paid the minimum wage, given decent accommodations, and otherwise respected, the Bracero Program's terms were widely ignored.[46]

Urban Mexicans also found it difficult to establish a separate sense of identity that was acceptable to the dominant Anglo culture. In the late 1930s, in response to the new movie and jazz cultures, second-generation African American and Mexican American youths in the inner city began to wear so-called zoot suits, a loose-fitting garment that one scholar has called a "refusal: a subcultural gesture that refused to concede to the manner of subservience."[47] In June 1943, riots broke out when white servicemen chased zoot-suit-clad Mexican youth down the city streets, angered by their apparent failure to enroll in the armed services. Sporadic clashes also took place between white servicemen and blacks in Watts and Pasadena. These events followed the August 1942 Sleepy Lagoon incident, in which twenty-two Mexican American youths were charged with the murder of a young compatriot at a water-filled gravel pit in East L.A. Wrongly treating the incident as gang-related, the Los Angeles Police Department (whose reputation for racial prejudice was going from bad to worse) submitted a report to the grand jury that "declared Mexicans inherently criminal and biologically prone to violence."[48] Seventeen of the youths were found guilty in the largest mass trial in Los Angeles history.

But the most serious example of increased racial tensions in this period was the incarceration of 112,000 Japanese Americans, from all across the nation, in internment camps for the duration of the war. Having been gathered in at assembly centers such as the Santa Anita race track, the first few thousand Japanese Americans from L.A. were sent early in 1942 either to the Manzanar internment camp, on the eastern side of the Sierras, or to Poston in Arizona. The rest were relocated to other camps throughout the western United States. The total number of Japanese Americans from the Los Angeles area who were interned during the war eventually reached more than forty thousand.[49]

Two-thirds of the relocated Japanese American families were composed of American citizens, and they were not, of course, imprisoned simply for security reasons. Most Japanese American internees found, for example, that they had lost most of their property and savings when they sought to recover them at the end of the war. The virulent hostility that was displayed towards the Japanese in Los Angeles during and after the war was in part the result of a heightened fear of the "yellow peril" and in part a manifestation of the sense of outrage at presumed betrayal that has frequently surfaced in the American psyche during and after its participation in foreign wars.

Urban development in rapidly industrializing Los Angeles also had consequences that helped restructure the city's ethnoracial order. In the early 1950s, for example, several thousand Mexican Americans were evicted from their traditional neighborhood in Chavez Ravine, near downtown, to make way for a new baseball stadium. This was only one of numerous urban renewal projects, including the building of the freeway system, that affected the minority community disproportionately.[50] But despite these travails, the 1940s and 1950s were not a period of complete gloom for ethnic minorities in the City of the Angels, nor for their white allies. For instance, by 1950 the African American community had succeeded in entering Watts on a large scale; from 1940 to 1950, the numbers of blacks there had jumped from 8,814 to 92,117. This concentration of blacks brought white flight, but it also provided the African American community with a strong geographical base and turned Watts into by far the largest black residential area in the city.[51]

Despite layoffs from the defense plants when victory came in 1945, numerous African Americans, as well as a smaller number of Mexican Americans and others just entering the Los Angeles labor market, were able to build on their wartime experience to gain a much firmer foothold in a wide range of previously all-white occupations. The majority of workers in these two groups who had obtained jobs in steel, auto, and rubber retained them after the war, thanks largely to the willingness of CIO unions to accept them into membership and to defend their positions. Many black and Mexican army veterans reentering civilian industry again worked as janitors, domestic servants, or unskilled laborers, but by 1950 approximately one-third of the males in these two groups had been placed in manufacturing jobs. They, and their sons after them, were to remain employed in heavy industry until the deindustrialization of Los Angeles began in the 1980s. An increasing number of black and Mexican women also found employment in government work, teaching, and the food industry after the Second World War.[52] These minorities also had a rich and successful associational life of their own. Politically, for example, Mexican Americans and blacks were now beginning to become important. In the depression year of 1934, the muckraking novelist and radical reformer Upton Sinclair ran a vigorous and effective campaign for governor on his EPIC (End Poverty in California) platform. He panicked the white business elite when he won the primary election and received substantial minority support for his cooperative food production ideas.[53]

By this time, a significant number of both African American and Mexican American immigrants had also been drawn into the Democratic party as a result of the reforms of the New Deal. Blacks were recruited via neighborhood political organizations and the 1936 union endorsements of the CIO, Mexicans via the efforts of the Mexican American Movement, a voluntary organization that had originated to serve young Chicanos in the YMCA. Although a far smaller proportion of Mexicans than blacks voted at this time (because far fewer Mexicans were citizens), the increase that took place in the number of applications for citizenship in the 1934–36 period suggests a rising political consciousness in the Mexican American community.[54] Most of those who did vote in the 1936 and 1940 elections undoubtedly supported the Democrats. This political affinity, like the anti–zoning law campaign and the unionization efforts of the CIO, helped ethnic and racial minorities to draw together on a classwide basis, instead of being pushed apart into ethnic separatism.

In spite of their confinement to inadequate housing and semiskilled and unskilled jobs, by 1950 most blacks were also far better off financially than they had been in the South, just as most Mexican immigrants were better off than they had been in Mexico. This was particularly true during the boom years of the Second World War. Movie houses filled up, dance halls thrived, the minority communities took pride in their decorated war heroes, and a common spirit of patriotism submerged many social divisions.[55] When victory came in 1945, most ethnic and racial minority groups in Los Angeles looked forward to the future with considerable optimism.

POSTWAR DEVELOPMENTS IN LOS ANGELES COUNTY

For much of the period between 1950 and 1970, it was not difficult to maintain this sense of optimism. Once more Los Angeles grew dramatically, and despite many bitter struggles, the Civil Rights movement of the 1960s lifted the hopes of minority communities across Southern California. Hollywood again boomed; oil poured from area wells into tankers anchored outside Long Beach harbor; aircraft, shipbuilding, and auto assembly plants continued to thrive; and thousands of new industrial jobs were created as capital flowed in and real estate developers drove the conurbation relentlessly across the coastal plain.

So much urban growth had also taken place between the former suburban islands that by 1970, the term suburban island had become obsolete. To be sure, some of the older, wealthier outlying white communities managed to preserve their earlier status. These communities included college towns like Pasadena and Claremont, as well as older coastal cities such as Santa Monica and Pacific Palisades. Fighting back against the urban sprawl, they were able to retain their quiet, tree-lined streets. Here, a largely white community of midwestern retirees, Jewish liberals, and Anglo-Saxon professionals maintained the myth of suburbia.

But these previously established suburban communities were no longer typical of Southern California's urban sprawl. "Semi-autonomous urban zones" is a better description for the large number of new cities that once more sprang up all over Los Angeles County in the period between 1950 and 1970. One reason for adopting the new term is that most of the former suburban islands were no longer isolated from each other by citrus groves, hay fields, or small truck farms, as they had been before the Second World War. Except for a few holdouts, most of the Japanese, Mexican, and other farm workers who had earlier cultivated the land between the islands had either become gardeners, service employees, or small businessmen or had taken urban jobs. A second reason is that places like Glendale, Alhambra, and Norwalk now had downtowns, if not industries, of their own. Most white professionals continued to commute to their downtown commercial and government offices, but a growing minority did not work in downtown Los Angeles at all. Instead, they remained on the west side, commuting the few miles from Santa Monica to Beverly Hills or from Pacific Palisades to Hollywood to transact their daily business. Thus was born the polycentric conurbation (some called it the city without a downtown) of Los Angeles that we still see today.[56]

In one sense, then, the lesson to be drawn from the developments of the 1950s and 1960s is that the city of Los Angeles and its environs became more segregated in the postwar years than it had been in the past. Until the 1950s, the west side, the San Fernando Valley, and the vast housing tracts then being built eastwards along the San Bernardino and Santa Ana freeways were very largely white. South Central and the inner city, on the other hand, continued to be populated by people of color. But if we focus on the new outer ring of cities and break the 1970 population down into its ethnic components, a different picture emerges. By 1970, most minority groups, with the notable exception of African Americans, had broken out of their downtown enclaves and spread far and wide among the white population. The Mexican American community, in particular, which the 1970 census designated Spanish American, had by then established significant enclaves for itself in places as far apart as San Fernando, Long Beach, and El Monte. Some of these places, like San Fernando, were longstanding Mexican communities that had simply grown larger, but others were newly established. The same tendency to expand outwards was embraced by numerous second- and third-generation Japanese and Chinese, as well as by a scattering of newly arrived Koreans.[57]

One reason for this new spread of minority communities throughout Los Angeles County was the final defeat of the racially exclusive residential covenants by laws such as the Open Housing Act of 1968. Another was the establishment of the freeway system in the 1950s and 1960s, which opened up to general settlement regions that had hitherto been exclusively suburban. A third and more important reason was the growth of a small but substantial middle class among second-generation Mexicans and blacks, as well as among both the Chinese and the Japanese. Some upwardly mobile elements of these groups could now afford to abandon their downtown apartments or tiny suburban houses and move farther out of the city to take public or professional service jobs in the new communities that were springing up in the more remote parts of the county.

Middle-class growth had always been rapid in Los Angeles, differing in some respects from that of other American cities.[58] Because L.A. lacked a smokestack industry in the nineteenth century, most early Anglo settlers were not factory workers when they first arrived. They were small tradesmen, artisans, or would-be entrepreneurs. Many of these people were putative members of the middle class. So too were some of the native Mexican ranchers and shopkeepers, although after being dispossessed by Anglo landowners many in this group became downwardly mobile. Quite a few Japanese had also been restaurateurs or truck farmers from the beginning. And as we have seen, some of the initial cadre of African Americans who came out from the Midwest to settle in Pasadena or on Central Avenue in the 1920s were teachers or pharmacists. As a minority of blacks moved further up in the social hierarchy, however, they tended to stay close to home. Except for a community established in Altadena, the new black middle-class communities of the 1950s and 1960s were located in places like Baldwin Hills and View Park, neither of which was very far from South Central Los Angeles.[59]

SPREADING OUT INTO THE FIVE-COUNTY AREA, 1950–1970

If most upwardly mobile blacks stayed close to their original places of settlement after the Second World War, this tendency was not necessarily true of other social groups. After completing their war service in 1945, quite a few enterprising whites took advantage of the G.I. Bill to further their education and subsequent careers. Although they were outnumbered by other, long-distance migrants entering the Los Angeles basin, by 1970 some of these newly skilled professionals were attracted by a new burst of industrial development that was beginning to occur even beyond the boundaries of Los Angeles County. These new areas of development to the south and east of the city were more than twenty miles from downtown.

The new phase of outward expansion was foreshadowed in 1957 when aerospace pioneer Howard Hughes bought 350 acres of land on which to develop Hughes Aircraft Company in Fullerton, Orange County. As the Cold War intensified, other big entrepreneurs bought up large tracts of land for industrial development in and around small rural communities in Riverside, San Bernardino, and San Diego counties. This heralded the blossoming of Southern California's military industrial complex.[60]

It must be emphasized that in 1970, when the period covered by this chapter comes to an end, the spread of high-tech industry beyond the boundaries of Los Angeles County was still in its infancy. Most of Orange County, like the other rural counties to the south and east of the city, was still covered by citrus groves and farms. But already in 1965 bedroom communities for Los Angeles were growing up in northern Orange County, because south Los Angeles County had become fully developed.[61] Ten years later Fullerton, Buena Park, and Irvine in Orange County, along with other small towns in Riverside and San Bernardino counties, became the models for a new form of urban development, one for which even the designation "semi-autonomous urban zone" would soon become obsolete. Such zones had implied the existence of downtowns that to some extent marked off one urban community from another. But the multicentered metropolitan regions that spread across the five-county area of Southern California in the 1980s and 1990s were postsuburban communities in which shopping malls, industrial parks, and office complexes ran into each other in one continuous ribbon.

In 1970, except for pockets of native Mexicans and a few second- or third-generation Asians living in old-style citrus centers like Santa Ana,[62] these newly emerging metropolitan areas were largely populated by young, skilled, middle-class Anglo-Saxon professionals, some of whom had moved south and east from the old downtown. Other residents in the newly settled areas came from elsewhere in California or from out of state. Since the population census for Los Angeles, Orange, Riverside, San Bernardino, and San Diego counties has been used by the other contributors to this volume as their main statistical unit of analysis, it will be employed here to offer some overall insights into the changing character of the Southern California labor force between 1940 and 1970.

In the years after 1940, the region's economy became transformed in both size and composition. By 1970, the region contained close to three million jobs; thus it employed virtually three times as many people as it had three decades before. Reflecting the wartime and then cold war booms in defense work, which had spilled over into other activities in goods production, that much-larger economy gave pride of place to manufacturing. Now almost five times larger than it had been three decades before, the factory complex in South Central Los Angeles and elsewhere employed over a quarter of the region's work force. Before the war, manufacturing workers had worked in the durable and the nondurable goods industries in almost equal numbers; now durable manufacturing had emerged as the region's leader, containing not only the bulk of factory employment but also its best-paying, most stable, most highly unionized jobs. Though not quite as important, the public sector had also grown at rates well above the regional growth rate, as had professional services, a sign of postindustrial shifts to come. By contrast, agriculture, never a big employer but always a key sector in terms of the value of its output, shed employees as suburbs replaced farms and as the remaining growers replaced workers with machines. In relative terms, personal services was also a losing sector; employing more than 10 percent of the region's labor force in 1940, it accounted for less than 4 percent of the jobs three decades later.

In general, the sustained boom of the post–World War II period had a beneficial effect on all ethnic groups. In absolute terms, whites were the biggest gainers during these growth years, when Los Angeles exerted its greatest attraction for migrants from elsewhere in the United States. But the steady infusion of white workers into the region's economy masked a *relative* decline in their prominence in that economy; holding 82 percent of the region's jobs in 1940, whites retained only 71 percent three decades later. When the economy is broken down by sector, whites actually lost jobs in only two sectors of note, agriculture and personal services, both of which declined overall during this period. But the white *share* of jobs eroded significantly in nondurable manufacturing, which in these years grew more slowly than did the region's heavy industrial sector. In other sectors, whites retained shares of jobs that were roughly proportional to their share of the region's total employment.

Thus, the hidden story of the postwar boom is the growing economic importance of the region's minorities of color, as can be seen from figures 2.3 and 2.4. The Second World War and the labor shortages it induced gave black workers a foothold in the region's industrial complex that steadily expanded in years to come. Three percent of the region's labor force in 1940, African Americans came to fill 7 percent of the greatly expanded economic base three decades later. Growth largely occurred through diffusion. In 1940, almost half of all African Americans were still working in personal services; they were grossly underrepresented in every other sector save the public sector, where their share of employment equaled their share of all

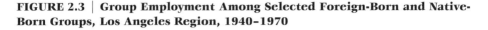

FIGURE 2.3 | **Group Employment Among Selected Foreign-Born and Native-Born Groups, Los Angeles Region, 1940–1970**

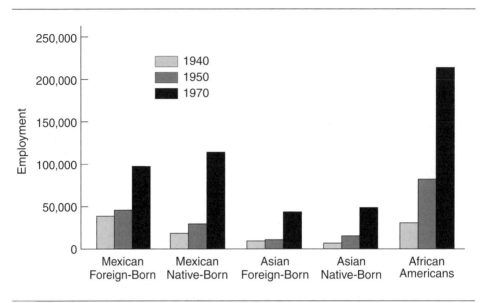

jobs in the region. Despite the industrial breakthroughs created by the war, personal service still ranked as the number one employer in 1950. Even though every sector but agriculture saw substantial increases in black employment, large gains in share occurred only in durable manufacturing and in public employment, where by 1950 African Americans had already achieved a position of significant overrepresentation. The next two decades of prosperity did far more to improve the black job profile. In 1970, the public sector emerged as the leading employer, followed by manufacturing, trade, professional services, and only then by personal services. Good times were not enough to overcome discriminatory obstacles, however; employers in the region's light manufacturing—and lower wage—industries proved very willing to hire African Americans. But this was not true of their counterparts in the booming durable manufacturing complex. Consequently, black employment in nondurable manufacturing stood at close to parity in 1970, but durable manufacturing remained a sector of considerable underrepresentation.

The trajectory followed by the Mexican-origin labor force contrasts with the black pattern in more than one respect. For Mexican-origin workers, this was a period of relative stability. Mexican-origin workers held 6 percent of the region's jobs in 1940 and 7 percent three decades later; by 1970, the majority of these workers were native-born, reflecting the minor role of im-

FIGURE 2.4 | **Group Employment as Share of Total Employment, Selected Ethnic Groups, Los Angeles Region, 1940–1970**

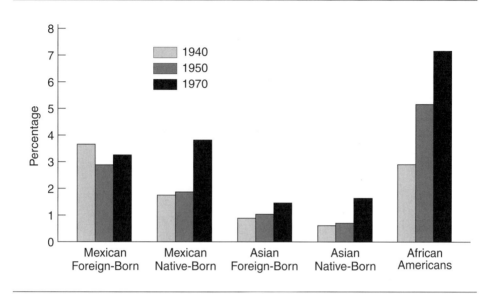

migration in these years. Like African Americans, Mexicans changed their industrial configuration, but in quite different ways. Heavily concentrated in agriculture at the beginning of the period, Mexicans shifted into industry and trade. By 1970, durable and especially nondurable manufacturing had become sectors of considerable Mexican overrepresentation; with these clusters in place, Mexicans established the networks that would subsequently connect employers with the massive number of immigrants who arrived after 1970.

Compared with both blacks and Mexican Americans, Asians represented a very small portion of the region's work force during these years—2 percent in 1940, 3 percent thirty years later. In this period, Asian Angelenos were still either of Chinese or Japanese descent, and as with Mexican Americans, the 1940–70 period witnessed the emergence of a native-born generation.

However, two general trends should be noted concerning Japanese and Chinese employment in the Southern California labor force during this period. The first—paralleling the Mexican American experience—is the decline, both relatively and absolutely, that occurred in the numbers working in agriculture. This drop reflected, among other things, the decline in the number of Japanese-owned truck farms in highly urbanized Los Angeles. The second is the diffusion of Asians into other sectors of the economy, especially into professional services like health, education, and engineering. Among American-born Asians, an especially high number—8,400 in all—had also moved into government employment by 1970.

If we look at changes in the relative position of different ethnic groups in the 1940–70 period, a couple of additional points are worth making, if only to correct some popular misconceptions. One such misconception, based on a tendency to read the present back into earlier periods of Los Angeles' history, is to assume that the city has always been heavily populated by immigrants from Mexico. It is important to stress again just how small both the American- and foreign-born Mexican population of Los Angeles still was in 1970. As we have already noted, in that year, when the five-county area held more than seven million people, the overall number of Mexican American workers was still only 211,500. Of these, almost half were born in America. A second point, which is needed as a minor corrective to the argument made earlier in this chapter about the relative decline of white Europeans in the labor force, is to note the ongoing dominance of Anglos in the highest-paid sectors of the labor force. Already in 1970, the overall class bifurcation of Los Angeles tended to be between whites and people of color.

RACIAL AND ETHNIC FRAGMENTATION AND ITS SOCIAL AND POLITICAL CONSEQUENCES, 1960–1970

Despite major disparities between the fortunes of whites and people of color, this postwar expansion in both the size and the geographical settlement patterns of Southern California's labor force had many positive effects. It brought advantages to most groups in terms of income and home ownership. But except for the few who managed to move up in the class structure, it did not do much to advance the interests of those who had been living in the ghetto areas of Los Angeles proper.

The continuing—indeed accelerating—isolation of the poor blacks and Mexicans who lived in the eastside barrios of downtown Los Angeles or in South Central between 1950 and 1970 was due partly to continued unspoken racism in job and housing applications and partly to the poor quality of the segregated public education system in the inner city. As William J. Wilson has shown, emerging class differences between middle- and working-class blacks also isolated the latter still more from mainstream employment.[63] A third reason, in the case of foreign-born Mexicans, was the rapid growth in the number of illegal immigrants who entered the inner city during the 1970s and 1980s. Poorly educated, speaking little English, and subject to harassment and arrest by the Immigration and Naturalization Service (INS), these new migrants developed into a subgroup that merely reinforced the isolation of the now heavily overcrowded East L.A. barrio.[64]

Paradoxically, therefore, the spread of immigrant communities through-out the Los Angeles basin, particularly the leapfrog manner in which mid-dle-class enclaves were established, contributed to the city's ethnoracial fragmentation. In turn, this fragmentation reinforced the political exclu-sion of most people of color, a phenomenon that had existed since the turn of the century. This weakness can be attributed not only to overt racism, but to the limited and multijurisdictional character of Los Angeles city gov-ernment, which permitted the growth of politically sovereign and fiscally independent suburban enclaves within its borders.

The political weakness of the Mexican American community became particularly noticeable after the Second World War, and prevented it from bargaining successfully for housing, city patronage, and other benefits. There were, of course, other reasons for Mexican political impotence. Gerry-mandering, for example, also played an important role. Another reason was a growing movement against integration. Although the number of Mexican immigrants taking out citizenship papers steadily increased in the 1950–70 period, many Mexicans were still reluctant to do so, particularly some immigrant members of a new generation of young Chicanos (native-born Mexican Americans). Building on the cultural nationalism of prewar activ-ists, as well as on the rise of a new sense of ethnic pride, these young people challenged the integrationist policies of mainstream organizations like the League of United Latin American Citizens (LULAC), the G.I. Forum, and the Political Association of Spanish Speaking Organizations (PASSO), favoring a more explicitly nationalist approach. This development tended to split the Mexican American community along generational lines. A similar trend occurred among blacks. In fact, by the late 1960s a minority of Los Angeles Chicanos—a term that by then had become politically correct—were openly following the separatist policies propounded by Malcolm X and other black radicals.[65]

Mexican Americans suffered another political setback in the 1960s when white liberals on the Westside were fashioning a new Democratic co-alition between the Jewish and African American communities. This move brought many benefits to those two groups, but it ignored the fair represen-tation of Mexican Americans on the City Council. In 1962, when City Coun-cilman Edward R. Roybal was elected to Congress after having served the Eastside since 1949, African American Gilbert Lindsay was appointed to fill Roybal's term. This action angered many Chicanos and was the first overt sign of the serious split between the black and Mexican communities that was to have such serious consequences in the 1980s and 1990s. The failure to replace Roybal with another Mexican American left the Chicano commu-nity without representation on the City Council for almost a quarter of a century.[66] But geographical fragmentation also contributed to Mexican American political impotence. In an illuminating essay comparing Los Angeles and San Antonio in this period, Carlos Navarro and Rodolfo Acuna attributed the greater political strength of the Mexican American community in the latter city to just this factor.[67]

At first sight, the African American community of Los Angeles was in a much better position to take advantage of its wartime gains than the Mexican American community was. It was large, geographically concentrated, and in possession of a sophisticated network of political clubs, black ministers, and professionals. The clubs included the NAACP, the Phyliss Wheatley Club, and the Los Angeles Forum. African Americans also had a much longer tradition of political action than Mexican Americans had. Black political leaders had begun running for the Los Angeles City Council as early as 1915. Besides electing several members to the council, the black community triumphed in 1973 when the Democratic coalition of Westside Jews, Anglo liberals, and African Americans from South Central elected Tom Bradley mayor of Los Angeles. This victory seemed to put L.A. on a par with Detroit, Newark, and other cities where African Americans exercised decisive political power. Surely the black community of Los Angeles could now take rapid strides towards economic opportunity, political influence, and racial acceptance.[68]

Despite major advances on a number of fronts, these gains were not achieved. To the contrary, the Watts uprising of August 1965 revealed an inner-city black population torn apart by anger, frustration, and despair. The six days of rioting, which resulted in thirty-four deaths (twenty-eight of them black), $40 million in property damage, and the importation of almost fourteen thousand national guard troops, seared the national conscience. It also resulted in increased economic distress, not for the whites against whom the anger was largely directed but for the African American community itself. What long-range circumstances in the African American experience of Los Angeles can explain this social breakdown?

In 1965, it was not poverty as such that played the main causal role. Nor can the "first-world, third-world" juxtaposition between different areas of the city (which is a plausible explanation for Los Angeles' ethnic and racial ills in the 1980s and 1990s) be used to explain the Watts riot. To be sure, many unskilled African Americans in South Central L.A. were poor, particularly recent arrivals from the rural south, but a significant proportion of the male population was still employed in nearby industrial plants. Ideological differences between the integrationist generation and youthful black nationalists may have played a role, as they did among Chicanos in East L.A. But overcrowding, ethnoracial fragmentation and isolation, coupled with outrage over the racially restrictive Rumford Housing Ordinance of 1963 (which was repealed by referendum vote in 1964) probably played more important roles. So too did the long history of humiliation and abuse from which black Angelenos had suffered in previous years.[69]

Ironically, the very success that African Americans had secured in overcoming the racially restrictive housing covenants of the 1910–50 era contributed to the dissolving of the connective tissues that earlier had bound them together. These covenants (and the community self-reliance they had engendered) meant that in the 1930s and 1940s most better-off black families in the Central Avenue district had shopped at the same stores as the poorer ones, attended the same churches and cinemas, and drunk at the same bars. Once the racial barriers to moving out of the inner city were broken down, however, it became fashionable for middle-class blacks to patronize white stores and to make use of other citywide facilities that they had been denied earlier. "When these [local] bonds were stretched by the struggle for equal rights" in the 1960s, Lonnie G. Bunch has written, "the black populace's cohesiveness began to slip away, thus inhibiting effective communal responses to economic and social problems."[70]

The corollary to this development, which also affected the Mexican American community, was the growth during the 1970s of social and economic distance between the African American working class of South Central Los Angeles and the newly emerging black bourgeoisie in the suburbs. The black Angeleno professionals who were fortunate enough to escape from the poorer sections of Watts did not go as far afield as the Asian and Mexican American middle classes; they relocated in View Park and Baldwin Hills instead. But that move was sufficient to deprive the older black community of a significant proportion of its investment capital, experienced leaders, and wealthier local businesses. When coupled with government neglect and generational conflicts over integration versus separatism, this ethnoracial fragmentation had severe social consequences. As Los Angeles expanded still further in the 1980s and 1990s, this fragmentation process was reproduced to some extent among other immigrant groups as well.

CONCLUSION

Besides massive changes in the economy, two fundamental influences were at work in Southern California between 1900 and 1970 that helped shape the modern city of Los Angeles. One was geographical in character, deriving from the peculiar nature of the climate and the terrain. The other was ethnoracial, stemming from the unique combination of immigrant and ethnic groups who settled in the region.

While these two influences were mutually interactive, the second was more heavily dependent upon the first. Once a modern transportation system, along with sufficient water, had become available and the extent of the area's natural resources had become known, the breadth and depth of Southern California's coastal plain appeared to afford unlimited opportunities for urban growth. In social and cultural terms, the development not only of a large urban community but of the two other spatial forms we have examined—the suburban island and the interurban agricultural zone—

became possible. The suburban islands enabled the dominant Anglo-Saxon majority to try, for a time with much success, to reproduce and preserve inviolate the cultural values and social apparatus of the small midwestern town. The agricultural zones enabled citrus and vegetable growers to develop a secondary agricultural economy based upon Mexican and Asian labor. African Americans who migrated to the region either from the Midwest or from the South in the first half of the century did not participate in the development of either of these two structures. Instead, for the most part, they were drawn into the industrial segment of the Los Angeles economy, which developed in the southern and eastern portions of the city after 1930.

By 1970, the agricultural sector of the economy had shrunk to minimal proportions. Many of the citrus groves that had been planted in the rural areas of the Los Angeles five-county region had been ripped out, to be replaced by a postsuburban spatial form best described as a multicentered metropolitan region, not as a city in the conventional European or American sense. Heavily dependent on the automobile, the Los Angeles model of the multicentered metropolitan region has recently influenced urban development in other parts of the country as well.

Many other influences have affected the cultural character of the Southern California region, from the climate to the so-called four ecologies—*surfurbia, foothills, plains,* and *autopia*—that Reyner Banham selected as the defining attributes of the conurbation.[71] But it is the ethnoracial order, which both affected and in turn was affected by the particular way in which the metropolis developed, that has constituted the main focus of this essay.

In this review of the influences that have shaped that order, I believe a strong case can be made for the argument put forward at the outset: that it was the class and cultural gap that opened up in the 1920s between incoming white Protestant midwesterners, on the one hand, and Catholics, Jews, and immigrants of color, on the other, that mainly determined the uneasy racial and ethnic relations between Anglos and others that persist in Los Angeles to this day.

In part, class conflict developed between the downtown Anglo business elite, who both drew members from the suburban islands and supplied the islands with new residents, and Los Angeles' multiracial and multi-ethnic working class, especially during the CIO's halcyon days in the 1930s and 1940s. The upper reaches of that multiethnic working class, it must be remembered, were themselves white. In part, too, class conflict has reflected internal economic differences within and between immigrant groups of color, as for example in the 1933 Mexican farm workers' strike against their Japanese employers in the El Monte berry fields.[72] In addition, the cultural clashes that took place between Protestant midwesterners and people of color were sometimes class conflicts in a disguised form.

But when we focus upon the major cultural conflicts that occurred in Los Angeles between 1920 and 1970, we find that they very often resulted from attempts to impose the Protestant values of small-town, rural America—modified to some extent by urban Progressivism—upon out-groups consisting of Catholics, Jews, and people of color. The major emphases of these values were temperance and churchgoing, economic individualism and social conformity, the pursuit of rural arcadia in the form of single-family dwellings, and an easy assumption of white social and economic superiority. The imposition of these values peaked in the two decades between 1909 and 1929. Progressive Mayor George Alexander's election to office in 1909 was followed by major efforts to Americanize Mexicans, Asians, and recent European immigrants and to exclude both African Americans and Jews who would not conform. The growth of intolerance—present everywhere in the city but highest in the suburban islands—was reinforced during and after the First World War by calls for patriotic conformity and immigration restriction, by the consolidation of the power of the downtown business elite, and by the influx of large numbers of upwardly mobile white townsfolk from the Midwest who sought to preserve in Los Angeles what they feared they had lost at home.

During these and the following years, however, challenges to the Anglo power structure arose that, while seeming to have little in common, all conflicted in one way or another with white Protestant values. Consider some examples: The Shenk rule angered African Americans because it fused white racial arrogance with an argument about the price of beer; Mexicans (many of whom were Catholics) and blacks objected to the school segregation that forced them to accept educational facilities inferior to those in the white Protestant suburbs; restrictive zoning codes were protested in an attempt to break down white, small-town exclusiveness; and the Zoot Suit Riots can, in part, be interpreted as a manifestation of Anglo anger against nonconformity in dress. Nor was it a coincidence that the most strenuous demands for Japanese internment after Pearl Harbor came from Los Angeles, not the Department of the Army in Washington.[73]

Of course, most of the Protestant small town values that fused with those of the downtown business elite during the 1920s have since been challenged, and many of them have been overthrown. But the past is still present, and not just in the restless dynamism that has endowed Los Angeles with its persistent appeal. Social and economic tensions continue to plague L.A.—and while those differences are deeply imbued with class conflicts, their origins lie in the struggle over values that accompanied the shaping of the ethnocultural order examined in this chapter.

Notes to Chapter 2

1. For a caustic and insightful analysis that uses a "first world, third world" paradigm to examine Los Angeles' current economic and social problems, see Mike Davis, *City of Quartz: Excavating the Future in Los Angeles* (London: Verso, 1990).

2. See Edward Soja, Rebecca Morales, and Goetz Wolf, "Urban Restructuring: An Analysis of Social and Spatial Change in Los Angeles," *Economic Geography* 59 (1979): 80–106; and Rob Kling, Spencer Olin, and Mark Poster, eds., *Posturban California: The Transformation of Orange County Since World War II* (Berkeley: University of California Press, 1991), 5–11.

3. David Clark, *Los Angeles, A City Apart* (Woodland Hills, Calif.: Windsor Publications, 1981), 18; Robert M. Fogelson, *The Fragmented Metropolis: Los Angeles, 1850-1950,* 2nd ed. (Berkeley and Los Angeles: University of California Press, 1993), chapter 1.

4. Clark, *Los Angeles,* 15.

5. Pauline V. Young, "Assimilation Problems of Russian Molokans in Los Angeles," (Ph.D. thesis, University of Southern California, 1930), chapter 1.

6. William M. Mason and John A. McMinistry, *The Japanese of Los Angeles* (Los Angeles: County Museum of Natural History, 1969), 8.

7. Quoted in George J. Sanchez, *Becoming Mexican American: Ethnicity, Culture and Identity in Chicano Los Angeles, 1900–1945* (New York: Oxford University Press, 1993), 76.

8. Mason and McMinstry, *Japanese of Los Angeles,* 3–7; Roger Daniels, *The Politics of Prejudice: The Anti-Japanese Movement in California and the Struggle for Japanese Exclusion* (New York: Atheneum, 1969), 27–105.

9. Quoted in Lonnie G. Bunch, "A Past Not Necessarily Prologue: The Afro American in Los Angeles," in Norman M. Klein and Martin J. Schiesl, eds., *20th Century Los Angeles: Power, Promotion and Social Conflict* (Claremont, Calif.: Regina Books, 1990), 101.

10. Bunch, "A Past," 103–4.

11. Sanchez, *Becoming Mexican American,* 75.

12. Fogelson, *Fragmented Metropolis,* 64–66.

13. For the numbers of "new" European immigrants entering Pittsburgh, see John Bodnar, *Lives of Their Own: Blacks, Italians, and Poles in Pittsburgh, 1900–1960* (Urbana: University of Illinois Press, 1982).

14. Clark, *Los Angeles,* 148–49.

15. Fogelson, *Fragmented Metropolis,* 74. See also Bruce Henstall, *Sunshine and Wealth: Los Angeles in the Twenties and Thirties* (San Francisco: Chronicle Books, 1984).

16. Kenneth T. Jackson, *Crabtree Frontier: The Suburbanization of the United States* (New York: Oxford University Press, 1985), 5.

17. Carey McWilliam, *Factories in the Fields: The Story of Migratory Farm Labor in California* (Santa Barbara: Peregrine Smith, 1935).

18. Ernesto Galarza, *Merchants of Labor, The Mexican Bracero Story* (Santa Barbara: McNally and Loftin, 1964), 24–25.

19. Galarza, *Merchants of Labor,* 32; Sanchez, *Becoming Mexican American,* chapter 2.

20. William Deverell, "The Neglected Twin: California Democrats and the Progressive Bandwagon," in William Deverell and Tom Sitton, eds., *California Progressivism Revisited* (Berkeley: University of California Press, 1993), 90–92.

21. Sanchez, *Becoming Mexican American,* chapter 4.

22. Judith R. Raftery, "The Invention of Modern Urban Schooling: Los Angeles, 1885–1941" (Ph.D. thesis, University of California at Los Angeles, 1984), chapter 5.

23. Sanchez, *Becoming Mexican American,* 99–105.

24. John Laslett and Mary Tyler, *The ILGWU in Los Angeles, 1907–1988* (Inglewood, Calif.: Ten Star Press, 1989), 80–101.

25. Davis, *City of Quartz,* 119–20; Neal Gabler, *An Empire of Their Own: How the Jews Invented Hollywood* (New York: Macmillan, 1988).

26. Donald Tuero Hata and Nadine Ishitani Hata, "Asian American Angelenos: Model Minorities and Indispensable Enemies," in Klein and Schiesl, *20th Century Los Angeles,* 68.

27. Sanchez, *Becoming Mexican American,* chapter 3.

28. Bunch, "A Past," 120–21.

29. Sanchez, *Becoming Mexican American,* 77.

30. Clark, *Los Angeles,* 148–49.

31. Fogelson, *Fragmented Metropolis,* 128–34; Myrna Donohoe, "Workers' Response to Plant Closures: The Case of Steel and Auto in Southwest Los Angeles, 1935–1986" (Ph.D. thesis, University of California at Irvine, 1987), chapter 1.

32. Arthur C. Verge, *Paradise Transformed: Los Angeles During the Second World War* (Dubuque: Kendall Publishing Co., 1993), 85–88.

33. For the rise of the CIO in Los Angeles, see Louis B. Perry and Richard S. Perry, *A History of the Los Angeles Labor Movement, 1911–1941* (Berkeley: University of California Press), chapters 11–15.

34. Keith E. Collins, *Black Los Angeles: The Maturing of the Ghetto, 1940–1950* (Saratoga, Calif.: Century Twenty One Publishing Co., 1980), 20.

35. Sherna Gluck, *Rosie the Riveter Revisited: Women, War and Social Change* (Boston: Twayne Publishers, 1987).

36. Hata and Hata, *Asian American Angelenos,* 81–83; Sucheng Chan, *Asian Americans: An Interpretative History* (Boston: Twayne Publishers, 1991), 131–42.

37. Greg H. Hise, "The Roots of the Postwar Region: Mass-Housing and Community in California, 1920–1950" (Ph.D. thesis, University of California at Berkeley, 1992), chapter 4.

38. Verge, *Paradise Transformed,* 58–59.

39. Collins, *Black Los Angeles,* 18–19.

40. Collins, *Black Los Angeles,* 25.

41. Lawrence B. DeGraff, "The City of Black Angels: Emergence of the Los Angeles Ghetto, 1890–1930," *Pacific Historical Review* 39 (1970): 333–52.

42. Quoted in Verge, *Paradise Transformed*, 47.

43. Collins, *Black Los Angeles*, 21.

44. James N. Gregory, *American Exodus, The Dust Bowl Migration and Okie Culture in California* (New York: Oxford University Press, 1989), 83–89.

45. Abraham Hoffman, *Unwanted Mexican Americans in the Great Depression: Repatriation Pressures, 1929–1939* (Tucson: University of Arizona Press, 1974).

46. Galarza, *Merchants of Labor*, 13–20.

47. Sanchez, *Becoming Mexican American*, 265.

48. Quoted in Sanchez, *Becoming Mexican American*, 266. See also Mauricio Mazon, *The Zoot-Suit Riots: The Psychology of Symbiotic Annihilation* (Austin: University of Texas Press, 1984).

49. Roger Daniels, *The Decision to Relocate the Japanese* (Malabar, Calif.: R. E. Krieger Publishing Co. 1975), 47–53.

50. Jo Hindman, "Homes Into Kindling: Urban Renewal, Our Latest Demolition Team 'Home Wrecking A Specialty,' " *American Mercury* 89 (1959): 20–24.

51. Collins, *Black Los Angeles*, p. 48.

52. Verge, *Paradise Transformed*, 111.

53. Floyd Dell, *Upton Sinclair, A Study in Social Protest* (New York: AMS Press, 1984), 248–81.

54. Sanchez, *Becoming Mexican American*, 255–61.

55. Verge, *Paradise Transformed*, chapter 7.

56. Davis, *City of Quartz*, chapter 4.

57. Chan, *Asian Americans*, chapters 4–5.

58. For a comparative discussion of the growth of the middle class in Los Angeles and several other major American cities, see Frederic Cople Jaher, *The Urban Establishment: Upper Strata in Boston, New York, Charleston, Chicago and Los Angeles* (Urbana: University of Illinois Press, 1982).

59. E. Frederick Anderson, *The Development of Leadership and Organization Building in the Black Community of Los Angeles* (Saratoga, Calif.: Century Twenty One Publications, 1980), chapter 9.

60. Roger W. Lotchin, *Fortress California 1910–1961: From Warfare to Welfare* (New York: Oxford University Press, 1992).

61. Kling, Olin, and Poster, *Posturban California*, 5.

62. Kling, Olin, and Poster, *Posturban California*, chapter 9.

63. William J. Wilson, *The Truly Disadvantaged: The Inner City, The Underclass, and Public Policy* (Chicago: University of Chicago Press, 1987), 41–48.

64. For a recent study of undocumented Mexican immigrants, see Leo Chavez, *Shadowed Lives: Undocumented Workers in American Society* (New York: Collins, 1992).

65. Sanchez, *Becoming Mexican American*, chapter 11.

66. Carlos Navarro and Rodolfo Acuna, "In Search of Community: A Comparative Essay on Mexicans in Los Angeles and San Antonio," in Klein and Schiesl, *20th Century Los Angeles,* 203–7.

67. Navarro and Acuna, "In Search of Community," 205–6.

68. Bunch, "A Past," 121.

69. The most illuminating account of the Watts riot of 1965 is still the McCone Commission report entitled *Governor's Commission on the Los Angeles Riots,* 18 vols. (Los Angeles: State of California, 1966). See also Robert M. Fogelson, "White or Black: A Critique of the McCone Commission Report on the Los Angeles Riots," *Political Science Quarterly* 82 (1967), 218–47.

70. Bunch, "A Past," 121.

71. Rayner Banham, *Los Angeles: The Architecture of Four Ecologies* (Hammondsworth, England: Penguin Books, 1973).

72. Charles B. Spaulding, "The Mexican Strike at El Monte, California," *Sociology and Social Research* 18 (1963), 571–80.

73. For evidence on this point, see Daniels, *Decision to Relocate,* 114–19.

CHANGING
DEMOGRAPHICS, 1970–1990

(See photo captions on next page)

Population Change: Immigration and Ethnic Transformation

Georges Sabagh and Mehdi Bozorgmehr

LOS ANGELES WAS a small Mexican pueblo when California was admitted to the Union in 1850. The first federal census of California in that year showed that Los Angeles had 3,518 inhabitants, most of them of Mexican origin. Los Angeles remained a small town until 1880, when its population reached 30,000; from then on a remarkable demographic story unfolded. In a relatively short time, as we saw in the preceding chapter, L.A. experienced a population explosion, becoming the premier migrant metropolis of the United States and attracting Americans from all over the country, especially from the Midwest. This new "gold rush"—in which sun, palm trees, orange groves, beaches, and land speculation replaced gold as the lure— was "the most extended period of sustained growth ever experienced by an equally compact region of the United States."[1] Los Angeles continued to be a haven for midwesterners during the Great Depression of the 1930s and throughout the postwar years.

This chapter recounts L.A.'s demographic story, the most striking feature of which is its successive population surges. Until the 1970s, migrants from other regions of the United States accounted for most of the spurts in population growth. Suddenly in the 1970s, the tidal waves of immigration to the Southern California shores altered the region's ethnic character. Demographically speaking, Los Angeles has recaptured its early pueblo features, thanks to the sizable population of Mexican Americans. But at the same time it has become the "capital of the Third World,"[2] because of the additional influx of Central Americans, Asians, Middle Easterners, and other groups.

DEMOGRAPHIC DYNAMISM OF LOS ANGELES

The extension of the railroad to Los Angeles in the 1870s linked the city to other regions of the United States and greatly facilitated the mass movement of people. It was to the advantage of the railroad companies, which had extensive landholdings, to provide cheap transportation and to publicize aggressively all the marvels of this new "heaven on earth." Many Americans—and more particularly midwesterners, who had the easiest access to the railroad heading to Los Angeles—quickly responded to this message. Figure 3.1 vividly captures the demographic consequences of this mass movement of people. In just thirty years, the population of the Los Angeles region multiplied tenfold, from about 100,000 in 1890 to nearly 1 million in 1920. In the next ten years, the population more than doubled to reach 2.2 million in 1930. The automobile, which had appeared after the turn of the century, was quickly adopted by Angelenos as their favorite mode of transportation; already in the 1920s there were more cars in L.A. than any other city in the United States, and by the late 1930s Angelenos had nearly a million cars.[3] The automobile further facilitated the movement of people and their dispersal over a wide territory, a phenomenon that has since become a hallmark of Los Angeles.

Although the depression years of the 1930s slowed the pace of popula-

FIGURE 3.1 | Population Trends, Los Angeles County and Outlying Counties, 1850–1990

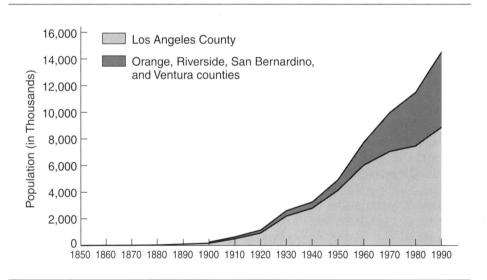

tion growth, the demographic effects of bad times were felt only briefly. The outbreak of the Second World War in 1939 and the sharp increase in the demand for warplanes triggered a massive expansion of L.A.'s aircraft industry, where employment multiplied tenfold from 15,000 to about 150,000 in only five years (1939–44).[4] Thanks to the postwar prosperity, the population of the Los Angeles region resumed its rapid growth, exceeding 4 million in 1950.

Los Angeles continued to expand in the following decades. As a result of U.S. involvement in the Korean War in 1953 and the ensuing Cold War with the Soviet Union, employment in the aerospace and related defense industries swelled further.[5] During the buildup of the defense complex and other related industries, L.A. continued its quick climb to the heights of the metropolitan hierarchy. In 1930, Los Angeles ranked fourth among the nation's largest metropolitan areas, with only about one-fifth as many people as New York; by 1960, the L.A. region had moved to the number two spot, with half as many people as New York. Unlike New York, however, Los Angeles held on to a predominantly Anglo population mix. All that changed in the following decades, when the unanticipated flood of immigrants transformed Los Angeles beyond recognition. It is this story that commands our attention in the pages that follow.

POPULATION GROWTH OF THE LARGEST
U.S. METROPOLITAN REGIONS

Of all the giant metropolitan regions in the United States, Los Angeles is the most demographically dynamic. Since 1960, the populations of Los Angeles, San Francisco, and the Miami metropolitan regions have increased much more rapidly than those of New York, Chicago, or Philadelphia (see table 3.1).[6] While Miami's population expanded more rapidly than Los Angeles' in the 1960s and 1970s, it was also a much smaller region. Although not among the five largest, Miami is included in table 3.1 since it is a diverse metropolis with a large Hispanic population.[7] Indeed, Miami continues to receive considerable publicity as a haven for Cuban and Haitian refugees.

Even though metropolitan population growth declined notably throughout the nation during the 1970s, the gap between the two California and three Eastern metropolitan regions widened. Newcomers poured into Los Angeles, San Francisco, and Miami; New York and Philadelphia saw residents depart in excess of the number of migrants who replaced them. Chicago nearly stood still.

In the 1980s, the older metropolitan areas experienced a slow growth in their populations. Beneath the stability, however, lay considerable churning. Many immigrants moved to New York and Chicago, in particular, but not in

TABLE 3.1 | Growth of Los Angeles and Other Major Metropolitan Areas, 1960–1990

Metropolitan Areas	Population in 1,000s				Percent Change		
	1960	1970	1980	1990	1960–70	1970–80	1980–90
Los Angeles CMSA	7,752	9,981	11,498	14,531	28.8	15.2	26.4
Los Angeles PMSA	6,039	7,042	7,478	8,863	16.6	6.2	18.5
Balance of CMSA	1,713	2,939	4,020	5,668	71.6	36.8	41.0
New York CMSA[a]	16,175	18,072	17,540	17,953	11.7	-2.9	3.1
New York PMSA	8,759	9,077	8,275	8,547	3.6	-8.8	3.3
Balance of CMSA	7,416	8,995	9,265	9,406	21.3	3.0	1.5
Chicago CMSA[b]	6,935	7,779	7,937	8,066	12.2	2.0	1.6
Chicago PMSA	5,527	6,093	6,060	6,070	10.2	-0.1	0.2
Balance of CMSA	1,408	1,686	1,877	1,996	19.7	11.3	6.3
San Francisco CMSA[c]	3,723	4,754	5,368	6,253	27.7	12.9	16.5
San Francisco PMSA	1,332	1,482	1,489	1,604	11.3	0.0	7.8
Balance of CMSA	2,391	3,272	3,879	4,650	36.7	18.6	19.9
Philadelphia CMSA[d]	5,131	5,749	5,681	5,899	12.0	-1.2	3.8
Philadelphia, PA and NJ PMSA	4,343	4,824	4,717	4,857	11.1	-2.2	3.0
Balance of CMSA	788	925	964	1,042	17.4	4.2	8.1
Miami-Fort Lauderdale CMSA	1,269	1,888	2,644	3,193	48.8	40.0	20.8
Miami-Hialeah PMSA	935	1,268	1,626	1,937	35.6	28.2	19.1
Balance of CMSA	334	620	1,018	1,256	85.6	64.2	23.4

SOURCES: U.S. Bureau of the Census, *State and Metropolitan Areas Data Book 1986* (Washington, D.C.: GPO, 1986), 22, 82, 202, 262; U.S. Bureau of the Census, *State and Metropolitan Areas Data Book 1991* (Washington, D.C.: GPO, 1991), 2, 30, 44, 58.

NOTE: CMSA = Consolidated Metropolitan Statistical Area; PMSA = Primary Metropolitan Statistical Area

[a] New York-Northern New Jersey-Long Island, Connecticut

[b] Chicago, Illinois-Gary, Indiana-Lake County, Wisconsin

[c] San Francisco-Oakland-San Jose, California

[d] Philadelphia, Pennsylvania-Wilmington, Delaware-Trenton, New Jersey

Figures given are subject to possible correction for undercount and overcount

sufficient numbers to compensate for the exodus of natives. Natural increase (the excess of births over deaths) helped to make up for some of these out-flows, yielding a small population gain in New York and Chicago.

The populations of Los Angeles, San Francisco, and Miami, however, skyrocketed. Miami still had a large elderly population, so while it received a large number of Cuban exiles, its high death rate kept natural increase down. Reflecting a tilt toward the West Coast, San Francisco grew more rapidly than the Eastern metropolitan regions but more slowly than Los Angeles, which benefited from both high rates of immigration and a high rate of natural increase.

Since 1990, the Los Angeles region has continued to grow, although at a slower pace, reaching 15.3 million in July 1994.[8] Its 5.5 percent rate of increase, while trailing behind Miami's (6.7 percent), is higher than San Francisco's (4.2 percent). Philadelphia and New York continue to have the lowest rates of growth, and the gap between New York and Los Angeles is becoming ever smaller. Surprisingly, the Chicago region has experienced a demographic renewal with a 3.5 percent increase, almost equal to that of San Francisco.

The mushrooming of the Los Angeles suburbs, the balance of the Consolidated Metropolitan Statistical Area (CMSA) in table 3.1, has been spectacular, contributing further to the region's metropolitan sprawl.[9] The rapid postwar suburbanization continued in all six metropolitan regions, but it was most rapid in Los Angeles and Miami. San Francisco had the next highest rate of suburban growth, but its rate was only half that of the Los Angeles region. New York had the highest rate of suburban expansion among Eastern metropolitan regions. Even if the figures in table 3.1 are corrected for census underenumeration, Los Angeles would still be the most dynamic of any giant metropolitan region in the United States.[10]

Thus, the demographic history of the past hundred years has put Los Angeles on a trajectory that should lead it to a position as the nation's premier metropolitan place. If the growth rates of the recent past continue, Los Angeles by the twenty-first century will be home to a population of nearly twenty million, surpassing New York as the nation's largest metropolitan region. The severe economic recession of the early 1990s may delay this scenario, but only a catastrophic earthquake, known popularly as "the big one," can postpone it indefinitely.

One striking feature of giant American metropolitan areas in the 1990s is the numerical importance of ethnic minorities. In 1990, minorities already made up a substantial share of the population of New York, Chicago, and San Francisco, but they were the demographic majority in Los Angeles (see figure 3.2). Philadelphia, which has attracted fewer recent immigrants, has the smallest proportion of minorities. On the other hand, the much smaller Miami metropolitan area has drawn so many immigrants that they have become the overwhelming majority. There are marked differences, however, in the ethnic composition of the minority populations of the above six metropolitan regions. African Americans constitute about one-fifth of the population of Chicago, New York, Philadelphia, and Miami, but they are less than 10 percent of L.A.'s and San Francisco's populations. Asians are much more concentrated in Los Angeles and San Francisco than in the other metropolitan areas. Although San Francisco has the highest Asian percentage, Los Angeles has the largest number of Asians. Hispanics, particularly Mexican Americans, are on their way to becoming a demographic majority in Los Angeles; in 1990 they already made up one-third of the population of the region. In Miami Hispanics are becoming a demographic majority even more rapidly than they are in Los Angeles, but Miami's Latinos are mostly Cuban Americans and are not as numerous as Mexicans in Los Angeles. Furthermore, the post-Castro Cuban "golden exiles" started a thriving ethnic enclave economy in Miami, an adaptation trajectory that is markedly different from that of Mexican labor migrants in L.A.[11]

FIGURE 3.2 | **Distribution of Major Ethnic Groups, Los Angeles and Other U.S. CMSAs, 1990.**

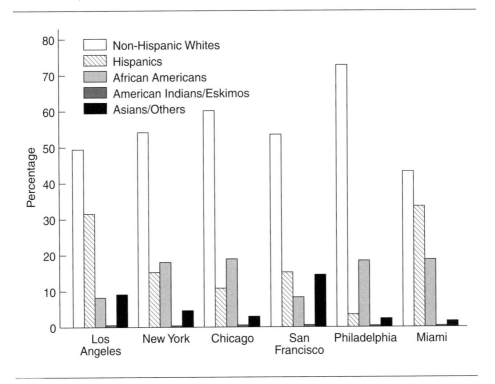

THE SOURCES OF LOS ANGELES' POPULATION DYNAMISM

Los Angeles has always grown through migration, but over the past fifty years, the movements from afar have varied greatly, in both origins and tempo. Natural increase has also added to the region's demographic dynamism, though not necessarily in synchronization with the arrival of migrants from abroad or elsewhere in the United States.

Net internal migration to Los Angeles County exceeded one million persons in the war years of the 1940s and accounted for three-quarters of the population increase.[12] The volume of net migration remained at a high level (1.2 million persons) in the 1950s. Reflecting the process of suburbanization, net migration accounted for more than three-quarters of population growth in the peripheral counties of Orange, Riverside, San Bernardino, and Ventura during the 1950s. The 1960s were an ominous turning point in L.A. County's net migration boom. Net migration plummeted to one-fourth its 1950s level and accounted for only one-fourth of population growth. By the 1970s, Los Angeles County experienced a loss of 123,000 persons through net migration. It was only because of a fairly high level of natural increase that L.A.'s population grew. The picture was very different in the four suburban counties (see figure 3.1 and table 3.1). These counties attracted people not only from Los Angeles County but also from other parts of the United States. Net migration in the outer counties reached nearly 1 million in the 1960s, dropped somewhat in the 1970s, but rebounded to 1.3 million in the 1980s. In these periods, net migration still accounted for about three-fourths of the population growth.

The massive international migration waves of the late 1970s and the 1980s made a big difference in the demographic saga of the Los Angeles region. In the 1970s, if it had not been for international migration Los Angeles County would have lost about 1 million people through net migration instead of the 123,000 it did lose.[13] In the 1980s, there was a dramatic reversal of this trend. In Los Angeles County, net migration increased to nearly half a million people, whereas in the Los Angeles region it increased to 1.8 million. International migration accounted for much of this spectacular reversal, particularly for Los Angeles County. Between 1970 and 1990, the dramatic increases from 11 to 32 percent foreign-born in Los Angeles County and from 10 to 27 percent in Greater Los Angeles make clear the demographic contribution of immigrants. Additional data on previous place of residence also document the demographic contribution of international migration. For Los Angeles County, the number of in-migrants—migrants from within the United States—in the five years preceding the 1980 and 1990 censuses increased slightly from 1.2 million to 1.4 million. But L.A. County's share of recent international migrants increased from slightly under 40 percent to nearly 50 percent. During 1975–80, Los Angeles County experienced a net loss through internal migration of 217,000 non-Hispanic whites but a net gain of 177,000 Hispanics.[14] The massive immigration of the 1980s counteracted somewhat the non-Hispanic white loss but added substantially to the Hispanic gain. For the Los Angeles region in 1985–90, the loss of 135,000 non-Hispanic whites through net internal migration was balanced by a gain of 149,000 international migrants.[15] While Hispanics also experienced a net loss of 49,000 through internal migration, they gained a staggering 488,000 immigrants. Surprisingly, Asians gained population both through net internal migration (37,000) and substantial immigration (212,000). Neither internal nor international migration contributed much to changes in the black population between 1985 and 1990.

Recent information on immigrants' intended metropolitan area of residence suggests that Los Angeles continues to be a magnet for immigrants in the 1990s. According to the latest figures, of the nearly one million immigrants admitted to the United States in fiscal year 1992, 130,000 indicated Los Angeles as their intended place of residence.[16] Moreover, Los Angeles attracts a large number of undocumented immigrants, probably more than any other place in the United States. Since the vast majority of the undocumented are from Mexico, L.A.'s proximity to the Mexican border explains its strong attraction. Of the 1.8 million who applied for permanent resident status under the Immigration Reform and Control Act (IRCA) in 1990, 35 percent resided in Los Angeles County, as compared with only 6 percent in New York. In the Los Angeles region as a whole, there were over three-quarters of a million applicants for legalization.[17] As of January 1, 1992, it is estimated that there were as many as 1.5 million people who either received amnesty or were still unauthorized residents in Los Angeles.[18] California Governor Pete Wilson and others used these large estimates of undocumented immigrants and their alleged burden on social services to convince the majority of California's electorate to pass Proposition 187, which denies public medical care and schooling to the undocumented. Since the vast majority of them are Hispanic, the passage of this proposition disproportionately hurts a single ethnic group and, despite claims to the contrary, is discriminatory.

In summary, Los Angeles has always been a migrant town, but in a very short time it has changed from a magnet for internal migrants to one for international migrants. As a consequence, L.A. now has more Mexicans, Central Americans, Asians, and Middle Easterners than any other metropolitan area in the United States. These two features of L.A.'s population change make it unique.

ETHNIC DIVERSIFICATION OF LOS ANGELES

Despite the impressive growth of the Hispanic and African American populations between 1930 and 1960 (see chapter 2), Los Angeles remained an essentially Anglo metropolis. In 1960 in both Los Angeles County and the region, at least eight out of ten residents were non-Hispanic whites.[19] Moreover, non-Hispanic white migrants from other states of the United States vastly outnumbered African and Mexican American internal migrants.

In the following thirty years, however, the region's demographic makeup was transformed. The predominance of whites ended; their numbers declined somewhat between 1970 and 1980, remained stagnant in the next ten years, and by 1990 had slipped to just under half of the region's population. Nevertheless, in 1990 there were still 6.9 million non-Hispanic whites in Greater Los Angeles. Unlike the pattern in the prior decades, increases in the size of the African American population did little to alter the ethnic mix; between 1960 and 1990, the relative demographic importance of the African American population increased only slightly. Rather, the change resulted from growth among Hispanics and Asians. The Hispanics increased from one-tenth of the region's population in 1960 to one-third in 1990, and Asians grew from 2 to nearly 10 percent.[20]

Within Los Angeles County itself, the process of ethnic change took place at an even more rapid pace. Between 1960 and 1990, the Hispanic percentage jumped from 11 to 36 and the Asian percentage from 2 to 11. If the greater underenumeration of Hispanics could be taken into account, it would be clear that by 1990 there were almost as many Hispanics as non-Hispanic whites in Los Angeles County.[21]

Outside the L.A. core, Anglos made up two-thirds of the population in the four suburban counties in 1990—still the majority, but a drastic fall-off from the peak levels of Anglo predominance recorded in 1960. Other groups made substantial gains; African Americans rapidly suburbanized, and Hispanics and Asians, their numbers swollen by immigration, moved to the suburbs in even larger numbers than did African Americans.

There has been a marked increase in the ethnic diversity of Los Angeles' population as measured by the index of entropy.[22] For both Los Angeles and the Los Angeles region, this index doubled between 1960 and 1990. Most of the increase in diversity, however, occurred between 1960 and 1980. Ethnic diversity also increased in the four outlying counties of the Los Angeles region, but at a lower level than that of Los Angeles. Table 3.2 presents population trends for specific ethnic groups from 1970 to 1990.

As we saw earlier, Los Angeles started as a Mexican pueblo, and Mexican Americans have always been an important element of the population of Los Angeles. Because of changes in the classification of Mexican Americans, it is difficult to have comparable counts of Mexican Americans for the 1930–

90 period. Before 1940, Mexican Americans were classified as non-whites, but under pressure from the Mexican government the Census Bureau reclassified Mexicans as whites instead of nonwhites in the 1940 census. As a consequence, native Mexican Americans whose parents were born in the United States were not identifiable in the 1940 census. Spanish surnames were used to identify Mexican Americans in the 1950 and 1960 censuses, but this system did not distinguish them from other Latinos. To remedy this inadequacy, a new question on Hispanic origin was introduced in the 1970 census and was used in subsequent censuses. In spite of these changes in classification and underenumeration, the Mexican American population of Greater Los Angeles more than tripled between 1970 and 1990 when it reached 3.7 million (see table 3.2 and figure 3.3). By 1990 the Mexican population was more than half as large as the non-Hispanic white population.

Central Americans, mainly Salvadorans, who were nearly nonexistent

FIGURE 3.3 | **Population of Ethnic Groups, Los Angeles Region, 1970–1990**

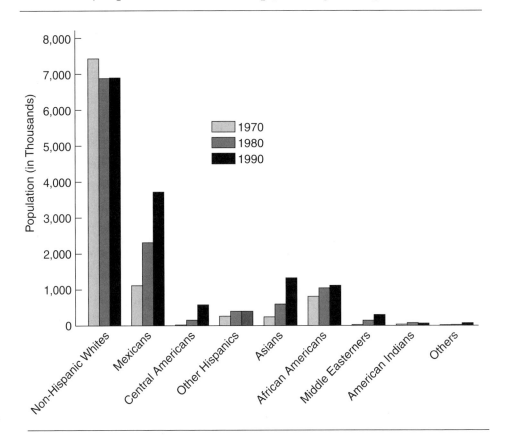

in L.A. in 1970, numbered more than half a million by 1990. Their influx balanced the stagnation in growth of the Hispanic population originating from South America and at the same time added a new element of diversity to the Hispanic population. Despite the more satisfactory classification of Hispanics on the basis of origin, the actual number of Mexicans and Central Americans would be substantially higher if we could adjust the census figures for undercount.

Although Asians have lived in Greater L.A. since the latter half of the nineteenth century, the Asian population also has burgeoned with recent immigration. The number of Asians increased spectacularly from about a quarter of a million in 1970 to 1.3 million in 1990. To the Japanese and Chinese groups who made up the bulk of Asian residents in the 1960s, the new immigration added a much more diverse Asian-origin population. The Japanese were L.A.'s largest Asian-origin group in 1980, but they lost their historical preeminence when the Chinese surpassed them in 1990. The Filipinos were the next largest Asian group in 1990, followed by the Koreans and the Japanese. The population of Filipinos, Vietnamese, Koreans, and Asian Indians more than doubled in the 1980s.[23] In the 1980–90 decade, the Japanese were the slowest-growing Asian group, and the Chinese were the most rapidly growing. Because Japan was so prosperous in this period, the Japanese had no desire to leave their homeland, and Japanese immigration was minimal. As a result, the Japanese population fell from first to fourth place in size, the Chinese rose from third to first place, and the Koreans from fourth to third. Los Angeles has no "Little Manila" Filipino enclave. Nonetheless, despite their residential invisibility, Filipinos were the second most numerous Asian immigrant group in both 1980 and 1990.[24]

The African American population increased at a much slower rate than either the Hispanic or the Asian populations. Still, with 1.1 million persons in 1990, African Americans are a sizable minority in the Los Angeles region. Although American Indians are the smallest of any ethnic group in Los Angeles, they make up the largest native American concentration in any metropolitan area in the United States. Their numbers nearly quadrupled between 1970 and 1980 but then declined to 63,000 in 1990; this decline, however, may reflect both increasing underenumeration and changes in definitions. While Middle Easterners are a small ethnic group compared with Asians, Hispanics, and African Americans, they experienced the most rapid growth of any group, increasing nearly sixfold between 1970 and 1990. By 1990, there were 300,000 Middle Easterners in Greater Los Angeles.

COMPONENTS OF ETHNIC POPULATION CHANGE

A variety of factors account for the changing size of L.A.'s major ethnic groups, but those factors affect each group differently. Asians, for example, have increased primarily because of their massive immigration of the past thirty years, African Americans largely because of an excess of births over deaths, and Mexicans because of high rates of both immigration and fertility. This section seeks to identify the sources of ethnic population change, sorting out the effects of internal migration, international migration, mortality, and fertility. Although data for such an analysis are not readily available, U.S. census data provide some clues to the relative importance of immigration, internal migration, and fertility.

The contribution of immigration, especially its recent waves, to the population growth of ethnic groups varies widely. Nearly all the growth of the Central American population can be attributed to recent immigration, most of it in the 1980s (see figures 3.4 and 3.5 and table 3.2). Immigration also accounts for a large share of Asian and Middle Eastern rapid population growth. The bulk of Asian immigration has occurred since 1965, the year when American immigration legislation was liberalized. On the other hand, Middle Eastern immigration has occurred mostly since 1975, in response to changing economic and political conditions in the Middle East. The foreign-born segment of the already large Mexican American community increased noticeably from 25 percent in 1970 to 46 percent in 1990 (see figure 3.4 and table 3.2); this group gained nearly one million persons through immigration in only one decade, the 1980s (see figure 3.5).

FIGURE 3.4 | Percentage Foreign-Born by Ethnic Groups, Los Angeles Region, 1970–1990

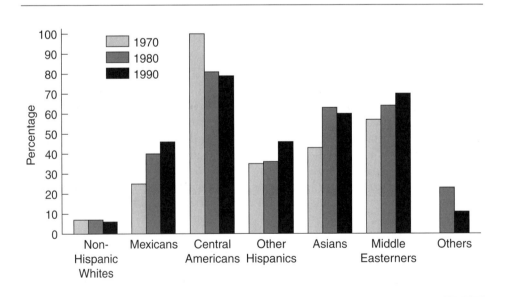

FIGURE 3.5 | **Selected Foreign-Born Ethnic Groups by Year of Immigration, Los Angeles Region, 1970–1990**

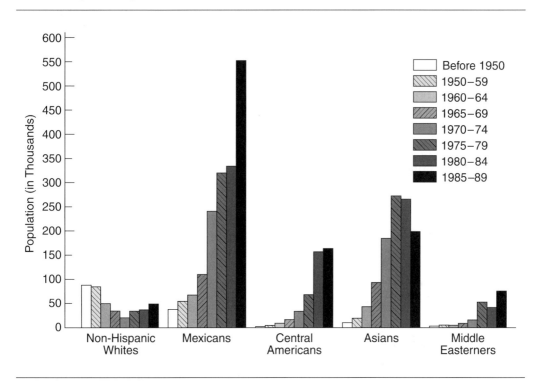

Immigration contributed the least to the population growth of non-Hispanic whites and African Americans (see figure 3.4 and table 3.2). The foreign-born share of non-Hispanic whites dropped from 7 percent in both 1970 and 1980 to 6 percent in 1990. More significantly, however, most of this immigration is old and goes back to 1965 and earlier. African Americans born abroad increased from nearly 0 to 2.7 percent between 1970 and 1990.

Data on state of birth indicate the magnitude of lifetime internal migration. Internal migration is much more important than international migration for non-Hispanic whites and African Americans; 40 to 50 percent of these groups were born in other states of the United States. By contrast, internal migration was less significant than international migration for Asians and Hispanics; fewer than 10 percent of them reported that they were born in other states.

On the whole, mortality levels are fairly low for all ethnic groups in the Los Angeles region, and with groups that have a low mortality rate, higher fertility is likely to contribute to their rapid population increase. One must also take into account the indirect contribution of immigrants through their higher fertility. Data on the number of children ever born to married women at the end of their childbearing years provide a good measure of overall fertility levels. Hispanics have the highest fertility rate of any native-born or foreign-born group, as can be seen in figure 3.6; they have retained that lead although their fertility rates have declined over the past twenty-five years, with the average fertility rate of four children in 1970 falling to three by 1990. Non-Hispanic whites, as well as Asians and other immigrants, have much lower rates, which did not exceed two children on average in 1990. The fertility of both non-Hispanic whites and Asian immigrants declined between 1970 and 1990. For immigrants who arrived prior to 1970, this decline can be attributed mainly to their adaptation to the American norm of smaller families. For the more recent immigrants, fertility decline in the countries of origin may explain why they have fewer children.

Data on the native-born given in figure 3.6 suggest that the second and later generations generally have smaller families than the immigrant generation. Fertility differences among the various ethnic groups, although still noticeable, declined somewhat between 1970 and 1990. For the native-born in 1990, fertility ranged from a high of 2.5 children among Hispanics to about 1.8 among non-Hispanic whites. African Americans' fertility was only slightly lower than that of Hispanics.

FIGURE 3.6 | Number of Children Born per Married Woman Aged 35–44, by Ethnic Group, Los Angeles Region, 1990

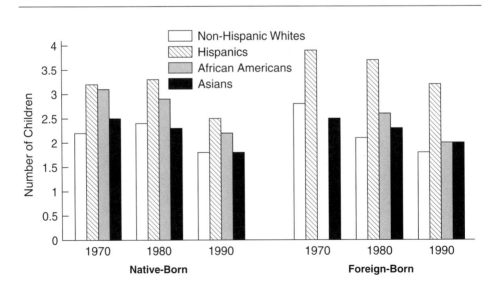

High rates of fertility and of international migration have kept the Hispanic population growing faster than any of the region's other ethnic groups; those factors are likely to continue and to exercise the same effect in the future. Hispanics are likely to have higher age-specific mortality rates, normally a constraint on growth, but the population's youthful age structure has an offsetting impact, yielding lower overall death rates. By contrast, international migration has been the central force propelling the rapid growth of the Asian population: given this population's lower fertility, its future growth will depend entirely on additions from outside, either through continued international migration or through internal migration, although the latter is a relatively unlikely source.

SHIFTING IMMIGRANT ORIGINS

International migration is not a new phenomenon in Los Angeles. The last three decades, however, have brought marked changes in immigration, both an increasing scale and a radical shift in origins from Europe to the Third World, particularly Mexico, Central America, and Asia. Between 1900 and 1930, about 17 percent of L.A. County's population was foreign-born (see figure 3.7), a rate slightly higher than that of the United States.[25] Partly as a result of the Great Depression, the immigrant population in Los Angeles dropped sharply to about 10 percent of the total and stayed at that level until the big explosion in immigration began in 1970. By 1990, the foreign-born accounted for 33 percent of the population of Los Angeles County and slightly less of the metropolitan region, a figure substantially higher than the 8 percent foreign-born for the United States.

The massive new immigration is one of the most striking sociodemographic phenomena of the last three decades, not only in Los Angeles but in the United States as a whole. The new immigration to the United States included 13.6 million persons legally admitted and about 3 million estimated to have arrived illegally from 1961 to 1989.[26] The only other comparable period of massive immigration was 1891–1920, when 18.2 million persons were admitted to the United States. What is distinctive about the new immigration is its composition by countries of origin. According to Thomas Muller and Thomas Espenshade, who described it as the "fourth wave" of immigrants, the new immigration is characterized not only by the predominance of Asians and Hispanics but also by greater diversity and "sharp cultural differences among immigrant subgroups."[27] These features are even more pronounced in Los Angeles than in the nation as a whole.

The massive immigrant influx to Los Angeles involved a dramatic shift in origins. Although Los Angeles never experienced a mass European immigration comparable to that of the East Coast cities, Europeans were the most important foreign-born population until 1960. After 1960, the size of the

FIGURE 3.7 | Percentage of Population Foreign-Born, Los Angeles Region and Los Angeles County, 1900–1990

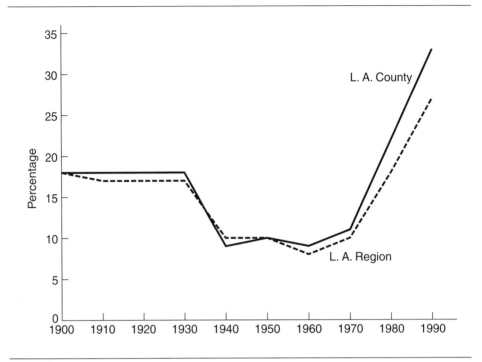

European-born population, mostly non-Hispanic whites, declined. As European numbers dropped and newcomers from the rest of the world headed for L.A., the share of Europeans among the foreign-born shrank to 5 percent in 1990. Only the countries of the former Soviet Union continued to funnel a sizable immigrant flow toward Los Angeles, though not for the entire period with which we are concerned. The number of Russian immigrants declined by half between 1960 and 1980 but then nearly doubled in the 1980s, as a result of the influx of Jewish and Armenian refugees.

After 1960, the newcomers to the Los Angeles region predominantly came from the Third World; by 1990, the number of Angelenos who had been born in Latin America, Asia, or the Middle East had increased from nearly 534,000 twenty years before to about 3.5 million. This rise transformed the national origins mix of the region's foreign-born residents. In 1960, Third World immigrants were about half as numerous as the European foreign-born; by 1990, their numbers were nine times greater (see table 3.2).

From 1970 to 1990, Latin America, and more particularly Mexico, con-

TABLE 3.2 | **Population of Specific Ethnic Groups by Nativity, Los Angeles Region, 1970–1990**

	1970[a]	1980	1990
Hispanics			
Salvadoran NB	—	7,560	60,058
Salvadoran FB	4,800	54,060	241,509
Guatemalan NB	—	6,040	32,431
Guatemalan FB	3,500	32,780	126,837
Other Central Amer NB	—	15,500	31,362
Other Central Amer FB	14,100	38,360	87,800
Mexican NB	830,000	1,380,200	2,000,472
Mexican FB	283,900	928,660	1,717,911
Other Hispanic NB	171,400	256,680	214,046
Other Hispanic FB	91,900	142,280	185,083
All Hispanics	1,399,600	2,862,120	4,697,509
Native-born	1,001,400	1,665,980	2,338,369
Foreign-born	398,200	1,196,140	2,359,140
Asians and Pacific Islanders			
Japanese NB	88,600	108,300	123,345
Japanese FB	32,200	45,240	57,094
Chinese NB	26,800	36,160	75,649
Chinese FB	29,000	80,420	231,361
Vietnamese NB	—	4,200	26,597
Vietnamese FB	—	44,120	116,293
Filipino NB	19,300	32,200	81,080
Filipino FB	24,700	80,100	203,138
Korean NB	4,200	11,960	36,322
Korean FB	9,200	64,740	155,568
Asian Indian NB	1,800	6,960	16,321
Asian Indian FB	2,900	20,540	56,851
Other Asians NB	6,900	22,860	55,113
Other Asians FB	10,600	38,280	91,827
All Asians	256,200	596,080	1,326,559
Native-born	147,600	222,640	414,427
Foreign-born	108,600	373,440	912,132
Middle Easterners			
Armenian NB	8,600	17,880	33,089
Armenian FB	9,300	34,520	81,956
Iranian NB	1,300	3,240	12,276
Iranian FB	2,400	22,420	63,249
Arab NB	8,300	22,280	33,449
Arab FB	7,000	25,140	46,585
Israeli NB	2,200	3,520	5,846

TABLE 3.2 | *(Continued)*

	1970[a]	1980	1990
Israeli FB	4,600	7,900	14,270
Other ME NB	4,700	4,380	5,962
Other ME FB	4,000	2,820	3,864
All Middle Easterners	52,400	144,100	300,546
Native-born	25,100	51,300	90,622
Foreign-born	27,300	92,800	209,924
Non-Hispanic Whites[b]			
Native-born	6,577,500	6,425,560	6,494,372
Foreign-born	506,000	450,980	398,884
African Americans			
Native-born	778,700	1,026,800	1,114,269
Foreign-born	2,300	17,000	31,415
American Indians			
Native-born	20,300	75,580	61,978
Foreign-born	200	1,280	575
All Others			
Native-born	9,800	17,480	61,996
Foreign-born	6,000	5,200	7,324
Total Native-born	8,868,600	9,485,340	10,576,033
Total Foreign-born	1,090,300	2,136,840	3,919,394

[a] 5 percent sample for Hispanics and 15 percent sample for all other groups. Because the numbers are based on samples, the total populations in this table do not agree with table 3.1.
[b] Excluding Middle Easterners

tributed the most to the immigrant population of the Los Angeles region. In 1990, L.A. had 2.4 million persons who had been born in Latin America, 1.7 million of them in Mexico. Asians ranked next in importance to Latin Americans, numbering nearly 1 million in 1990.

Middle Easterners also headed for L.A. in significant numbers, creating the largest metropolitan concentration of Middle Easterners in the United States. In a mere twenty years, 1970–90, their numbers increased sixfold, yielding a population of 300,000 that was dominated by a mix of Armenians, Iranians, Arabs, and Israelis. While the number of African immigrants also rose sharply during this period, this gain began from a tiny population base; by 1990, L.A.'s African immigrant population was still very small (see table 3.2).

Growth was accompanied by increased diversity among the newcomers from the Third World. Even though immigration yielded a huge net gain over the course of the next two decades, Mexico's share of foreign-born Latinos decreased steadily from 1970 to 1990. Political turmoil in Guatemala and civil war in El Salvador made for a massive flow of refugees searching for safe havens; many found safety in L.A., which saw its foreign-born population from El Salvador and Guatemala mushroom from about 8,000 in 1970 to 368,000 in 1990 (see table 3.2). Despite this recent trend, persons born in Mexico still account for about half of all the foreign-born in the Los Angeles region. The composition of the immigration from Asia also changed. The end of the U.S. involvement in Vietnam precipitated a sizable migration of Vietnamese to the Los Angeles region. The greater U.S. economic or military involvement in Korea and Taiwan also facilitated emigration from those two countries.

Immigration has made an important contribution to the growth of specific groups such as Filipinos, Chinese, and Mexicans. It accounts for about half of the growth of the Mexican population, about three-quarters of both the Chinese and Filipino population increase, and most of the Vietnamese and Iranian population growth.

GRAYING ANGLOS AND YOUTHFUL LATINOS

Although immigration has been a driving force of demographic change, shifts in age structure and differences in fertility have also contributed powerfully to the region's changing ethnic mix. Latinos are now dominant among the region's children and adolescents, a development that reflects their higher fertility rates. By contrast, non-Hispanic whites make up the bulk of the elderly population. Thus, Los Angeles, thanks to its Latinos, has become younger, even while the rest of American society has begun to gray.

Figures 3.8, 3.9, and 3.10 show ethnic differences in the age structure of the region's population in 1970, 1980, and 1990 respectively; together they paint a portrait of dramatic change. The most startling transformation was the increasing ethnic diversity of children, adolescents, and young adults. In 1970, persons younger than twenty-five were overwhelmingly non-Hispanic white, but by 1990 they became a Latino majority. If we add Asians and African Americans to Latinos, ethnic minorities made up over 60 percent of youthful Angelenos, compared with only 30 percent in 1970. This was the most dramatic ethnic transformation of young Angelenos under twenty-five years of age in the whole history of Los Angeles. Thus, in a mere twenty years, young Anglos became the new demographic minority in the Los Angeles region. On the other hand, older Anglos remained the overwhelming majority throughout this period. In 1990, the latter still made up three-quarters of the population sixty-five years and older in the Los Angeles region.[28]

These ethnodemographic trends have far-reaching implications. They

FIGURE 3.8 | **Age Profile of Ethnic Groups, Los Angeles Region, 1970**

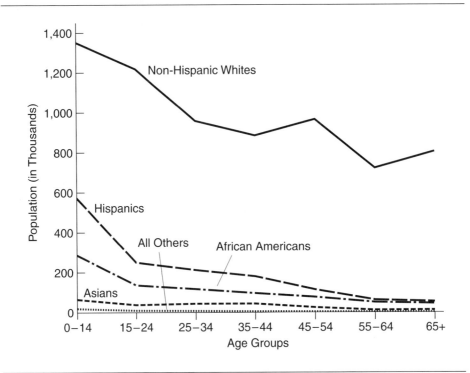

are immediately reflected in the composition of the student population of the Los Angeles public schools. Between 1970 and 1990, the Hispanic share of the student population rose from 20 percent to 63 percent, and the non-Hispanic white segment dropped sharply, from 50 percent to 14 percent. Meanwhile, the share of Asian students nearly doubled, from 4 percent to 7 percent in these schools.[29]

The overwhelming presence in schools of children of immigrants, many of whom have a limited knowledge of English, has had a tremendous impact on Los Angeles' public schools. In spite of limited funds, these schools have had to develop special curricula to satisfy the needs of these children. Some schools, such as Fairfax High, where the influx of Hispanic and Asian students has transformed the student body, have been successful in initiating these programs. On the negative side, some Anglo parents perceive these changes as detrimental to their children's education. Many who can afford it send their children to private schools, while others have moved to suburbs in search of schools with fewer minorities. This factor has indirectly contributed to "white flight" and Anglo suburbanization.

FIGURE 3.9 | **Age Profile of Ethnic Groups, Los Angeles Region, 1980**

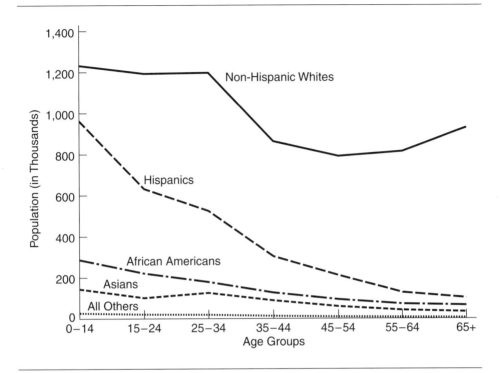

As the supporters of Proposition 187 have amply publicized, a number of students in Los Angeles and other California public schools are children of undocumented immigrants. Their education will be at risk if Proposition 187 is implemented. But regardless of their legal status, immigrant students pose a serious challenge to Los Angeles' public schools to provide an education that is sensitive to their multicultural and multilingual backgrounds.

The ethnic diversity of youth has carried over to the local universities and colleges, albeit at different rates. For instance, the University of California at Los Angeles (UCLA) has become one of the most ethnically diverse universities in the United States. In the fall of 1994, 29 percent of UCLA's freshman class were white/Caucasian (including Middle Easterners), 43 percent were Asian and Pacific Islanders (including Filipinos),[30] 14 percent were Chicano/Mexican American, 5 percent were Latinos/other Latin Americans, 8 percent were African Americans, and 1 percent were American Indians.[31] Because UCLA has very strict admission policies, this composition does not reflect L.A.'s ethnic population mix. Asians are vastly overrepresented, blacks are very slightly underrepresented, but Mexican Americans are grossly underrepresented.

FIGURE 3.10 | **Age Profile of Ethnic Groups, Los Angeles Region, 1990**

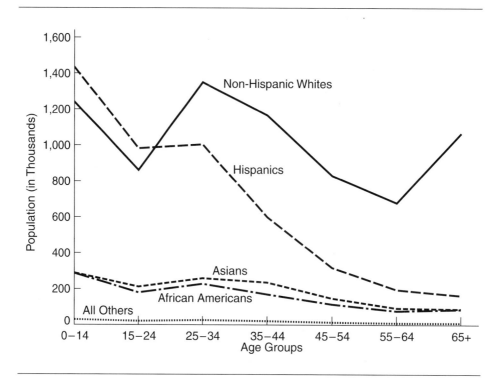

Perhaps the most important consequence of the changing age profile is its impact on the distribution of the labor force by age and ethnic group. In 1970, non-Hispanic whites were clearly the majority in the younger labor force aged 25–34. By 1990, they became the minority, numbering 1.4 million versus 1 million Hispanics and nearly half a million Asians and African Americans. Non-Hispanic whites were still the vast majority in the oldest labor force age group of 55–64 years. If increasing age implies seniority, security of employment, better jobs, and higher incomes, Hispanics, Asians, and African Americans are at a disadvantage, a conclusion reached by other authors in this book.

In voting, non-Hispanic whites are increasingly likely to endorse candidates and ballot measures that favor the elderly population. By contrast, Asians, African Americans, and particularly Hispanics will support programs aimed at improving schools and providing employment for young adolescents and young adults. To the extent that non-Hispanic whites oppose such programs, it will bring them in conflict with Hispanics, African Americans, and Asians. For example, immigrants in Los Angeles protested California Governor Pete Wilson's veto of a bill that would have financed

English proficiency classes.[32] During the days preceding the November 1994 election, there were massive walkouts and demonstrations by Hispanic and other high school students against Proposition 187. After California voters approved the proposition, many Hispanic groups allied with other groups to challenge its legality.

LOOKING INTO THE FUTURE

What has happened to the population of the Los Angeles region since 1990? Local newspapers are full of stories of families leaving Los Angeles for better lives elsewhere. Late in 1993, the *Los Angeles Times* asserted that Los Angeles is experiencing its "largest exodus . . . this century."[33] This exodus has been attributed not only to the economic recession of the early 1990s but also to natural disasters, such as the devastating Northridge earthquake in January 1994. "Fleeing Los Angeles: Quake is the last straw" read one headline in the *New York Times*.

Despite the bad news, the Los Angeles region keeps on growing. Persistent immigration, albeit at lower levels, continues to swell the population base. According to one estimate, average net annual migration to the Los Angeles region fell to 41,000 during the first four years of the 1990s, from the much higher figure of 156,000 recorded during the 1980s. Not all parts of the region have fared equally well in the contest for new arrivals. Los Angeles County experienced a net out-migration of 152,000 between 1990 and 1994; by contrast, the four suburban counties enjoyed a yield of 311,000 persons through net in-migration.[34]

Although migration continued, it lost place to natural increase as the most important contributor to population growth during the 1990s. During the first four years of the 1990s, natural increase was responsible for an average annual addition of 221,000 people—a large jump relative to the 1980s, when natural increase contributed 147,000 new Angelenos each year.[35]

Of course, these high rates of natural increase are an immediate legacy of immigration, most importantly the growth of the region's immigrant Hispanic population. The estimated total fertility rate of Los Angeles has increased steadily ever since 1984, when 2,090 babies were born per year for every one thousand women, as compared with 2,650 in 1988. In 1984, by contrast, fertility rates for the United States as a whole fell well below the Los Angeles levels, and though they subsequently increased, the proportional increase failed to match L.A.'s gain. Youthful, and with higher age-specific fertility rates than other ethnic groups, L.A.'s expanding Hispanic population contributes to population growth both directly and indirectly.

Will the demographic future of the Los Angeles region be different from the present? Or will L.A. witness the rapid population growth, ethnic diver-

FIGURE 3.11 | Total Population and Population of Major Ethnic Groups, Los Angeles Region, Actual 1990 and Projected to 2020

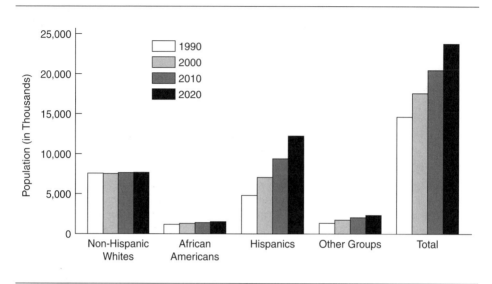

sification, and re-Latinization that were typical of the 1970s and 1980s? The higher fertility of both native- and foreign-born Hispanics and continued immigration from Mexico and Central America imply a continued Latinization of the future population of the Los Angeles region, and especially of L.A. County. The official population projections prepared by the California Department of Finance (see figure 3.11) point in just this direction.[36] These projections estimate that the population of the Los Angeles region will increase substantially from slightly under 15 million in 1990 to nearly 24 million in the year 2020.[37] Much of this increase is likely to result from the expansion of the Latino population from nearly 5 million in 1990 to 12 million in 2020. This continued Latinization of the population is particularly noticeable among the youth of Los Angeles County, half of whom were Latinos in 1990. By 2020, the Latino share of youth may increase to 70 percent.[38] Thus, no matter what projection methods are used, multi-ethnicity and Latinization, particularly of the youth, will characterize the future of the Los Angeles region.

CONCLUSION

This chapter has documented the demographic dynamism of the Los Angeles metropolitan region and the sudden and radical transformation of its ethnic composition under the impact of the massive new immigration of the 1970s and 1980s. Thanks to immigration, this once-provincial urban region has become a vibrant cosmopolitan metropolis.

With a population exceeding 15 million, Los Angeles is the next largest metropolitan region after New York in the United States; its population is expected to surpass New York's in the twenty-first century. L.A.'s demographic history has been characterized by a dynamism unequaled by any other giant metropolitan region. At the beginning of the twentieth century, it had only a quarter of a million persons, a relatively small population compared with other metropolitan regions. In the decades that followed, dramatic population spurts occurred, brought about by massive internal migrations from other parts of the United States. This population boom ended abruptly with the onset of the Great Depression but reappeared with even more vigor during and after the Second World War with new waves of internal migrants. Prior to the 1970s, the relatively small foreign-born population consisted predominantly of Europeans. In spite of past demographic dynamism, Los Angeles was headed to zero population growth in the 1970s, when waves of immigrants from the Third World, particularly from Mexico, Central America, and Asia, suddenly flooded its shores. This new immigration submerged the relatively small European stock. More importantly, it gave back to Los Angeles its demographic dynamism while also radically altering its ethnic mix and making the region highly diverse. In the process, Los Angeles also recaptured its Latin origin, becoming the largest Mexican metropolis outside of Mexico City and the largest Salvadoran settlement outside of San Salvador. Los Angeles now also has the largest Korean, Filipino, and Iranian diaspora populations in the Western world. In the 1980s, Los Angeles replaced New York as the principal magnet for the new immigration, further contributing to its diversity and growth.

The new immigration contributed indirectly as well as directly to the demographic dynamism of Los Angeles. The noticeably higher fertility of the large Hispanic population, particularly of its sizable foreign-born component, partly accounts for Los Angeles' higher fertility rates and rates of population growth. Both immigration and fertility explain the wide differences in age profiles among the various ethnic and racial groups of Los Angeles. The non-Hispanic white population is aging so rapidly that its children, adolescents, and young adults are now a minority. The youth of Los Angeles have become overwhelmingly Hispanic. The opposite is true for the elderly, among whom the non-Hispanic whites still are the vast majority.

The end of the cold war with the Soviet Union and the drastic reduction of military expenditures triggered an economic recession and increasing unemployment in the Los Angeles region, returning the region to slow population growth. This is amply illustrated by numerous newspaper stories on the topic, but it is also documented by official estimates of the State of California. In the years 1990–94, Los Angeles County experienced a negative net migration of about 152,000 persons, but because of substantial natural increase, it continued to grow slowly to an estimated 9.2 million on January 1, 1994.[39] Whether this trend is reversed or not in the immediate future, it is clear that Los Angeles will experience further ethnic diversification and Latinization. By the year 2010, the Hispanic population of the Los Angeles region is projected to exceed the non-Hispanic white population by nearly 2 million; by 2020, the difference between these two populations may exceed 4 million. Schools and other social institutions in Los Angeles will have to adapt to face the challenge of an irreversible ethnodemographic transformation that started in the 1970s. Barring a major catastrophe, by the beginning of the twenty-first century Los Angeles will emerge as the largest metropolitan region of the United States, replacing New York's two-century dominance of urban America.

Notes to Chapter 3

1. Quoted from George J. Sanchez, *Becoming Mexican American: Ethnicity, Culture, and Identity in Chicano Los Angeles, 1900–1945* (New York: Oxford University Press, 1993), 71.

2. This characterization is from the subtitle of David Rieff, *Los Angeles: Capital of the Third World* (New York: Simon and Schuster, 1991).

3. George W. Robbins and L. Deming Tilton, *Los Angeles: Preface to a Master Plan* (Los Angeles: The Pacific Southwest Academy, 1941), 103.

4. Allen J. Scott. *The Technopoles of Southern California* (UCLA Research Papers in Economic and Urban Geography, no. 1, July 1989), 41.

5. Employment in the aerospace industry tripled between 1950 and 1955, accounting for half of all manufacturing employment. See Scott, *Technopoles,* 42.

6. Five metropolitan regions with populations of at least five million each in 1980 are included. In 1990, these five accounted for about 41 percent of the population of all metropolitan regions (CMSAs or Consolidated Metropolitan Statistical Areas) and one-fifth of the total population of the United States.

7. Alejandro Portes and Alex Stepick, *City on the Edge: The Transformation of Miami* (Berkeley and Los Angeles: University of California Press, 1993).

8. U.S. Bureau of the Census. *Estimates of the Resident Population of States and Counties, and Percent Change 4/1/90 to 7/1/94* (Press release CB94-204, issued 1/18/95).

9. The Los Angeles CMSA encompasses an area of 33,210 square miles, which is much larger than the 7,658, 7,403, 5,660, and 5,351 square miles for the New York, San Francisco, Chicago, and Philadelphia CMSAs, respectively (U.S. Bureau of the Census, *State and Metropolitan Area Data Book 1986* (Washington, D.C.: Government Printing Office, 1986). Even if we exclude its extensive desert and mountain areas, Los Angeles is still a geographically vast metropolitan region.

10. The population data for all ethnic groups, more particularly African Americans, Hispanics, and American Indians, are affected by underenumeration. According to an estimate prepared by the U.S. Bureau of the Census (press release, June 13, 1991), for the total resident population of the United States in 1990, underenumeration expressed in percentages were: total population, 2.1; blacks, 4.8; Hispanics, 5.2; American Indians, 5.0; and Asian and Pacific Islanders 3.1. The range in these estimates for the 95 percent confidence interval were: 1.7 to 2.5, 4.2 to 5.4, 4.6 to 6.0, 2.9 to 7.1, and 2.2 to 4.0, respectively. In 1990, after adjustments for underenumeration, the population of Los Angeles County increased from 8,863,164 to an estimated 9,292,000 (U.S. Bureau of the Census, press release, June 13, 1991).

11. Alejandro Portes and Robert Bach, *Latin Journey* (Berkeley and Los Angeles: University of California Press, 1985).

12. Because of the unreliability of birth and death data prior to 1940, we limit the analysis of the relative contributions of net migration and of natural increase to the last fifty years (1940–90). See Georges Sabagh, "Los Angeles, A World of New Immigrants: An Image of Things to Come?" in *Migration Policies in Europe and the United States,* Giacomo Luciani, ed. (Dordrecht, Netherlands: Kluwer Academic Publishers, 1993), 106, for data on net migration.

13. Thomas Muller and Thomas J. Espenshade, *The Fourth Wave: California's Newest Immigrants* (Washington, D.C.: The Urban Institute, 1985).

14. U.S. Bureau of the Census. *Gross Migration for Counties: 1975 to 1980* (Washington, D.C.: Government Printing Office, 1984).

15. We would like to thank Mark Ellis of UCLA's Geography Department for making the 1990 census figures available to us. It should be noted that the net gains through migration are only for internal migration.

16. These data refer to both adjustments to permanent residence and admissions in fiscal 1992 (U.S. Immigration and Naturalization Service, *1992 Statistical Yearbook* [Washington, D.C.: U.S. Government Printing Office, 1993], 64). Another 60,000 selected the counties of Orange, Riverside, San Bernardino and Ventura.

17. U.S. Immigration and Naturalization Service. *1990 Statistical Yearbook* (Washington, D.C.: Government Printing Office, 1991), 95.

18. Manuel Moreno et al., *Impact of Undocumented Persons and Other Immigrants on Costs, Revenues and Services in Los Angeles County.* Unpublished Report, Los Angeles County Urban Research Section, 1992, 25.

19. In 1960, Hispanics refers to persons with Spanish surnames.

20. In 1960, the population data for Hispanics are based on Spanish surnames and are not strictly comparable to data from the 1970, 1980, and 1990 censuses. For the first time, the 1970 census included a question on "Spanish origin." In Los Angeles County in 1970, there were 911,004 persons with Spanish surnames and 1,289,311 persons of Spanish origin (U.S. Bureau of the Census, *1970 Census of Population, Persons of Spanish Origin* (Washington, D.C.: Government Printing Office, 1973). Thus, it is possible that if data on Spanish origin were available in 1960, the percent Hispanic would have been greater than shown in table 3.3.

There are also problems in the comparisons between the 1970 and 1980 censuses. According to Bean and Tienda, part of the growth of the Hispanic population between 1870 and 1980 "is an artifact of improvement in the coverage of the Hispanic population resulting from a change in the design of census questionnaires and from the initiation of an effective public relations campaign aimed at reducing undercount among ethnic populations." See Frank Bean and Marta Tienda, *The Hispanic Population of the United States* (New York: Russell Sage Foundation, 1987), 58.

21. The estimated undercount of Hispanics in the United States in 1980 ranges between the figures of 1.9 percent undercount for whites and 7.7 percent undercount for blacks (see Bean and Tienda, *Hispanic Population,* 58). For estimates of underenumeration of Hispanics in Los Angeles in 1980–81, see David M. Heer and Jeffrey S. Passel, "Comparison of Two Methods for Estimating the Number of Undocumented Mexican Adults in Los Angeles County," *International Migration Review* 21 (1987): 1446–73.

22. The greater the diversity, the higher the index of entropy.

23. It should be noted that, in 1980, Orange County had only 19,333 Vietnamese, fewer than Los Angeles County, but by 1990, the 71,822 Vietnamese in Orange County exceeded those in Los Angeles County and were the largest Asian group. The Chinese, with a population of 41,403, were the next most numerous group, and the Koreans, with a population of 35,919, were the third largest. The most rapidly growing Asian groups in Orange County were the Vietnamese and Asian Indians, whose population quadrupled in ten years. The population of Chinese, Koreans, and Filipinos tripled in the same period. These data suggest a process of suburbanization among some Asian groups between 1980 and 1990. See U.S. Bureau of the Census, *1980 Census of Population,* vol. 1 *Detailed Population Characteristics, California.* (Washington, D.C.: Government Printing Office, 1983); U.S. Bureau of the Census, *1990 Census of Population, Social and Economic Characteristics, California* (Washington, D.C.: Government Printing Office, 1993).

24. See further Mehdi Bozorgmehr, Georges Sabagh, and Ivan Light, "Los Angeles: Explosive Diversity," in Silvia Pedraza and Ruben Rumbaut, eds., *Origins and Destinations* (Belmont, Calif.: Wadsworth, 1996), 346–59.

25. U.S. Bureau of the Census, *We the American . . . Foreign Born* (Washington, D.C.: Government Printing Office, 1993), 2.

26. U.S. Immigration and Naturalization Service, *1989 Statistical Yearbook* (Washington, D.C.: U.S. Department of Justice, 1990).

27. Muller and Espenshade, *Fourth Wave.* It should be noted that there were smaller waves of Asian and Hispanic immigration going back to the second half of the nineteenth century.

28. It may be noted, however, that between 1980 and 1990 there was a doubling in the number of aged Hispanics and Asians and Pacific Islanders and a slight increase in the number of aged African Americans.

29. Los Angeles Unified School District, *Ethnic Survey Report, Fall 1990* (December, 1990).

30. Filipinos are counted separately.

31. *UCLA Today,* December 16, 1994.

32. *New York Times,* Monday, November 11, 1991.

33. *Los Angeles Times,* October 2, 1993.

34. California Demographic Research Unit, *Total, Military, Civilian Population, Crude Birth Rates, and Components of Change for California Counties and the State,* Report E-6 (Sacramento: Department of Finance, 1994).

35. California Demographic Research Unit, *Total, Military, Civilian Population.*

36. Population projections for the state of California prepared by the U.S. Bureau of the Census suggest that the projection of the California Demographic Research Unit of the State Department of Finance may have markedly underestimated future Asian population growth and slightly overestimated future Hispanic population growth. For the year 2020, the U.S. Bureau of the Census projected 9.7 million Asians and Pacific Islanders in California, compared with 5.7 million projected by the California Demographic Research Unit. The comparable figures for Hispanics are 17.4 million and 20 million. See U.S. Bureau of the Census, *Population Projection by States by Age, Race, and Hispanic Origin: 1993–2020; Current Population Reports.* ser. P-25, no. 1111 (March, 1994); California Demographic Research Unit, *Projected Total Population of California Counties, Report 93 P3, Official State Projections* (Sacramento: Department of Finance, 1993).

37. As compared with the estimated population of 15.4 million for the Los Angeles region on January 1, 1994, a projected population of 17.5 million for this region in 2000 implies an unlikely rapid acceleration of population until the end of the century. It is likely that later projections of the future population of the Los Angeles region will be adjusted downward.

38. California Demographic Research Unit, *Projected Total Population of California Counties.*

39. California Demographic Research Unit. *Total, Military, and Civilian Population,* 19.

Residential Patterns: Avoidance, Assimilation, and Succession

William A. V. Clark

THE NORTHRIDGE earthquake struck Los Angeles on January 17, 1994, delivering a social as well as a seismic shock. When the trembling stopped, the region began the long, hard work of recovering from its most recent natural disaster, only to receive a geography lesson that it had not expected to learn. The earth had shaken hardest in the San Fernando Valley, where white middle-class homeowners had replaced orange groves barely a generation ago. But in the aftermath of the catastrophe, Angelenos discovered that the epicenter of the quake had become home to a fast-growing concentration of newcomers from abroad. For anyone who still thought of the San Fernando Valley as Southern California's quintessential suburban enclave, the sight of thousands of immigrants milling in the Valley's streets and camped in its parks showed how profoundly the region had changed.

If the Northridge earthquake provided a window into the new residential reality in Los Angeles, the full details of the region's evolving ethnic geography are not yet clear. Los Angeles seems to portend an emerging multicultural United States, but changes at the regional level are not necessarily played out at the community levels where people live and mix. The image of regional diversity may well be a statistical artifact that conflicts with patterns of homogeneity and segregation at the local level and the varying local scales of block and census tract. It is also possible that life at the local level is every bit as diverse and heterogeneous as the statistics for the region would suggest but the mixing is just a passing phase. Does the multiethnic world uncovered by the Northridge earthquake provide an indicator of immigrant assimilation into a mixed society of old-timers and newcomers? Or does it point to a continuing pattern of ethnic succession, in which one group will move out in an effort to avoid another?

These are the questions addressed by this chapter as it seeks to tell the story of Los Angeles' new ethnic geography. It will take up the issue of the relative level of mixing—how much of each group exists in different communities and neighborhoods—and identify the extent, location, and pace of ethnic diversity in the residential structure of Los Angeles. The first sections of the chapter examine the aggregate patterns of residential diversity between 1970 and 1990, asking how the patterns of diversity change as one moves from broader areas to smaller scales. The latter sections examine the pace of ethnic and racial change in the past decade and explore the evidence of change or persistence in the process of succession. The chapter concludes by seeking to interpret the numbers, probing for signs that might point to increasing integration or new patterns of segregation.

THE THEORETICAL CONTEXT OF SEPARATION AND SEGREGATION

Studies of the residential mosaic—the patterns of ethnic and residential separation—form a rich component of the literatures of sociology, demography, and geography. In various ways, social scientists have tried to understand how our society has created its patterns of separation, avoidance, and assimilation. Traditionally, the immigrant enclaves were presented as transitional stages on the road to eventual acceptance and integration into the larger American society.[1] As developed by the Chicago school, the model posits initial separation followed by long-term assimilation. At first, the ethnic group sticks together, but only in order to integrate more successfully into the larger society at a later time. Thus, the immigrant enclave provides both haven and opportunity.

Counterposed to this earlier pattern of separation followed by assimilation is an alternative model of residential change characterized by persistent efforts at avoidance. In this framework, the barriers to mixing result from extensive and pervasive white flight, as whites move first to nearby suburban areas and later to communities even farther removed from the urban core and its ethnoracial concentrations. Of course, other considerations—most importantly, the quest for the suburban life, combined with a desire for distance from inner-city ethnic groups—fuel the outward flow of whites. But whatever the precise mix of factors, L.A.'s white population has consistently gravitated away from the center and toward the periphery— yesterday in the San Fernando and San Gabriel valleys, today in Simi Valley and other newer areas beyond the confines of Los Angeles County.

These concepts of separation and assimilation, generated by the urban ecology school, provided a rich context for studies of segregation, especially those focusing on African Americans and whites. The early studies of neighborhood structure and neighborhood change sought to describe and measure the levels of separation among various ethnic and racial groups. Later studies evaluated the variation in residential patterns and examined the roles of economics, residential choice, and discrimination in the creation of separate neighborhoods.[2] The causes of separation across residential neighborhoods remain a subject of ongoing debate, with one camp emphasizing choice and self-selection, and the other, racial avoidance and its associated barriers to residential integration and assimilation.[3] In the past, both processes affected the residential patterns of European immigrants and their descendants, and a similar mix of causal conditions seems to impinge on the newcomers of today. Preferences for particular combinations of ethnic neighbors continue to play an important role in deciding where individual families choose to reside.[4] But not all groups have the same preferences; whites and Asians clearly have stronger preferences for neighborhoods of their own race or ethnicity than do Hispanics and blacks.[5] Groups also differ in their ability to exercise their choices; financial considerations make a major difference, but so too do barriers thrown up by other groups. In the end, varying preferences and the process of distancing create communities of interest and, therefore, of separation in the structure of residential neighborhoods.[6] Hence, the combinations of preferences and avoidance may be reinforcing patterns of separation that perhaps were seen initially as providing havens in the assimilation process.

THE TREND OF SEGREGATION AND MULTI-ETHNICITY

Rapid ethnic in-migration is yielding important changes in the residential mosaic all across the United States, as a number of indicators show. One such shift has to do with the older simple dichotomy between black and white communities, which no longer appears relevant, especially in the larger metropolitan areas but also in certain other regions of the country. Los Angeles, New York, Chicago, and four other cities of more than half a million residents lack a majority of any ethnic group (see figure 4.1). In another group of cities, majorities of non-Hispanic whites live alongside mixtures of minority ethnic/racial groups that, when combined, make up 30 to 50 percent of the population base. Ten of California's cities of 50,000 people or more no longer have an ethnoracial majority of any kind (see figure 4.2). In sum, diversity at the citywide level is on the increase.

But change at the aggregate level has uncertain implications for residential segregation, especially for the trajectory followed by the African American community in large metropolitan areas. On the basis of an analysis of changes during the 1970s, Douglas Massey and Andrew Gross concluded that although there were some signs of decreasing segregation, these changes

FIGURE 4.1 | Population Distribution of Major Ethnic Groups in Cities of 500,000 or More Without an Ethnic/Racial Majority, 1990

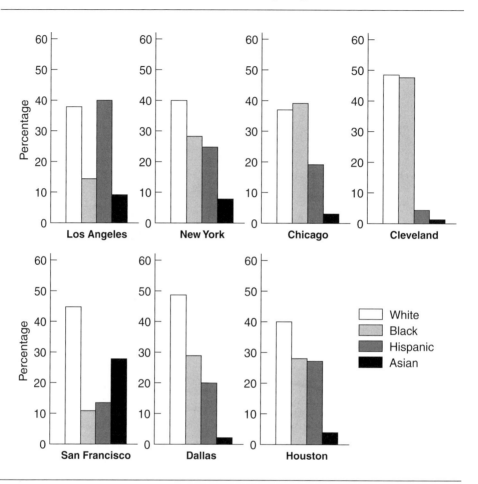

were limited to a small number of residential areas where the number of African Americans was relatively small.[7] Other evidence points to differences between older and newer metropolitan areas in the type of neighborhood transitions; in the older cities of the East, limited amounts of new construction and acute levels of black poverty and deprivation maintain high levels of residential segregation,[8] whereas newer, Western cities may be providing an exception to the long-established succession rule, whereby the process of transition, once begun, continues until the formerly dominant ethnic group is entirely replaced by another.[9] Still other studies, based on 1990 census data, support the view that unique racial segregation dy-

The Labor Market: Immigrant Effects and Racial Disparities

Paul Ong and Abel Valenzuela, Jr.

OVER THE PAST twenty-five years, the influx of Latino and Asian immigrants to Los Angeles has transformed the region's population, a change that has reconfigured and complicated race relations, particularly as they pertain to economic issues. The pattern of white racism against blacks and Latinos has shifted to a more nuanced and convoluted one of multiracial and multi-ethnic configurations. This transformation in race relations is symbolized by the differences between the 1965 Watts uprising and the 1992 civil unrest in Los Angeles. According to the Kerner Commission, the 1965 Watts uprising, like the other urban riots of that period, was rooted in white-on-black racism, which was the underlying cause for an unequal society.[1] This form of racism certainly has not disappeared,[2] but there is something new in the air. It is best described as interethnic minority conflict, which in Los Angeles involves competition between Latinos and African Americans over housing, jobs, and political power.

This chapter focuses on the job competition between Latino immigrants and young African Americans with low levels of education. Such workers are primarily concentrated in low-skill occupations and are more likely than their better-educated brothers to compete with the immigrant workers, who also concentrate in the low-wage sector. The competition between these groups is potentially explosive because of the impact of the enormous flows of immigrants from Mexico and other parts of Latin America. Black/Latino conflict also presents a political dilemma between two principles of public policy. On the one hand, there is a commitment to eliminating—or at least ameliorating—the grave economic problems facing African Americans. Granted, this obligation is neither universally held nor vigorously pursued by the state. In fact, most accomplishments in the civil rights realm result from the political struggles undertaken by African Americans.[3] Still, we would argue that the United States has adopted a commitment to racial equality for African Americans and, by extension, to other minorities as public policy. The second principle is this country's cherished tradition as a nation of immigrants. Like the principle of racial equality, the country has not always practiced what it espouses, particularly in its long history of anti-Asian immigration restrictions.[4] Nonetheless, the United States has been among the most open and generous countries in terms of immigration policy, especially after the elimination of racially biased quotas in 1965.

Interestingly, three decades ago there was a synergy between the African American civil rights movement and the efforts to eliminate discriminatory immigration laws. The cry for domestic racial justice meshed with the demand from Third World countries for equality and dignity in the postcolonial era after the Second World War. It was not coincidental that both major civil rights and immigration reform acts were passed in the mid-1960s. Subsequent events have further entangled the two dynamics. Modern immigration has created a new force within the civil rights movement, because a majority of the newcomers are from Asia and Latin America. These new immigrants belong to populations that historically were victims of discrimination, and to varying degrees they continue to experience unfair treatment in the labor market, educational institutions, and politics. In recent years, these groups have become much more active in the voting and educational rights movements through advocacy and litigation.[5]

The principles of ameliorating inequality for minority groups and welcoming new immigrants clash when newcomers compete for jobs with African Americans or other indigenous minority groups. Economic conflict and subsequent tension among minority groups can easily undermine the civil rights movement. Worse, this tension is simultaneously stirring a conservative backlash against civil rights and generating a nativist movement bent on stopping immigration. The challenge facing California—indeed the entire nation—should not involve choosing one principle over the other. Unfortunately, the existing political debates do not go far in this direction. If the country is to attack racial inequality and develop a sensible immigration policy, it must explicitly acknowledge the material conflicts over scarce resources. At the same time, the undesirable employment outcomes for African Americans must not be seen merely as an immigration-related problem but as symptomatic of an increasingly unequal and discriminatory labor market.

Understanding the encounters of new immigrants and African Americans requires a theoretical and empirical assessment of the nature and extent of competition for scarce resources, rather than a denial of the very possibility that one group might displace or adversely affect another. Although immigrants and African Americans may be competing in a number of arenas, employment is probably of principal importance. The public seems to perceive that immigrants are taking jobs away from African Americans, a view shared by many commentators, expert and otherwise. Studies undertaken during the 1980s, using data from the 1970s, generally showed that immigration had little or no adverse impact on African Americans. There are grounds for calling these findings into doubt, however. Methodological issues raise questions about validity,[6] and in any case there is no reason to believe that immigration exercised the same effects during the 1980s, when the foreign-born inflow moved to new levels, as it did a decade before. Indeed, some authors in this book argue that the impacts may be larger than previously thought (see, for example, chapter 13). While the problem, to the degree that it exists, is a national one, the effects are particularly important and profound for Los Angeles, given its status as the center of present-day immigration to the United States.

This chapter begins with a theoretical discussion of how an increased supply of immigrants can directly and indirectly affect the labor-market outcomes of native workers, how persistent discrimination and racial segmentation continue to affect African Americans, and how these two processes interact. The second section contains our estimates of the impacts of increased immigration and of racially based disparities on employment and earnings. We found adverse effects for African Americans stemming from the presence of low-skilled Latino immigrants. We do not blame the poor labor-market outcomes of African Americans solely on immigrants, however; we argue that continuing structural and labor-market discrimination are even greater factors. The chapter concludes by returning to the broader question of how immigration has transformed race relations and how race politics, in turn, have been changed. The statistical analyses that are the basis for this chapter are contained in the chapter appendix.

LABOR MARKET EFFECTS OF IMMIGRATION: A THEORETICAL FRAMEWORK

Theory cannot predict the impact of immigration on native minorities, especially on African Americans. The relevant theories point to forces and factors that at times offset each other, and at other times interact and reinforce each other. Consequently, outcomes depend on prevailing circumstances, such as the state of the economy and the composition of the immigrant and nonimmigrant populations. This ambiguity makes an empirical accounting important in discerning the extent of job competition. Nonetheless, a theoretical framework is crucial in guiding the empirical work and in interpreting the findings.

We use a paradigm based on economics to study the labor-market impacts of immigration. This approach examines the interaction between market forces and institutional arrangements, which are defined as supply, demand, economic choices made by agents, and linkages operating across markets. The following discussion draws from traditional labor economics to answer the question of how the influx of foreign-born labor affects the established labor force in general and African Americans in particular.[7] Traditionally these effects include substitution, complementary, and growth effects. Given our position that immigration effects must be studied in a broader context of factors that disadvantage African Americans, the theoretical discussion is extended to include institutions related to race—that is, discriminatory behavior by employers and labor-market segmentation associated with race.

Political and scholarly discussions have focused on what economists call the *substitution effect.* Substitution occurs where a profit-maximizing firm replaces workers from one group with workers from another group or chooses one group over the other because of differences in the cost of labor. The workers from the two groups must be able to undertake similar tasks, although it is not necessary that they perform equally effectively or productively.[8] Substitution is more likely to occur where skill requirements are minimal or where skills of the two groups are comparable. The choice is based on the labor cost of output, which is a function of labor productivity and the wage bill. The wage bill includes monetary payments to workers and all other related costs, such as benefits, taxes, and other items. Although the logic of substitution has been defined in simple economic terms, the underlying concepts of labor productivity and cost can be expanded to include elements of control. Clearly, employers see a controllable labor force as more productive and less costly in the long run than a more militant labor force. In more concrete terms, employers have a preference for a labor supply that is less unionized or more difficult to organize.

The substitution effect is quite noticeable in sectoral-based case studies of specific industries. An example is Waldinger's study of hotels and restaurants throughout Los Angeles, which found a strong employer preference for immigrants over African Americans.[9] This situation is perhaps magnified if the immigrant is without papers (that is, illegal), because employers believe that undocumented workers will work harder and under more exploitative conditions for fear of deportation. To employers, a docile worker who labors long hours for almost nothing and does not complain is certainly preferable to a worker who demands the minimum wage, decent working conditions, and other rights.

The limitation of sectoral studies is that they ignore possible complementary effects, which are more difficult to observe because they are more diffuse and often appear at points of production beyond those at which substitution occurs. A complementary effect is seen when an increase in the supply of immigrant labor expands the demand for native workers. For example, an increase in low-skilled immigrants is likely to add to the demand for high-skilled native workers in industries that require both types of labor. To the degree that the incorporation of low-wage, low-skilled immigrant labor translates into a more competitive position for firms and a correspondingly greater demand and output for goods and services, then immigration also creates a corresponding increase in the demand for high-skilled native workers. Skill difference, however, is not the only factor that can help create complementary effects between native and immigrant labor; language and legal status are others. For example, some jobs require command of a specific language—English, in most instances—in the interaction with workers, clients, and management. Similarly, most employment, particularly in the public domain, requires a high degree of documentation, including a green card, a social security number, and other forms difficult to obtain without legal status.

In addition, the presence of new immigrant workers can have growth effects, expanding the demand for native labor by increasing the total amount of resources available to the economy with the result that total real output rises.[10] In some regions, immigrants are crucial to the replenishment and expansion of labor markets. They provide the opportunity for business expansion and global competitiveness in a wide range of low-wage industries. They function as local and regional agents of job creation. As people migrate out of a region to find better jobs, immigrants take the low-skill, bottom-of-the-ladder jobs that were left behind. At the same time, immigrants generate the demand for numerous support-related jobs that African Americans and other groups can fill, in health care, education, government, retail, and a host of other occupations and industries—clearly all indirect complementary effects.

Past studies have shown that the net outcome of these effects is not significant. Displacement of native laborers is mostly negligible, according to the findings of several national,[11] regional and metropolitan,[12] and sectoral/industrial studies.[13] Overall, immigrants tend to complement native laborers, according to labor-market studies conducted at the national and industrial/sectoral level. Nor do immigrants seem to affect the average wage of native laborers in any significant manner. The majority of national[14] and regional and metropolitan studies[15] confirm that immigrants impact wages of native-born coethnic workers only slightly. Only coethnic U.S.-born workers with fewer skills are likely to be harmed, but even here, the impacts are relatively small.

Unfortunately, it is unclear whether the findings from these studies apply to the 1980s. Many of the above studies concern the 1970s, and those using more recent data rely on samples that are too small to reveal metro-

politan-level effects. As we stated at the beginning of this section, the underlying theories do not predict any particular outcome. As conditions change,
it is quite possible that outcomes also change. Analysis of more recent data
indicates that the impact of immigration has become greater, particularly
among earlier immigrant and minority subgroups.[16] The question of what
has happened, then, is an empirical one, which we will address later in this
chapter.

Given our argument that the immigrant effects must be contextualized,
it is equally important to discuss theories on the role of race in influencing
labor-market outcomes for African Americans. Institutionalized values and
behavior that shape discriminatory personnel actions at the level of the
firm or below powerfully affect employment outcomes for this population.
These institutional factors also operate at a more aggregate level, where race
influences the allocation of labor in various segments of the labor market.
Consequently, a disproportionate number of minorities cluster in the segments of the labor market where wages are low, employment is unstable,
and competitive forces are rampant.

Discrimination against African Americans has long hurt their ability to
enter many kinds of jobs and to earn equal pay with whites. Labor-market
discrimination is evident in the significant differences in wages or employment among races and ethnic groups that remain after such factors as education, experience, and skill are taken into account. Today, race is as pervasive as ever in mediating job hiring, setting wages, and concentrating
workers in particular occupations. Some neoclassical theorists have argued
that labor-market discrimination cannot exist in a perfectly competitive
economy (that is, a market in equilibrium, in which information about jobs
is freely available), because employers who practice discrimination will be
driven out of the market by their competitors who do not discriminate and
hire workers based on productivity outputs.[17] Labor markets in Los Angeles
and other large cities, however, are far from being markets in equilibrium;
information regarding job openings and hiring is rarely accessible to all.
Furthermore, the persistence of disparities in employment and earnings between blacks and whites[18] indicates that such a competitive market is seldom found.

In part, the problem is that competitive conditions predicated on equal
access to information do not exist. Even though blatant racial bigotry has
waned, racism has remained central to determining labor market outcomes.
Statistical discrimination occurs when an employer believes (correctly or
not) that African Americans are less productive than whites and uses this
belief in making hiring decisions.[19] Researchers in Chicago have shown empirically that employers rely primarily on race and its interaction with
class and residency in their hiring decisions. They found that African
Americans were typecast as unskilled, uneducated, illiterate, dishonest, un-
motivated, lacking initiative, involved with drugs and gangs, not under-

standing work, lacking personal charm, unstable, lacking a work ethic, and having no family lives or role models.[20] Given this discriminatory practice, it is not surprising that African Americans are concentrated in what is known as the secondary labor market.[21]

While race is an important factor in influencing the distribution of the labor force in the various segments of the labor market, its effect is not the same as that predicted from a strict model of racial segmentation. Instead, labor-market segmentation is rooted in more fundamental forces and relations, including the degree of market competition in an industry, the strength of established workers in controlling on-the-job training and the production process, the presence of unions, and the type of labor control used by firms.[22] In one formulation, segmentation theory breaks the labor market into two parts: the *primary sector,* with high wages and benefits, better working conditions, opportunities for acquiring on-the-job training, and employment security; and the *secondary sector,* with low wages and few if any benefits, poor working conditions, limited training, and little job stability. Another formulation divides the labor market into several sectors. For our purpose, it is not crucial which classification is more accurate. The point is that race is used to allocate workers across segments and to strengthen the segmentation. In this process, African Americans and other minorities are disproportionately forced into the least desirable sector. The result is a racial segmentation of the labor force. It is not perfectly distributed, of course, since there are minorities in every sector, but racial divisions are significant enough to produce racial disparities that cannot be totally explained by differences in human capital.

Segmentation has two implications. First, it brings together immigrant impacts and the racial effects caused by the concentration of African Americans in the secondary sector. Concentration creates a disproportionate number of black workers who are forced to compete with low-skilled immigrants for jobs. The presence of both types of labor within the secondary sector can increase overcrowding in which the greater supply of labor leads to downward pressure on wages and increased unemployment.[23]

Second, blacks experience the immigrant effect differently, depending on their location in the labor market. As we stated earlier, racial division in the U.S. labor market is not perfect—that is, it is not equivalent to a race-based caste system—so that outcomes for African Americans depend on the sector in which they are located. Although many blacks find themselves in direct competition with immigrants, other blacks (and native minorities) work in sectors that are insulated from direct competition with immigrants.[24] Although skill levels and education influence the scope and force of direct competition, other factors come into play; native workers may be employed in unskilled jobs but nevertheless enjoy protection from job competition through union contracts or civil service, examples of institutional barriers that prevent the incorporation of many immigrant workers. Under these conditions, immigrant and native-born labor complement one another in different sectors of the economy. Likewise, because blacks, even those with less education, work in segments that vary in institutional barriers and other characteristics that reduce immigrant penetration, immigration can have the effect of promoting even greater disparities among African Americans.

EFFECTS ON JOBLESSNESS AND EARNINGS: EMPIRICAL FINDINGS

This section summarizes our empirical analysis of the impacts of immigration and racism on African Americans. As in most empirical work in this field, the findings do not constitute direct proof of the validity of our theoretical framework. The findings are, however, consistent with our position. The main objective of the analysis is to derive the extent or magnitude of the phenomenon. One limitation is that, in many cases, the findings provide information on the net effects alone, particularly in the case of offsetting substitution and complementary effects. This limitation is also true for factors that work in combination with one another, such as racial discrimination and racial segmentation. Indeed, our findings are consistent with the point made in the previous section that many African Americans are insulated from job competition with immigrants by their concentration in public sector jobs.

Our analysis focuses on the impact of immigration on the joblessness and earnings among black males aged 18–24 and on those aged 18–64 who have no more than a high school education. We chose these populations because they are concentrated in the low-pay, high-turnover secondary sector and are thus the most susceptible to job competition. The analysis of joblessness and earnings is based on a comparison of outcomes in Los Angeles County with those in fifty-five other metropolitan statistical areas MSAs). The choice of Los Angeles County rather than the five-county Los Angeles region ensured consistency with the census definition of metropolitan areas for comparison purposes. Through the use of multivariate techniques, we attempted to estimate how immigration has disadvantaged blacks in Los Angeles relative to their counterparts in other metropolitan areas, after taking into account both individual and regional factors (see the appendix to this chapter for details). Our findings indicate that immigration increases joblessness among African Americans, with a larger net impact coming from the presence of Latino immigrants with limited education than from those with higher levels of education. On the other hand, we found no detectable net impact on earnings.

Tables 6.1 and 6.2 present labor force estimates and ratios for the various metropolitan categories used in our study. While Los Angeles has a relatively small percentage of the African American labor force, it has a very

TABLE 6.1 | **Labor Force Estimates**

	All 56 MSAs (in 1,000s)	L.A. MSA	
		(in 1,000s)	(%)
Young black males	377.4	20.1	5.3
Less-educated black males	1,578.6	72.6	4.6
Recent immigrants	758.5	278.2	36.7
Recent Latino immigrants	326.3	194.7	59.7
Recent less-educated immigrants	443.5	203.0	45.8
Recent less-educated Latino male immigrants	253.6	170.0	67.0

large percentage of the immigrant labor force. Moreover, the immigrant to black ratios are very high in Los Angeles, as table 6.2 reveals in the case of Latino immigrants; the ratios are about ten times higher than the average for the other fifty-five MSAs. Consequently, the immigrant impacts found for Los Angeles should be higher than those in other parts of the United States.

Table 6.3 contains the findings for joblessness, which is defined as being without a job, not in school or the military, and not disabled.[25] A comparison of raw rates indicates that joblessness is more prevalent in Los Angeles than in other metropolitan areas among both young and less-educated blacks. The differences in observed rates underestimate the disparity between Los Angeles and the other fifty-five MSAs, because blacks in Los Angeles are on average better educated and thus should have a lower jobless

TABLE 6.2 | **Labor Force Ratios**

	L.A. MSA	55 MSAs Without L.A.	L.A. Relative Ranking
Recent immigrants to:			
Young black males	13.8	2.1	2[a]
Less-educated black males	3.8	0.6	2[a]
Recent Latino immigrants to:			
Young black males	9.7	0.9	1
Less-educated black males	2.7	0.3	1
Recent less-educated Latino immigrants to:			
Young black males	8.5	0.7	1
Less-educated black males	2.3	0.2	1

[a]San Francisco-Bay Area is ranked first because of the large number of Asian immigrants and smaller number of African Americans.
NOTE: Column 1 shows ratio of immigrants in various categories to young black males and less-educated black males. For example, the first number in column 1 indicates that there were 13.8 recent immigrants in Los Angeles for every one young black male.

TABLE 6.3 | **Black Joblessness by Metropolitan Areas**

	Young Black Males Aged 18–24 (%)	Less-Educated Black Males Aged 18–64 (%)
Los Angeles	46	37
55 other MSAs	40	30
Raw difference	+6	+7
Adjusted for age and education	+9	+8
Estimated net impact of Latino immigration	+7	+5

SOURCE: See appendix to chapter 6.

rate. After adjusting for education and age, we find that the gap between this region and the other fifty-five MSAs is about a percentage point higher. Amazingly, most of the difference is associated with the level of recently arrived less-educated Latinos. The estimated net effects on joblessness in Los Angeles, reported in the last row of table 6.3, are the combination of jobless-inducing substitution and employment-inducing growth from immigration.

Estimates of the impacts on earnings are listed in table 6.4, which is based on workers who earned more than $1,000 in 1989. A comparison of the geometric means shows that earnings tend to be considerably higher in Los Angeles than elsewhere, even after controlling for age and education. Although the larger flow of immigrants depresses African American earnings indirectly through joblessness, the presence of immigrants also ap-

TABLE 6.4 | **Black Earnings by Metropolitan Areas**

	Young Black Males Aged 18–24	Less-Educated Black Males Aged 18–64
Geometric Mean		
Los Angeles	$10,600	$15,600
Other MSAs	$ 9,100	$14,200
Difference	16%	10%
Controlling for age and education	13%	9%
Estimated impact of Latino immigration	1%	3%

SOURCE: See appendix to chapter 6.

pears to have a complementary effect in increasing the earnings of those African Americans who are employed. Consequently, we estimate that Latino immigration generates a small but positive net effect on earnings.

Thus Latino immigration to Los Angeles affects the labor market chances of African Americans in two different ways: It increases joblessness but (slightly) boosts earnings for those with a job. These results are consistent with the hypothesis that when imperfect racial segmentation exists, increased immigration produces greater employment polarization among African Americans. Clearly, there are those whose earnings and employment are adversely affected. When there are substitutable immigrant workers, employers do prefer to hire them, and prevailing wages may fall below the normally acceptable (that is, reservation wage) rate of African Americans, thus producing joblessness. On the other hand, those who remain employed are either unaffected by this change or benefit in terms of greater opportunities and higher wages. In other words, immigration appears in some instances to widen and in other instances to narrow the economic gap of African Americans.

Our findings are also consistent with other regional studies showing that African Americans are concentrated in public sector employment[26] and therefore are insulated from direct competition with immigrants. We argue that immigrants have a complementary effect for African Americans in public sector employment that derives from the increased demand that legal and illegal immigrants place on public services and agencies. Public sector employment growth in Los Angeles between 1970 and 1980[27] and again between 1980 and 1990 has been documented in this book and in other studies. As the demand for public services, programs, and personnel has grown because of population growth, largely from immigration, African American employment in this sector has increased.

While these findings indicate measurable impacts of Latino immigration,[28] not all aspects of immigration are bad for African Americans in Los Angeles. At least two other factors are at work here. First, our own analysis indicates that other immigrants appear to have a positive, or net complementary, effect on African Americans. The presence of Asian and other (non-Hispanic and non-Asian) immigrants is not related to higher black unemployment rates but is positively related to higher black earnings. Second, the cheap goods and services that immigrants provide benefit many segments of society. For many professionals and better-paid workers, the Latino immigrant population is a major provider of child care and other domestic support work.[29]

Moreover, the impact of Latino immigrants on African Americans should be placed in the context of racism in the labor market. Indeed, we find sizable racial effects on joblessness and earnings. These disparities hold for both 1970, prior to the massive influx of immigrants, and 1990. In terms of sampling and techniques, the analysis of racial effects parallels the immigration effects just described; the major difference is that the reference group is U.S.-born non-Hispanic whites in the Los Angeles region. If race in itself is unimportant, then we should observe no difference between black and white workers with identical characteristics and they would be equally affected by immigration. On the other hand, significant differences between white and black workers would be consistent with the presence of racial discrimination. The sample of African Americans from 1970 is large enough to undertake an analysis only for Los Angeles County; for 1990, we examine both Los Angeles County and the rest of the Los Angeles region.

As table 6.5 shows, joblessness among African Americans is considerably higher than it is among non-Hispanic whites, even after controlling for schooling and age.[30] Moreover, the racial gap increased between 1970 and 1990. By the latter year, the rates for blacks in Los Angeles were nearly three times higher. Even after adjusting for schooling and age, the rates were 50 percent higher. Compared with African Americans in Los Angeles, blacks in the other counties of the region fared better, but they also experienced considerably higher joblessness than their non-Hispanic white counterparts. Some of the joblessness among blacks is a result of higher unemployment rates; that is, a relatively larger proportion were out of work but still seeking employment. This strongly indicates that blacks are more likely to be in the secondary labor market, where turnovers and frequent unemployment are prevalent.

Additional unpublished data from the census shed light on how the ra-

TABLE 6.5 | Joblessness in Los Angeles Region by Race

	L.A. County		Los Angeles Region Without L.A. County
	1970 (%)	1990 (%)	1990 (%)
Young adult males			
White	21	16	16
Black	37	46	39
Difference	16	30	23
Controlling for age and education	13	24	18
Less-educated adult males			
White	10	13	12
Black	19	35	27
Difference	9	22	14
Controlling for age and education	7	19	11

SOURCE: See appendix to chapter 6.

cial differences in joblessness are generated, but these factors themselves are likely to be linked to race. For example, years of schooling and educational degrees understate racial differences because the quantitative numbers do not reveal systematic disparities in the quality of education. Other research in the Los Angeles region indicates that at each level of schooling minority students do not perform as well as whites on standardized tests.[31] In other words, the number of years of schooling understates differences in human capital. While the limitations to our analysis make it difficult to pinpoint the magnitude and source of the racial effect on joblessness, there is no question that being African American rather than white severely disadvantages a worker in Los Angeles.

Black/white inequality is also seen in annual earnings, even after controlling for schooling and age, as table 6.6 shows. All amounts are reported in 1989 dollars. For each group, earnings tended to be lower in 1989 than in 1969, consistent with the national trend of declining real wages for those with fewer skills. The racial gap increased slightly between 1969 and 1989, and the disparities in Los Angeles are more pronounced than in the other four counties. Taken together, the findings indicate that earnings for young African Americans are about one-fifth lower than for their white counterparts and three-tenths lower among less-educated black males. As with the analysis of joblessness, it is impossible to identify unambiguously how the

TABLE 6.6 | Earnings in Los Angeles Region by Race

	L.A. County		Los Angeles Region Without L.A. County
	1969	1989	1989
Young Adult Males			
Geometric Mean			
White	$14,600	$14,100	$13,800
Black	$11,600	$10,600	$11,300
Difference	−21%	−25%	−18%
Adjusted	−19%	−21%	−18%
Less-Educated Adult Males			
Geometric Mean			
White	$26,200	$23,000	$22,900
Black	$17,700	$15,700	$16,000
Difference	−32%	−32%	−30%
Adjusted	−30%	−30%	−27%

SOURCE: See appendix to chapter 6.

racial differences are generated. One implication of the findings, however, is that relatively more blacks than whites are employed in low-wage positions, the type of jobs that are likely to be in the secondary labor market.

The analyses show that both Latino immigration and racism play significant roles in disadvantaging African Americans in terms of joblessness and earnings. The estimates suggest, however, that racial discrimination and segmentation are more important factors in determining joblessness and earnings for blacks. The additional joblessness associated with racial disparity is three to four times greater than that associated with immigration, and all the adverse impacts on earnings stem from racial disparity. But, the impacts of racism and immigration are not unrelated. The differences between young adults and less-educated adults in tables 6.3 and 6.4 support this contention. The higher concentration of blacks in the secondary labor market, where the bulk of low-skilled Latino immigrants have been incorporated, exposes blacks to greater job competition and perhaps contributes to their increased joblessness rates and their lower earnings relative to non-Hispanic whites. Finally, in an issue we did not analyze, the effects of racism (discriminatory practices and segmentation) and immigration may be further compounded as they interact with imports. George Borjas and Valerie Ramey argue that immigration and imports are highly correlated and may have the same impacts on native workers.[32] Thus, some of the substitution effect associated with immigration would also be caused by growing numbers of imports. Moreover, immigrant workers are most likely to be incorporated into the domestic sectors that are under import pressures. In other words, these jobs would have been lost even if there had been no immigrants.

POLICY IMPLICATIONS AND CONCLUSION

While our findings indicated that immigration—particularly of Latinos with limited education—increased joblessness among African Americans, there seemed to be no detectable net effect on earnings. This study also showed that the impact of Latino immigrants on African Americans should be placed in the context of racism in the labor market. The finding of a persistent black/white differential is consistent with a national pattern of higher joblessness and lower earnings for African Americans than for non-Hispanic whites, even after controlling for schooling and age. In this regard, African Americans in Los Angeles are no different from African Americans in other regions of the country, many of whom live in areas with very little immigration. The explanation for our findings is complex. African Americans start with the disadvantage of having less education, a product of a biased and ineffective educational system. This racial bias is magnified in the labor market, which concentrates African Americans in the secondary sector, where they are likely to be confined. Our study showed that while increased joblessness for African Americans is connected to increases in Latino immigration, endemic racism also plays a central role.

Our findings present a serious challenge to the simultaneous pursuit of civil rights for African Americans and maintenance of our heritage as a nation of immigrants. Some use job competition between Latino immigrants and African Americans (and possibly other U.S.-born minorities and more established immigrants) as a rationale for stopping immigration. For example, one group has called for a moratorium on all immigration because "high levels of immigration, legal and illegal, have adversely affected U.S. minorities, particularly African Americans, in terms of job opportunities, social benefits, and political power."[33] This position is at best incomplete. As our study showed, immigration can be beneficial. Generalizing about all immigration is an exercise in misleading polemics. Furthermore, in the fight for black equality in this country, a sound policy must include efforts to eradicate endemic racism. To focus on immigrants as the only source of disadvantage to African Americans scapegoats an already vulnerable group and misses the point that other factors, such as labor market discrimination and segmentation, are more important in explaining African American inequality. Even worse, focusing solely on immigration brings out a form of nativism that ultimately reinforces racially based prejudices.

Rhetorical anti-immigrant arguments may be easily dismissed, but political activists involved in minority rights movements can also fall into an ideological trap. Some would regard such a conflict as job competition as a strategy of divide and conquer perpetuated by those in power or would dismiss it as based on cultural misunderstandings. One could argue that, with experience and education, those at the bottom would come to see their shared plight and unite in a common struggle. This position, however, flies against the material reality and an emerging political and nationalist sentiment within minority communities. It would be unfair to insist on Third World solidarity while ignoring a real cost of immigration borne by African Americans. There is a fundamental problem of racism, which not only seriously disadvantages minorities but also magnifies the impact of immigration on some communities; recognizing this factor, however, does little to address the immediate harsh reality. Indeed, there is a rising anti-immigrant sentiment among native-born minorities, often in the form of growing resentment toward undocumented aliens, who in Los Angeles are almost always defined as Latinos. This resentment became vividly clear in a pre- and post-election poll[34] on minority voter support for the 1994 California Proposition 187.[35] Statewide exit polls showed that 47 percent of African American and Asian voters and 23 percent of Latino voters supported this proposition.[36] Other related and national polls have shown strong minority, including Latino, support for more stringent immigration laws.[37] But, as we have noted, anti-immigrant politics is not easily confined to attacks on illegal immigration, for it easily spills over as a nativist attack on all immigrants.

The task before us, then, is finding ways to lower the uncomfortable trade-off imposed by job competition. One approach to be seriously considered is enforcing border policies and increasing the role of economic objectives in formulating immigration policy. The weak enforcement of border policies creates a large undocumented population that is at the heart of the immigration debate. While stringent enforcement will not stop undocumented immigration, it can stem the flow to some degree and thus reduce the supply of less-skilled workers. Controlling the border, however, is not the same as attacking those already in the United States, whose rights need to be protected. It is important to note that they are here because of lax enforcement policies and an implicit policy that supports employers who have become accustomed to and even dependent on cheap immigrant labor. By establishing roots in Los Angeles and participating in economic activities, including the labor market, consumerism, and tax outlays, undocumented immigrants have, in our opinion, some rightful claim to be a part of this society. In addition we must have fair levels of legal immigration to fulfill our obligations as an immigrant country and to meet our labor demand. In doing so, we must avoid reintroducing race and nationality quotas into laws governing immigration and support policies that favor economic growth. Immigration laws have legitimacy from a civil rights perspective only when they are nondiscriminatory.

We should be equally concerned about attacking the underlying racism that unfairly concentrates African Americans into the very sector adversely affected by immigration. Civil rights policy needs to continue to amend past and present injustices in the educational, political, and economic areas with an explicit realization that immigrants also belong to America and, by extension, are entitled to civil rights.

The idea of ameliorating inequality for African Americans and other minority groups while simultaneously welcoming new immigrant groups has had a short and tumultuous history in the United States. Nevertheless, these two principles have in part been adopted into and shaped by public policies that have strained relationships between majority and minority groups, often resulting in demagoguery and minority scrapegoating regarding voting rights, affirmative action, discrimination suits, and exclusionary immigration laws. To pursue our historical tradition of immigration is to propose fair laws and to realize that both immigration policy and the United States have changed over the past several decades. Likewise, the civil rights movement—founded to combat white discrimination and oppression towards blacks—has evolved to include the concerns of Latinos, Asians, and other minority groups. Indeed, the membership rolls of Latino and Asian civil rights organizations have swelled since they first emerged in the mid-1960s—not coincidentally when the landmark immigration law was passed, prompting the massive immigration that continues to the present. As immigrants from Latin America, Asia, and other continents continue to arrive, their place in the civil rights community becomes tenuous while affirmative action, voting rights, and other policies that aid minorities are being dismantled. A main point of contention in the current affirmative action debate is whether immigrants should be beneficiaries of laws designated for the native-born minorities. In the end, the American principles of welcoming immigrants and protecting the rights of African Americans and others need not be mutually exclusive.

Appendix

DATA

The samples for the analyses were drawn from the 5 percent 1990 Public Use Microdata Samples (PUMS) and include individuals in the fifty-six metropolitan areas with the largest numbers of U.S.-born young African American males. The Los Angeles sample, which is used to study racial disparity in jobs and earnings in this region, also includes other U.S.-born respondents. The samples on employment are restricted to those who were not enrolled in school, enlisted in the military, disabled, or foreign-born. In the analysis of joblessness, the sample of young males is limited to those aged 18–24 at the time of the census, and the sample of less-educated males is limited to those with no more than a high school education and aged 18–64 at the time of the census. In the analysis of annual earnings, the sampling is based on the age of the respondents minus one. For example, the sample of young males comprises those aged 19–25. This adjustment is made because earnings reported in the 1990 census pertain to 1989. The analysis of earnings includes only those workers who earned more than $1,000 in 1989.

The analyses in this appendix use a common set of conceptual variables, whose values are determined according to the particular issue. When microdata are used, *jobless* refers to a dichotomous variable denoting whether the individual was employed or not during the census week. When the variable is used at the metropolitan level, it refers to the percent of the relevant population that was not employed, and this percentage can either be the observed raw rates or the rates adjusted for age and education. The latter rates are estimated by the authors. The analyses using microdata incorporate data on an individual's educational attainment and age. The latter can be transformed into potential years of labor market experience, which is approximated by the difference between the age at the time of the census and the age at the time of leaving school. To estimate the substitution and complementary effects, we use a ratio of the supply of immigrants to the supply of blacks. The immigrant supply includes those in the labor force who entered the United States during the 1980s. This population is further disaggregated by ethnicity and skill levels.

The metropolitan level analyses include several other structural variables that are important in explaining intermetropolitan variations: growth, manufacturing jobs as a percentage of all jobs, the percent of the labor force that is unionized, and the prevailing wage level. The *growth* variable at the metropolitan level is defined as the square root of population growth between 1980 and 1990. This specification performs better than the linear form. The manufacturing and unionization rates were provided by Evelyn Blumenberg. The prevailing wage level is defined as the log of the annual earnings of native non-Hispanic white males aged 35–44 with a bachelor's degree. This population is the least affected by immigration, and its geographic mobility is likely to generate earnings that represent the intermetropolitan regional compensations to produce equilibrium wages in economic terms.

ANALYSIS OF BLACK JOBLESSNESS BY METROPOLITAN AREAS

Analysis of intermetropolitan joblessness is based on a two-part model. The first stage uses logit regression with microdata to estimate intermetropolitan variations in joblessness probability after controlling for educational attainment and age. The regression also includes a dummy for the Los Angeles metropolitan area. "Less than HS" refers to individuals who have at least an eighth-grade education but less than a high school education. The estimated parameters are reported in table 6.7.

The same model is then extended by using a set of metropolitan dummy variables for each of the fifty-five MSAs, with Los Angeles being the excluded category. The results are converted into probabilities using the formula $[p/(1-p)]c$, where p is the observed probability of being jobless for the entire sample and c is the estimated coefficient. In this context, the probability for a given MSA represents the estimated difference between the jobless rates for Los Angeles and for that MSA, after controlling for age and education.

The second part of the jobless analysis examines whether variations at the metropolitan level are related to any of a number of variables, including the number of recent-immigrant workers relative to the number of young or less-educated blacks. We examined several measures of immigration, including total number of immigrants, immigrants disaggregated by ethnicity alone, immigrants disaggregated by educational level alone, and immi-

TABLE 6.7 | Logit Regression of Black Joblessness

	Young Black Males (Aged 18–24)	Less-Educated Black Males (Aged 18–64)
Constant	15.82***	3.39***
Less than HS	0.07**	0.32***
High school	−0.96***	−0.51***
Some college	−1.04***	
College degree	−1.99***	
Graduate degree	−1.60***	
Age	−1.30***	−0.21***
Age squared	0.03***	0.00***
Los Angeles	0.36***	0.38***
N	19,338	76,811
Adj R^2	.07	.06

$*p<.10$ $**p<.05$ $***p<.01$

grants disaggregated by ethnicity and educational level. A comparison of the numerous runs indicated that the effects appear when the immigrant population is limited to those with no more than a high school education disaggregated by ethnicity. The regressions are weighted by the size of the male African American population in the appropriate age category for each metropolitan area. The results for this specification are reported in table 6.8.

The estimated net impact of Latino immigration is calculated as the sum of the direct impact through the Latino Ratio (see table 6.2) and the indirect impact through population growth. The direct effect is the coefficient for Latino Ratio times the value for Los Angeles. The indirect effect through growth assumes that the contribution of Latino immigration is equal to net growth for the total Los Angeles population. In fact, Latino immigration in the 1980s was larger than net gain to the total; thus the estimated contribution to lowering joblessness is on the conservative side.

BLACK EARNINGS BY METROPOLITAN AREAS

The analysis of intermetropolitan earnings among blacks is based on a two-part model similar to the analysis of intermetropolitan joblessness. The first stage uses linear regression with microdata, with the log of annual earnings as the dependent variable and a set of independent variables including educational attainment, age, and a dummy variable for the Los Angeles metropolitan area. The estimate parameters are reported in table 6.9. The same model is then extended by using a set of metropolitan dummy variables for

TABLE 6.8 | **Analysis of Intermetropolitan Black Male Joblessness**

	All 56 MSAs	Without L.A.	Unadjusted
Young black males			
Constant	35.31 ***	35.18 ***	37.81 ***
Latino ratio	1.95 ***	2.78 ***	1.64 ***
Asian ratio	−1.07	−1.05	−2.20
Other ratio	−0.03	−0.52	0.85
Growth	−2.18 ***	−2.30 ***	−2.26 ***
% Mfg	−0.02	0.01	0.01
% Union	0.37 ***	0.35 ***	0.37 **
Adjusted R^2	.67	.66	.66
Less-educated black males			
Constant	23.40 ***	26.35 ***	27.91 ***
Latino ratio	5.69 ***	6.74 ***	5.29 ***
Asian ratio	5.38	5.02	2.76
Other ratio	−10.00	−10.45	−6.01
Growth	−1.86 ***	−1.89 ***	−1.88 ***
%Mfg	−0.01	−0.00	−0.01
% Union	0.40 ***	0.39 ***	0.35 ***
Adjusted R^2	.72	.71	.70

*$p < .10$ **$p < .05$ ***$p < .01$

TABLE 6.9 | **Regression Analysis of Log of Earnings**

	Young Black Males (Aged 18–24)	Less-Educated Black Males (Aged 18–64)
Constant	2.51 ***	6.95 ***
Less than HS	−0.05 *	−0.11 ***
High school	0.25 ***	0.16 ***
Some college	0.31 ***	
College degree	0.62 ***	
Graduate degree	0.75 ***	
Age	0.46 ***	0.11 ***
Age squared	−0.01 ***	−0.00 ***
Los Angeles	0.13 ***	0.09 ***
N	16,101	59,709
Adjusted R^2	0.13	0.18

*$p < .10$ ***$p < .01$

each of the fifty-five MSAs, excluding Los Angeles. The estimated coefficients, then, represent average earnings in the other MSAs relative to those in Los Angeles, after accounting for education and age.

The second part of the earnings analysis examines whether intermetropolitan differences are related to the presence of recent-immigrant workers. As in the analysis of joblessness, several measures of immigration were examined, and the results indicated that the effects are produced by immigrants with no more than a high school education disaggregated by ethnicity. Growth was initially included but proved to be statistically insignificant. Moreover, since it is colinear with other independent variables, its inclusion can introduce biases in the estimated parameters. The regressions are weighted by the size of the male African American labor force in the appropriate age category for each metropolitan area. The results for the final specification are reported in table 6.10.

The estimated net impact of Latino immigration on black earnings is calculated as the sum of the direct impact through the Latino Ratio and the

TABLE 6.10 | Analysis of Metropolitan Variation in Black Earnings

	All 56 MSAs	Without L.A.
Young black males		
Constant	−5.930***	−6.050***
Prevailing wages	0.587***	0.598***
Latino ratio	0.031***	0.037**
Asian ratio	−0.039	−0.040
Other ratio	0.097**	0.093**
% Mfg	−0.005**	0.005*
% Union	0.006**	0.006**
Jobless	−0.014***	−0.014***
Adjusted R^2	.69	.68
Less-educated black males		
Constant	6.377***	−6.513***
Prevailing wages	0.600***	0.612***
Latino ratio	0.054*	0.080*
Asian ratio	0.052	0.043
Other ratio	0.063	0.049
% Mfg	−0.001	−0.000
% Union	0.010***	0.010***
Jobless	−0.009***	−0.009***
Adjusted R^2	.58	.57

*$p<.10$ **$p<.05$ ***$p<.01$

indirect impact through joblessness. The direct effect is the coefficient for Latino Ratio times the value for Los Angeles. The indirect effect through joblessness is based on the direct effects of Latino immigration on joblessness based on the results reported in the preceding section.

JOBLESSNESS AND EARNINGS IN THE LOS ANGELES REGION

The analysis of racial disparities in joblessness and earnings between blacks and non-Hispanic whites (tables 6.11 and 6.12) uses the same basic models described in the two preceding sections. Joblessness is modeled using logit regressions, and earnings are modeled using linear regressions. The 1990 regressions are weighted by the personal weights reported in the

TABLE 6.11 | **Logit Regressions of Male Joblessness**

	L.A., 1970	L.A., 1990	Rest of L.A. Region
Young Male Adults			
Constant	−0.214**	−0.315***	−0.440***
High school	−0.768***	−0.773***	−0.887***
Some college	−0.867***	−1.628***	−1.679***
College degree	−1.130***	−2.032***	−2.200***
Graduate degree	−1.787***	−1.095***	−2.381***
Experience	−0.220***	−0.321***	−0.192***
Experience squared	0.413*	3.223***	1.050***
Black	0.738***	1.316***	1.180***
Latino	−0.021*	0.144***	0.120***
Asian	0.596**	0.207***	0.328***
N	3,611	6,782	5,137
Adj R^2	.035	.109	.074
Less-Educated Males			
Constant	−1.279***	−1.336***	−1.399***
Experience	−0.117***	−0.083***	−0.100***
Experience squared	0.208***	0.141***	0.194***
Less than HS	0.562***	0.672***	0.717***
Black	0.656***	1.213***	0.896***
Latino	0.068*	0.176***	0.149***
Asian	0.170*	−0.026*	−0.134***
N	18,164	21,023	17,210
Adj R^2	.046	.084	.052

*$p<.10$ **$p<.05$ ***$p<.01$

Table 6.12 | Regressions of Male Earnings

	L.A., 1970	L.A., 1990	Rest of L.A. Region
Young adult males			
Constant	8.582***	8.705***	8.653***
High school	0.406***	0.299***	0.347***
Some college	0.621***	0.582***	0.674***
College degree	0.976***	0.862***	0.934***
Graduate degree	1.159***	1.304***	1.312***
Experience	0.232***	0.219***	0.214***
Experience squared	−1.174***	−1.616***	−1.378***
Black	−0.212***	−0.237***	−0.199***
Latino	−0.033*	−0.062***	−0.075***
Asian	−0.083*	−0.044*	−0.027*
N	3,490	6,758	5,341
Adj R^2	0.137	0.140	0.148
Less-Educated Males			
Constant	9.484***	9.355***	9.286***
Experience	0.070***	0.071***	0.084***
Experience squared	−0.121***	−0.113***	−0.147***
Less than HS	−0.188***	−0.246***	−0.246***
Black	−0.350***	−0.363***	−0.321***
Latino	−0.196***	−0.164***	−0.159***
Asian	−0.202***	−0.173***	−0.161***
N	16,945	18,078	15,592
Adj R^2	0.176	0.205	0.211

*$p < .10$ **$p < .05$ ***$p < .01$

PUMS. The major modification is that racial variables are used rather than metropolitan variables.

Notes to Chapter 6

1. *The Report of the National Advisory Commission on Civil Disorders* (Washington, D.C.: U.S. Government Printing Office, 1988).

2. Gunnar Myrdal, "The War on Poverty," *The New Republic* 150 (1964): 14–16; Joe R. Feagin and Vera Hernan, *White Racism: The Basics* (New York: Routledge Press, 1994); Derrick Bell, *Faces at the Bottom of the Well: The Permanence of Racism* (New York: Basic Books, 1992).

3. Michael Omi and Howard Winnant, *Racial Formation in the United States, From the 1960s to the 1980s* (New York: Routledge Press, 1986).

4. Paul Ong and John Liu, "U.S. Immigration Policies and Asian Migration," in Paul Ong, Edna Bonacich, and Lucie Cheng, eds., *The New Asian Immigration in Los Angeles and Global Restructuring* (Philadelphia: Temple University Press, 1994), 45–72.

5. For example, in Los Angeles the Mexican American Legal Defense and Education Fund (MALDEF) and the Asian Pacific Legal Center (APLC) are involved in redistricting and other litigations.

6. Indeed, many of these studies are based on assumptions that limit analyses. For example, economic impacts of immigration, at a national or aggregate level, are always found to be negligible; thus, local or regional impacts are often presumed or inferred to be minimal. Another assumption of past studies on this topic is the treatment of the labor market as one entity, when in fact the labor market is composed of many different jobs, industries, and occupations.

7. See, for example, Michael J. Greenwood and John M. McDowell, "The Labor Market Consequences of U.S. Immigration," *Journal of Economic Literature* 24 (1986): 738–72; Mark Killingsworth, "Effects of Immigration into the United States on the U.S. Labor Market: Analytical and Policy Issues," in Mary M. Kritz, ed., *U.S. Immigration and Refugee Policy: Global and Domestic Issues* (Lexington, Mass.: Lexington Books, D. C. Heath and Company, 1986), 249–68.

8. This requirement can be modified when wages and prices induce firms to change their production methods and capital infrastructure, in turn altering skill requirements for labor. Immigration can also increase the share of income going to capital relative to labor. See D. Usher, "Public Property and the Effects of Migration Upon Other Residents of the Migrant's Country of Origin and Destination," *Journal of Political Economy* 85 (1977): 1001–1020.

9. Roger Waldinger, "Who Makes the Beds, Who Washes the Dishes? Black/Immigrant Competition Reassessed," in Harriet O. Dulup and Phanindra V. Wannara, eds., *Immigrants and Immigration Policy: Individual Skills, Family Ties, and Group Identities* (Greenwich, Conn.: JAI Press, 1966).

10. Killingsworth, "Effects of Immigration."

11. George J. Borjas, *Friends or Strangers: The Impact of Immigrants on the U.S. Economy* (New York: Basic Books, 1990); Frank D. Bean, Lindsay Lowell, and Lowell J. Taylor, "Undocumented Mexican Workers and the Earnings of Other Workers in the United States," *Demography* 25 (1988): 35–52; Jean B. Grossman, "The Substitutability of Natives and Immigrants in Production," *Review of Economics and Statistics* 64 (1982): 596–603; James Stewart and Thomas Hyelak, "An Analysis of the Earnings Profiles of Immigrants," *Review of Economic Statistics* 66 (1984): 292–303.

12. Joseph G. Altonji and David Card, "The Effects of Immigration on the Labor Market Outcomes of Natives," in Richard B. Freeman and John M. Abowd, eds., *Immigration, Trade, and the Labor Market* (Chicago: University of Chicago Press, 1990); Julian L. Simon and Stephen Moore, 1988, "The Effect of Immigration upon Aggregate Unemployment: An Across-City Estimation," unpublished typescript taken from Julian L. Simon, *The Economic Consequences of Immigration*

(Cambridge, Mass., and Washington: Basil Blackwell and CATO Institute, 1989); Thomas Muller and Thomas Espenshade, *The Fourth Wave: California's Newest Immigrants* (Washington, D.C.: Urban Institute Press, 1985); Richard Reischauer, "Immigration and the Underclass," *The ANNALS of the American Academy of Political and Social Science* 501 (1989): 120–31.

13. Gregory F. DeFreitas, "The Earnings of Immigrants in the American Labor Market" (Ph.D. diss., Columbia University, 1980); Richard Mines and Philip L. Martin, "Immigrant Workers and the California Citrus Industry," *Industrial Relations* 23 (1984): 139–49; Roger Waldinger, *Through the Eye of the Needle: Immigrants and Enterprise in New York's Garment Trades* (New York: New York University Press, 1986); Thomas Bailey, *Immigrant and Native Workers: Contrasts and Competition* (Boulder, Colo.: Westview Press, 1987).

14. Grossman, "The Substitutability of Natives and Immigrants"; Allen G. King, B. Lindsay Lowell, and Frank D. Bean, "The Effects of Hispanic Immigrants on the Earnings of Native Hispanic Americans," *Social Science Quarterly* 67 (1986): 672–89; George J. Borjas, "The Impact of Immigrants on the Earnings of the Native-Born," in Vernon M. Briggs and Marta Tienda, eds., *Immigration: Issues and Policies* (Salt Lake City: Olympus, 1984); Borjas, George J., "Assimilation, Changes in Cohort Quality, and the Earnings of Immigrants," *Journal of Labor Economics* 3 (1985): 463–89; George J. Borjas, "Self-Selection and the Earnings of Immigrants," *American Economic Review* 77 (1987): 532–53; George J. Borjas, "Immigrants, Minorities, and Labor Market Competition," *Industrial and Labor Relations Review* 40 (1987): 382–92; Robert J. LaLonde and Robert H. Topel, "Labor Market Adjustments to Increased Immigration," in Richard B. Freeman and John M. Abowd, eds., *Immigration, Trade, and the Labor Market* (Chicago: University of Chicago Press, 1990); Frank Bean, Lindsay Lowell, and Lowell J. Taylor, "Undocumented Mexican Workers"; Joseph Altonji and David Card, "The Effects of Immigration"; George J. Borjas, Richard B. Freeman, and Lawrence F. Katz, "On the Labor Market Effects of Immigration and Trade," in George J. Borjas and Richard B. Freeman, eds., *Immigration and the Workforce: Economic Consequences for the United States and Source Areas* (Chicago: University of Chicago Press, 1992).

15. Barton Smith and Robert Newman, "Depressed Wages Along the U.S.-Mexico Border: An Empirical Analysis," *Economic Inquiry* 15 (1977): 51–66; Thomas Muller and Thomas Espenshade, *The Fourth Wave: California's Newest Immigrants* (Washington, D.C.: The Urban Institute, 1985); Kevin F. McCarthy and Roberto B. Valdez, *Current and Future Effects of Mexican Immigration in California* (Santa Monica: Rand Corporation, 1985); Richard D. Reischauer, "Immigration and the Underclass"; David Card, "Changing Wage Structure and Black-White Wage Differentials," *American Economic Review* 84 (1994): 29–33.

16. Robert H. Topel, "Regional Trends in Wage Inequality," *American Economic Review* 84 (1994): 17–22; Howard Wial, "Immigration and the Distribution of Earnings," Immigration Policy & Research Working Paper Series (Washington, D.C.: U.S. Department of Labor, 1994); Abel Valenzuela, Jr., "Immigrants, Minority Workers, and Job Competition: A Comparative Analysis of New York and Los Angeles, 1970 to 1980" (Ph.D. diss., Massachusetts Institute of Technology, 1993).

17. Gary Becker, *The Economics of Discrimination* (Chicago: University of Chicago Press, 1957).

18. John Bound and Richard B. Freeman, "What Went Wrong? The Erosion of Relative Earnings of and Employment Among Young Black Men in the 1980s," *Quarterly Journal of Economics* 107 (1992): 201–32; Frank Levy and Richard Murnane, "U.S. Earnings Levels and Earnings Inequality: A Review of Recent Trends and Proposed Explanations," *Journal of Economic Literature* 30 (1992): 1333–81; David Card, "Changing Wage Structure and Black-White Wage Differentials," *American Economic Review* 84 (1994): 29–33; Francine Blau and Andrea Beller, "Black-White Earnings Over the 1970s and 1980s: Gender Differences in Trends," *Review of Economics and Statistics* 74 (1992): 276–86.

19. Owen Fiss, "A Theory of Fair Employment Laws," *University of Chicago Law Review* 38 (1971): 235–314; Lester Thurow, *Generating Inequality* (New York: Basic Books, 1975).

20. Joleen Kirschenman and Kathryn Neckerman, " 'We'd Love to Hire Them, But . . . ': The Meaning of Race for Employers" in Christopher Jencks and Paul E. Peterson, eds., *The Urban Underclass* (Washington, D.C.: The Brookings Institution, 1991).

21. William Dickens and Kevin Lang, "The Reemergence of Segmented Labor Market Theory," *American Economic Review* 78 (1988): 129–34.

22. Peter B. Doeringer and Michael J. Piore, *Internal Labor Markets and Manpower Analysis* (Lexington, Mass.: Lexington Books, 1971); David M. Gordon, Richard Edwards, and Michael Reich, *Segmented Work, Divided Workers: The Historical Transformation of Labor in the United States* (Cambridge: Cambridge University Press, 1982); Michael Reich, *Racial Inequality: A Political-Economic Analysis* (Princeton: Princeton University Press, 1981); Richard B. Freeman and James Medoff, "New Estimates of Private Sector Unionism in the United States," *Industrial and Labor Relations Review* 32 (1979): 143–74; Richard B. Freeman and James Medoff, "The Two Faces of Unionism," *Public Interest* 57 (1979): 69–93.

23. Barbara Bergmann, "Occupational Segregation, Wages and Profits When Employers Discriminate by Race or Sex," *Eastern Economic Journal* 1 (1974): 103–10.

24. Michael J. Piore, *Birds of Passage: Migrant Labor and Industrial Societies* (Cambridge: Cambridge University Press, 1979).

25. We realize that by excluding those with disabilities, we potentially keep out a differentially large number of African Americans, depending on our definition of disability. As a result, our study might have shown an even stronger effect if we had included those disabled but potentially employable.

26. See chapter 13 in this volume and Cordelia Reimers and Howard Chernic, "Hispanic Employment in the Public Sector: Why is it Lower Than Blacks'?" in Edwin Melendez, Clara Rodriguez, and Janice Berry-Figueroa, eds., *Hispanics in the Labor Force* (New York: Plenum Press, 1991).

27. Abel Valenzuela, Jr., "Immigrants, Minority Workers, and Job Competition."

28. Immigration may also have an effect by decreasing internal migration of blacks into Los Angeles. An analysis of geographic mobility, based on available aggre-

gate data, indicates that immigration decreases net African American migration to this region, and the effect is traced to Latino immigration. Immigration thus serves to moderate the effects on earnings and joblessness by minimizing the growth in the supply of African American labor.

29. Stuart Silverstein, "Domestics: Hiring the Illegal Hits Home," *Los Angeles Times,* October 28, 1994, A1.

30. African Americans tend to be both younger and less-educated than whites in Los Angeles. Among young males between the ages of 18 and 24 who were not in school, 33 percent of African Americans in 1990 had less than a high school education, compared with 21 percent for non-Hispanic whites. At the same time, 35 percent of the African Americans were under the age of 21, compared with only 27 percent of non-Hispanic whites.

31. Eulalio Castellanos, Luz Echavarria, and Yvette Galindo, "Educational Inequality," in Paul M. Ong, *The Widening Divide: Income Inequality and Poverty in Los Angeles* (Los Angeles: Graduate School of Architecture and Urban Planning, UCLA, 1989).

32. George J. Borjas and Valerie A. Ramey, "Rising Wage Inequality in the U.S.: Causes and Consequences—Time Series Evidence on the Source of Trends in Wage Inequality," *American Economic Review* 84 (1994): 10–16.

33. Yeh Ling-ling, "America Needs a Time Out From Immigration," *Hayward Daily Review,* October 21, 1994.

34. Mark DiCamillo and Mervin Field, "Anti-Illegal Immigrant Measure, Proposition 187, Continues to Draw Strong Voter Support." The Field Poll, Release #1731, September 27, 1994; Paul Feldman, "The Times Poll: 62% Would Bar Services to Illegal Immigrants," *Los Angeles Times,* September 14, 1994.

35. Proposition 187 was designed to deny social services to undocumented aliens. The official ballot measure, which was overwhelmingly passed by the voters of California (61 percent), mandates that "illegal aliens are ineligible for public social services, public health care services (unless emergency under federal law), and attendance of public schools. Requires state/local agencies report suspected illegal aliens."

36. *Los Angeles Times* exit poll, November 10, 1994.

37. Rodolfo O. de la Garza, et al., *Latino Voices: Mexican, Puerto Rican, and Cuban Perspectives on American Politics* (Boulder, Colo.: Westview Press, 1992).

Self-Employment: Mobility Ladder or Economic Lifeboat?

Ivan Light and Elizabeth Roach

STAGGERING UNDER the quadruple blows of national recession, slumping housing values, reduced defense spending, and long-term exportation of jobs, Greater Los Angeles became an official ex-paradise in the 1990s.[1] An influential report found that Los Angeles suffers "urban, industrial, and social decay comparable to the worst of the Eastern metropolises."[2] In actuality, Greater Los Angeles' deterioration was underway long before the riot and arson of April, 1992 attracted media attention.[3] In the preceding decade many whites had left Greater Los Angeles, turning "California, Here I Come" into "California, Here I Go." Apparently, however, the revised lyrics did not reach Central America or Asia, from which an even more sizable number of immigrants seeking opportunity arrived in the Golden State. Ironically, Los Angeles became America's new Ellis Island, a first-stop for immigrants in search of the American dream, just as native whites began to abandon the region.[4]

If the region's economy had remained strong into the 1990s, Greater Los Angeles could more easily deliver the American dream today as New York City delivered it a century ago. With its vast immigrant populations, startling ethnic diversity, bankrupt local governments, and declining economy, however, Los Angeles is putting the American dream of material abundance to its severest historical test.[5]

In this situation, self-employment strongly influences the economic welfare of all the ethnoracial groups that make up Greater Los Angeles. One reason is the sheer prevalence of self-employment in the region. Los Angeles has long had more self-employed workers than other re-

193

gions, and in the last generation, the region's self-employment rate has increased faster than that of the United States. Greater Los Angeles simply has so many self-employed workers that one cannot ignore their welfare.[6]

A second reason is the continued centrality of self-employment to upward economic mobility. Abraham Lincoln called the progression from wage employment to self-employment the "natural course of labor" and proposed to guarantee this right to blacks as well as to whites. Although Lincoln's fairness to blacks was unusual, his view of self-employment was not. Long before Lincoln, Benjamin Franklin had already understood self-employment as the standard path from working class to middle class. After Lincoln, Horatio Alger's juvenile novels continued this positive view of self-employment as the obvious means by which industry and thrift were rewarded.[7] Currently, self-employment remains a key to middle-class status and welfare for native whites as well as immigrant and ethnic minorities.

Unfortunately, a third reason for the importance of self-employment is less reassuring. Now, as ever, self-employment provides a recourse of desperation for the underemployed or unemployed.[8] Just as the lifeboats come out when a ship goes down, so self-employment rates rise as job opportunities sink. Precisely this scenario affects Greater Los Angeles. Because of job exportation, Greater Los Angeles experienced rising unemployment and declining real incomes between 1970 and 1990.[9] Some of the region's self-employment developed because households started a business when wages stopped or simply failed to keep pace with living costs. The remarkable growth of women-owned businesses owes much to this situation.[10]

Self-employment as regional mainstay, traditional route up the ladder, and lifeboat are three aspects of this complex subject, and they operate simultaneously. At any moment in time, successful people are latching onto self-employment as a means of economic ascent, while struggling people are undertaking self-employment to survive hard times. Presumably the proportion of ascent-oriented self-employment increases on the upward leg of the business cycle just as the proportion of survival-oriented self-employment increases on the downward leg. But whether the business cycle is at its trough or its peak, both types are always present in the self-employed population.

The business cycle is not, however, the only influence upon the balance of successful and struggling people in the self-employed population. Ethnicity affects this balance in three basic ways. First, entrepreneurial ethnoracial and ethnoreligious groups can exploit opportunities more effectively than others.[11] This influence has always been a factor in Greater Los Angeles, where the movie industry rose to world preeminence on the entrepreneurial skills of Jews. These skills enable Jews and other entrepreneurial minorities to prosper in business. Therefore, when immigration increases the proportion of entrepreneurial minorities in a region, that region's average entrepreneurial competence increases, driving up the proportion of positive, ascent-oriented firms in the self-employed population and increasing regional self-employment.[12] The immigration that brings about this new, ascent-oriented self-employment we call an *entrepreneur influx.*

Second, when immigrants outstrip the job supply in a migration-reception region and saturation looms, migration networks seeking to find employment for new immigrants begin to produce more self-employed workers and fewer wage and salary workers.[13] We call this *network-driven self-employment,* because the momentum of immigration forces up the self-employed population. Some of this network-driven self-employment is ascent-oriented, but most is survivalist. In an extreme but theoretical case, when a job supply in the destination economy is exhausted, a migration continues only when all new immigrants employ themselves. As such a situation develops, the network-driven self-employment of immigrant groups can drive up regional self-employment even in deteriorating business climates.

Third, even when economic conditions are generally improving or generally deteriorating, ethnic occupational and industrial niches need not rise and fall in unison. Because immigrant and ethnic minorities, including native-born whites, cluster in identifiable niches and do not spread evenly over the industrial landscape,[14] changing economic conditions usually affect ethnoracial groups unequally. Sometimes even drastic economic change impacts some ethnic niches a lot, others a little, and still others not at all. Declining ethnic occupational and industrial niches mean deteriorated job markets for their inhabitants, whose reaction to the disintegration of a formerly secure niche takes the form of survival-oriented self-employment. Normally the growth of this defensive self-employment increases the affected group's self-employment rate.

Naturally, these three causes need not coincide in a single region; there can be regions of immigrant reception in which one or two of these causes operate without the others. Wherever all three causes converge, however, one can expect self-employment rates to rise the most. This convergence happened in Los Angeles between 1970 and 1990. In that twenty-year period, Greater Los Angeles experienced a hyperentrepreneurial influx, largely but not exclusively consisting of Asian, Russian, and Middle Eastern immigrants. It also experienced network-driven Latino and Asian self-employment arising from migration-induced pressure on the job supply; and it experienced survival-oriented self-employment arising from decay of the longstanding industrial niches of native workers, especially native whites to be discussed in chapter 14. All three contributed to the region's increased dependence upon self-employment.

CHANGING PATTERNS OF SELF-EMPLOYMENT

To document this claim, we turn first to Greater Los Angeles' self-employment between 1970 and 1990. The region witnessed job exportation increasing unemployment rates, and stagnant living standards throughout this twenty-year period, as chapter 8 will detail. Nonetheless, rates of aggregate self-employment increased markedly. Combining all four major ethnoracial categories, we found that total self-employment in Los Angeles increased from 10.4 percent of the labor force in 1970 to 12.2 percent in 1990, a 17 percent increase. As a result of this rate increase, Greater Los Angeles had 142,464 more self-employed workers in 1990 than it would have had if the 1970s self-employment rate had remained unchanged until 1990.

These increases in self-employment were not, however, uniform among all the ethnoracial groups and categories in this diverse region. Figure 7.1 shows that the four major ethnoracial categories experienced unequal self-employment growth. The largest proportional change occurred among non-Hispanic whites; Hispanics also registered a substantial gain. Asian rates changed little, though that modest increase began from a very high base, indicating that Asians have maintained a high self-employment rate even as the Asian economic presence has massively expanded. Black self-employment rates remained virtually unchanged.

Distinguishing the proportions of incorporated versus unincorporated self-employment enables us to ascertain how advantageous increased self-employment was for each of the four major ethnoracial groups. Incorporated self-employment means an incorporated business; unincorporated self-employment means a proprietorship, possibly a very small firm. Incorporated business firms are bigger and more lucrative on average than unincorporated businesses, and are more likely to propel their owners into the ranks of the affluent. Incorporated self-employment epitomizes sheer economic success, the American dream, whereas unincorporated self-employment may represent only a tiny Mom-and-Pop store that keeps a struggling family off welfare.

Incorporated self-employment increased among all four ethnoracial groups (Asians, whites, blacks, and Hispanics) in the twenty-year period. Indeed, incorporated self-employment experienced the highest growth of any industrial class in the twenty-year period. These were boom years for access to big money. Among whites and Hispanics, the incorporated self-employed more than doubled their percentage share of the labor force. Incorporated self-employment rose among blacks as well, though only by half a percentage point and from a minuscule base; among Asians, the incorporated self-employed more than tripled their share.

Changes in unincorporated self-employment were mixed. Among blacks and Asians, unincorporated self-employment declined, but the shift toward incorporated self-employment boosted the already high self-employed rate for Asians. By 1990, 3 out of every 100 Asians were in incorporated self-employment, the most remunerative type. This shift was economically advantageous; it meant that prosperous proprietors became a bigger segment of the Asian self-employed, Mom and Pop a smaller share. On balance, therefore, this shift improved the business mix of the Asian self-employed,

FIGURE 7.1 | **Self-Employment Among Selected Groups, Los Angeles Region, 1970–1990**

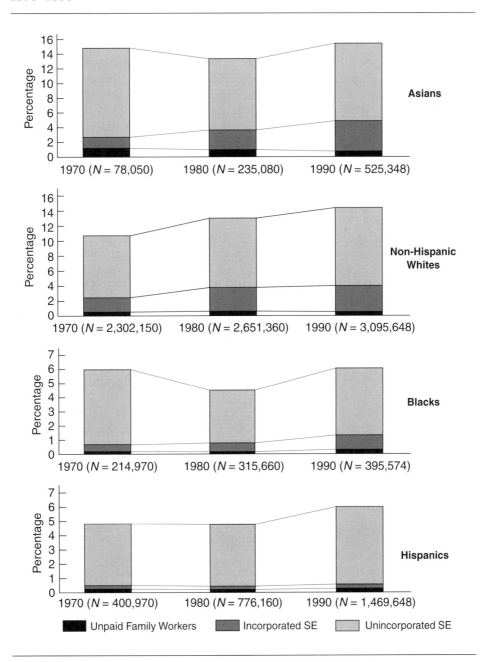

NOTE: Charts show self-employment as a percentage of total employment for that group.

even as overall self-employment rates moved upward and numbers—reflecting the immigrant influx—went through the roof.

For whites and Hispanics, two decades of change were less advantageous. Both groups experienced an increase in incorporated and unincorporated rates. Thus some of the increase in overall self-employment rates represented a real growth in the numbers of newly rich people, as incorporated self-employment permitted new white and Hispanic entrepreneurs to move up into a high income level. On the other hand, however, the increase of unincorporated self-employment resulted from overcrowded Hispanic employment niches and the crumbling of longstanding white employment niches.[15] These mixed results signal economic conditions that permitted some whites and Hispanics to achieve entrepreneurial success while compelling others to scrounge for alternatives to vanishing jobs.

Immigration from Mexico and Central America produced network-driven self-employment during the 1980s. The rapid influx of low-skilled immigrants presented the Greater Los Angeles labor market with more unskilled workers than employers could hire. One predictable result was the growth of informal employment, with street-corner labor markets providing this service. Another result was deflection of underemployed Hispanic immigrants into marginal self-employment.[16] Between 1980 and 1990 the number of unincorporated foreign-born Hispanic self-employed grew from 18,480 to 54,768, tripling their number even though the number of jobs in Greater Los Angeles did not even double in this decade. At the same time, the mean years of education of these self-employed Hispanics declined, even though the general level of education in the labor market increased 10 percent in the same period. The predictable result was a decline in the real earnings of these immigrant entrepreneurs.

In incorporated self-employment, the saturation effect hit even harder. While the number of incorporated foreign-born Hispanic self-employed tripled, their average educational attainment dropped, and their real money earnings declined 30 percent. In sum, by 1990, Los Angeles had three times more immigrant Hispanic business owners than a decade earlier, but these foreign entrepreneurs were less educated than their predecessors, and they made far less money. At the low end of the self-employment spectrum, among the poorest and least educated Hispanic entrepreneurs, a big informal economy had emerged, prompting the quip that Los Angeles had become "the Capital of the Third World."[17]

Of course, figure 7.1 shows nothing about the national-origin communities that made up the four ethnoracial categories of white, Hispanic, Asian, and black. Table 7.1 compares the self-employment rates of fourteen selected ethnoracial groups in 1970, 1980, and 1990, including native-born Russians (largely Jews)—a white ethnic group with a continuing entrepreneurial propensity—and other native whites. Self-employment rates increased among all the foreign-born groups. Growth in self-employment was

TABLE 7.1 | **Self-Employment Rates in the Los Angeles Region, 1970–1990 (Selected Immigrant and Ethnic Groups, Ages 25–64, Employed)**

	1970[a] (%)	1980 (%)	1990 (%)
Salvadoran FB	3.9	3.8	7.0
Guatemalan FB	N/A	3.3	7.8
Mexican NB	4.7	5.3	6.3
Mexican FB	4.8	4.0	6.7
Japanese NB	18.6	15.1	10.9
Chinese NB	20.5	10.7	11.2
Chinese FB	11.5	16.5	16.6
Filipino FB	3.4	3.5	5.2
Korean FB	3.6	24.8	34.6
Blacks NB	6.3	4.4	5.8
Armenian FB	N/A	24.3	27.2
Iranian FB	N/A	20.9	27.8
Russian NB	N/A	22.9	23.4
Other white NB	10.1	12.0	13.3

[a]The 1970 data should be interpreted with caution, since for most groups the sample sizes are less than 50.

not universal in Greater Los Angeles, however; the native-born pattern was quite mixed. Among native-born Chinese and Japanese, self-employment rates declined hugely in the twenty years, presumably because, as a result of declining racism, these native-born Asians found more opportunity in the general labor market than they once had. Among native blacks and native whites of Russian descent, self-employment rates were stable. The only native-born groups among whom self-employment rates actually increased were non-Russian-origin native whites and Mexicans, whose rates each increased about one-third.

SELF-EMPLOYMENT INCOME

The desirability of self-employment depends upon the income it affords. Self-employment is unattractive when its money returns are skimpy in comparison with wages. If the self-employed earn more than wage and salary earners, then self-employment is financially attractive.[18] Where such a scenario prevails, market capitalism still delivers the American dream of upward economic mobility through ownership of one's own business. The dream seems to live on in Los Angeles, a surprise since the nation's self-employed generally earn less than wage and salary workers.[19] Contrary to the national pattern but in conformity with the region's historically high entrepreneurship, Greater Los Angeles' self-employed earn more than employees in every decennial year from 1970 to 1990. Table 7.2 shows that, except for Hispanics in unincorporated self-employment in 1990, mean earnings of both the incorporated and the unincorporated self-employed

TABLE 7.2 | Mean Earnings of Ethnoracial Groups, Los Angeles Region, 1970–1990 (Ages 25–64)

	1970 ($)	1980 ($)	1990 ($)	Index
Whites				
Employees				
Private	11,236	21,416	44,044	392
Government	11,438	20,913	40,980	358
Self-employed				
Incorporated	23,290	45,764	92,155	396
Unincorporated	20,871	24,768	48,151	231
Blacks				
Employees				
Private	7,031	15,207	31,534	448
Government	8,775	16,613	34,875	397
Self-employed				
Incorporated	12,066	40,894	54,808	454
Unincorporated	11,273	18,896	42,617	378
Hispanics				
Employees				
Private	8,164	13,588	23,186	284
Government	9,300	14,718	29,853	321
Self-employed				
Incorporated	21,678	32,382	44,981	207
Unincorporated	12,613	18,397	29,599	235
Asians				
Employees				
Private	9,186	17,200	34,336	374
Government	10,913	19,066	37,233	341
Self-employed				
Incorporated	18,951	32,754	66,007	348
Unincorporated	16,366	23,468	41,889	256

NOTE: Index = 1990/1970 × 100

exceeded the mean earnings of coethnic private sector or government employees in 1970, 1980, and 1990. For example, the mean earnings of incorporated black self-employed were $54,808 in 1990 and the mean earnings of unincorporated black self-employed were $42,617 in that year. Both means exceeded the mean earnings of black employees in the private sector and the government sector.[20]

A second issue is the growth of self-employment income relative to growth of wage income. Even if average self-employment incomes exceed average wage incomes, as they do in Greater Los Angeles, an eroding relative advantage of self-employment spells deteriorating advantage; unless interrupted, this deterioration ultimately leaves average self-employment incomes abreast of or even behind average wages. When this declining trend of relative self-employment income accompanies an increasing rate of self-employment, we conclude that poor job prospects have driven so many former employees into defensive self-employment that money returns declined in self-employment. When relative incomes are steady or increasing, we might attribute increases in self-employment to demand-side causes. But when people are flocking into declining self-employment, we infer that they are fleeing deteriorating conditions in the wage sector. Such a scenario is definitely not the American dream.

In general, Greater Los Angeles experienced precisely such a network-driven deterioration of unincorporated self-employment income between 1970 and 1990. The index numbers (see Table 7.2) show the increase in self-employment income between 1970 and 1990 for each ethnoracial category. By comparing the index numbers of the four categories, one can see where self-employment earnings kept pace and where they declined in twenty years. Happily, the situation was by no means all bad. Income declines did not affect the incorporated self-employed, the wealthiest sector of the entire labor force. The financial return of incorporated self-employment kept pace with the wages of private-sector workers among blacks and whites, but not among Asians and Hispanics. Among Hispanics, the income of the incorporated self-employed increased only 73 percent as much as did Hispanic wage income in the private sector.

Unfortunately, conditions were much worse among the unincorporated self-employed, for whom the growth in self-employment incomes of all four ethnoracial categories fell behind the growth in income of each group's private wage and salary workers. Whites sustained the severest deterioration of their income. Among whites, unincorporated self-employment incomes increased only 45 percent as much as did the income of wage and salary workers in the private sector. Other ethnoracial categories suffered smaller but still serious damage. The incomes of unincorporated Asian self-employed workers increased only 56 percent as much as did the wages and salaries of Asian employees in the private sector. Unincorporated blacks and Hispanics increased their incomes 80 percent and 73 percent as much as did coethnic employees in the private sector. As a result of this adverse trend, the incomes of self-employed workers were lower relative to private sector workers in 1990 than they had been in 1970, even though average self-employment incomes were still higher than average wages in the private sector. Only among whites and Hispanics did the growth of unincorporated self-employment also exceed the growth of private wage and salary employment, suggesting influx-driven deterioration of unincorporated self-employment.

THE SELF-EMPLOYMENT BONUS

Human capital is an individual's investment in personal productivity, the value a worker adds. The usual measures of human capital are years of formal education and years of work experience. If the self-employed had more human capital than wage and salary workers, one might explain their superior earnings as returns on their educational investment.[21] Similarly, if the average human capital of the self-employed declined, then one would expect their relative earnings advantage to decline, too. Conceivably the self-employed earned more than coethnic wage and salary workers because they were better educated on average, even though their margin of educational superiority declined between 1970 and 1990. Additionally, one must consider the possibility that the self-employed were older than coethnic employees, spoke better English, were married, and so forth. Any of these conditions could explain away the income advantage of the self-employed. That is, if the self-employed earned more, possibly it was because they were older or spoke better English rather than just because they were self-employed.

A *self-employment bonus* is the income advantage of self-employment over wage or salary employment net of individual productivity. The usual measures of productivity are human capital, age, English proficiency, and other factors that affect wages. Where a self-employment bonus exists, a switch into self-employment occasions a real increase in income just because self-employment is more lucrative than wage or salary employment. Table 7.3 uses ordinary least squares regression to estimate the size of any self-employment bonus in 1990. The first column shows the absolute self-employment bonus, obtained by subtracting wage or salary earnings from self-employment earnings. It contrasts thirteen important ethnoracial groups. In each of these groups, the self-employed earned a bonus, but the size of the bonus varied. It was smallest among foreign-born Mexicans, Salvadorans, and Guatemalans, largely working-class groups. The bonus was largest among native-born persons of Russian extraction—mostly Jewish—but Iranians, Armenians, Chinese, Japanese, Koreans, and blacks also received self-employment bonuses of $10,000 or more in 1990. These data are quite compatible with those in table 7.2. They show that the self-employed earned a bonus, and that Hispanic groups earned a smaller bonus than non-Hispanic groups, possibly as a result of network-driven self-employment.

The second column of table 7.3 adjusts the self-employment bonus for human capital and other variables that might spuriously inflate it.[22] This procedure enabled us to ascertain whether the self-employed really earned more because of self-employment or whether their higher earnings were due to superior personal productivity. When statistically evaluated, these census data showed that the self-employment bonus was real. Except for Armenians, whose bonus was enhanced, the statistical adjustment always reduced the size of the bonus, but it never eliminated it. Every group, including native whites, obtained an economic bonus for self-employment. Net of human capital, age, English proficiency and other factors, the self-employed simply earned more than did wage or salary earners. The differences were not small in any category, but they were largest for Armenians, Iranians, and Russians. Among the Hispanics, the adjusted self-employment bonuses were smallest but still appreciable. Apparently the migration-driven increase of Hispanic self-employment had reduced the self-employment bonus but did not eliminate it.

These results support the mixed conclusions drawn earlier in this chapter about self-employment in the twenty-year period. By 1990, the self-employment bonus had frayed, but Los Angeles was by no means a region in

TABLE 7.3 | Self-Employment Bonus Among Selected Groups, Los Angeles Region, 1990 (Employed Males Aged 25–64 Years Old)

	Self-employment Bonus ($)	Adjusted Self-employment Bonus ($)
Salvadoran FB	4,012	3,797
Guatemalan FB	6,768	5,120
Mexican NB	10,101	9,067
Mexican FB	6,452	4,737
Japanese NB	13,330	12,698
Chinese NB	19,713	14,232
Chinese FB	15,437	12,993
Filipino FB	9,326	7,624
Korean FB	14,474	9,941
Black NB	14,119	13,467
Armenian FB	14,989	15,158
Iranian FB	17,806	15,067
Russian NB	21,875	17,336

which the American dream had collapsed, although its payoffs declined. Despite all the area's economic problems and the heavy immigration to the region, even Hispanic immigrants—generally the poorest and least prepared of any immigrants—could still settle in Greater Los Angeles and obtain upward economic mobility if they started their own business.

ENTREPRENEURSHIP AMONG IMMIGRANTS

Thanks to relentless media coverage of immigrant entrepreneurship, the American public has come to view immigrants as entrepreneurial miracleworkers.[23] Playing on this popular impression in the late 1980s, at the height of the regional real estate boom in Greater Los Angeles, Vietnameseborn Tom Vu purchased long, haranguing television commercials that taunted white Americans with their failure to match his rags-to-riches career in real estate.[24] Vu had a point in that immigrants are normally more entrepreneurial than native-born persons of the same ethnoracial origin. This reliable difference has persisted over one hundred years of census records. The usual explanation fastens upon the relative disadvantage of the immigrants in the labor force. Speaking English poorly, lacking recognized educational credentials, and not having access to existing referral networks, immigrants must also face hiring discrimination based on accent, national origin, or religion. For these reasons, it is argued, immigrants have more to gain in self-employment than do native workers.[25]

This classic situation certainly existed in Greater Los Angeles in 1990. Table 7.4 compares the self-employment of foreign- and native-born men and women of the four principal ethnoracial categories. The self-employment rate of foreign-born white, Asian, and black men exceeds the rate of their native-born coethnics. Similarly, the self-employment of foreign-born white, Asian, and Hispanic women also exceeds the self-employment of their native-born coethnics.[26] Only the self-employment of foreign-born Hispanic men and foreign-born black women failed to exceed that of their native-born coethnics. In this sense, the census data show that as immigrants crowded into Los Angeles, they raised the region's aggregate self-employment rate over what would have been expected from a comparable influx of native-born coethnics.

Although the superior entrepreneurship of the immigrants buffered their impact on labor markets, relieving sources of potential competition with native workers, the buffering effect would have been even greater had all the immigrants demonstrated the self-employment rate of Koreans or Iranians (table 7.1). Indeed, the buffering impact would have been much greater if all the immigrants had matched even the self-employment level of native-born whites. Immigrants did not all do that, as tables 7.1 and 7.4 show, although they should have had consistently higher self-employment

TABLE 7.4 | **Wage Employment and Self-Employment, Los Angeles Region, 1970–1990**

	1990 Self-employed (%)	Index, 1970–1990[a]	
		Wage and Salaried	Self-employed
White NB			
Men	19.0	108	150
Women	10.7	151	280
White FB			
Men	34.0	124	210
Women	14.0	145	197
Black NB			
Men	7.6	153	150
Women	3.7	201	179
Black FB			
Men	8.8	N/A	N/A
Women	2.8	N/A	N/A
Asian NB			
Men	13.6	209	105
Women	6.5	264	226
Asian FB			
Men	21.8	984	1,438
Women	12.5	1,074	N/A
Hispanic NB			
Men	8.2	191	245
Women	4.5	271	627
Hispanic FB			
Men	8.0	659	817
Women	6.1	746	1,793

[a] Index = 1990/1970 × 100

rates than native whites if disadvantage in the labor market were the only determinant of self-employment.

Explaining the intergroup differences requires an examination of the resources of class and ethnicity that immigrants brought with them.[27] Arguably, as Timothy Bates maintains, intergroup differences like those in table 7.1 arose because native whites had more class resources than did others and outperformed them for this reason, just as some of the immigrants had more class resources than the native whites.[28] To unravel this issue, table 7.5 compares the adjusted and unadjusted odds ratio of self-employment among thirteen native- and foreign-born groups. Native-born white men are the omitted category against whom the other groups' odds of self-employment are compared. The raw odds ratio records the odds of male self-

**TABLE 7.5 | Raw and Adjusted Odds Ratios of
Self-Employment, Los Angeles Region, 1990
(Selected Groups of Employed Men Aged 25–64)**

	Raw Odds Ratio	Adjusted Odds Ratio
Salvadoran FB	0.40	0.43
Guatemalan FB	0.46	0.51
Mexican NB	0.49	0.50
Mexican FB	0.45	0.47
Japanese NB	0.88	0.86
Chinese NB	0.89	0.95
Chinese FB	1.29	1.36
Filipino FB	0.39	0.32
Korean FB	2.47	3.46
Black NB	0.49	0.47
Armenian FB	2.17	2.89
Iranian FB	2.08	2.76
Russian NB	1.83	2.02

employment in each immigrant or native-born group relative to the odds of native-born white self-employment.[29] The adjusted odds ratio shows the same odds net of productivity, English proficiency, work limitation, and marital status.[30]

Even taking full account of individual productivity, the native-born white men had lower odds of self-employment than did foreign-born Chinese, Korean, Armenian, and Iranian men.[31] They also had lower odds of self-employment than native-born men of Russian descent, a heavily Jewish category, who were twice as likely to be self-employed as comparable native white men. One cannot explain away this difference on the strength of human capital, marital status, or work limitation. On the other hand, even net of individual productivity, the native-born white men had higher odds of self-employment than native-born Mexican, Japanese, Chinese, and black men. They also had higher odds of self-employment than foreign-born Salvadoran, Guatemalan, Mexican, and Filipino men. One cannot explain away these differences on the grounds of human capital, either.

These results certainly support the view, found already in the literature, that immigration raises the aggregate self-employment of immigrant-reception areas. But they do not prove that all immigrants are miracle-workers, a common extrapolation. In actuality, some immigrants are less entrepreneurial than native whites, and some are more entrepreneurial. Thus, the degree to which immigration increases regional self-employment depends upon the exact ethnoracial composition of the immigrant population. In the specific case of Greater Los Angeles, some immigrants had high-entrepreneurship, others low; that is, some immigrant groups had higher self-employment rates than native whites, others lower. This balanced mix increased regional entrepreneurship more than would have an immigration composed exclusively of Central Americans, but less than would have an immigration composed exclusively of Iranians.

CONCLUSION

As a means of economic self-defense against deteriorating labor markets, self-employment was most important to whites. Of all the ethnoracial groups and categories in the Greater Los Angeles mosaic, whites suffered the most economic damage from job exportation. After all, whites had the most to lose. They had enjoyed the lion's share of the stable blue-collar and middle-management jobs that globalization exported. As jobs were shipped away, whites experienced the largest loss of jobs. The huge exodus of whites from Greater Los Angeles, documented in this volume and elsewhere, is evidence of the economic damage whites sustained in this period.[32] Further evidence is seen in the drastic increase in white self-employment, especially the self-employment of white women.

Jobs exportation did not hurt Asians as much as whites. Despite global restructuring, native-born Asian men have made strong employment gains in the last two decades. These gains cannot be attributed to the Asians' education levels, which were no higher than those of whites. Long subjected to employment discrimination, native-born Asian men had clustered in low-return self-employment in self-defense. As employment discrimination lifted and Asian men moved into jobs for which their qualifications fit them, otherwise deteriorating labor market conditions actually drew Asian men from self-employment into wage and salary employment. The reduction of discrimination in the labor market benefitted Asian men more than any loss of jobs to global restructuring had harmed them. Foreign-born Asian men and Asian women lagged about a generation behind native-born Asian men in this respect.[33] Labor market conditions improved less radically for Asian women, among whom self-employment in new immigrant-staffed industries offered an avenue for upward income mobility. Either way, both Asian men and Asian women improved their economic situation in this period.

Our data do not show defensive self-employment among blacks in these two decades. Blacks had neither immigration nor job exportation to stimulate their self-employment. Despite modest increases, black women's self-employment rates have stagnated at a persistently low level over the course of the twenty-year period reviewed in this chapter. A small percentage of blacks, however, did succeed in shifting to high-income, incorporated self-employment; this growth contributed to the expansion of the region's black middle class, a trend documented in greater detail in chapter 13 of this book. In view of blacks' economic vulnerability, our failure to find evidence of unemployment-driven, defensive self-employment deserves attention. The explanation, we conclude, derives from the already desperately marginal position of blacks in 1970. Severely disadvantaged, blacks had less to fear from restructuring than others. It is possible that restructuring drove blacks further down into crime and the informal economy, activities the census statistics do not chart.[34] Therefore, our data may not record increased economic stress among blacks so well as they do among whites.

Like native-born Asian men, native-born Hispanic men made gains in the labor market despite restructuring. We suppose that, like Asian men, the native-born Hispanic men also benefited more from reduction in discrimination than they suffered from restructuring. These exported jobs would not have gone to Hispanics even if they had remained in Los Angeles. The effects of restructuring are most visible among foreign-born Hispanic men and Hispanic women. These groups' self-employment rates increased along with the share of total income they received from self-employment. The increases are moderate, but one could interpret them as evidence of mild distress arising from diminished earning opportunities in the wage economy. The drastic increase in Hispanic women's labor force participation spilled over into a more drastic increase in Hispanic women's self-employment.[35] By implication, the Hispanic women were not finding all the jobs they wanted and turned to self-employment. Of course, those low-wage jobs they did find are among the most prominent effects of restructuring. In this sense, Hispanic women were major beneficiaries of restructuring, which created jobs they could get.

The attractions of Greater L.A. are more than just the mild climate. The hope of riches is still another important reason people come to Los Angeles, whose state motto ("Eureka [I have found it]") comes straight out of the Gold Rush of 1848. To a large extent, immigrants and internal migrants got what they came for through self-employment. As a route of economic ascent, business ownership still offers the American dream to the people of Greater Los Angeles, native and immigrant alike.[36] Just opening a business of their own permitted workers of all ethnic and nativity backgrounds to increase their income. Indeed, for whatever reason, entrepreneurship was more profitable in Greater Los Angeles in the last generation than it was in the rest of the United States.

We must observe, however, that self-employment is more complex than the American dream, important as that is. In particular, one cannot explain the increased self-employment rate in Greater L.A. on the basis of increased opportunities. Rather, much of Los Angeles' increased self-employment arose from economic distress, the bitter side of free enterprise. Whites and Hispanics saw this bitter side more than did black and Asian entrepreneurs, for whom the last two decades were altogether beneficial. For the native whites, twenty years of job exportation had created a less attractive labor market than had existed in 1970. As the best jobs moved out of California, many whites sold their houses and moved out, too. Among those who stayed, many households increased labor market participation to compensate for declining or static real incomes of the male breadwinner. The rush of native white women into the job market was paralleled by their rush into poorly paid self-employment. This strategy reduced unemployment rates and enabled many working families to remain self-supporting.

Among Mexican and Central American immigrants, a different, more difficult scenario unfolded. The Hispanic workers increased in number because of immigration as well as because of the increased labor force participation of women, a double stress. The network-driven growth of Hispanic entrepreneurs certainly drove down the rewards of business ownership among this group to a greater extent than any other. In a way, however, the Hispanic situation was superior to what the whites faced. They were developing new economic niches in garment manufacturing, gardening, and hotel and restaurant work as the whites were losing their comfortable niches. Admittedly the Hispanic niches were poorly paid, but getting a bad job may be easier to endure than losing a good one.

Notes to Chapter 7

1. This list excludes drought, fire, and riot, disasters that also befell the region. On the riot, see Ivan Light, Hadas Har-Chvi, and Kenneth Kan, "Black/Korean Conflict in Los Angeles," in Seamus Dunn, ed., *Managing Divided Cities* (Keele, U. K.: Ryburn, 1994), 72–87.

2. David Friedman, *The New Economy Project: Final Report* (Los Angeles: The New Vision Business Council of Southern California, 1994).

3. "Los Angeles is covered with areas that are characterized by abandoned factories, high unemployment, high rates of out-migration, deskilling of jobs, wage reductions and shifts from industrial to service jobs; automobile, tire, and steel industries being the primary examples of this trend." Marta Lopez-Garza, "Immigration and Economic Restructuring: The Metamorphosis of Southern California," *California Sociologist* 12 (1989): 119.

4. Ivan Light and Parminder Bhachu, "Introduction: California Immigrants in World Perspective," in Ivan Light and Parminder Bhachu, eds., *Immigration and Entrepreneurship* (New Brunswick, N.J.: Transaction, 1993), 1–24; Yen Le Espiritu, "Immigration and the Peopling of Los Angeles," in Gerry Riposa, ed., *The City of Angels* (Dubuque, Iowa: Kendall/Hunt, 1992), 67–82. Apparently the bad news had not penetrated the White House, either. See Ronald Brownstein, "L.A. Left Out of Urban Aid Program, U.S. Officials Say," *Los Angeles Times*, December 20, 1994.

5. Mehdi Bozorgmehr, Georges Sabagh, and Ivan Light, "Los Angeles: Explosive Diversity," in Silvia Pedraza and Rubén Rumbaut, eds., *Origins and Destinies: Immi-*

gration, Race, and Ethnicity in America (Belmont, Calif.: Wadsworth, 1995), 346–359.

6. Nancy Rivera Brooks, "What's Entrepreneurial, Small, Private, and Young? The Typical L.A. County Firm, a New Study Says," *Los Angeles Times,* October 24, 1994.

7. See chapter 7 of Ivan Light and Carolyn Rosenstein, *Race, Ethnicity, and Entrepreneurship in Urban America* (Hawthorne, N.Y.: Aldine de Gruyter, 1995).

8. John Benson, *The Penny Capitalists* (New Brunswick, N.J.: Rutgers University Press, 1983). Even the homeless turn to self-employment. See Steven Balkin, "Entrepreneurial Activities of Homeless Men," *Journal of Sociology and Social Welfare* 19 (1992): 129–50.

9. Edward W. Soja, *Postmodern Geographies* (London: Verso, 1989); Ivan Light, "Los Angeles," in Mattei Dogan and John Kasarda, eds., *Giant Cities of the World: Problems and Policies,* vol. 2 (Beverly Hills: Sage Publications, 1987), 56–96; Walter Russell Mead, "Economy Keeps Improving, Why Aren't Clinton's Polls?" *Los Angeles Times,* September 9, 1994.

10. Karyn A. Loscocco and Joyce Robinson, "Barriers to Women's Small-Business Success in the United States," *Gender and Society* 5 (1991): 511–32.

11. See Light and Rosenstein, *Race, Ethnicity, and Entrepreneurship,* chapter 1.

12. Steven J. Gold, "Patterns of Economic Cooperation among Israeli Immigrants in Los Angeles," *International Migration Review* 28 (1994): 114–35; Ivan Light and Angel Sánchez, "Immigrant Entrepreneurs in 272 SMSAs," *Sociological Perspectives* 30 (1987): 373–99.

13. Ivan Light, Parminder Bhachu, and Stavros Karageorgis, "Migration Networks and Immigrant Entrepreneurship," in Ivan Light and Parminder Bhachu, eds., *Immigration and Entrepreneurship,* 25–49.

14. Ivan Light, *Cities in World Perspective* (New York: Macmillan, 1983), chapter 12; John R. Logan, Richard D. Alba, and Thomas L. McNulty, "Ethnic Economies in Metropolitan Regions: Miami and Beyond," *Social Forces* 72 (1994): 691–724. For a discussion of ethnic niches, see Roger Waldinger, "The Making of An Immigrant Niche," *International Migration Review* 28 (1994): 3–30.

15. Mexican American wages declined as a result of the relentless immigration as well. George Vernez found that the wage gap for Mexican immigrants deteriorated relative to white men and to native-born men of Mexican origin. Mexican male wages declined from 67 percent of white men's wages in 1960 to 60 percent in 1980 ("Mexican Labor in California's Economy," in Abraham F. Lowenthal and Katrina Burgess, eds., *The California-Mexico Connection* [Stanford: Stanford University Press, 1993], 150).

16. Norma Chinchilla and Nora Hamilton, "Central American Enterprises in Los Angeles." Report to the Inter-University Program for Latino Research and to the Social Science Research Council (Los Angeles, 1988).

17. David Rieff, *Los Angeles: Capital of the Third World* (New York: Touchstone, 1991).

18. Self-employment increases the mean earnings of groups even when the self-employed earn *less* than wage and salary workers, provided the new self-employed

are recruited from the previously unemployed or otherwise unemployed, as is indeed most commonly the case. See Ivan Light and Stavros Karageorgis, "The Ethnic Economy," in Neil Smelser and Richard Swedberg, eds., *Handbook of Economic Sociology* (New York: Russell Sage Foundation, 1994), 647–71. Using national longitudinal data, David S. Evans and Linda S. Leighton found that the switch into self-employment was greater from the status of unemployment than from wage employment. The previously unemployed are those new entrepreneurs whose last previous job status was unemployment; the otherwise unemployed means new self-employed workers who would have been unemployed had they sought wage employment instead of opening a business. Even low-income self-employment is more remunerative than unemployment. ("Some Empirical Aspects of Entrepreneurship," *American Economic Review* 79 (1989): 519–35.

19. Light and Karageorgis, "Ethnic Economy," 653.

20. This consistent relationship does not mean that every time a worker switched from wage or salary employment into self-employment the worker's earnings increased. It does imply, however, that taken in the aggregate, increases in a category's self-employment rates increased the mean earnings of the category. In this narrow economic sense, increased self-employment was always desirable throughout this twenty-year period.

21. Alejandro Portes and Min Zhou, "Gaining the Upper Hand: Economic Mobility among Immigrant and Domestic Minorities," *Ethnic and Racial Studies* 15 (1992): 491–522.

22. *The adjusted self-employment bonus* equals the multiple regression coefficient for the self-employment variable. For each group, separate multiple regressions are conducted. The dependent variable is the 1989 earnings. These are mean CPI-adjusted (1982/1984) earnings (wage/salary income plus self-employment income) with a minimum of $1,000; negative earnings are rounded to 0; no-earnings and no-weeks-worked-in-1989 are eliminated in the analysis. The regressions are for all currently employed (April 1990) workers, aged 25–64, in Greater Los Angeles. The independent variables are:

> Education (dummy coded; reference category = high school, less than high school, some college, college graduate)
> Years of experience (age − years of education − 6)
> Years of experience squared
> English proficiency (dummy coded; reference category = not very well, "good" English, "fair" English)
> Marital status (married with spouse present versus all other statuses)
> Work limitation (no work limitation versus work limitation)
> Full-time work (35 + versus fewer than 35 hours/week)
> Weeks worked in 1989 (number of weeks worked)
> Self-employed (yes, no)
> Period of immigration (dummy coded)

The adjusted numbers (column 2) tell us how much more or less the self-employed earn compared with other employees within each group, after controlling for human capital characteristics.

For all groups, both the adjusted and the unadjusted numbers are greater than zero, indicating that self-employed workers earn more than non-self-employed workers, before and after controlling for human capital characteristics. For example, self-employed native-born (NB) Russians earn $17,336 (column 2) more than non-self-employed NB Russian workers, all else being equal. Except for foreign-born (FB) Koreans, groups that are more likely to be self-employed than NB other whites (for example, FB Chinese, FB Armenian, FB Iranian, NB Russian) earn an additional $10,000 or more per year from self-employment, after controlling for human capital characteristics.

23. We do not deny the contribution immigrants have made to economic welfare. For a statement of this argument, see Thomas Muller, *Immigrants and the American City* (New York: New York University Press, 1993).

24. Vu was selling his real estate self-study course to the television public in this way.

25. See Light and Sánchez, "Immigrant Entrepreneurs."

26. "The number of self-employed women rose 68 percent between 1972 and 1982, whereas there was a 24 percent increase in the number of self-employed men. During the 1980's the increase in the number of women owning small businesses was five times greater than that for men." (Karyn A. Loscocco and Joyce Robinson, "Barriers to Women's Small-Business Success," 512.)

27. Okori Akpa Uneke, "Inter-Group Differences in Self-Employment: Blacks and Chinese in Toronto" (Ph.D. diss., University of Toronto, 1994); Timothy Bates, "Social Resources Generated by Group Support Networks May Not Be Beneficial to Asian Immigrant-Owned Small Businesses," *Social Forces* 72 (1994): 671–89.

28. But Alejandro Portes and Min Zhou reject this claim, noting that economists have neglected self-employment's contribution to minority mobility because of their "almost exclusive concentration on the relationship between human capital and wage levels." "Gaining the Upper Hand," 495.

29. *The raw odds ratio* = the ratio of the odds of persons in a particular group being self-employed to the odds of NB whites being self-employed.

$$\frac{\text{percent self-employed (group)}}{\text{percent self-employed (NB whites)}}$$

For example, for FB Salvadorans the ratio is:

$$\frac{0.064}{0.161} = 0.40$$

30. The *adjusted odds ratio* = the anti-logged group coefficient from the logistic regression. The regression is a total-employed-population pooled regression with a dummy for each comparison group, with the reference group (NB other whites) omitted. The dependent variable in the logistic regression is self-employment, and the independent variables are as follows:

Education (dummy coded; reference category = high school, less than high school, some college, college graduate)

Years of experience (age − years of education − 6)

Years of experience squared

English proficiency (dummy coded; reference category = not very well, "good" English, "fair" English)

Marital status (married with spouse present versus all other statuses)

Work limitation (no work limitation versus work limitation)

After controlling for background and human capital characteristics, the adjusted numbers are in most cases very similar to the raw numbers; the exceptions are FB Koreans, FB Armenians, and FB Iranians. For example, for FB Koreans the difference between adjusted and raw figures is rather large—2.5 versus 3.5; in this case, after controlling for human capital characteristics, propensity for self-employment increases.

Groups with adjusted odds ratios greater than one have a greater propensity for self-employment than do NB other whites, all else being equal. Among these groups are FB Koreans, FB Chinese, FB Armenians, FB Iranians, and NB Russians. For example, FB Koreans are 3.5 times more likely to be self-employed than NB other whites, all else being equal.

Groups with adjusted odds ratios less than one have a lesser propensity for self-employment than do NB other whites, all else being equal.

31. The results of this analysis replicate comparable analyses that utilized 1980 census data rather than 1990 data. See Ivan Light and Carolyn Rosenstein, *Race, Ethnicity and Entrepreneurship,* chapters 3 and 4.

32. Ivan Light and Parminder Bhachu, "California Immigrants in World Perspective," 5–8.

33. Keiko Yamanaka and Kent McClelland, "Earning the Model Minority Image: Diverse Strategies of Economic Adaptation by Asian-American Women," *Ethnic and Racial Studies* 17 (1994): 79–114.

34. See Enzo Mingione, "Informalization, Restructuring, and the Survival Strategies of the Working Class," *International Journal of Urban and Regional Research* 7 (1983): 319–22. See also Mercer L. Sullivan, *Getting Paid: Youth Crime and Work in the Inner City* (Ithaca: Cornell University, 1989) and Min Zhou, "Underemployment and Economic Disparities among Minority Groups," *Population Research and Policy Review* 12 (1993): 139–57.

35. Paul M. Ong, "Immigrant Wives' Labor Force Participation," *Industrial Relations* 26 (1987): 297.

36. And these businesses often provided good jobs to coethnics. "The growing Chinese-Vietnamese ethnic economy appears to be providing relatively highly paying jobs for a significant number of refugees. Coethnics who have close ethnic or familial ties to successful entrepreneurs are often able to use this social capital to obtain employment or become self-employed in ways that promote upward mobility." (Steven J. Gold, "Chinese-Vietnamese Entrepreneurs in California," in Paul Ong, Edna Bonacich, and Lucie Cheng, eds., *The New Asian Immigration in Los Angeles and Global Restructuring* [Philadelphia: Temple University Press, 1994]: 219.)

The Manufacturing Economy: Ethnic and Gender Divisions of Labor

Allen J. Scott

THE DEMOGRAPHIC changes that have swept across Los Angeles in recent decades have had profound effects on the economic as well as the social life of the metropolis. Several earlier chapters in this volume have described how ethnicity plays a central role in the ordering of the region's labor markets. Over much of the present century, as chapter 1 recounts, African American, Latino, and Asian workers have been largely excluded from core sectors. Recent immigrants, in particular, have been drawn disproportionately into the expanding low-wage sector, and this phenomenon in turn appears to have had negative consequences for the employment prospects of less-skilled African Americans, as chapter 6 describes. These trends are all subsumed within the wider transformation of L.A.'s ethnic and gender division of labor. It is this transformation and the ways in which it has worked itself out over the post–Second World War decades that I seek to describe in this chapter.

This chapter focuses on divisions of labor in Los Angeles' manufacturing economy. Although manufacturing does not constitute the totality of the economy of the metropolitan region, it is of critical importance, and it has been the engine behind the extraordinary growth that the region has experienced from the 1940s down to the very recent past. Manufacturing also lends itself well to an exploration of ethnic- and gender-sorting processes in the division of labor, as it breaks down into a large number of individual sectors whose employment profiles often differ greatly in their sociocultural features. I begin by describing some of the more important trends in employment in Los Angeles over the post war decades, as represented above all by the vast expansion of the immigrant labor force. Next, I analyze the manner in which various social and ethnic attributes of the labor force function as important criteria in the assignment of individuals to manufacturing sectors, focusing on the contrasts between immigrants and natives. Finally, I argue that the shifting relationships between a variegated labor force on the one hand and a complex division of labor on the other have had profound impacts on the development of Los Angeles' manufacturing economy over the last three or four decades. I conclude by drawing out a few policy implications from the analysis, with particular reference to the cheap-labor predicament that increasingly threatens the prosperity and viability of the region's manufacturing base.

PATTERNS OF EMPLOYMENT, 1950–1990

Over much of the post–Second World War period the five counties that make up the Los Angeles region grew at a remarkably rapid rate. In 1950, close to 2 million people were employed in the manufacturing and nonmanufacturing sectors combined. By 1970 total employment had increased to 3.9 million, and in 1990 it stood at 6.9 million. This remarkable rate of growth is traced out more fully in tables 8.1, 8.2, and 8.3, where the employment figures for the region are broken down by one-digit industries (the most aggregate expression in official statistics of the sectoral division of labor), cross-classified by nativity, gender, and race.

Table 8.1 shows that in 1950 manufacturing was by far the largest one-digit sector in Los Angeles, with 23.1 percent of all employment. Retail trade and professional services occupied second and third places, respectively. At this time, the region's labor force as a whole was predominantly made up of native-born workers, with white males dominating by far. Native-born and foreign-born women constituted 30.6 percent of the labor force, and African Americans (almost all of them native-born) just 5.1 percent. Foreign-born workers as a whole—most of them of European origin—made up 12.6 percent of the labor force in 1950. Hispanic and Asian immigrants represented only a minuscule proportion of the working population at this time.

By 1970 manufacturing had become an even larger element of Los Angeles' economy, as table 8.2 shows, accounting for 26.2 percent of all jobs. Professional services had also been growing rapidly in the 1950s and 1960s, and by 1970 this industry had surpassed retail trade to become the second largest one-digit sector in the region. Women's employment increased to 38.1 percent, and African Americans marginally improved their representation in the labor force, accounting for 6.9 percent of the total. The foreign-born constituted 12.3 percent of all workers, almost identical to the corresponding figure for 1950. It should be noted that among the re-

TABLE 8.1 | Employment by One-Digit Sectors, Los Angeles Region, 1950

	Native-born[a]		Foreign-born[a]		African Americans[a]	Total Employment in Sector
	Male	Female	Male	Female		
Agriculture	2.7	0.3	1.3	0.1	0.1	88,571
Construction	6.2	0.3	0.9	0.0	0.4	146,232
Manufacturing	15.5	4.8	2.1	0.7	0.8	459,115
Transportation & public utilities	5.6	1.4	0.5	0.1	0.4	150,301
Wholesale trade	3.4	0.8	0.5	0.2	0.1	98,327
Retail trade	9.7	6.2	1.7	0.7	0.7	362,836
FIRE[b]	2.6	2.0	0.4	0.2	0.2	102,008
Business services	2.7	0.6	0.3	0.1	0.2	74,298
Personal services	1.9	3.9	0.6	0.6	1.4	138,848
Professional services	3.8	5.3	0.5	0.4	0.4	199,499
Public administration	3.4	1.3	0.2	0.1	0.4	96,949
Other	2.4	0.7	0.3	0.1	0.1	68,721
Total Employment	1,191,165	544,042	186,345	64,154	101,284	1,985,706

SOURCE: U.S. Department of Commerce, Bureau of the Census, *Census of Population and Housing, 1950: Public Use Microdata Samples.*
[a] Data are given as percentages of total employment.
[b] Finance, insurance, and real estate.

gion's foreign-born workers, Asians and especially Hispanics were starting to become much more prominent than they had previously been. These incipient changes in the character of the foreign-born work force can be ascribed largely to the Immigration and Nationality Act of 1965, which abolished national-origin quotas for immigrants to the United States.[1]

Table 8.3 shows that in the year 1990 professional services (with 20.7 percent of the total labor force) had become Los Angeles' leading one-digit sector, with manufacturing just slightly behind (with 19.6 percent). The table also indicates that, in addition to professional services, other service industries in the region have become markedly more important in recent years. Other dramatic changes can be observed. Throughout the 1970s and 1980s women (including female immigrants) had continued to move into

TABLE 8.2 | Employment by One-Digit Sectors, Los Angeles Region, 1970

	Native-born[a]		Foreign-born[a]		African Americans[a]	Total Employment in Sector
	Male	Female	Male	Female		
Agriculture	0.9	0.2	0.4	0.1	0.1	60,900
Construction	4.2	0.3	0.5	0.0	0.3	195,500
Manufacturing	16.3	5.9	2.7	1.4	1.6	1,012,000
Transportation & public utilities	4.4	1.5	0.4	0.1	0.4	248,900
Wholesale trade	2.8	1.1	0.4	0.2	0.2	173,700
Retail trade	8.3	6.2	1.2	0.8	0.8	641,100
FIRE[b]	2.6	2.7	0.3	0.3	0.3	227,900
Business services	2.7	1.2	0.4	0.2	0.4	174,200
Personal services	1.1	2.3	0.3	0.5	0.6	158,500
Professional services	6.1	9.7	0.7	1.0	1.5	673,800
Public administration	3.4	1.5	0.2	0.1	0.7	198,600
Other	1.5	0.7	0.1	0.1	0.1	91,500
Total Employment	2,095,200	1,286,800	292,100	182,500	267,900	3,856,600

SOURCE: U.S. Department of Commerce, Bureau of the Census, *Census of Population and Housing, 1970: Public Use Microdata Samples.*
[a] Data are given as percentages of total employment.
[b] Finance, insurance, and real estate.

the labor force in large numbers; in 1990 they accounted for 43.3 percent of the total. Foreign-born workers as a whole, with 32.6 percent of all jobs, also greatly increased their presence. Of the foreign-born workers, Hispanics now account for significantly more than half, but Asians too are becoming very important in the region's work force. By contrast, the relative representation of African American workers in the region's economy has remained more or less stable in comparison with the situation in 1970, and it has actually declined in manufacturing.

Thus, over the postwar period but especially since about 1970, momentous changes have occurred in the economy of the Los Angeles region as a

TABLE 8.3 | Employment by One-Digit Sectors, Los Angeles Region, 1990

	Native-born[a]		Foreign-born[a]		African Americans[a]	Total Employment in Sector
	Male	Female	Male	Female		
Agriculture	0.5	0.2	1.0	0.1	0.0	126,718
Construction	3.9	0.5	2.2	0.1	0.2	465,731
Manufacturing	7.5	3.6	5.5	3.0	0.9	1,350,376
Transportation & public utilities	3.4	1.7	1.1	0.4	0.8	458,758
Wholesale trade	2.2	1.1	1.2	0.5	0.2	340,182
Retail trade	5.1	5.0	3.7	2.1	0.8	1,095,395
FIRE[b]	2.5	3.5	0.8	1.1	0.6	541,247
Business services	2.4	1.5	1.5	0.6	0.4	420,764
Personal services	0.6	1.1	0.6	1.3	0.2	245,970
Professional services	5.4	10.4	1.8	3.0	1.9	1,425,524
Public administration	1.7	1.2	0.3	0.2	0.5	232,127
Other	1.4	0.8	0.3	0.2	0.2	194,104
Total Employment	2,529,580	2,115,311	1,380,051	871,955	467,530	6,896,897

SOURCE: U.S. Department of Commerce, Bureau of the Census, *Census of Population and Housing, 1990: Public Use Microdata Samples.*
[a] Data are given in terms of percentages of total employment.
[b] Finance, insurance, and real estate.

whole. What are the factors underlying these changes? To address this question, we look more closely at the evolution of the region's manufacturing system and its associated labor force.

MANUFACTURING IN LOS ANGELES: A SECTORAL PROFILE

Manufacturing in the Los Angeles region has long been focused on three major groups, or ensembles, of sectors: (1) low-technology, labor-intensive (or "craft") industries, such as textiles, clothing, furniture, and printing; (2)

high-technology industries, composed primarily of aerospace and electronics sectors; and (3) metallurgical and machinery industries. There has also always been a wide variety of other manufacturing sectors in the region, including such industries as food processing, petroleum refining, chemicals, plastics, and—now largely moribund—automobile assembly.

The changing structure of employment in these ensembles is presented in table 8.4. This table was constructed by assigning individual manufacturing sectors (as given in the censuses for 1950, 1970, and 1990) to the three industrial ensembles identified above, plus a residual category representing all those sectors not specifically assigned to an ensemble. This task inevitably involves much arbitrariness, especially as the census sectors are redefined at frequent intervals, so the results must be treated with some caution. Three major points emerge from a scrutiny of table 8.4. First, employment in low-technology, labor-intensive industries in Los Angeles had been retreating in relative terms over the period from 1950 to 1970, but then clearly blossomed again over the period from 1970 to 1990. This resurgence can, in part, be related to large increases in the region's immigrant labor force. Second, the relative position of high-technology industry grew strongly over the 1950–70 period but has stabilized or even retreated somewhat in more recent years. Third, employment in both the metallurgical/machinery and the "other" category has, again in relative terms, decreased gradually over the entire period. Of course, these remarks disguise enormous shifts and variations within each of the major ensembles, and some of these more detailed changes will be discussed later in this chapter. In absolute terms, employment in each of the three ensembles increased strongly from 1950 to 1990.

These ensembles tend to have definite locational expression in the Los Angeles region. The low-technology, labor-intensive industries are heavily concentrated in districts lying close to downtown Los Angeles, the high-technology industries tend to form dense clusters around the periphery of

TABLE 8.4 | Principal Manufacturing Ensembles of Los Angeles, 1950, 1970, and 1990

	Percentage of Total Employment		
	1950	1970	1990
Low-technology labor-intensive	29.0	16.3	26.4
High-technology	19.7	34.2	31.9
Metallurgical and machinery	18.7	17.5	16.1
Other	32.6	32.0	25.6
Total manufacturing employment	459,115	1,102,000	1,350,375

SOURCES: U.S. Department of Commerce, Bureau of the Census, *Census of Population and Housing, 1950, 1970, and 1990: Public Use Microdata Samples.*

the region, and the metallurgical and machinery industries occupy a swath of terrain corresponding to the older industrial quarters of the region, stretching from the eastern San Fernando Valley around the eastern reaches of central Los Angeles and down through South Central Los Angeles to northern Orange County. This locational pattern is of special interest, because there are strong interdependencies between its main outlines and the social geography of the region. These interdependencies involve, on the one hand, the tendency of workers to occupy residential locations that have ready access to their place of work and, on the other hand, the tendency of employers to seek out locations that provide access to a preferred labor force. Thus, there is always a rough but definite spatial correlation between places where individuals of particular ethnic groups are employed and the places where the same individuals reside.[2]

THE MANUFACTURING WORK FORCE

Tables 8.5 to 8.7 indicate how the manufacturing labor force of Los Angeles in 1950, 1970, and 1990 breaks down by social and ethnic category. Again, we observe the proliferating diversity of the labor force, especially after 1970, superimposed upon an overall pattern of growth. Changes from census to census in the definitions of some of the racial and ethnic categories, however, make it necessary to exercise care when making comparisons among the tables. In particular, the definition of "Hispanic" varies greatly from one census to another, and there is almost certainly some underestimation of the number of Hispanics involved in 1950 and 1970 as compared with 1990.

TABLE 8.5 | Employment in Manufacturing by Ethnic Group, Los Angeles, 1950

	Native-born[a]		Foreign-born[a]		Total Employment
	Male	Female	Male	Female	
White	63.6	18.9	6.9	2.2	420,910
African American	2.2	1.1	0.0	0.0	15,159
Hispanic	0.6	0.5	2.0	0.9	18,308
Asian	0.6	0.2	0.0	0.5	4,243
Other	0.1	0.0	0.0	0.0	495
Total Employment	307,878	95,077	41,477	14,683	459,115

SOURCE: U.S. Department of Commerce, Bureau of the Census, *Census of Population and Housing, 1950: Public Use Microdata Samples.*
[a] Data are given as percentages of total manufacturing employment.

TABLE 8.6 | Employment in Manufacturing by Ethnic Group, Los Angeles, 1970

	Native-born[a]		Foreign-born[a]		Total Employment
	Male	Female	Male	Female	
White	48.2	16.2	4.7	1.8	717,300
African American	3.9	2.0	0.1	0.0	60,600
Hispanic	8.9	3.8	5.0	3.1	209,800
Asian	0.9	0.3	0.4	0.4	20,500
Other	0.2	0.1	0.0	0.0	3,800
Total Employment	628,300	227,100	103,600	53,000	1,012,000

SOURCE: U.S. Department of Commerce, Bureau of the Census, *Census of Population and Housing, 1970: Public Use Microdata Samples.*
[a] Data are given as percentages of total manufacturing employment.

Four essential points emerge from a scrutiny of these tables:

1. From 1950 to 1990, white males—both native-born and foreign-born—accounted for a steadily decreasing share of manufacturing employment.
2. The proportion of women in the manufacturing labor force rose from 24.3 percent in 1950 to 33.7 percent in 1990. In 1950, only 3.2 percent of the labor force comprised foreign-born women whereas in 1990 the figure amounted to 15.3 percent. The latter circum-

TABLE 8.7 | Employment in Manufacturing by Ethnic Group, Los Angeles, 1990

	Native-born[a]		Foreign-born[a]		Total Employment
	Male	Female	Male	Female	
White	28.4	12.6	3.1	1.2	611,657
African American	2.8	1.8	0.1	0.1	64,998
Hispanic	5.7	3.2	20.0	10.8	534,287
Asian	1.0	0.6	5.0	3.2	130,478
Other	0.4	0.2	0.1	0.0	8,955
Total Employment	515,271	247,770	380,632	206,703	1,350,375

SOURCE: U.S. Department of Commerce, Bureau of the Census, *Census of Population and Housing 1990: Public Use Microdata Samples.*
[a] Data are given as percentages of total manufacturing employment.

stance results principally from the large inflow of Hispanic and Asian women into manufacturing jobs in the region.

3. In general, Hispanic and—to a lesser extent—Asian foreign-born workers have come to represent an extraordinarily strong presence in the region's manufacturing labor force, especially since 1970. In 1950, Hispanic immigrants represented 2.9 percent of all manufacturing employment in the region, but by 1990 they represented 30.8 percent. In spite of the presumed statistical underestimation of the Hispanic category for 1950, these figures probably express a reasonably accurate order of magnitude of change. Asian immigrants constituted 0.5 percent of all manufacturing workers in 1950 and 8.2 percent in 1990.

4. African Americans, by contrast, have remained a minor element in Los Angeles' manufacturing labor force over the postwar decades. In 1950 they accounted for 3.3 percent of all manufacturing employment in the region, and in 1970 they had increased their share to 6.0 percent; in 1990, however, their representation had fallen back to 4.8 percent. Indeed, over the decade 1980–90 the number of African Americans in manufacturing jobs in the region actually declined in absolute terms, from 76,020 to 64,998.

Manufacturing labor markets in Los Angeles have thus gone through massive transformations in recent decades, especially as a result of the large-scale entry of Third World immigrants and women into the employment system. As will be seen later in the chapter, the situation is actually more complex than this, for beneath this dominant pattern there is considerable additional social and ethnic variation. These same tendencies are seen in all the great industrial centers of the United States, though they have arguably gone furthest in Los Angeles, and they have resulted not just in transformations of the local manufacturing labor force but in major changes in the complexion of urban society itself.

MANUFACTURING WAGES

Immigration and feminization also appear to have been associated with intensifying downward pressures on wage rates.[3] In constant 1989 dollars, the average weekly wage earned in manufacturing in Los Angeles in 1950 was $335; in 1970 it was $607, and in 1990 $596. Thus, the average manufacturing wages in Los Angeles, after experiencing significant increases in real values over the 1950s and 1960s, were flat or declining slightly over the 1970s and 1980s.[4]

But manufacturing labor markets also have been subject to increasing bifurcation in recent years, and average wage data conceal even more pronounced drops in wage rates in the bottom segments of the work force. If we array manufacturing sectors according to the average wages that they pay, we find that in 1950 those sectors lying in the lowest one-third employed just 10.7 percent of all manufacturing workers, with the top third employing 45.1 percent. By 1990, however, employment in the lowest one-third had increased to as much as 23.9 percent of the labor force, while employment in the top third showed a slight decrease to 40.7 percent. As a corollary, the middle tier has effectively been eviscerated, falling from 44.2 percent of the labor force in 1950 to 25.4 percent in 1990, a finding that is in accord with the claim that the region's labor force in general is subject to a "disappearing middle" phenomenon.[5] The expansion of the pool of low-wage workers as a result of immigration and feminization is no doubt a causal factor in the wage declines seen in the region. At the same time, it seems likely that sharply intensifying global competition too has put severe downward pressure on manufacturing wages, thereby encouraging employers to seek out, more than ever before, low-wage immigrant and women workers.

The existence of a generalized inverse relation between wages and immigration/feminization is shown in table 8.8, in which three regressions of the quantitative interrelations between these latter variables in Los Angeles' manufacturing system are summarized for the years 1950, 1970, and 1990. For each regression, the observations are represented by individual manufacturing sectors as defined by the relevant census. Sectors with fewer than a thousand workers were eliminated from the analysis, though doing so never involved deletion of more than seven or eight observations from the total set. The regressions define the statistical association between the average weekly wage (in current dollars) per sector on the one side and the proportions of foreign-born workers and females per sector on the other. A statistical deficiency of the regressions is that the two latter variables tend to be highly correlated with one another. Changes in census definitions of industrial sectors create difficulties in making intertemporal comparisons, but once this has been said, a remarkably consistent set of results appear in table 8.8. In each of the three census years under investigation here, the presence of foreign-born and female workers in any sector is strongly and negatively correlated with the average wage rate. In the case of the foreign-born, this negative association has intensified greatly over time, as suggested by the beta-coefficients in table 8.8. The latter circumstance is no doubt related to the fact that the stream of immigrants entering the manufacturing labor force has increasingly—though by no means wholly—been made up of unskilled, low-wage workers from Third World countries.[6] We would, of course, expect many other variables (such as size of establishment, education, experience, and unionization rates) also to have significant effects on wages, though detailed sectoral and regional data of this sort are not easily obtainable over extended time periods.

TABLE 8.8 | **Regression Analyses of the Effects of Nativity and Gender Differentials on Wages in Los Angeles' Manufacturing Industries**

	1950	1970	1990
A-value	70.12	202.01	729.36
Proportion foreign-born			
b-coefficient	−46.51	−88.48	−405.68
Standard error	27.39	33.07	44.73
Beta-coefficient	−0.24	−0.30	−0.68
Proportion females			
b-coefficient	−28.34	−77.71	−183.54
Standard error	11.60	21.10	58.53
Beta-coefficient	−0.35	−0.42	−0.24
R^2	0.27	0.42	0.65
N	50	74	75

SOCIAL AND ETHNIC VARIATIONS AND THE DIVISION OF LABOR IN MANUFACTURING

How are workers belonging to different social and ethnic groups distributed over detailed manufacturing sectors in Los Angeles? Factor analysis, a statistical technique for extracting simplified structural dimensions from complex data sets, brings this question into sharp focus. The data sets examined by this method consist of three large matrices (one each for the years 1950, 1970, and 1990) whose rows are defined by manufacturing sectors and whose columns are defined by fourteen different combinations of nativity status (native-born or foreign-born), race and ethnic identity (white, African American, Hispanic, Asian), and gender.[7]

The data subjected to factor analysis were defined in terms of an index of representation for each social and ethnic group in individual manufacturing sectors.[8] An index greater than one signifies that members of a given group are employed in a given sector in disproportionately large numbers relative to the size of that sector; an index less than one indicates that they are employed in disproportionately small numbers. Because the index is liable to exaggerate error in industries where overall employment is small, all sectors with fewer than one thousand workers were again eliminated from consideration.

The factor analyses of these data are presented in table 8.9. In general, the results indicate that the region's industries became more complex and differentiated in social and ethnic terms with the passage of time and that

TABLE 8.9 | Main Ethnic Dimensions of Los Angeles' Manufacturing Labor Force: Rotated Factor Loadings

Variable			1950[a]	1970[b]		1990[c]		
Race/ethnicity	Nativity	Gender	Factor 1	Factor 1	Factor 2	Factor 1	Factor 2	Factor 3
White	NB	Male	-0.45	-0.43	-0.34	0.68	-0.51	0.36
White	NB	Female	0.24	0.83	-0.13	0.39	0.08	0.30
White	FB	Male	0.11	-0.02	-0.10	0.13	-0.14	0.67
White	FB	Female	0.48	0.65	0.37	0.14	0.72	0.06
African American	NB	Male	-0.05	-0.23	-0.21	0.82	-0.20	-0.03
African American	NB	Female	0.92	0.67	0.23	0.78	0.14	0.09
Hispanic	NB	Male	0.14	-0.66	-0.04	0.02	-0.73	-0.04
Hispanic	NB	Female	0.80	0.06	0.30	-0.03	0.18	-0.28
Hispanic	FB	Male	-0.08	-0.13	-0.12	-0.74	-0.23	-0.42
Hispanic	FB	Female	0.49	0.32	0.66	-0.43	0.75	-0.35
Asian	NB	Male	0.14	0.03	-0.09	0.45	-0.13	0.60
Asian	NB	Female	0.84	-0.05	0.68	-0.11	0.29	0.58
Asian	FB	Male	0.03	-0.42	0.29	0.19	0.29	0.61
Asian	FB	Female	0.83	0.03	0.78	-0.01	0.79	0.24
Sum of squared factor loadings			3.67	2.53	2.10	2.92	2.85	2.16

[a] $N = 50$
[b] $N = 74$
[c] $N = 75$

a dominant gender split in the early postwar years became interwoven in more recent years with additional ethnic, racial, and human capital characteristics. We must keep in mind that the detailed results to be described deal with broad social and ethnic variations *across* sectors and not detailed variations *within* sectors.

Analysis of 1950 data: Just one meaningful factor was extracted from the data for 1950. This factor describes a split in manufacturing labor markets, mainly along simple gender lines. An examination of the factor loadings presented in table 8.9 reveals that females of all racial and ethnic types are represented at the positive end of the factor, and males (especially white, native-born males) at the negative end. The factor analysis technique generates so-called factor scores (not shown here), which represent numerical expressions of the degree to which individual manufacturing sectors are describable by any factor. The factor scores indicate, unsurprisingly, that female workers have a high relative presence in industries like apparel, textiles, confectionery, and bakery products, whereas males have a high relative presence in industries like pulp and paper, paints and varnishes, and diverse metallurgical industries.

Analysis of 1970 data: For 1970, two main factors made their appearance. Together, they seem to represent a bifurcation and extension of gendered labor market structures. The first factor runs roughly parallel to the single factor identified for 1950, and it is characterized by females of all types at its positive end and by males at its negative end. The second factor evidently represents a more specialized kind of female-male split and the beginnings of a widening social variegation of the region's local labor markets because of immigration. It is characterized by mainly immigrant (Hispanic and Asian) females at its positive end (in industries like apparel, plastics, and various food industries), and by native-born males at its negative end (in industries like metal-working, machinery, and drugs).

Analysis of 1990 data: A further marked increase in the social and cultural differentiation of the labor force is evident in the data for 1990. Three meaningful factors emerged. Factor 1 reveals that a massive social segmentation of Los Angeles' manufacturing labor markets had occurred. At the positive pole, the factor is represented by mainly native-born workers (including whites and African Americans, males and females) employed in high-wage, stable jobs concentrated in sectors dominated by large establishments such as aircraft and parts, missiles, and industrial chemicals. At the negative pole, the factor is represented by foreign-born workers of both sexes in low-wage, unstable jobs in small-plant sectors like textiles and furniture. These interpretations are bolstered by the observation that the scores for factor 1 correlate strongly and positively with (a) average wage rates, (b) workers' educational levels, (c) job stability, measured as the average number of weeks in the year that workers were gainfully employed, and (d) average size of establishment. Factor 2 represents the same generalized gender split that made such a strong appearance in the analyses for 1950 and 1970, though in the labor market data for 1990 it is relegated to second place. The factor is identifiable in terms of two polarities, namely (a) females of varied social and ethnic types in a wide variety of sectors such as knitting mills, apparel, confectionery, cosmetics, and electrical machinery, and (b) an equally diverse group of males in sectors such as blast furnaces and steelworks, ordnance, and construction machines. Factor 3 picks up on an industrial technology dimension. On the one side, it identifies a labor-force segment made up of whites and Asians (but otherwise undifferentiated by nativity or gender), and on the other side a segment made up of Hispanics (again, without further social differentiation). The factor scores indicate that the former segment is associated with industries such as computers, drugs, and medical instruments and the latter with industries like textiles, pottery, leather. Thus, factor 3 gives expression to the special and contrasting employment characteristics of high- and low-technology industry.

Despite the difficulties of cross-temporal comparisons of the census data used here, the factor analytic results displayed in table 8.9 reconfirm the observation that manufacturing labor markets in Los Angeles have become increasingly multidimensional over the last several decades. This clearly reflects the increasing heterogeneity of Los Angeles' population over the postwar years, and the progressive expansion and diversification of the region's industrial base. Thus, a simple split between male- and female-dominated sectors in 1950 became by 1990 a series of much more intricately textured labor market specializations as represented by assorted combinations of race, ethnicity, nativity, and gender. Simple gender divisions, while still of major significance, today are interpenetrated by other kinds of effects. In particular, foreign-born Hispanics of both sexes now occupy the least favorable labor market positions in the region's economy. These findings indicate that employers have taken advantage of the rising demographic complexity of the labor force and have been able to differentiate their intake of labor on the basis of a wide variety of social and cultural markers. In turn, as the following section describes in greater detail, this has led to some remarkable fine-tuning of the match between the characteristics of various industries and the personal attributes of their workers.

HISPANIC AND ASIAN IMMIGRANT WORKERS

One of the principal factors underlying the diversification of manufacturing labor markets in Los Angeles has been the surge of immigrants arriving from Latin America and Asia, and a fuller analysis of the role of these immigrants in the local employment system is needed. In this section, the historical approach adopted in previous sections has been dropped in favor of a detailed synoptic view of data from the 1990 census alone. In part this shift in emphasis is due to the relative recency of the large-scale Hispanic and Asian incursions into the region's manufacturing labor force; in part it is a strategy for focusing more intently on the social and ethnic articulation of the division of labor as such. Our point of departure is an analysis of contrasts in educational attainments and wages between these two groups.

Education and Wages

Hispanic and Asian immigrant workers employed in manufacturing in the Los Angeles region tend to occupy positions toward the bottom end of the labor market. There are certain exceptions to this, however, and there are significant differences between the two groups in terms of qualifications and earning power.

In table 8.10, data on years of education for immigrant Hispanic and Asian workers employed in manufacturing in the region are given by length of residence in the United States and by gender. On the whole, they show that more recent immigrants tend to have lower levels of educational attainment than less recent immigrants. The data also show that male Hispanics and Asians have higher educational attainment levels than their female counterparts. In addition, and across the board, each cohort of Hispanics has markedly lower educational levels than the equivalent Asian cohort.

The data given in table 8.11 indicate that these educational differences are fairly faithfully reflected in differences in earnings, with Asians on average having higher wage levels than Hispanics. Even immigrant Asian females tend to earn more than their Hispanic male counterparts. The simple correlation coefficient between the two sets of data in tables 8.10 and 8.11 is 0.80, suggesting that a significant part of the difference in earnings power between Hispanics and Asians is due to their educational differences.[9] That

TABLE 8.10 | Average Years of Education of Hispanic and Asian Immigrants Employed in Manufacturing in Los Angeles, by Length of Residence, 1990

Length of Residence in U.S.	Hispanics		Asians	
	Male	Female	Male	Female
0–4 years	8.26	7.89	13.12	11.57
5–9 years	8.50	7.81	13.46	12.11
10+ years	8.42	8.01	14.49	12.60

SOURCE: U.S. Department of Commerce, Bureau of the Census, *Census of Population and Housing, 1990: Public Use Microdata Samples.*

TABLE 8.11 | Average Weekly Wages of Hispanic and Asian Immigrants Employed in Manufacturing in Los Angeles, by Length of Residence, 1990

Length of Residence in U.S.	Hispanics		Asians	
	Male	Female	Male	Female
0–4 years	$252.57	$205.20	$541.60	$299.47
5–9 years	$348.14	$243.02	$572.49	$333.22
10+ years	$471.26	$303.27	$748.76	$503.53

SOURCE: U.S. Department of Commerce, Bureau of the Census, *Census of Population and Housing, 1990: Public Use Microdata Samples.*

said, there appear to be definite residual effects due to both length of residence in the United States and gender. Income differences between the two ethnic groups are most emphatic for recent immigrants, and the male-female earnings divide remains pronounced.

Sectoral Allocations of Hispanic and Asian Immigrant Workers

These differences between Hispanic and Asian immigrants are superimposed on and, in turn, reflected in the sectoral division of labor in manufacturing, often in extremely subtle ways. A preliminary sense of these intertwined relationships may be gleaned from table 8.12, which presents a composite picture of the relative prevalence of Hispanic and Asian immigrant workers (divided by gender) in detailed manufacturing sectors in Los Angeles for the year 1990.[10] Table 8.12 reveals four principal trends:

1. Hispanic male immigrants are widely distributed over Los Angeles' manufacturing industries, but they are found especially in industries characterized by heavy materials-handling labor processes and often noisy or dirty working conditions, such as the wood-products and metallurgical industries.[11]

2. Hispanic female immigrants are concentrated above all in labor-intensive craft industries marked by small establishment size; examples are the clothing, textiles, and leather-products industries. They are also to be found in some of the electrical and electronic industries of the region, where they commonly work in assembly functions.

3. Asian male immigrants are predominantly concentrated in the region's high-technology industries, where their generally superior educational attainments enable them to move rapidly into the middle and even upper tiers of the labor force.

4. Asian female immigrants are split into two main groups. One of these is in the region's craft industries, where, it would seem, Asian

age of 8.2 years of schooling.[14] Bringing somewhat higher skills, the more recent immigrants should do better than their predecessors; when we compare the real earnings of immigrant cohorts at the end of the decade during which they moved to the United States, however, we see that each successive cohort does worse. As figure 9.3 shows, the gap, relative to comparably aged whites, also grows.

The pattern of declining earnings represents a puzzle of considerable note. The literature links the erosion of immigrants' earnings to changes in the composition of the immigrant stream that have produced an immigrant work force of "lower quality" or skill, yet educational levels among Mexican migrants to Los Angeles have risen, albeit modestly. An alternative explanation is that changes in the region's economic structure may have drawn successive waves of newcomers into low-skill occupations out of which there are few avenues of escape. Indeed, even as the immigrant economic base expanded, and massively so, Mexicans moved into a relatively narrow tier of occupations and industries in the low-skill sector. Occupational segregation was a distinguishing feature of the Mexican immigrant job scene in 1970, as table 9.1 clearly shows. But segregation intensified in the following decades, with Mexican immigrants becoming increasingly dissimilar to almost all groups, and especially to Chicanos and African Americans.

Occupational segregation reflects the workings of two forces: those that

FIGURE 9.3 | Earnings Among Three Cohorts of Mexican Immigrants and Comparably Aged Native Whites, Los Angeles Region, 1969–1989

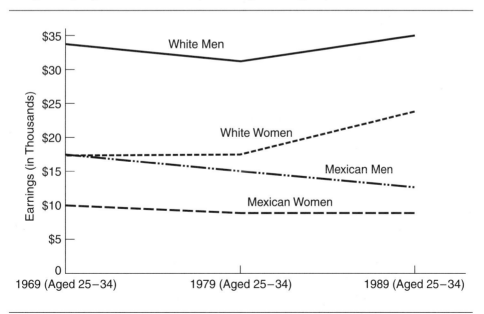

TABLE 9.1 | Index of Occupational Dissimilarity for Mexican Immigrants, Los Angeles Region, 1970–1990

	1970	1980	1990
Black NB	.44	.49	.55
Mexican NB	.33	.36	.43
White NB	.56	.59	.59
Central Amer FB	N/A	.29	.23
Asian FB	.58	.51	.54
Asian NB	N/A	.61	.65

Note: See chapter 1 and appendix for an explanation of the index of dissimilarity.

exclude Mexican immigrants from others, on the grounds of race and skill, and those that connect Mexicans to their compatriots, on the grounds of familiarity and mutual exchange. Just as the other groups studied in this book did, newcomers from Mexico moved into jobs alongside veteran settlers, establishing distinctive clusters or niches. As they did so, the degree of clustering in niches substantially increased, but the quality of these concentrations remained poor. As table 9.2 shows, few of the niches provide opportunities for public-sector or self-employment; the great majority are to be found in the region's manufacturing sector, and most of the jobs require low levels of education.

In a labor market characterized by sex segregation, gender has steered men and women into different niches. Some concentrations—for example, groundskeepers or construction laborers—are overwhelmingly dominated by men; others, such as textile sewing machine operatives, are mainly female. But in contrast to the niches established by Central Americans, the region's other large Latino population, the great majority of the Mexican niches tend to be male-dominated. And even classic "women's occupations,"

TABLE 9.2 | Occupational Niches, Mexican Immigrants, Los Angeles Region, 1970–1990

	As Percentage of Group's Employment	Mean Years of Education	Characteristics of Employment, as Percentage of Niche Employment				Mean Earnings ($)
			PubSec (%)	Self-Empt (%)	Mfg (%)	Mgr/Prof (%)	
1970	58	6	0	4	54	2	15,247
1980	65	6	3	3	53	0	10,252
1990	72	7	3	5	41	0	17,055

like sewing, have seen an influx of immigrant men, reflecting the pressure to find work.

Immigrants cluster in occupations because contacts with established workers help newcomers find jobs. In the process, the massively growing numbers of Mexican immigrants have been packed into a relatively narrow tier of occupations; by 1990, 72 percent of Mexican immigrants worked in occupations that could be classified as Mexican immigrant niches.

The immigrant story is typically one of toil and travail, but this survey of the Mexican immigrant experience in Los Angeles suggests that the rewards for hard work have been exceedingly slim. Only the older settlers show any economic improvement over the past twenty years, and even in their case the glass is at best half-filled. The cohort of the 1960s saw their real earnings advance steadily from the beginning to the end of the period, in gains that were far from trivial. But native whites, and particularly native white males, generally did better, with the result that the white/immigrant gap did not decline. More disturbing is the fate of subsequent cohorts, who not only slipped further behind native whites with each decade but failed to recapture the very modest earnings of their predecessors. As I have shown, earnings erosion seems linked to a pattern of concentration in the lowest-paid and lowest-status occupations.

ASSIMILATION AMONG NATIVE-BORN MEXICANS

The conventional immigrant story is one of starting on the bottom and slowly moving ahead. As the preceding section showed, the experience of the veteran Mexican settlers in Los Angeles provides some approximation of this oft-told tale, but the trajectory of the more recent arrivals veers off in a different, downward direction, and over time they get further behind. Whatever the troubles of the first generation, the second generation expects—and is expected—to do better. The adult Chicanos currently living and working in Los Angeles are also the descendants of earlier immigrants, who presumably moved to the region when conditions were neither as severe nor as competitive as they are today. This background suggests that Chicanos may well be replicating the earlier experience of the descendants of the European foreign-born, advancing beyond the bottom-level positions to which the immigrants were consigned and evolving into an emergent middle class. On the other hand, the City of Angels never dealt its Mexican immigrants a particularly promising hand. Consequently, there is reason to suspect that prior hindrances to progress have not been overturned and that Chicanos, like African Americans, encounter barriers that leave them at the bottom of the labor market. Which, then, offers the appropriate comparison, the immigrant experience or the African American experience?

During the years 1970–90 L.A.'s native-born population saw a period of upgrading and improvement, and Chicanos were no exception. On most counts—education, earnings, and self-employment—Chicanos were doing better in 1990 than they were twenty years before; on the other hand, so too were native whites and blacks. Little progress toward closing the original gap thus seems to have been made.

Cohort analysis confirms the modest rate of change undergone by L.A.'s Chicanos over the two decades. Indeed, the pattern of disadvantage relative to whites persists even when focusing on the relatively small cohort of Mexican Americans who entered the economy at age 25 to 34 during the boom times of the 1970s. Unlike Mexican immigrants, this group of Chicanos no longer fell at the very bottom of the earnings curve; in fact, men did slightly better than similarly aged African Americans, though Chicanas' earnings ranked lowest among women. Still, male and female Mexican Americans found themselves some distance behind whites from start to finish (see figure 9.4). Real earnings grew for all groups during the two decades after 1970, but whites did best, increasing the earning gap with both cohorts of Chicanos.

While Chicanos who entered the region's labor market in the 1960s improved their situation in succeeding years, their position in the region's ethnic hierarchy remained the same: somewhere in the lower-middle reaches, above the foreign-born but behind native whites. It might be

FIGURE 9.4 | **Earnings Among a Cohort of Native-Born Males and Females, Los Angeles Region, 1969–1989**

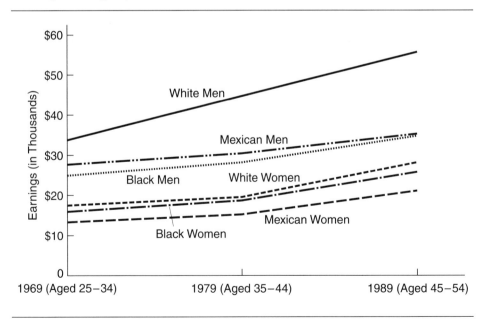

thought that the prospects for the more recent cohorts would be better, for reasons having to do with shifts on both the demand and the supply sides. Changes in employer practices, in the regulatory environment, and in a greater acceptance of—or at least accommodation to—diversity may have diminished the discriminatory pressures that were still quite strong when the cohort of the 1960s entered the labor market. And subsequent cohorts are likely to have better schooling and therefore to be more attractive job candidates at a time when employers are paying a growing premium for education.

Unfortunately, the experience of L.A.'s Chicano workers, both male and female, has not yet fulfilled the predictions of this rosy scenario. Chicano schooling levels rose, but most of the change occurred during the 1970s and involved a sharp increase in the proportion completing secondary school, not college; though these gains narrowed the educational gap, successive white cohorts retained a commanding lead. The region's burgeoning econ-omy, combined with changes in marital and family patterns, lured a grow-ing proportion of Chicanas into the labor force, virtually erasing the sizable interethnic differences that had previously existed. Among Chicanos, em-ployment rates eroded; the decline, though not quite as severe as the loss among blacks, stood in sharp contrast to the persistently strong employ-

FIGURE 9.5 | **Earnings Among Three Cohorts of Native-Born Males and Females, Los Angeles Region, 1969–1989**

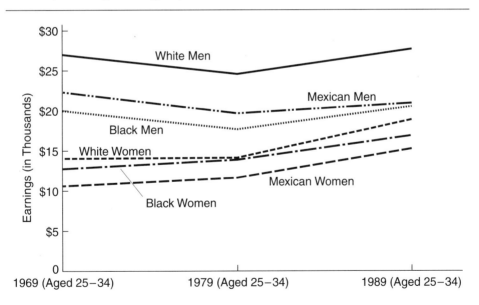

ment rates among comparably aged white men. Chicanos' earnings stagnated during the 1970s; while the earnings of the 1980s cohort surpassed their predecessors', native whites did still better during that decade, producing a growing ethnic gap. Though earnings among all groups of native-born women grew modestly in the two decades after 1970, in relative terms Chicanas ended the period where they began—at a considerable lag behind whites.

If persistent earnings disparities characterize both Chicanos and Mexican immigrants, the sources of those disparities appear to differ. Economic restructuring drew the growing number of new immigrant arrivals into an ever-expanding low-wage sector, where the increased immigrant concentration in a narrow tier of niches drove wages down. Chicanos, however, moved in very different directions. On the one hand, they diffused out of their traditional niches into the broader labor market (see table 9.3). Between 1970 and 1990, the Chicano job mix increasingly overlapped with the distributions of other groups; by the latter date, Chicanos were occupationally more segregated from Mexican immigrants than from any other group. Simultaneously, the level of concentration in occupational niches, which had been lower but still comparable to the immigrant pattern of 1970, substantially declined; by 1990, just over one-fifth of Chicanos worked in occupations that could be classified as ethnic niches, in contrast to 35 percent two decades before.

On the other hand, Chicanos developed new niches that were far removed from the immigrant concentrations (see table 9.4). In comparison with the earlier period, the niches of 1990 were less likely to be in manufacturing, more likely to be found in the public sector, and more likely to involve jobs that required a high school degree. A few salient cases highlight the extent and the nature of change. In 1970, Chicanos clustered in occupations like assembler, construction laborer, and gardener that they then shared with the foreign-born but that have now become "immigrant jobs." By 1990, "heavy truck drivers," a virtually all-male occupation in which Chi-

TABLE 9.3 | **Index of Mexican-American Occupational Dissimilarity, Los Angeles Region, 1970–1990**

	1970	1980	1990
Mexican FB	.33	.36	.43
Central Amer FB	N/A	.40	.23
Black NB	.34	.24	.21
White NB	.28	.33	.28
Asian FB	.47	.38	.35
Asian NB	N/A	.39	.34

TABLE 9.4 | Occupational Niches, Native-Born Mexicans, Los Angeles Region, 1970–1990

	As Percentage of Group's Employment	Mean Years of Education	Characteristics of Employment, as Percentage of Niche Employment				Mean Earnings ($)
			PubSec (%)	Self-Empt (%)	Mfg (%)	Mgr/Prof (%)	
1970	35	9	5	5	57	3	21,275
1980	40	10	15	4	42	0	14,635
1990	22	12	25	4	16	5	28,920

canos averaged close to $36,200, ranked as the single largest niche. The other major concentrations spanned a range of low-skill white-collar and middle-to-high-skill blue-collar jobs, including the mainly female occupations of typist and receptionist and the mainly male jobs of heavy equipment operator, police officer, and mail carrier.

Relative both to the recent past and to the immigrant situation, the newly emerging niches represent a change for the better. But these new niches neither provide opportunities for professional or managerial employment nor allow for much self-employment—quite in contrast to the mix of professional and business niches found among the Middle Eastern and many of the Asian groups. While more rewarding than the immigrant concentrations, most Mexican American occupational niches are still low-paying. The exceptions, of course, involve some of the skilled blue-collar occupations, but economic restructuring is likely to reduce the future demand for workers in these types of jobs.

Nonetheless, the characteristics of the Mexican American niches are unlikely to explain the sizable disparity between Chicano and native-white earnings. Some of that gap reflects differences in characteristics that employers value and reward commensurately; though they are better schooled than the immigrants and, as chapter 5 showed, much more likely to speak English well, both male and female Chicanos have not yet achieved the same levels of education as native whites. A statistical procedure that gives Chicanos and blacks the same characteristics as native whites shows that Mexican Americans and African Americans would make a good deal more if they had the same skills and other labor-market and familial characteristics shared by whites. But the same procedure shows that even adjusting for these traits, Chicanos and blacks remain substantially behind whites in earnings, and more so in 1989 than in previous years (see figures 9.6 and 9.7). The recent changes in the region's labor market appear to have increased the racial bonus enjoyed by whites, reinforcing the preexisting barriers to Chicano progress.

FIGURE 9.6 | Earnings Gap Between Selected Ethnic Groups and Native-Born White Males, Los Angeles Region, 1969–1989

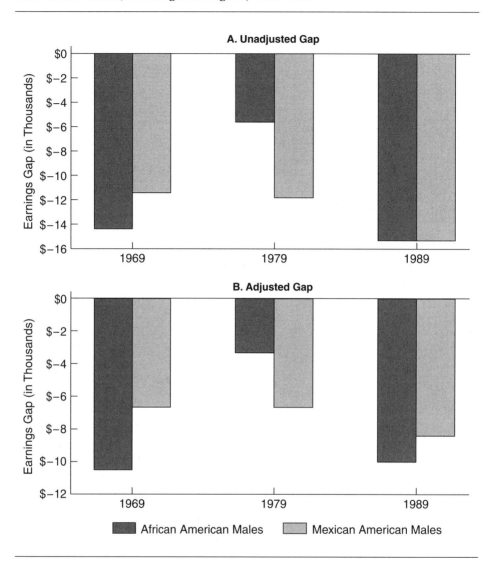

SCHOOLING AND THE PROSPECTS FOR THE YOUNG

While the experience of adult Chicanos is disappointing, the fate of the next generation might still be better—assuming, of course, that they receive the education they need to get ahead. That hope is clouded, not only by the

FIGURE 9.7 | **Earnings Gap Between Selected Ethnic Groups and Native-Born White Females, Los Angeles Region, 1969–1989**

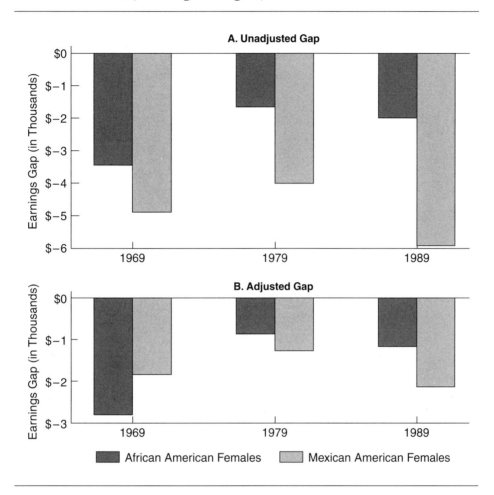

schools' historic failure to respond to the needs of Mexican American children but by the extraordinary fiscal and administrative problems that the region's school systems are now encountering, just when they need to absorb an unprecedented number of immigrant children. The census is by no means the ideal vehicle for assessing educational progress, since it tells us little about actual school performance, and the data we glean from it—for example, on years of school completed—can be considered no more than distant proxies for skills that students may have actually learned. But the census does allow us to paint a portrait of attendance patterns at various levels of schooling, and this picture, while limited, has value. Overall, a distressingly large portion of the region's Mexican-origin youth—more than among any other group—are not finishing high school, and far too few are attending college. Among the youthful population as a whole, both native- and foreign-born youth, the proportion of adolescents enrolled in high school has dropped significantly since 1970, and very little advance of any kind can be seen.

There is better news once the youthful population is disaggregated by nativity status, since natives accounted for a much larger share of the younger Mexican-origin population in 1970 than they did twenty years later. Breaking this population down into three groups—foreign-born who came to the United States after the age of ten, foreign-born who came to the United States before the age of ten, and native-born—shows that teenage high school dropout rates have gone down for each group, and college attendance rates for slightly older youth have gone up for each group since 1970. In each decade, the 1.5 generation puts in a better performance than the foreign-born, and the native-born do better still. And the changes among the native-born provide considerable grounds for cheer; relative to native whites, native-born Mexicans were doing much better in 1990 than they were two decades before.

But the cheers should not get too loud. Table 9.5 shows that despite improvements, native-born Mexicans still rank highest among the region's native-born groups in their dropout rates (see the data in chapter 11 on Asians for further comparison). Fully one-quarter of 18–24-year-old Chicanos have not completed high school—not a good omen considering the declining wages for low-skilled work and the increasing premium employers are placing on a college education or more. Moreover, the dropout rates for foreign-born Mexicans are truly stratospheric; granted, some of these immigrants are probably already in the labor market and in some sense should not be classified as dropouts, since many may have last entered a classroom in elementary school prior to migration to the United States. Still, the foreign-born, even as restrictively defined here, make up a very large proportion of younger Mexican-origin Angelenos; the consequences of their failure to obtain a high school education will drag down their earnings—and employment chances—for years to come. Thus, there is little likelihood to expect that sizable components of the region's varied Mexican-origin population will make a breakthrough into the skilled, better-paying jobs needed for middle-class status in years to come. Rather, they are likely to experience persistent working-class status, which means exposure to labor-market conditions that are currently unfavorable and probably will not improve.

This sketch of labor-market trends among L.A.'s Chicanos does indeed show progress, but of a very modest sort. The cohort of native-born Mexican Americans who were young adults in 1970 was doing somewhat better twenty years later; likewise, recent cohorts have encountered a more favorable economic environment than did their predecessors. Thus, the evidence

TABLE 9.5 | Educational Attendance and Completion Levels, Los Angeles Region, 1970–1990

	1970 (%)	1980 (%)	1990 (%)
High school dropouts, aged 16–19			
All Mexicans	26	43	41
First generation	65	63	58
1.5 generation	23	28	23
Native-born	21	19	15
Native-born black	15	11	13
Native-born white	11	11	8
High school dropouts, aged 18–24			
All Mexicans	43	48	45
First generation	70	74	64
1.5 generation	31	39	38
Native-born	36	29	25
Native-born black	21	17	18
Native-born white	13	13	11
College attendance, aged 18–24			
All Mexicans	11	13	18
First generation	2	4	8
1.5 generation	15	15	21
Native-born Mexican		19	28
Native-born black	13	26	29
Native-born white	25	30	38

from Los Angeles does not support a view that Chicanos are stuck at the bottom of the economic ladder, but it does show that Chicanos have gained economic security through concentration in stable working-class occupations. And these modest gains seem inconsistent with the optimistic view that Mexican Americans experience "the fluidity of the sort expected for unranked groups in the American system."[15] Rather, Chicanos resemble African Americans on most socioeconomic criteria, faring better than the region's increasingly impoverished immigrants but not showing significant progress in the race to catch up with whites.

If the past two decades have yielded meager fruit, prospects for future generations seem worrisome, especially since the numbers entering the labor force will be large. As long as the Chicano school performance record lags behind all other groups, improving school completion rates and greater movement to higher education provide little hope that the Chicanos who come of age in the twenty-first century will move on to a burgeoning middle class. The best hope seems to be for more of the same—entry into the ranks of the solid working class. The continued shrinkage of the region's high-wage manufacturing sector puts even that scenario into doubt.

ETHNIC PERSISTENCE

The traditional social science perspective sees the fluidity of ethnic boundaries as a distinguishing feature of the ethnic experience in the United States; in a sense, the literature on assimilation can be read as an attempt to describe and analyze the process by which ethnic boundaries change.[16] But there is considerable doubt that the conventional assimilation framework helps in understanding the Chicano case. "Few groups," writes Carlos Arce, "have had as consistent a history of collective identity, of pronounced preferences for ethnic group labels, and of resistance to assimilationist tendencies or forces."[17] And even an optimistic analyst like Donald Horowitz concedes that in the Mexican American case "group boundaries have become more and more permeable, less and less ascriptive, *without* producing assimilation."[18]

Thus, the Mexican American case is distinctive, and for good reason. After several decades of residence in the United States, the descendants of European immigrants found themselves sharply removed from the homeland and cut off from new arrivals; consequently, substantial shifts in group boundaries occurred within two to three generations. But L.A.'s Mexican community has been composed of immigrants living alongside a multigenerational, U.S.-born population. Consequently, considerable group attachment persists even among the native-born, although Chicanos clearly differ from immigrants and show evidence of significant assimilation.

Residential Segregation

Residential segregation is a relatively new feature of the Mexican experience of living in Los Angeles, as chapter 2 has shown. Although the combination of suburbanization, urban renewal, and persistent discrimination led to greater separation after the Second World War, Mexican Americans were considerably less segregated than African Americans. In the 1960s, the Mexican American pattern was one of "moderate" segregation "characterized by a paucity of established enclave areas, few succession areas, and many areas of recent entry."[19] All this changed with the massive upswing of immigration. In the 1960s, most of the census tracts gaining Hispanic residents were also gaining white residents, and relatively few of the tracts gaining Hispanic residents were losing whites. During the 1970s, the pattern changed decisively. Most of the neighborhoods that had gained Hispanic residents during the 1960s subsequently lost Anglo residents, as did most areas newly entered by Hispanics.[20]

The trends of the 1970s deepened and accelerated in the following decade. Writing about Los Angeles County in the early 1980s, Muller and Espenshade described the Mexican population as located in and around its traditional enclaves, most importantly East Los Angeles and two smaller communities, San Fernando and Azusa, both of which had grown out of earlier settlements established by agricultural workers.[21] Indeed, these were areas of extraordinarily high density, where Mexicans made up 75 percent or more of the population (see figure 9.8). But even then, immigration had led to widespread spilling over into areas of traditionally lower Mexican density. By 1980 Mexicans were living all over the San Gabriel Valley, often at densities of over 50 percent; they had established a significant presence in Long Beach and other South Bay communities, and they had begun to infiltrate the mainly black areas of Watts, Compton, and Inglewood.

Ten years later, the traditional barrios of Los Angeles County still retained a significant Mexican presence—in fact, in greater densities than ever before, as chapter 4 has described. But the areas of very high concentration now covered a broader spread, and the once clearly demarcated clusters of East Los Angeles and Azusa were virtually connected in a single mass (see figure 9.9). At the center of the county, the Mexican population had moved south and west, spreading deeply into the traditional African American ghetto in South Central Los Angeles and establishing significant concentrations in Watts, Compton, and Inglewood. The once-isolated settlement in San Fernando was now at the heart of a growing concentration, which was diffusing into the previously white heartlands of the San Fernando Valley south and west, the Santa Clarita Valley to the north, and even the newly developed exurban settlements on the county's very northern boundaries. Only in the highly affluent communities along the western coast did Mexicans encounter barriers of housing cost—and possibly discrimination—that were sufficiently high to block the growth of noticeable clusters.

Diffusion has had a paradoxical result. The 1970s saw increasing segregation from whites; comparisons of segregation indices for 1980 and 1990 (see table 9.6) point to continuing changes but of a more subtle nature. In the 1980s, Mexicans moved into areas of the region that had previously had few if any Mexican residents. Consequently, the distribution of the region's Mexican and Anglo populations became more similar over the course of the decade, as shown by a slight decline in the white/Mexican index of dissimilarity (D). The exposure index (P*), which measures the likelihood of contact with members of one's own or another group, tells a different story. Increasing Mexican densities involved less frequent contact with whites; on average, whites made up 64 percent of the typical tract in which Mexicans lived in 1980 but only 54 percent ten years later. Diminished contact with whites went hand in hand with greater exposure to other Latinos, most of whom were Mexicans, as the very low exposure indices of Mexicans relative

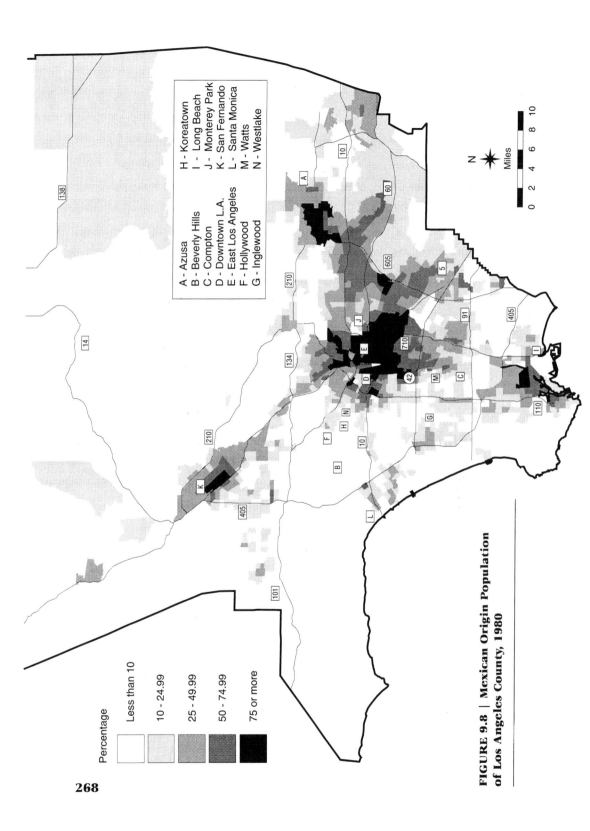

FIGURE 9.8 | Mexican Origin Population of Los Angeles County, 1980

Percentage

Less than 10

10 - 24.99

25 - 49.99

50 - 74.99

75 or more

A - Azusa
B - Beverly Hills
C - Compton
D - Downtown L.A.
E - East Los Angeles
F - Hollywood
G - Inglewood
H - Koreatown
I - Long Beach
J - Monterey Park
K - San Fernando
L - Santa Monica
M - Watts
N - Westlake

N

Miles

0 2 4 6 8 10

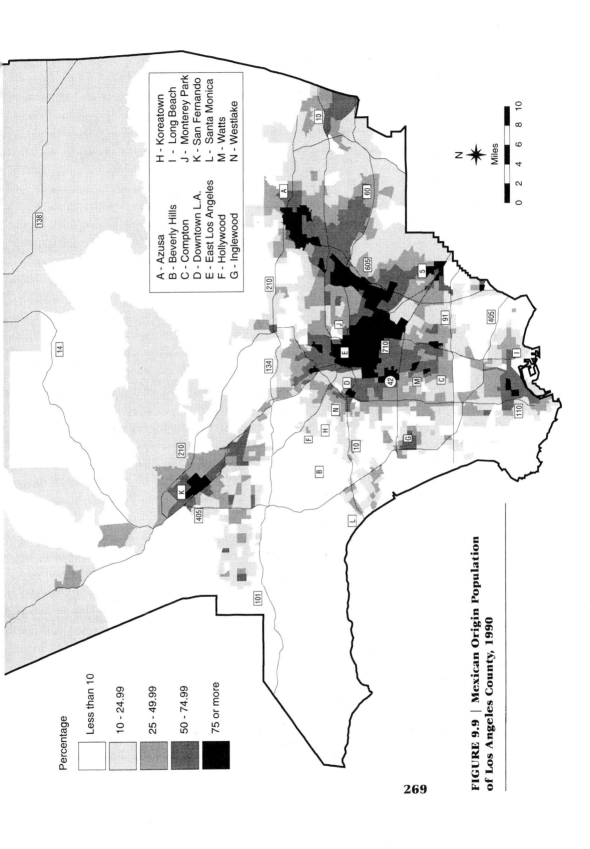

Percentage

Less than 10

10 - 24.99

25 - 49.99

50 - 74.99

75 or more

A - Azusa
B - Beverly Hills
C - Compton
D - Downtown L.A.
E - East Los Angeles
F - Hollywood
G - Inglewood

H - Koreatown
I - Long Beach
J - Monterey Park
K - San Fernando
L - Santa Monica
M - Watts
N - Westlake

N

Miles

0 2 4 6 8 10

**FIGURE 9.9 | Mexican Origin Population
of Los Angeles County, 1990**

TABLE 9.6 | **Residential Indices of Dissimilarity (D) and Exposure (P*), Los Angeles Region, 1980–1990: Mexican-Origin Population**

	1980		1990	
	D	P*	D	P*
Whites	.50	.64	.47	.54
Asians	.55	.05	.54	.08
Chinese	.67	.01	.67	.02
Filipinos	.61	.01	.56	.02
Koreans	.72	.01	.72	.00
Japanese	.65	.01	.65	.00
Vietnamese	.70	.04	.65	.01
Blacks	.71	.08	.58	.08
Latinos	.08	.49	.08	.55
Mexicans		.43		.46
Salvadorans	N/A	N/A	.53	.03
Guatemalans	N/A	N/A	.54	.01

to Salvadorans and Guatemalans indicate. The situation for the Central American groups, described in chapter 10, is quite the opposite, reflecting the size differences between the region's Mexican population and its newly arrived Central American immigrants; on average, the latter swim in a heavily Mexican sea, and their presence is not noticeable to the region's Mexican residents.

On balance, then, residential changes brought greater exposure to a broadly Latino but dominantly Mexican world. Moreover, any evidence of declining segregation, as Clark has already argued in this book, seems suspicious, more an artifact of the time when the census clock stopped rather than anything of more lasting value. The trend for Mexican/black segregation may be the best case in point; there was less segregation in 1990 than a decade earlier, but only because Mexicans were entering the South Central area from which blacks were leaving, a retreat that has certainly not ended its course. However durable or transitory current levels of segregation may be, the fact remains that Mexicans are at very best somewhat segregated from the myriad groups that make up the region's ethnic mix. More importantly, they are increasingly likely to be exposed to other Mexicans and Hispanics and less likely to rub shoulders with whites, a trend that points strongly in the direction of growing separation.

Intermarriage

Residential integration is not only an indicator but a facilitator of assimilation, since it is in mixed residential settings that closer contacts and relationships are likely to be made. Marriage is the most important of those relationships that can maintain or blur ethnic boundaries; it therefore matters that Mexican Americans have historically been less likely to out-marry than white ethnics but a good deal more likely to do so than African Americans, for whom a caste-like situation with respect to marriage has until recently applied.

In the first part of the twentieth century, as George Sanchez has shown, most Mexican Angelenos tended to in-marry; in his sample of married Mexican Americans, 83 percent were in-married, a high proportion, though one reflecting the newness of the community and the large number of foreign-born adults.[22] By the 1960s, before the advent of the new immigration and during a time of second-generation dominance, about 40 percent of Chicanos were marrying partners from outside the group;[23] by the mid-1970s, half of all Mexican American marriages in California were exogamous, the highest rate for Chicanos in the entire United States.[24]

By 1990, of course, the adult Mexican-origin population was heavily tilted toward the foreign-born; not surprisingly, then, endogamy prevailed. In 1990, 85 percent of all married Mexican-origin women living in Los Angeles were married to Mexican-origin men, as table 9.7 shows. The tendency toward in-marriage reflects the advent of the immigrants, whose marital decisions were often made prior to movement to the United States. Among those who met their partners after they arrived in Los Angeles, other factors are likely to have encouraged endogamy, most importantly the propensity to interact with other Mexicans in a Spanish-speaking monolingual environment and the expansive impact of immigration on the pool of potential partners.

TABLE 9.7 | Rates of In-marriage, Los Angeles Region, 1990

	Married Women In-married (%)	Odds Ratio of Marrying Within Group
White	93.2	99.6
Black	94.2	2,407.5
Asian	83.3	524.0
Hispanic	86.2	153.9
Mexican	85.1	154.3
Native-born	71.9	13.3
Aged 25–35	65.8	6.3
Aged 55–64	83.2	65.8
Foreign-born	92.8	121.2
Aged 25–35	92.6	88.3
Aged 55–64	93.4	160.3

Whatever the precise mix of factors that produce endogamous marriages among the immigrants, in-marriage rates decline when we focus on the native-born alone. They fall still further when we distinguish younger from older women, indicating that the earlier tendencies toward assimilation, at least as measured in terms of intermarriage, remain alive and well.

Still, the dynamics of Mexican American intermarriage appear profoundly affected by the compositional shifts produced by immigration and the related demographic shifts in the region's population, as can be seen by comparing the figures in column one of table 9.7, which show the in-marriage rate, with the figures in column two, which show the odds that Mexican women will marry Mexican men, compared with the odds of non-Mexican women doing the same. Column two tells us that younger Mexican women, in sharp contrast to their older peers, are not much more likely than anyone else to marry a Mexican man. But column one indicates that the great majority of younger Mexican women nonetheless marry Mexican men, given the large number of available Mexican partners as well as the other factors that normally promote endogamy.

Just what today's patterns mean for the future is hard to tell, since for the most part the large generation of children who are the offspring of the post-1965 immigrants were not yet of marriageable age as of 1990. But once they begin to marry, as they are almost certainly doing as of this writing, the ample availability of Mexican mates will induce considerable in-marriage. And the fact that in-marriage rates for younger native-born Mexican women appear to have increased suggests greater endogamy, and hence slower assimilation, in years to come.

Language

Though the United States has been a mass importer of non-English-speakers for the past two hundred years and more, "the American experience," as noted in one major review of the immigration literature, "is remarkable for its near mass extinction of non-English languages."[25] If no group seems exempt from this seemingly universal trend toward English monolingualism, the various Spanish-speaking groups do seem to follow the main drift at a slightly slower pace. Moreover, language maintenance is closely related to the degree of immigrant self-sufficiency and isolation. Since immigration seems to have produced greater segregation of L.A.'s Mexican-origin residents, it may have also altered the patterns of language change.

David Lopez has examined this issue in ample detail in chapter 5; here I quickly expand on his treatment (see table 9.8). As Lopez shows, almost all Mexican immigrants speak Spanish at home; native-born Mexican Americans are more likely to speak English in this setting, though a large proportion continue to use Spanish at home.[26] Among the immigrants, English language facility improves with the amount of time spent in the

TABLE 9.8 | Language Use by Mexican-Origin Population, Los Angeles Region, 1980–1990

	1980 (%)	1990 (%)
Speak Spanish in the home		
Foreign-born	97.5	96.0
Native-born	63.5	62.4
Aged 5–24	56.8	63.9
Aged 25–44	66.7	50.3
Aged 45–64	84.4	76.3
Aged 65 & older	83.2	82.7
Speak English Well or Very Well		
Foreign-born	47.4	51.2
Migrated pre-1960	67.0	71.7
Migrated 1960–70	57.3	65.8
Migrated 1970–80	39.6	58.7
Migrated 1980–90		41.4

United States; among the longest-established residents, the great majority report that they speak English "very well." For the native-born, the relationship between age and use of Spanish moves in an opposite direction, with Spanish much more likely to be used at home by older than by younger Chicanos.

In broad outlines, these data show that L.A.'s Mexican Americans are like most other groups; English becomes more prevalent with the advent of newer generations and younger cohorts. Clearly, and as Lopez argues, the shift toward English occurs somewhat more slowly among Mexicans and Mexican Americans than among many of the region's other ethnic groups. But the fact that the basic pattern persists deserves considerable note, especially since growing immigrant numbers and densities have led to greater segregation in contexts other than the home and hence to more occasions to interact in Spanish. Moreover, the 1990 pattern is generally consistent with the language reports recorded by the 1980 census, indicating that immigration has not significantly altered the relationships between generation and age, on the one hand, and language use, on the other. While the proportion of younger Chicanos speaking Spanish at home was greater in 1990 than it had been ten years before, this change is likely to reflect the greater proportion of young people with foreign-born parents rather than a shift in the underlying trend.

In summary, this survey of ethnic change among the region's Mexican Americans points to considerable diversity. While a substantial segment of the native-born population continues to speak Spanish, others do not. Similarly, significant portions of the community marry coethnics and live in segregated neighborhoods, even though segregation from whites remains at moderate levels and younger Mexican American women show a considerable propensity to marry outside the group.

Thus, Mexican American Los Angeles is clearly a community in change; to the extent that ethnic behaviors persist, continuing group attachment is a product of recent migration and its replenishment of the cultural life of longstanding Chicano communities. But the fact that the region's Chicanos seem to be on the road toward social assimilation remains paradoxical in light of their record of very modest economic progress. The comparison with African Americans heightens the puzzle; while Chicanos have clearly moved much farther down the road toward integration with Anglos, this social change does not seem to have done much to help Chicanos get ahead. Whatever the impediments to Chicano—and, more broadly, Mexican American—progress, the solution does not seem to lie in entering the social and cultural mainstream.

CONCLUSION

The stories of the immigrant and native-born Mexicans of Los Angeles are surprisingly similar. Both Mexican immigrants and Chicanos move ahead as they age, but progress is modest and can be measured only in absolute terms; on a relative scale, the record shows slippage. Moreover, such good news as there is applies only to the earlier and smaller cohorts who entered the region's economy at a particularly promising time. The immigrants of the 1980s are doing worse than their counterparts of the 1960s after a comparable passage of time. Though the portrait of the native-born is not quite so bleak, it is disappointing to note that the Mexican Americans who came of age in the 1980s were no better off than the cohort that entered adult life two decades before. Clearly, the traditional ethnic saga of hard labor followed by rewards does not apply.

One could argue that the skill characteristics of the region's Mexican-origin population explain this reversal of fortune, since both immigrants and Chicanos still suffer from relatively low skills. But relative to whites, Mexican Americans lagged behind two decades ago. The problem is in how to account for economic erosion, when schooling levels have in fact advanced in the past twenty years, especially among the native-born.

To locate the obstacles to Mexican American progress, we must turn to the changes that have restructured the region's economy. Restructuring has operated with a dual effect, wiping out well-paying, stable jobs in industries like steel, automobiles, and tires that were once an important part of the economic landscape, while encouraging the development of a downgraded manufacturing sector in industries like garments, electronics, and plastics. These shifts yield a one-two punch, eroding opportunities in the type of durable manufacturing jobs that traditionally employed Mexican Americans while expanding demand among those employers on the lookout for the cheapest, most easily exploited work force—a quest that leads them to the immigrant population.

With their progress stalled, Mexican Americans in Los Angeles have few grounds for the optimism that pervades traditional approaches to the immigrant and ethnic experience in the United States; the barriers that hinder Mexicans and Chicanos in their search for advancement seem stronger than the obstacles that impeded earlier groups of immigrants from Europe. In this respect, their experience has been closer to that of African Americans though not identical to it. As will be seen in chapter 13, black Angelenos do not find themselves in one single group at the bottom of the ladder; the African American trajectory, rather, is one of bifurcation, with a significant portion moving into the middle-class while another portion is sunk in poverty. Similar diversity does not hold in the Mexican American case; immigrants consistently rank at the bottom of the economic scale, with Chicanos one notch above in working-class and lower-middle-class occupations.

So dismal a scorecard makes for anxiety about the future, in which today's young Mexican-origin population will play an increasingly important part. Unfortunately, the people of Los Angeles seem unwilling to confront reality, opting instead for a search for scapegoats on whom they can blame the region's social and economic ills. Rather than encouraging investment in the future, the anti-immigrant campaigns are sowing the seeds of bitterness, to be reaped by tomorrow's generation with vengeance.

Notes to Chapter 9

1. In this chapter, *Mexican* and *Mexican-origin* are used as general terms to refer to the population of Mexican origin residing in the U.S., regardless of nativity or generational status. *Immigrant* or *foreign-born* is used when referring to those born in Mexico, while *native-born* is used to refer to those born in the U.S. Occasionally, *Mexican American* and *Chicano* are used to refer to the native-born population.

2. Donald Horowitz, "Conflict and Accommodation: Mexican Americans in the Cosmopolis," in Walker Connor, ed., *Mexican Americans in Comparative Perspective* (Washington, D.C.: Urban Institute Press, 1985), 68.

3. Leo Grebler, Joan Moore, Ralph Guzman, and Associates, *The Mexican-American People: The Nation's Second Largest Minority* (New York: Free Press, 1970), 95.

4. Frank Bean and Marta Tienda, *The Hispanic-Origin Population of the United States* (New York: Russell Sage Foundation, 1986).

5. Leobardo Estrada, et. al., "Chicanos in the United States: A History of Exploitation and Resistance," *Daedalus* 110 (1981): 103–131.

6. Estrada, "Chicanos in the United States," 129.

7. Rebecca Morales and Paul Ong, "The Illusion of Progress: Latinos in Los Angeles," in Rebecca Morales and Frank Bonilla, eds., *Latinos in a Changing U.S. Economy* (Newbury Park, Calif.: Sage, 1993), 56.

8. Linda Chavez, *Out of the Barrio: Toward a New Politics of Hispanic Assimilation* (New York: Basic Books, 1991), 305.

9. Joan Moore and Harry Pachon, *Hispanics in the United States* (Englewood Cliffs, N.J.: Prentice-Hall, 1985).

10. Albert Camarillo, *Chicanos in California* (Sparks, Nev.: Materials for Today's Learning, 1990).

11. Douglas Massey, et al., *Return to Aztlan: The Social Process of International Migration from Western Mexico* (Berkeley: University of California Press, 1987).

12. Gilda Ochoa, "Intra-Ethnic Relations in La Puente" (Paper presented at the American Sociological Association annual meetings, Los Angeles, August 1994).

13. There are drawbacks to using multiple census year data to gauge longitudinal change in an immigrant population. One issue is that undocumented immigrants, a significant portion of the Mexican immigrant population, may not be counted in the census when they have recently arrived. They are more likely to be counted in later census years, when they have resided in the United States longer, their fear of deportation has lessened, and they may have legalized their immigration status. The size of the cohort thus increases over time as more immigrants are counted. On the other hand, return migration and mortality should cause the size of the immigrant cohort to decrease. For instance, Mexican immigrants who come for short stays and return to Mexico are counted soon after their arrival, but then disappear from later censuses after their return to Mexico. Return migration is probably more likely to occur among younger immigrants than older ones. Mortality also plays a significant role in decreasing the size of the cohort over time, since mortality increases with age. The increase in the size of the cohort who arrived between 1960 and 1969 from 19,900 as counted in the 1970 census to 28,640 as counted in the 1980 census suggests that undocumented immigrants may indeed have been undercounted in 1970 and included in later censuses. On the other hand, the decrease in the size of the cohort between 1980 and 1990, from 28,640 to 24,839, suggests that return migration and mortality occurred to a larger extent between these two points. Overall, it appears that the changes in cohort size across the three census years are not large enough to invalidate the cohort analyses in this chapter.

14. While these are the averages for men, the averages for the same-aged women in the same immigrant cohorts are virtually identical.

15. Donald Horowitz, "Conflict and Accommodation," 77.

16. For an example of just such an attempt, see Milton Yinger, "Assimilation in the United States: The Mexican Americans," in Walker Connor, ed., *Mexican Americans in Comparative Perspectives* (Washington, D.C.: Urban Institute Press, 1985).

17. Carlos Arce, "A Reconsideration of Chicano Culture and Identity," *Daedalus,* 110 (1981): 177–91.

18. Horowitz, "Conflict and Accommodation," 78; italics added.

19. Bean and Tienda, *The Hispanic-Origin Population,* 164.

20. Bean and Tienda, *The Hispanic-Origin Population,* 168. For further detail, see Douglas Massey and Brendan Mullan, "Processes of Hispanic and Black Spatial Assimilation," *American Journal of Sociology* 89 (1984): 836–76.

21. Thomas Muller and Thomas Espenshade, *The Fourth Wave: California's Newest Immigrants* (Washington, D.C.: The Urban Institute, 1985); for the history of these traditional enclaves, see Joan Moore, *Homeboys: Gangs, Drugs, and Prison in the Barrios of Los Angeles* (Philadelphia: Temple University Press, 1978), 14–17.

22. George J. Sanchez, *Becoming Mexican American: Ethnicity, Culture, and Identity in Chicano Los Angeles, 1900–1945* (New York: Oxford University Press, 1993), 138–39. Sanchez's findings are consistent with the results of a much earlier study by Constantine Panunzio, "Intermarriage in Los Angeles, 1924–1933," *American Journal of Sociology* 47 (1942): 690–701.

23. Frank G. Mittelbach and Joan Moore, "Ethnic Endogamy—the Case of Mexican Americans," *American Journal of Sociology,* 74 (1968): 50–62.

24. Robert Schoen, Verne E. Nelson, and Marion Collins, "Intermarriage among Spanish Surnamed Californians, 1962–1974," *International Migration Review* 12 (1978): 359–69; Moore and Pachon, *Hispanics in the United States,* 108–9.

25. Alejandro Portes and Rubén Rumbaut, *Immigrant America* (Berkeley: University of California Press, 1990), 182.

26. Note, however, that the census tells us nothing about the frequency of language switching and conditions under which it occurs.

Central Americans: At the Bottom, Struggling to Get Ahead

David E. Lopez, Eric Popkin, and Edward Telles

ALTHOUGH CHICANOS and immigrant Mexicans still constitute the overwhelming majority of the region's Latino population, Latino Los Angeles was fundamentally altered in the 1980s by the massive influx of immigrants from other parts of Latin America. Today Los Angeles is home to immigrants from throughout the Americas. Each new group has constructed its own array of ethnic institutions: restaurants, soccer and social clubs, and bewildering constellations of "hometown" organizations devoted to remembering and supporting the communities left behind. This chapter briefly surveys this new Latino diversity and then examines in depth the current status and prospects of the largest and most distinctive components of this new Latino immigration, Salvadorans and Guatemalans in Los Angeles.

Salvadorans and Guatemalans share a number of characteristics that make them particularly interesting examples of the new immigration to Los Angeles. The majority of both populations came to the United States in the past decade and a half, fleeing their homes for a combination of economic and political reasons. The communities are still overwhelmingly foreign-born, and most of those born in the United States are the children of recent immigrants; less than 3 percent of the adults are U.S.-born. In both communities a few of the migrants are middle class, but most are of humble origins and brought with them little in the way of educational or other resources. They have actively integrated into the Los Angeles economy, but mostly at the level of low-wage service and manufacturing jobs. Like most immigrant generations, they continue to speak their native language. Finally, and perhaps most importantly for the people in question, the Salvadoran and Guatemalan communities have two of the highest rates of undocumented status in the United States today; no circumlocution can avoid the fact that they are largely illegal, just at a time when California voters have chosen to "do something" about illegal immigration.

LATINO DIVERSITY IN LOS ANGELES

Mexican Americans still constitute the largest Latino subgroup at the national, state, and local levels; four-fifths of the Los Angeles area Latino population is Mexican American (see table 10.1). But Salvadorans, Guatemalans, and to a lesser extent other Central Americans are very important parts of today's Latino community in L.A. Their actual numbers are modest in comparison with Mexican Americans; the 580,000 Central Americans counted in the 1990 census[1] make up only 12 percent of the region's Latino population. But Los Angeles is home to 44 percent of all Central Americans in the United States and to well over half the Salvadorans and Guatemalans. In contrast, only 12 percent of those of South American origin live in Greater Los Angeles, and only small percentages of the Puerto Ricans, Cubans and Dominicans. Nationally, Central Americans already outnumber Cubans.

The numbers in table 10.1 suggest that we should concentrate on the Salvadoran and Guatemalan populations in Los Angeles, and selected comparisons of these groups with other Latino subgroups from Central and South America reinforce that conclusion. All these groups are predominantly foreign-born, but they vary considerably in schooling and in their current economic status. Guatemalans and Salvadorans have educational levels sharply lower than other Central Americans in the United States (only 34 percent and 38 percent have a secondary-school education or above, compared with 50 to 67 percent for other Central Americans). South Americans have distinctly higher educational levels (71 percent have secondary school or above); their incomes approximate the median for all U.S. households in 1990. Even the immigrant populations from Bolivia and Peru, two countries with low educational levels and dismal poverty, are markedly superior to the Salvadorans and Guatemalans in schooling and family income. What this fact suggests, of course, is that migrants from these relatively distant South American nations come from higher up in their national class structures. Salvadoran and Guatemalan migrants, in contrast, are much more representative of their countries' overall class structures, though their numbers include more college-educated persons than the population that stayed behind.

In sum, both for their quantitative importance and for their social distinctiveness, it makes sense to focus our analysis of other Latinos in Greater

TABLE 10.1 | **Hispanic-Origin Populations in Los Angeles Region and the United States, 1990**

	United States	Los Angeles Region	Percentage in Los Angeles Region
All Hispanics	21,900,000	4,714,000	22
Mexican	13,393,000	3,736,000	28
Puerto Rican	2,652,000	65,000	2
Cuban	1,053,000	60,000	6
Dominican	520,000	3,000	1
Central American	1,324,000	580,000	44
Salvadoran	565,000	302,000	53
Guatemalan	269,000	159,000	59
Nicaraguan	203,000	44,000	22
Other	287,000	75,000	26
South American	1,036,000	129,000	12
Other Hispanic[a]	1,922,000	141,000	7

SOURCES: National data from *1990 Census of Population: Persons of Hispanic Origin in the United States;* state data from *1990 Census of Population: Social and Economic Characteristics.*
[a] Includes Spaniards, "Spanish," and other general references to Spanish Hispanic origin.

Los Angeles on the Guatemalan and Salvadoran communities. Throughout the analysis we will also present some data for the other Central Americans, a mixed group composed of substantial numbers of Nicaraguans and Hondurans and a smaller proportion of Costa Ricans, Panamanians, and Belizeans. We will often use the term *Central Americans* to refer to a population whose majority is from El Salvador and Guatemala.

A STATISTICAL PORTRAIT OF CENTRAL AMERICANS IN LOS ANGELES

The rapid rise to predominance of Salvadorans and Guatemalans in Los Angeles is emphasized in figure 10.1, which shows the growth of all Central American subgroups in Greater Los Angeles from 1970 to 1990. In 1970 the Hispanic Central American republics had roughly equal and quite small populations in Los Angeles. With the exception of the Costa Ricans,[2] all these groups grew during the 1970s, but only the Salvadoran and Guatemalan communities experienced runaway growth. According to the 1990 census, 301,600 Salvadorans and 159,200 Guatemalans resided in Greater Los Angeles in 1990. For both groups, this meant a nearly fivefold increase from the 1980 population, when the two groups were already the largest in the region.

FIGURE 10.1 | Growth of the Central American Population, Los Angeles Region, 1970–1990

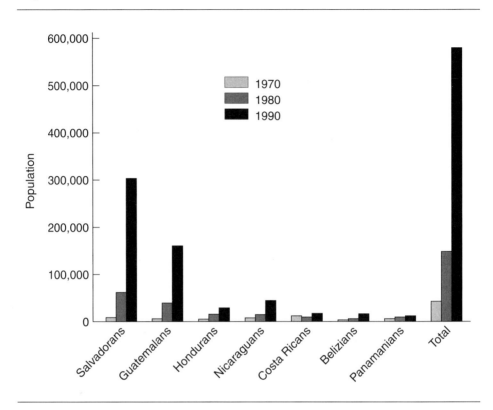

We have already seen that Salvadorans and Guatemalans stand out from other Latino subgroups in a number of respects. Their communities in Los Angeles differ significantly from those of other Central Americans and are even more distinct from the population at large. Table 10.2 compares a number of social and economic characteristics of Salvadorans, Guatemalans, and other Central Americans with non–Central Americans in Greater Los Angeles (including Mexicans). Perhaps the most striking figures relate to years of schooling; the Salvadoran and Guatemalan rates of high school graduation are half the rate of other Central Americans and little more than one-third the non–Central American rate. The proportions of college graduates are even more modest: one-third the rate for other Central Americans and one-seventh the non–Central American rate. It is worth emphasizing that these modest educational credentials are essentially what Central Americans have brought with them, from home societies in which even in the best of times schooling is much less available than in the United States.

TABLE 10.2 | Selected Characteristics of Central American Populations, Los Angeles Region, 1990

	Salvadorans	Guatemalans	Other Central Americans	All Others
Population	301,567	159,268	119,000	13.9 million
Foreign-born	80%	80%	74%	N/A
High school or above[a]	28%	30%	60%	77%
College graduate[a]	3%	4%	12%	24%
In labor force				
Men	93%	92%	91%	88%
Women	70%	68%	70%	68%
Unemployed[b]				
Men	8%	8%	7%	5%
Women	8%	8%	7%	4%
Median household income	$28,040	$29,260	$34,956	$47,441
Households below poverty line	25%	25%	21%	10%
Median household size	4.6	4.6	3.9	2.9
Median age[c]	26	27	24	34
fertility[d]	2.6	2.6	2.8	1.9

[a]Of population 25–64
[b]Of those in the labor force
[c]Foreign-born only
[d]Children ever born for women 35–44

The war in El Salvador and to a lesser extent in Guatemala severely curtailed education at the university and secondary levels, interrupting the schooling of an entire generation. It is too early to tell whether or not these newcomers will be able to make up their losses by going back to school in the United States. On the brighter side, we can expect that immigrant children and U.S.-born Central Americans will achieve much higher levels of education than the refugees who came as young adults.

Central American men in Los Angeles have higher than average labor force participation rates; the rates for women are both lower overall and not so different from non–Central Americans. Both men and women report distinctly above-average rates of unemployment.[3] The high labor force participation of Central American and Mexican immigrants, along with their correspondingly low public assistance rates[4] (less than half that of Hispanic natives), has been pointed to as evidence that they have a strong work ethic. Perhaps they do; certainly Salvadorans cherish the notion that they are a particularly hardworking lot. But then they have little choice; only a portion of the legal immigrants qualify for general welfare, and none of the undocumented do. Survival for Salvadorans in the United States—and of course in El Salvador as well—requires high levels of labor force participation.

Salvadoran and Guatemalan households in Los Angeles have median incomes only about 60 percent of that of non–Central Americans, and their poverty rates are 2.5 the non–Central American rate. The disparity in individual earnings is even worse but is compensated for somewhat by a larger number of wage earners in each household. On the other hand, Central American households are considerably larger than average, so that the per capita income of Salvadorans and Guatemalans is less than 40 percent that of non–Central Americans. (A more detailed look at incomes and the occupations that produce them will follow later in this chapter.)

Many factors account for the larger-than-average size of these households. Multiple impoverished but unrelated households crowd together far more frequently than among any of the region's other groups, Mexican immigrants excepted. But whether households are single or multiple, age and fertility play the crucial role. The median age of the population is markedly lower than that of non–Central Americans. Clearly this young age structure is due in considerable part to the fact that immigrants tend to be young adults in their childbearing years, but there is also evidence that these are comparatively high-fertility populations, not just young adults in their years of family formation. Their fertility rates are 37 percent higher than the non-Hispanic average.

The fact that immigrant Central American women tend to be in their childbearing years and appear to have above-average fertility has created a situation of increasing political importance in California: The native-born populations are disproportionately the young children of immigrants. The 1990 census showed that 89 percent of U.S.-born Salvadorans were under sixteen; over half were under the age of six. For Guatemalans the figures are 85 percent and 40 percent, respectively. Only 3 percent of the working-age adults are U.S.-born. Few of the parents of the U.S.-born children are citizens by birth or naturalization, and perhaps half the parents are in the United States illegally.

THE FLIGHT FROM WAR AND REPRESSION IN CENTRAL AMERICA

More than statistical averages distinguish the Salvadoran and Guatemalan stories from other Latino migration experiences; in both cases emigration was stimulated by the horrors of civil war and government terror and repression. These migrants are refugees, by any meaningful definition of the term, despite the U.S. government's resistance to recognizing this status.

The emergence of Central American immigrant communities in Los Angeles is one of Ronald Reagan's most ironic legacies to the region. Almost immediately after his inauguration in 1981, direct U.S. military assistance to El Salvador soared from zero in 1980 to $424 million in the 1981–84 period, leading to a rapid escalation of the war in that country and major disruption of the economy and the livelihood of many Salvadorans. Similarly, the war in Guatemala escalated with increased U.S. intervention, though often through foreign intermediaries. Political violence directly affected many people's lives as their close friends and family members were killed or tortured and their own lives were threatened. Under such conditions of instability and fear, there was little option but to bear the consequences or emigrate.

The result of these policies was massive devastation of the countryside in both El Salvador and Guatemala. Support for the Nicaraguan Contras also led to considerable disruption, but on a much smaller scale than in El Salvador and Guatemala, where scorched earth, strategic hamlets, and free-fire zones became commonplace. In some parts of highland Guatemala, Indians sympathetic to the rebels or just caught in the middle of the fighting had only two choices: to join a strategic hamlet and convert to Protestantism (this was the period of Rios Montt, the born-again president of Guatemala) or to flee. In El Salvador often only the latter option was available.

The years in which Salvadorans and Guatemalans immigrated to Los Angeles illustrate the relation between political violence in those two countries and immigration. Table 10.3 shows that almost one-quarter of all Salvadoran immigrants and about one-sixth of all Guatemalan immigrants residing in Los Angeles in 1990 had arrived in a period of only two years, 1980 and 1981, the height of violence in both El Salvador and Guatemala. After 1982 both immigration streams continued at a steady pace to the end of the

TABLE 10.3 | Period of Immigration of Selected Foreign-Born Populations, Los Angeles Region, 1990

	Salvadorans (%)	Guatemalans (%)	Other Central Americans (%)	Mexicans (%)
Before 1970	4	6	20	26
1970–79	22	22	22	33
Per year	2	2	2	3
1980–81	24	16	12	11
Per year	12	8	6	6
1982–84	16	15	12	8
Per year	5	5	4	3
1985–89	34	41	34	22
Per year	7	8	7	4

decade. We lack comparable data for the early 1990s, but the Immigration and Naturalization Service estimates that the rate of *unauthorized* immigration between 1990 to 1992 continued at about twice the rate indicated by census figures for the late 1980s.[5]

Although the war in El Salvador has ended and fighting in Guatemala has subsided, the uncertain future of these countries and the ongoing repression have kept many Central American immigrants from returning. Indeed, emigration has persisted despite declining political incentives to leave, and the INS figure just cited indicates that the United States is still the destination of choice. Sectors of the Salvadoran economy are thriving, but these largely relate to the development of services for middle-class and urban Salvadorans; nationwide unemployment continues to be high, and wages remain low. Continuing emigration is facilitated by the international migration networks of kin and *paisanos* (those from the same towns and regions) that developed during the peak of political violence in Central America. These networks guide Salvadorans and Guatemalans to housing and jobs in Los Angeles and other urban centers in the United States.

In the past few years a sense of stability has emerged in the Salvadoran and Guatemalan communities of Los Angeles and the rest of the United States. California's voters seem intent on disrupting this stability, but meanwhile Salvadorans and Guatemalans in the United States have become important contributors to the local economy, albeit in supporting roles rather than as economic stars. They have also come to play an increasingly important role in the economic stability of their home countries, especially of El Salvador. At least 8 percent of that nation's population now resides in the United States (see table 10.4); over half of these immigrants are in Los Angeles. Throughout the 1980s the remittances sent from the United States

TABLE 10.4 | Emigrant Populations in the United States in Relation to Population of Country of Origin, 1990

	Emigrants in U.S.[a]	Percentage in L.A.[a]	Country of Origin Population[b]	Emigrants as Percentage of Country of Origin Population[c]
El Salvador	458,700	53	5,252,000	8
Guatemala	216,000	59	9,197,000	2
Other Central American	366,400	20	14,442,000	2
Mexico	4,459,800	39	81,249,000	5

[a]*1990 Census of Population: Persons of Hispanic Origin in the United States.*
[b]From James Wilkie, 1990, *Statistical Abstract of Latin America* (Los Angeles: UCLA Latin American Center).
[c]Total counts derived by adding emigrant population in the United States to country populations from Wilkie, *Statistical Abstract.* In all cases emigrant population in the United States is at least 80 percent of total emigrants.

back to El Salvador became an important source of income to families and foreign exchange to the government. It has been estimated that by the end of the decade this remittance income was over $500 million, rivaling the foreign-exchange earnings of all Salvadoran exports.[6]

The economic impact of the remittance flow for Salvadorans residing in the United States is less clear. If generally accepted estimates of the magnitude of remittances are correct, then the average Salvadoran household in the United States sends over $6,000 back home each year. We view this figure with some skepticism, but if it is anywhere near correct, it constitutes a big bite out of the household economy for these low-income families, whose household incomes average about $22,000. The image of single men rooming together and sending their money back home to feed their hungry wives and children no longer describes the Salvadoran community in the United States, and it probably never did; only 16 percent of U.S. Salvadorans live without other family members.[7] Remittances may bind Salvadorans to their families and towns back home, but they may also constrain the immigrants from getting ahead in the United States.

THE LEGAL STATUS OF CENTRAL AMERICANS IN GREATER LOS ANGELES

In this period of anti-illegal-immigrant frenzy—that is, after the passage of Proposition 187 in California, which denies public education and health benefits to the undocumented—Salvadorans and Guatemalans constitute perhaps the most vulnerable national-origin groups in the United States, for three reasons. First, they are among the most undocumented of national-origin groups in the United States; second, they are poor and work in the marginal, nonformal sectors of the economy; third, their claims to refugee status have never been recognized by the U.S. government, and they are about to lose what temporary protection against deportation they have had.

In a recent paper,[8] the Immigration and Naturalization Service Statistical Division estimated that in 1992 there were 327,000 unauthorized Salvadorans and 129,000 unauthorized Guatemalans in the United States, 205,000 and 88,000 of them, respectively, in California. On the basis of these figures we estimate that the respective 1992 figures for Greater Los Angeles are 178,000 and 80,000.[9] The same INS estimates indicate that there are three times as many unauthorized Mexican nationals in the United States as unauthorized Salvadorans and Guatemalans combined, with the same relationship holding in Los Angeles. But viewed proportionately the picture is very different; the 1992 estimate of 1.3 million unauthorized Mexicans equals less than 10 percent of the total Mexican-origin population and roughly one-quarter of the entire foreign-born Mexican population. In contrast we estimate that 49 percent of the entire Salvadoran population in the United

States is undocumented; the estimate for Guatemalans is 40 percent. These rates are conservative estimates, and it is entirely possible that the proportion of undocumented is even higher in Los Angeles, which has the greatest concentrations of both these communities.[10]

Throughout the 1980s human rights groups took the side of Salvadoran refugees against the U.S. government, which denied that there was anything repressive about its puppet government in El Salvador and hence anything from which to flee. Nicaraguans fleeing Sandinista "totalitarianism," in contrast, were welcomed. By the end of the decade Salvadoran advocates had won a partial victory. Through the courts they had managed to have the asylum and deportation hearing processes slowed down. In the late 1980s Central American advocates won a pair of court cases, lending to revised INS procedures more sensitive to reasons that Salvadorans and Guatemalans gave for leaving their homes. These court victories also led to the establishment of Temporary Protected Status (TPS), which provided what the name implies for Salvadoran would-be refugees, pending changes in the situation in El Salvador. About 187,000 Salvadorans registered for TPS, two-thirds of the estimated unauthorized Salvadoran population at the time. Two years later TPS was renamed Deferred Enforced Departure (DED) and extended for another eighteen months, though only about half of the original TPS registrants reregistered.

The extended DED program was scheduled to expire December 31, 1994. The Clinton administration refused to extend the program itself, but it did allow DED holders to register for temporary work permits and also to apply for refugee status. As of the end of 1995 only a small proportion had done so, apparently because few believe they can actually qualify as refugees. In any case DED officially affects only 90,000 of the approximately 350,000 undocumented Salvadorans who lived in the United States in 1994; the status of the other 97,000 original registrants who did not reregister has never been clarified. Furthermore, the members of most Salvadoran families have a range of legal statuses, from native-born citizen children through various degrees of asylum and temporary protection to unauthorized; it is logical to assume that any major shift in immigration and refugee law affecting Salvadorans will affect most Salvadoran families in the United States. Those losing DED status can join the backlog of hundreds of thousands of Salvadorans and other Central Americans who have applied for political asylum, if they have not done so already. And there are a variety of other paths along which to pursue legal status in the United States. But the fact remains that at least half the Salvadorans in the United States are vulnerable to whatever policy shifts may affect the undocumented. Guatemalans, both because a smaller proportion of them are undocumented and because they have not had the dubious advantages of temporary protection, are somewhat less vulnerable.

Just as the passage of Proposition 187 has not, as of this writing, led to mass deportations or even immediate changes in public services for the undocumented, so the expiration of DED status will probably not have any immediate cataclysmic consequences. The INS has promised that "massive or immediate" deportations are not being contemplated. But it has put Salvadorans in the United States precisely where they do not want to be, in the spotlight of attention by immigration reform advocates. Dan Stein, Executive Director of Federation of Americans for Immigration Reform (FAIR), has recently been quoted as saying that "the time has come for Salvadorans to go home."[11]

SETTLEMENT PATTERNS

Building on a relatively small pre-Reagan-era Central American community, immigrants from El Salvador and Guatemala have made Los Angeles their primary destination, forming large Central American settlements and diversifying the region's large Latino population. In a decade's time, Central American migration to Los Angeles has been facilitated by the establishment of a sizable Central American community in the region, a large network of Central American organizations in Los Angeles, and daily direct flights between Central American capitals and LAX. Guatemalans and Salvadorans are spread throughout many of the humbler residential areas of Los Angeles, but the population and especially its cultural and political institutions are concentrated in the Pico-Union/Westlake district, just west of downtown Los Angeles. The population extends northwest into Hollywood and, in fact, more Central Americans live in and around Hollywood than in Pico-Union/Westlake. *Pupuserias,* restaurants serving Salvadoran dishes, have become commonplace in these districts, as have the advertisements of courier and moving companies claiming to deliver to just about any place in Central America.

Pico-Union/Westlake and Hollywood contain the largest concentrations of Salvadorans and Guatemalans but not the majority of these populations. Furthermore, even in the most densely Central American core areas, Central Americans are not a majority of the population, at least according to 1990 census figures.[12] In fact less than 10 percent of the Salvadoran and Guatemalan population of Los Angeles County are found in the twenty-three census tracts that make up the core of the Pico-Union/Westlake area. Countywide, fully 60 percent of Salvadorans live in census tracts with fewer than 10 percent Salvadorans. In other words, about one-fifth of the Salvadoran population lives in the Westlake/Hollywood core; another fifth lives in tracts that have some Salvadoran identity, but three-fifths of population live in tracts that, though predominantly Latino, have little Salvadoran identity.

We did not compile similar statistics for Guatemalans, but the data that follow suggest that they follow the Salvadoran pattern of core-plus-dispersion.

Table 10.5 gives the composition of the two distinctively Central American districts. In both Westlake and Hollywood[13] Central Americans, principally Salvadorans and Guatemalans, make up about one-third of the residents counted. Mexicans and other Latinos constitute another third of the Westlake population, and about a quarter of the Hollywood residents. Asians together with a few blacks make up about a fifth of each neighborhood, and about one-fifth of Hollywood is white (including Armenians and other immigrant white ethnics). Perhaps the most striking fact about the Westlake figures is the near absence of non-Hispanic whites, who constitute only 6 percent of the population, in contrast to the 72 percent who are Latino. Whereas Westlake is a predominantly Latino neighborhood of mixed origins, the census data show that Hollywood, with its complex white ethnic population and its more diverse Asian population (the Asians

TABLE 10.5 | Ethnic Composition of Two Central American Districts in Los Angeles, 1990

	Pico-Union/ Westlake (%)	Hollywood (%)
Ethnic Group		
Salvadoran	22	19
Guatemalan	11	9
Other Central American	3	3
Mexican	33	20
Other Hispanic	3	3
Asian	16	19
Black	3	4
White	6	20
Percentage of Five-County Population Residing in the Area		
Salvadoran	12	8
Guatemalan	12	8
Other Central American	6	4
Mexican	1	1
Other Hispanic	2	1
Total Population	1.2	0.7

counted in Westlake are predominantly Koreans), is even more heterogeneous.

Both these neighborhoods serve as receiving areas for newly arrived Central Americans. Though very overcrowded, the areas do offer affordable housing, as well as markets and other institutions that will seem familiar to Central Americans. And they are well situated for access to jobs located throughout the center and western half of the city. Westlake is adjacent to the major east-west bus lines running on Wilshire, Venice, and Pico Boulevards; Hollywood is served by the bus lines on Santa Monica Boulevard. In contrast, East Los Angeles, the core of Chicano Los Angeles, is essentially isolated from Los Angeles west of downtown. It can take an hour to go by bus from East L.A. to downtown; to get to the Westside requires an inconvenient transfer and at least another hour. Salvadorans and other Latino residents of the neighborhoods just west of downtown are in a much better position to find work serving the Westside and San Fernando Valley middle class.

Table 10.6 shows that Salvadorans and Guatemalans reside in pretty much the same neighborhoods throughout the region. Their distributions are not identical, as the Salvadoran-Guatemalan dissimilarity index of .31 indicates, but that is far and away the lowest index value between these two

TABLE 10.6 | **Segregation of Salvadorans and Guatemalans, Los Angeles Region, 1990**

	Indexes of Dissimilarity		Indexes of Exposure	
	Salvadorans	Guatemalans	Salvadorans	Guatemalans
All Hispanics			.57	.55
Salvadorans		.31	.10	.08
Guatemalans	.31		.05	.05
Other Central Americans	.44	.45	.02	.02
Mexicans	.53	.54	.36	.36
Blacks	.65	.65	.12	.12
All Non-Hispanic Whites	.77	.75	.21	.24
English ancestry	.79	.77	.02	.03
Russian ancestry	.82	.82	.00	.00
All Asians	.66	.66	.11	.10
Filipinos	.64	.64	.03	.03
Koreans	.70	.69	.03	.03
Chinese	.78	.79	.02	.01
Japanese	.77	.77	.00	.00
Vietnamese	.79	.78	.00	.00

groups and any other in the city. (See chapter 4 and the appendix for an explanation of segregation indices.) Both groups are more segregated from other Central Americans (index = .44–.45) and from Mexicans (index = .53–.54) than from each other. Salvadorans and Guatemalans are somewhat more segregated from Filipinos and African Americans (index = .64–.65). As Figure 10.2 shows, this moderate level of integration reflects the overlap of Central American and Filipino residence in the East Hollywood/Echo Park area and the dispersion of Central Americans throughout South Central Los Angeles. Their indexes of dissimilarity with most other ethnic groups hover in the high .70s, with the greatest level of segregation from those of "Russian" ancestry (our proxy for Jews). Of course there is also an economic dimension to these patterns: Salvadorans and Guatemalans are segregated from the most affluent neighborhoods of the city, where "Russians" are most likely to be found.

The right half of table 10.6 provides the exposure index, which takes group size into account and measures the average ethnic composition of the census tracts in which a particular group lives. Unlike the dissimilarity index, which essentially measures the isomorphism of the distribution of two populations, the exposure index actually measures the degree to which members of a given group rub shoulders on a daily basis with members of other ethnic groups. Central Americans are simply too few and too dispersed to constitute their own residential communities. These data show that Salvadorans tend to live in predominantly Latino neighborhoods, with Mexicans constituting by far the single largest other ethnic group present.

What explains the Central American residential pattern of core and dispersion? Above all, Central Americans live in neighborhoods that provide the essential combination of inexpensive housing and public transportation to jobs. They would doubtless prefer the suburban lifestyle of Cerritos or even Simi Valley, could they afford it. Parts of Pico-Union/Westlake and East Hollywood contain the remnants of elegant neighborhoods of large houses and substantial apartment buildings, but by the 1970s these proud structures had been neglected and subdivided to provide housing for the mix of Central American and other immigrants that had been arriving in the area for years. These housing units were no bargain, if one judges by value received for money, but they were among the least expensive housing available in areas from which service jobs could be reached. Better value for the dollar could be found in the northeast corner of the San Fernando Valley or southeast of downtown Los Angeles, but these distant neighborhoods did not offer the locational advantages of Pico-Union. They also lacked the Spanish-language services and core of Central American cultural life that had grown up in Pico-Union by the mid-1970s. This area therefore became, and continues to be, the logical first stop for new arrivals from Central America, the most likely place to get help in finding jobs and housing from *paisanos*.

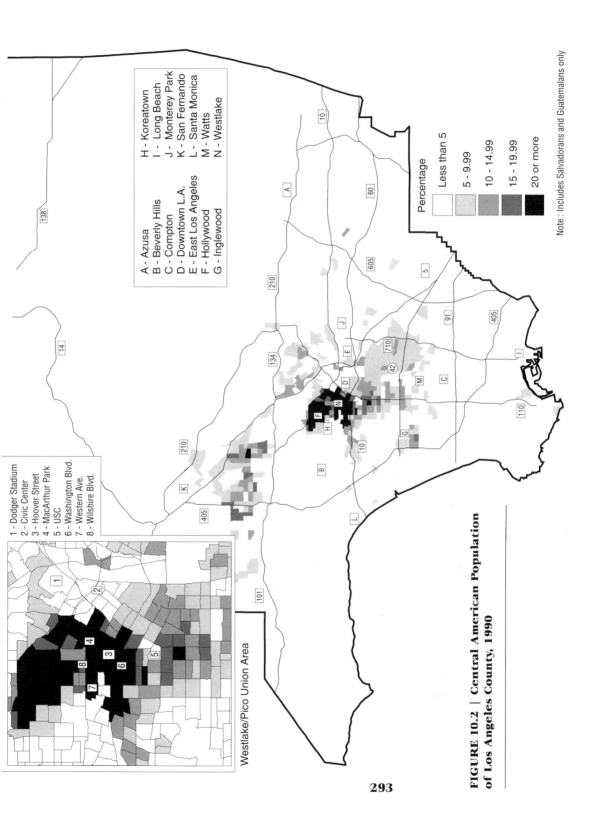

FIGURE 10.2 | Central American Population of Los Angeles County, 1990

A - Azusa
B - Beverly Hills
C - Compton
D - Downtown L.A.
E - East Los Angeles
F - Hollywood
G - Inglewood

H - Koreatown
I - Long Beach
J - Monterey Park
K - San Fernando
L - Santa Monica
M - Watts
N - Westlake

Percentage

Less than 5
5 - 9.99
10 - 14.99
15 - 19.99
20 or more

Note : Includes Salvadorans and Guatemalans only

1 - Dodger Stadium
2 - Civic Center
3 - Hoover Street
4 - MacArthur Park
5 - USC
6 - Washington Blvd.
7 - Western Ave.
8 - Wilshire Blvd.

Westlake/Pico Union Area

CENTRAL AMERICANS AT WORK

In a sense immigrant Central Americans are particularly well suited to fit into the new Los Angeles economy. They are not the highly educated and well-paid information workers who supposedly own the region's future, but they do the housecleaning and other dirty work that is needed to support the lifestyle of this emerging new class. This is not a pretty picture, of course; no one likes to see such a convergence of class and ethnicity at the lower levels of the occupational ladder. The apparent need for such labor has created a demand, however, and Central Americans have supplied the labor to fill that demand. They are hardly the first immigrant population to fill such a niche; the question is whether they will be able to move beyond it.

Central Americans currently toil in predominantly low-paying jobs that would seem to offer little more than day-to-day survival. Table 10.7 gives the major occupational groupings for immigrants from El Salvador, Guatemala, and Mexico in Greater Los Angeles, along with the total non-Hispanic population for perspective. The first point to make is the overall similarity for the three immigrant groups: they constitute an overwhelmingly blue-collar and service work force, with less than half the non-Hispanic rate of sales and clerical workers and only one-sixth as much representation in the professional-technical/managerial ranks. Overall more than 72 percent of the non-Hispanics are in white-collar occupations (managerial, professional-technical, sales and clerical) compared with 20 percent of the Salvadoran, Guatemalan, or Mexican immigrants. The other Central American immigrants are rather better off, with twice the white-collar rates of the other Latino groups. But Salvadorans, Guatemalans and Mexican workers appear to be a caste apart.

Despite the overall similarity in the occupational status of the Salvadoran, Guatemalan, and Mexican immigrants, there are some interesting differences. Mexicans are much more likely to be farm workers (and much more likely than Central Americans to reside in the less urbanized parts of Greater Los Angeles). Salvadoran and Guatemalan immigrants are almost twice as likely to be engaged in service occupations. Further breakdown of the occupational statistics indicates that this difference is particularly pronounced in household services, where Salvadorans and Guatemalans are five times as likely as Mexicans to be found. In fact, there are more Salvadoran and Guatemalan household workers than there are Mexican household workers, despite the much larger Mexican population base.

The comparison in table 10.7 with the total non-Hispanic population illustrates the magnitude of the gap between these immigrant populations and the mainstream. What about the second generation? As has been mentioned, the working-age native Central American population is simply too

TABLE 10.7 | **Occupational Distribution of Selected Foreign-Born Groups, Los Angeles Region, 1990 (Workers Aged 25–64)**

	Salvadoran (%)	Guatemalan (%)	Other Central American (%)	Mexican (%)	All Non-Hispanic (%)
Prof/Tech/ Managerial	7.3	6.9	18.0	7.3	42.0
Sales/Clerical	13.3	12.3	24.8	11.8	30.1
Crafts	15.4	17.4	13.6	18.7	10.6
Operative/ Transport	25.6	23.1	16.4	28.5	6.4
Service	31.1	32.0	21.0	18.4	8.3
Laborer	6.3	6.6	4.9	8.8	1.9
Farm	2.0	1.7	1.3	6.6	.7
Total Workers	108,240	56,866	39,529	692,189	4,063,573

small for statistical analysis, even if all national groups are combined. Statistical niceties aside, it is very problematic to project the status of the future second generation of Central Americans by the current status of today's native-born Central American population, who are the product of a very different era. It is worth pointing out, however, that the occupational profiles of native-born Mexicans and other Hispanics are dramatically different from the immigrant profiles in table 10.7; the majority of native-born Mexican American and other Hispanic workers are in white-collar occupations, though they have still not reached parity with Anglos, as chapter 9 has described. There is no guarantee that the children of the current Mexican and Central American immigrant generations will advance at the same rate, but neither is there persuasive evidence that future generations of Central Americans are headed into a dead-end underclass.

OCCUPATIONAL NICHES

It will surprise no one that Central American immigrants typically have jobs that are poorly paid and offer little in the way of security or advancement. The Los Angeles economy provides fewer and fewer "good" unskilled and semiskilled jobs, but it does offer abundant opportunities to work at low-paying dead-end jobs, the only ones for which the majority of Central American workers, with their modest educational and English language skills, are qualified.

TABLE 10.8 │ Occupational Niches for Central American and Mexican Immigrants, Los Angeles Region, 1990 (Index of Representation, Workers Aged 25–64)

	Salvadoran	Guatemalan	Other Central American	Mexican
Private servant	12.3	13.6	6.2	2.3
Textile sewer	6.6	4.9	3.7	4.4
Maid	5.7	5.8	3.9	3.5
Janitor	3.7	4.3	2.1	2.4
Cook	3.1	3.0	—	3.3
Assembler	2.4	1.8	1.9	1.5
Machine operator	2.8	3.4	—	3.9
Painter	3.4	4.3	—	1.9
Operative	2.8	3.3	2.8	4.2

Table 10.7 indicated some areas of Central American occupational concentration. Table 10.8 lists those occupations in which Salvadorans and Guatemalans are significantly more likely than the general population to be present. The most striking finding is the very high concentration of Salvadorans and Guatemalans in private service (as household workers, including cleaners and childcare workers in private homes). Salvadorans are overrepresented among the ranks of private servants by a factor of more than 12 and Guatemalans by a factor of more than 13. By contrast, Mexican immigrants were only 2.3 times as likely as the general population to be private servants. Salvadorans and Guatemalans are also five to six times as likely to be maids (housekeeping workers not in private households). The third occupation that stands out is textile sewing machine operators, with indexes of representation of 6.6 and 4.9, respectively.

There is an important gender dimension to these occupational niches; among Salvadorans and Guatamalans, 99 percent of the servants are female, the maids are 83 and 85 percent female, and the sewing machine operators are 80 and 62 percent female, respectively. The stereotype of Salvadoran and Guatemalan immigrant women as domestic workers and hotel maids is, then, all too true. These jobs represent the single most important occupation for them, and in fact, taken together these two comparatively small ethnic groups represent 36 percent of all the servants and 17 percent of the maids in Greater Los Angeles. Their reported earnings ($8,200–10,600) are also among the lowest for particular occupations in the region. Reported earnings for sewing machine operators are within the same range.

What about the men? The only male-dominated occupation with high levels of Central American representation is painter. But there are several jobs that Central American men and women share more or less equally and that have high levels of overall representation of Salvadorans and Guatemalans. These include janitor, cook, assembler, and machine operator; both nationalities are two to four times more likely than the general population to be found in these jobs. Jobs that have substantial proportions of male workers are somewhat better but still modestly paid; reported earnings range from $9,700 to $15,000.

The only other ethnic group with even marginally similar occupational concentrations are immigrant Mexicans. They too are heavily represented in occupations such as cook, construction laborer, sewing machine operator, and janitor. Mexican immigrants are also likely to be servants (index = 2.3) and maids (index = 3.5), but these indexes of representation are far below the rates for Central Americans.

The pattern of industrial niches for Central Americans, though not shown, follows the occupational niche pattern; private households, hotels, apparel and other manufacturers, and services are the largest employers, followed by auto repair shops, restaurants, and furniture repairers and manufacturers. Once again, the comparison with Mexicans is a composite of similarity and difference; Mexicans have an index of representation of at least 2.0 in most of the industries listed above, though with generally lower levels of presence than Central Americans, especially in service industries. The highest levels of Mexican immigrant representation occur in horticulture and agriculture.

Both occupational and industrial level data confirm that Central Americans make up more than one-third of the private household work force. Mexican immigrants account for another quarter. Central Americans also constitute substantial portions (14 to 17 percent) of the workers in the apparel and other service sectors. Mexican workers, because of their much larger numbers, constitute the largest single part of the workers in a variety of industries, such as apparel, furniture repair, and manufacturing; they are the absolute majority in horticulture and agriculture.

Another way to think about occupational niches and ethnicity is to ask how dependent a particular group is on the niches on which it has converged and what characterizes those occupations in which it has developed such dense concentrations. Table 10.9 answers those questions and compares Central Americans with other immigrant work forces. Salvadoran, Guatemalan, and Mexican workers are all more likely than Asian or other Central American immigrant workers to be in an occupational niche. Central American niches are also heavily populated by female workers, in contrast to Mexican niches. Finally, Central American immigrants are quite poorly educated and poorly paid. For comparison this table also includes

TABLE 10.9 | **Employment of Selected Foreign-Born Groups in Industrial Niches, Los Angeles Region, 1990**

	Percentage of Group in a Niche	Percentage of Niches in Manufacturing	Percentage Female	Mean Earnings ($)	Mean Years Education Among Niche Workers
Salvadoran	53	36	54	12,740	8
Guatemalan	54	30	50	12,877	8
Other Central American	32	38	62	15,891	10
Mexican	55	50	32	16,620	8
Asian	41	22	51	32,009	14

data for Asian immigrants; overall the latter are less likely to be in a niche (though more so than native-born Asians), the niches are less likely to be in manufacturing, and the earnings and education associated with the niche workers are substantially higher than for any of the Latino immigrant groups.

It is not hard to understand why Central American women are so heavily concentrated in domestic and related work, though the degree of overrepresentation is not easily explainable. Immigrant Central American women (and Mexican women of similar background) are willing to work for lower wages than native-born women; they have fewer alternatives, including the option of welfare, which is closed to most undocumented women. Another factor would seem to facilitate the presence of Central American women in domestic work, though it is difficult to say if it is cause or consequence: A larger proportion of Central Americans tend to reside closer to the middle-class neighborhoods of the Westside and the San Fernando Valley, where they are most likely to find employment. Each morning and evening MTA buses transport thousands of women from the Pico-Union/Hollywood areas along Wilshire, Santa Monica, Pico, and Venice Boulevards to the affluent Westside. To a lesser extent buses from the northern reaches of the Central American residential districts in Hollywood carry workers through the Cahuenga Pass and into Glendale and other parts of the San Fernando Valley. But these buses are carrying Mexican as well as Central American women; remember that Pico-Union/Westlake and Hollywood are home to as many Mexican as Central American workers (see table 10.5). The key difference is that the majority of Central Americans reside in areas accessible to the Westside, while Mexicans are concentrated in the more isolated areas east and south of Downtown Los Angeles.

EARNINGS

We have already seen that incomes of Central American workers are among the lowest in the region. Table 10.10 provides a more precise look at income differences, comparing the earnings of employed men aged 25–64. The earnings of native-born white men are the standard for comparison. All three of the native-born Latino groups earn about two-thirds of the white mean, but the earnings of the immigrant groups are all much lower, ranging from 23 percent to 43 percent of the white average. As expected, immigrants who have been in the United States longer have higher incomes, but they are far from catching up with native-born Latinos, let alone native whites.

In each case two income figures are given: the raw mean income and an adjusted mean that indicates how the group in question would do if it had the same set of background characteristics as native-born white men in Los Angeles. The logic of such an exercise is that any residual difference left after these background differences are standardized must be due to some unmeasured variable or set of variables. Often this residual difference is taken as a measure of discrimination, and if the adjustment procedure does indeed take into account key differences such as educational disparities, then that interpretation makes sense. In the case of recent immigrant populations, there are background differences that cannot easily be adjusted for: low levels of English competence, little familiarity with the occupations of advanced industrial economies, and educational backgrounds that do not easily translate year-for-year from one culture to another. It would be foolish simply to label the differences as discrimination. Whatever their explanation, the magnitude of these residual differences is considerable, espe-

TABLE 10.10 | Mean Earnings of Selected Groups, 1989 Dollars (Men Aged 25–64)

	Salvadoran		Guatemalan		Mexican	
	Raw	Adjusted[a]	Raw	Adjusted	Raw	Adjusted
Native-born	$30,627	38,518	26,723	42,936	30,974	37,848
Immigrated 1975–79	$17,653	20,039	19,959	31,486	17,481	24,370
Immigrated 1980–84	$15,336	21,477	14,437	20,939	14,764	21,277
Immigrated 1985–89	$10,552	13,675	11,774	18,770	11,752	18,169

NOTE: Mean earnings for native-born white men = $46,463.
[a] Adjusted to show how the group would do if it had the same background characteristics as native-born white men.

cially for the immigrant cohorts, for which the adjustment procedure yields only a modest effect in reducing the native-white/foreign-born gap. What this means is that even those few immigrants with substantial educational and work experience backgrounds have low incomes in comparison with whites with equivalent backgrounds. Outright discrimination could not account for all the difference, but on the other hand it should not be entirely discounted.

As table 10.10 shows, native-born Latinos have much higher incomes than immigrants. When adjusted for background differences with whites, the earnings gaps are substantially reduced, though hardly explained away. Even in these comparisons between native-born Latinos and whites it requires a leap of faith to attribute all the residual difference to discrimination in the job market; factors like educational quality and the subtler qualities of work experience and social and human capital are simply not measured by the Census Bureau. Still, we are on firmer ground arguing that discrimination is a major factor in explaining these gaps than in the comparisons involving immigrant Central American and Mexican workers.

A GLIMPSE OF THE FUTURE

The status of Central American immigrants in Greater Los Angeles is starkly clear and not likely to change greatly in their lifetimes. They will continue to be among the hardest-working and most poorly remunerated of Angelenos, almost literally a servant caste whose labor makes possible the emerging middle-class L.A. lifestyle: dual breadwinner families who entrust their lawns, their laundry, and their children to Central American and Mexican workers. But what about the children of the immigrants? Are they doomed to perpetuate this caste-like status? The Central American second generation consists of children and the yet-to-be-born (remember, half the Salvadoran second generation in 1990 was under the age of six). Even in the year 2000 there will be only the beginnings of a substantial Central American second generation in the work force. But some hint of the future can be gleaned from the current educational achievements of those immigrants who came as children, the so-called 1.5 generation.

Table 10.11 contains information on high school graduation and college enrollment and graduation for younger immigrants, comparing those who came as young children (ten or under, our operational definition of the 1.5 generation) with those who came as teenagers or young adults. Mexican and Central American immigrant youth are compared with Other Hispanics and European/Canadian immigrant youth, whom we know come from more advantaged backgrounds (see table 10.2). The data are suggestive, if hardly conclusive. In each comparison the Europeans/Canadians are doing

TABLE 10.11 | **Educational Trends for Selected Immigrant Groups, 1990**

	Mexican (%)	Central American (%)	Other Hispanic (%)	European/ Canadian (%)
In high school or graduated, aged 16–19				
First generation	42	65	81	86
1.5 generation	77	81	90	94
In college, aged 18–24				
First generation	8	16	31	42
1.5 generation	21	27	38	40
College graduates, aged 25–29				
First generation	3	4	16	30
1.5 generation	5	8	23	30

best, usually followed closely by the Other Hispanic group. More interestingly, Central Americans are clearly doing better than Mexicans in each comparison. The differences are not great, but they are consistent. Also consistent is the higher level of educational achievement of the 1.5 generation in each ethnic group. The Central American 1.5 generation is still far behind the better-off Other Hispanics and Europeans/Canadians, but they are doing better than their Mexican counterparts.

CONCLUSION

A combination of modest educational and English language skills has predictably shunted Central Americans to the lower levels of the Southern California occupational structure. They have found work in the marginal sectors of the service and manufacturing economy, sectors that are not likely to be stepping stones to better jobs for them or their children. Because perhaps half the immigrant generation is undocumented, many are forced to work in the informal fringes of the economy. The Central American second generation is too young and their numbers are too few to measure the degree to which they will be able to ride the hard work of their parents into the American mainstream.

On the other hand it must be emphasized that Central Americans are integrating into a mainstream, but of a different kind: the Mexican American/Latino mainstream. Latinos, with Mexican Americans at the core, are gradually becoming the single largest ethnic group in Greater Los Angeles. Politically they are still overwhelmed by Anglo voters; economically they are marginal, and socially they may be just barely acceptable. But a drive around Los Angeles (virtually any part will do) confirms what Central Americans know very well; the Latino Los Angeles of which they feel and are a part is not just another ethnic group among many. It is the emerging majority. Central Americans are an integral part of this emerging majority, and it is reasonable to assume that their future is tied to the future of the predominantly Mexican Latino population of Los Angeles generally.

Salvadorans and Guatemalans in L.A. work hard for modest returns. On the other hand, Central Americans did not come to Los Angeles expecting immediate entry into the ranks of information workers. They fled poverty exacerbated by oppressive governments and civil war and most probably judge themselves to be better off today than they were at home. Salvadorans and Guatemalans in Los Angeles face many legal and economic challenges that could disrupt lives and further endanger the communities' potential for upward mobility in the United States. But these hardworking immigrants are also playing an important and unique role in the region's economy, to the point that it is hard to envision Los Angeles without their labor. Other immigrant groups could probably take their places, but native-born citizens certainly will not. Los Angeles today needs Salvadorans and Guatemalans or other groups that can be similarly exploited.

Notes to Chapter 10

1. Estimates of the actual Central American and other Latino population often run far above the official census figures. Los Angeles Salvadoran community groups routinely estimate their current population at over 500,000, more than 50 percent higher than the highest official estimates; national estimates are as high as one million. Certainly the uncorrected census figures are lower than the true situation in 1990, but it is impossible to know the true size of the uncounted Central American and other Latino population. In this chapter, as throughout this volume, we are deriving most of our quantitative data from the 1990 census, which we know to be flawed and outdated but still the best source of quantitative data about the population of Greater Los Angeles. Later in the chapter we combine Census Bureau and INS data to make some estimates of the current size of the Central American population in the United States and the proportion that is undocumented. We do not use the higher estimates favored by community groups.

2. The remarkable steadiness of the Costa Rican population reflects a reduced level of immigration, though 69 percent of Costa Ricans in the United States are foreign-born. Impressionistic evidence suggests that immigrants from Costa Rica are more likely to taste the wonders of the United States and then return to this comparatively affluent and pleasant little nation. Perhaps the wisest course for U.S. immigration policy makers would be to figure out how to make more of Latin America like Costa Rica.

3. These high unemployment figures would seem to contradict the point made later in this chapter that Central American low-wage workers have continued to be able to find work in the midst of the recession. Indeed, if, as some economists argue, the informal/undocumented labor market in Greater Los Angeles is an efficient and self-regulating market, then why does not this high level of unemployment drive Central Americans to return home? First of all, census data may only poorly reflect the realities of this labor market, which includes so many undocumented workers and so much informal sector work. But even assuming that the data are valid, there is no great mystery here. Central American and Mexican workers in Greater Los Angeles do indeed respond to local labor market signals, but they do so in the context of labor markets in their home countries, where wages are much lower and unemployment much higher. In addition, there are the considerable costs associated with returning to their home country, particularly if they have families here. Therefore, it is quite rational for them to withstand long periods of unemployment—or, more likely, underemployment—without returning home. By the same line of reasoning, it is rational for them to seek work on "the corner," even if they are successful only two or three days a week.

4. The proportion of Salvadoran households receiving public assistance income is 7.1 percent, compared with 16.3 percent of native-born Hispanic households. Calculated from *1990 Census of Population: Persons of Hispanic Origin in the United States,* 153–73.

5. Robert Warren, "Estimates of the Unauthorized Immigrant Population Residing in the United States, by Country of Origin and State of Residence: October 1992," U.S. Immigration and Naturalization Service, April 1994.

6. Segundo Montes, *Las remesas que envian los salvadorenos de Estados Unidos* (San Salvador: UCA Editores, 1990) is among the more complete treatments of the subject; see also Juan Jose Garcia, *El Salvador: Remesas Internacionales y Economia Familiar* (Mexico: CEPAL, 1991). Estimates of total remittances per year by 1990 range from 150 million dollars to 900 million dollars; we suspect the figure is closer to the former, if only family-to-family assistance is counted.

7. The comparable figure for all U.S. Hispanics is 11 percent. Calculated from the *1990 Census of Population: Persons of Hispanic Origin in the United States,* 39–57.

8. Warren, "Estimates of the Unauthorized Immigrant Population."

9. The figures for Greater Los Angeles are derived by multiplying the state figures given by the INS by a proportion equal to the greater Los Angeles portion of the state's Salvadoran and Guatemalan population granted amnesty under IRCA.

10. We arrived at these estimates by combining information from the 1990 census and independent INS estimates of the undocumented population (see notes 1 and 8). The 10 percent undercount adjustment is a conservative figure for these populations in 1990. The net immigration figures come from the INS. More complex methodologies, utilizing data on IRCA legalization and adjusted estimates of the growth of the native-born population, produce population estimates in the same range.

	Salvadorans	Guatemalans
1990 census population count	565,000	269,000
10% undercount adjustment	57,000	27,000
Net immigration 1990–92 (INS)	40,000	29,000
Estimated 1992 population	661,000	325,000
Estimated 1992 undocumented population (INS)	327,000	129,000
Percentage undocumented:	49%	40%

11 *Los Angeles Times,* November 15, 1994, and December 3, 1994.

12 According to the field director of a major Los Angeles survey research organization, in some of the most densely populated Pico-Union census tracts there was almost no correspondence between the residential address lists provided by the Census Bureau and what their researchers found on the ground. Large old houses had been subdivided and then subdivided again, with garages and other outbuildings converted into tiny apartments. Workshops, warehouses, and the storage facilities of commercial buildings were also being used as residences. Alleys led to virtual neighborhoods of tiny apartments. We cannot estimate the prevalence of these hidden residences or the proportion of the Central American population living in them. But their existence should give pause and caution to researchers who fall into the trap of treating census data as if it were an accurate representation of reality.

13 These core areas are defined as places in which contiguous census tracts contain 20 percent or more Central Americans. The Westlake core runs from the Harbor Freeway west to about Crenshaw and includes parts of Koreatown and the mid-Wilshire areas as well as Pico-Union/Westlake. The Hollywood core is to the north and west of Westlake and includes parts of Echo Park.

Asians: The "Model Minority" Deconstructed

Lucie Cheng and Philip Q. Yang

"I THOUGHT I would never say this. But these new immigrants are ruining things for us," Jim Yamada, a third-generation Japanese American, said in disgust. "Asian Americans fought for decades against discrimination and racial prejudice. We want to be treated just like everybody else, like Americans. You see, I get real angry when people come up to me and tell me how good my English is. They say, 'Oh, you have no accent. Where did you learn English?' Where did I learn English? Right here in America. I was born here like they were. We really hated it when people assumed that just because Asian Americans looked different we were foreigners. It took us a long time to get people to see this point, to be sensitized to it. Now the new immigrants are setting us back. People see me now and they automatically treat me as an immigrant. I really hate that. The worst thing is that these immigrants don't understand why I am angry."

"Am I an Asian American? No, I am Vietnamese," Le Tran asserted. "Actually I am Vietnamese-Chinese. I came from Vietnam, but my ancestors were Chinese. Well, now maybe you can call me an Asian American. However, I don't usually identify myself that way." Her ethnic identity proves elusive. Some people tell her only those Asians born in the United States are Asian Americans; others say only Chinese, Japanese, Koreans, and Filipinos are Asian Americans, because their ancestors came here long ago and shared a history of discrimination; still others say one has to have citizenship or at least a green card to be Asian American. "It's all so confusing! Does it matter?" she asked.

"My husband is a *kongzhong feiren* (spaceman or trapeze flier)," sighed Mrs. Li, the wife of a Chinese immigrant engineer turned entrepreneur. "There is no normal family life. But I am glad that he isn't like so many other trapeze fliers who keep a 'wife' in every city." Dr. Li flies between Los Angeles, Taipei, Shenzhen, and Hong Kong every other month, managing a thriving garment manufacturing business. He anticipates tough competition from Taiwan entrepreneurs who are moving their plants to Indonesia to take advantage of cheap labor without the uncertain politics of the People's Republic of China.

These vignettes paint an initial portrait of L.A.'s changing Asian American communities. For Americans of Asian descent, ethnicity seems to have undergone periodic reconstruction. From the early immigration of the nineteenth century to the end of the Second World War, Asians in America identified themselves as distinct ethnic groups: Chinese, Japanese, and Filipinos. Each group was brought to the United States to meet the specific labor needs of the time and suffered the somewhat similar fate of discrimination, restriction, and exclusion. These similar experiences gave rise to a new identity constructed during the Civil Rights era. In order to gain political access, Chinese, Japanese, and Filipinos became "Asian Americans."[1] But no sooner was this new identity established than a new, post-1965 wave of immigrants from Asia coming from a wider range of countries called the concept of Asian American into question. Speaking different languages and engaging in distinct cultural practices, the new immigrants reversed, if only temporarily, the trajectory of pan-Asian integration. Their separate ethnic identities as Chinese, Japanese, Filipino, Indian, Korean, Vietnamese, Cambodian, and so forth strengthen—and are strengthened by—international ties that bind the global political economy.

Between 1970 and 1990, two migration streams from diverse Asian countries converged in Los Angeles.[2] The first was made up of highly educated Asian immigrants who joined the local professional-managerial class, usually on the lower rungs of the ladder, and slowly worked their way up. As new members of this class, which is becoming increasingly international, these immigrants are supported by the second stream, a large group of other Asian immigrants who fill the semiskilled and unskilled jobs in manufacturing and services. While Asian immigrant professionals serve as a link to the most advanced sectors of the world economy, the backward sectors are maintained by less-skilled immigrant labor.

Entrepreneurship is a common characteristic of Asian immigrants, as chapter 7 described. Although traditional Mom-and-Pop stores are still significant in the ethnic economy, Asian entrepreneurial businesses are increasingly diverse in size and scope. They not only fill niches in the local Los Angeles economy but create international business networks as well. For example, Chinese immigrants and Vietnamese refugees have played a unique role in the development of bilateral trade between the United States and their countries of origin, contributing to the privatization of the economy in China and Vietnam as well as to the transformation of businesses in Los Angeles. The restructuring of the world political economy has created not only multinational corporations but also an emerging group of transnational residents whose activities and presence weave together an international network of professional and business people. Asian participation in this network is gaining significance.[3] Once limited to jobs as professionals, entrepreneurs, and low-skilled laborers, Asian immigrants now include a growing number of capitalists looking for investment opportunities in the United States. Not only do their occupations reinforce capitalism as an economic system, but at the same time their influx to the United States and comparatively greater social mobility helps strengthen the capitalist ideology of meritocracy and its ethnoracial variant, the "model minority."[4]

On the other hand, the conditions that Asian immigrants encounter may not long support the optimism with which so many begin. The visibility and high profile of their residential enclaves and occupational niches in particular have tapped into undercurrents of racism and nativism deep in the American psyche. Many Asian Americans maintain that a "glass ceiling" keeps them from getting ahead, and these charges of discrimination have increased over the last decade. Anti-Asian violence has erupted in several major American cities. Alarmed by the resurgence of anti-Asianism, federal and state agencies have begun to monitor racial crime. An upsurge in hostility and discrimination, coupled with the changing Asian demographics, has made Pan-Asian solidarity an issue of necessity and urgency for all groups of Asian descent. Nevertheless, historical rifts and current relations among Asian groups also pose challenges to Asian American identity.

Asian immigrants are victims of racism in two ways. They suffer from discrimination from non-Asians, and yet, at the same time, many discriminate against other racial groups. Coming from very different national backgrounds, often also from more culturally homogeneous societies, some Asian immigrants seem quite intolerant of diversity. Cultural conflict aggravates already strained economic relations between Asians and other disadvantaged minorities. As victims of racism in the first sense, Asians are a progressive force for change. But Asian racism itself threatens to push the community toward conservatism.

This chapter focuses on the diversity of Asian Americans. What significant changes have occurred in the Asian American population in the past three decades? How well do Asians fare, and how do they adapt to the changing social environment? Do Asian experiences challenge or reinforce common stereotypes and concepts such as "model minority" and "glass ceiling" that are thought to be especially applicable to Asian Americans? Finally, what do the changing intergroup relations mean for Asian Americans, for the formation of a Pan-Asian ethnicity or coalition, and for the needs and aspirations of the reconstituted Asian ethnic groups? These are the main questions addressed in the following sections.

IMMIGRATION AND CHANGES IN ETHNIC COMPOSITION

The rapid restructuring of the Pacific Rim political economy, ushered in by a long-term crisis in advanced capitalism, the advent of the global economy, and the challenge of ascending East Asian states, has influenced profoundly the pattern of immigration to the United States in the last two and a half decades.[5] In 1965, fewer than 7 percent of all immigrants to the United States were from Asia. In 1970, the figure rose to 25 percent, and in 1980 to 44 percent. Although Asian immigration continues to rise in the 1990s, official statistics from the Immigration and Naturalization Service show that the Asian share of total immigration during the 1980s dropped to 22 percent. This decline is more illusory than real, however, largely reflecting the results of the 1986 Immigration Reform and Control Act (IRCA), which legalized a largely Mexican and Latin American–origin population, many of whom had arrived in the United States prior to 1982.[6]

Four general features distinguish the new wave of Asian immigration from the old: a larger size, a higher percentage of women, greater ethnic and socioeconomic diversity, and more extensive—as well as intensive—global linkages. These same features characterize Asian immigrants to Los Angeles. The Los Angeles region, a significant gateway of the Pacific Rim and an emerging "global city," is a favorite destination of post-1965 Asian immigration. In this multi-ethnic region, Asians have been the fastest-growing segment of the population over the past two and half decades, largely because of immigration. In 1970, 240,000 Asians lived in Los Angeles, about 2 percent of the total population. By 1990, with over 1.3 million Asians making up 9 percent of the total population, the Los Angeles region was now home to the single largest Asian population in the nation, far surpassing other major Asian centers such as San Francisco-Oakland, Honolulu, and New York. Between 1970 and 1990, the region's Asian population increased by 451 percent, ten times the regional average population growth rate (46 percent) and significantly more than the runner-up, the Latino population, which shot up by 236 percent. In contrast, the black population barely increased (.4 percent), and the white population declined (see chapter 3, especially figure 3.6).

While all Asian groups experienced large increases in absolute size and relative population share, rates varied considerably between 1970 and 1990. The Korean and Indian populations, each beginning with a small base, increased dramatically by more than 1,000 percent, while the already-established Chinese and Filipino groups showed impressive growth, 626 percent and 563 percent, respectively. The Vietnamese, who began to settle in Southern California after North Vietnam's conquest of the South in 1975, increased from 48,320 to 142,890 between 1980 and 1990, a 196 percent growth rate in one decade (see figure 11.1).

Vietnamese are the largest of several groups whose presence became visible after 1970. Cambodians and Laotians were also absent from the region before the American involvement in the Vietnam War and internal strife on the Indochinese peninsula led to their arrival. Korean immigration began in the early twentieth century in small numbers and increased after the Korean War, as war brides and orphans adopted by Americans arrived. It was not until 1965, the year in which the discriminatory national-origins quota system was abolished, that Koreans began moving to the United States in larger numbers. The change in immigration law also affected established groups such as the Chinese, Japanese, and Filipinos, whose foreign-born populations consist mostly of post-1965 immigrants. Most of the foreign-born Asians came after the enactment of the 1965 Immigration Act. In particular, almost all foreign-born Vietnamese, Koreans, and Asian Indians arrived after 1965.

The new immigration also ended the demographic predominance of the Japanese in transforming Asian American Los Angeles into a multi-ethnic community. In 1970, the Japanese, accounting for 51 percent of the region's Asian population, were the largest and dominant group. But with fewer immigrants and a low fertility rate, the Japanese lost their top-ranking position; no single dominant group replaced them in the new mix of Asian groups that emerged over the next two decades. By 1990, the Koreans stood third (with 14 percent of the region's Asian population), following the Chinese, with 23 percent, and the Filipinos, with 22 percent. Japanese, Vietnamese, and other Asians each accounted for somewhat more than 10 percent of the total Asian population in 1990.

The influx of new immigrants also reversed the earlier demographic dominance of the native-born, as figure 11.2 shows. In 1970, 57 percent of the Asian population in Los Angeles was made up of Americans by birth; twenty years later, they accounted for only 31 percent. From 1980 on, the foreign-born made up the majority of every Asian group except the Japanese. For almost all groups, the proportion of the foreign-born significantly increased from 1970 to 1980, but the increase slowed down in the next decade, and for the Vietnamese and Koreans the proportion even declined. A relatively youthful female immigrant population and lower immigration rates may both have contributed to this change.

Although early Chinese, Japanese, Filipino, and Korean American communities were largely bachelor societies, the situation changed after 1965, when U.S. immigration policies were revised to favor family reunification and large numbers of female immigrants began coming from Asia to Los Angeles. The large influx of Asian women generated nearly balanced sex ratios for the major Asian communities, which now have slightly higher

FIGURE 11.1 | Growth of Asian Population, Los Angeles Region, 1970–1990

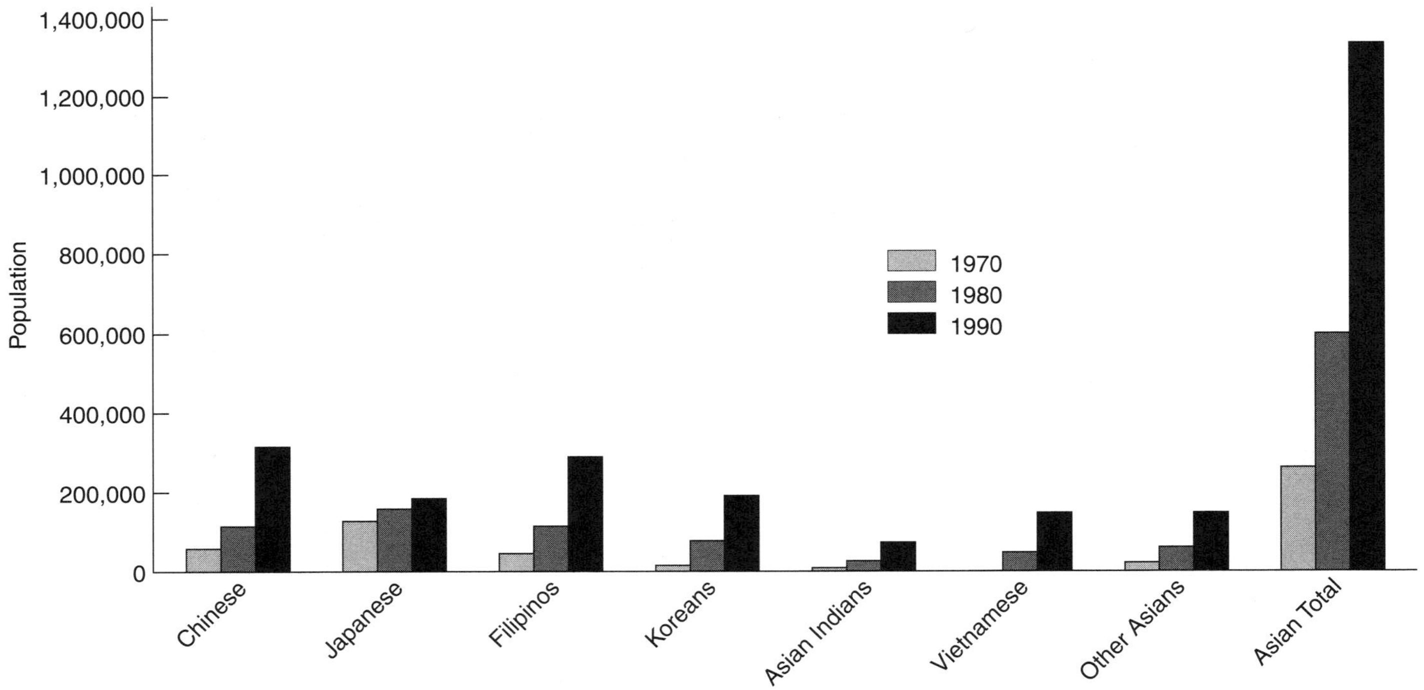

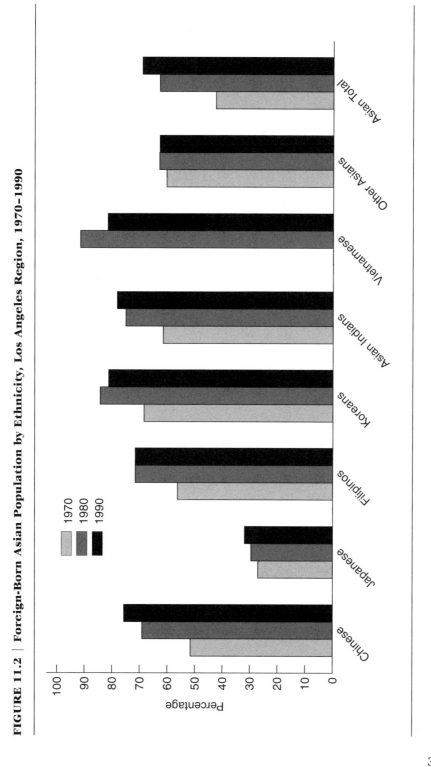

FIGURE 11.2 | **Foreign-Born Asian Population by Ethnicity, Los Angeles Region, 1970–1990**

311

proportions of females than males. The future sizes and compositions of the Asian populations will surely reflect the current ages of women immigrants admitted during the last two decades.

THE "MODEL MINORITY": IMAGE AND REALITY

The phenomenal surge of Asian immigration and the resulting changes in ethnic composition have hardly tarnished the image of Asian Americans as a "model minority." This portrayal began in the mid-1960s at a time of massive racial upheaval; the term was first used by the press to depict Japanese Americans who were struggling to enter the mainstream of American life and to laud Chinese Americans for their remarkable accomplishments.[7] These accounts conveyed the message that Japanese and Chinese Americans had achieved great success by overcoming discrimination with determination and hard work. Later extended to Asian Americans as a group,[8] the label filtered into college textbooks, where it further promoted the image of Asian Americans as minorities who "made it" in this "land of opportunity."

Ever since its inception, the model minority thesis has been a subject of considerable controversy, especially from critics who have argued that the image is racially stereotypic, empirically inaccurate, and no longer applicable to the changing Asian American population.[9] In their view, the label is also objectionable for its political implications, which cast America as a fair, open society and a real land of opportunity, where minorities can make it as long as they work hard. The concept thus counters the black militant claim that America is fundamentally a racist society, structured to keep minorities in a subordinate position. By extolling Asian Americans as a model minority, this critical literature asserts, the established world hopes to set a standard of behavior for other minorities.

Despite an unending barrage of attacks, the model minority image has persisted into the 1990s, quite alive if not entirely unscathed. The supporting literature often begins by citing the educational achievements of Asian Americans reported in data from the 1980 and earlier censuses.[10] Statistics for Los Angeles confirm the pattern of high levels of education and disproportionate representation in universities and colleges but demonstrate significant variations across groups. Compared with native-born non-Asian groups, U.S.-born Asians as a whole had higher levels of educational achievement in each census year. In 1990, for example, the average native-born Asian adult reported 14.2 years of schooling, the highest among all broad ethnic groups. Not all groups of native-born Asians were equally well-educated, however. While Chinese, Japanese, Koreans, and Asian Indians ranked ahead of native-born whites, Filipinos fell slightly behind and Vietnamese and other Asians fell substantially behind whites, with educational levels similar to or lower than those of native-born blacks and Hispanics. As a whole, Asian immigrants were less well-educated than their native-born coethnics. Though relatively small at the beginning of 1970, the immigrant-native gap widened in successive years, so that by 1990, the average Asian immigrant was slightly less well-schooled than the average native-white, a reversal of the pattern from twenty years before. As average schooling levels for most Asian immigrant groups either improved or stayed the same between 1970 and 1990, the slight decline in average education for the entire Asian group seems largely due to two factors: the influx of poorly educated Vietnamese and other Indochinese in the 1980s; and the arrival of female immigrants, whose educational levels were generally lower than those of their male counterparts (Filipinas excepted).

Data on the percentage distributions of educational level by ethnicity and nativity in 1990 (table 11.1) further substantiate the phenomenal accomplishments of Asian Americans in higher education, but again with great variation. Among native-born Asians every group outpaced native whites in completion of the college degree. Of particular note, is the disparity between Chinese Americans, among whom 65 percent had finished college, and native whites, among whom 31 percent had finished college. Japanese Americans, the other large group of native-born, also ranked well ahead of whites on this count, as did all the other smaller groups.

A similar pattern held up among immigrants, though with considerably greater variation. Once again, rates of college completion among all Asian groups substantially exceeded whites', Vietnamese excepted; even among the Vietnamese, almost half reported some college or more. At the other end of the spectrum, the immigrants were also underrepresented among the ranks of the poorly schooled with a high school degree or less, pointing to the continued selectivity of Asian immigration to Los Angeles; again, only the Vietnamese exceeded whites on this count.

While the schooling profile of adult Asian Americans shows some unevenness, a look at the educational performance of the younger generations erases any doubt. When it comes to school achievement and attainment, Asians leave all other groups far behind in the dust; and that generalization holds for *all* Asian ethnic groups, regardless of nativity and generational status, which we have broken down by adding a 1.5 generation to capture those immigrants who came as children under the age of ten. As table 11.2 shows, Asian teenagers aged 16–19 drop out of high school at a rate that is either under or comparable to the rate for whites; only Vietnamese and Filipino immigrants, who lag behind whites on so many other indicators, do worse on this count, by exactly one percentage point. At a slightly older age, Asians of every group—Vietnamese immigrants excepted—are more likely to complete high school than whites. As for college attendance, the Asian advantage is truly outstanding; every Asian ethnic and nativity group, with the exception of Filipino immigrants, surpasses whites in this

TABLE 11.1 | Distribution of Educational Attainment, Los Angeles Region, 1990 (Persons Aged 25 and Over)

	No School/Nursery (%)	Elementary School (%)	Some High School (%)	High School Graduate (%)	Some College (%)	College Degree or More (%)	Total
Asian							
Chinese							
FB	5.5	8.3	9.5	14.1	22.4	40.2	100.0
NB	1.2	0.7	2.0	7.5	23.2	65.4	100.0
Japanese							
FB	2.0	1.6	6.1	26.7	28.5	35.1	100.0
NB	0.3	0.5	3.1	17.1	35.1	43.9	100.0
Filipino							
FB	0.6	2.9	3.8	10.6	28.2	53.9	100.0
NB	0.7	0.9	7.3	19.3	39.4	32.4	100.0
Korean, FB	2.6	3.7	6.8	23.8	25.0	38.1	100.0
Indian, FB	2.3	3.2	8.1	12.2	19.0	55.2	100.0
Vietnamese, FB	7.3	9.3	19.4	15.4	30.3	18.4	100.0
Other ethnic groups							
White, NB	0.3	0.9	8.1	22.0	37.9	30.8	100.0
Black, NB	0.8	2.5	16.6	24.8	39.6	15.8	100.1
Hispanics							
NB	1.5	6.6	23.2	27.9	30.7	10.0	100.0
FB	10.4	38.1	20.8	13.5	12.4	4.8	100.0

TABLE 11.2 | Educational Attendance and Completion Levels, Select Groups, Los Angeles Region, 1990

	Japanese (%)	Chinese (%)	Vietnamese (%)	Filipino (%)	Korean (%)	Asian Indian (%)	Mexican (%)	White[a] (%)
High school dropouts, aged 16–19								
First generation	3	6	9	9	6	6	58	6
1.5 generation	N/A	2	5	4	4	5	23	6
Native-born	3	0	5	3	3	0	15	8
High school dropouts, aged 18–24								
First generation	5	7	16	9	6	7	64	8
1.5 generation	1	4	6	4	3	3	38	9
Native-born	4	2	9	8	3	2	25	11
College attendance, aged 18–24								
First generation	64	64	49	40	52	51	8	42
1.5 generation	54	60	60	61	71	69	21	40
Native-born	59	79	53	55	71	71	28	38

[a]White foreign-born and 1.5 generation are immigrants born in Europe or Canada.

315

respect. Chinese Americans attend college at twice the white rate, and native-born Asian Indians and Koreans are not that far behind. Numbers like these account for the growing Asian presence in higher education, so easily seen on the campuses of the elite universities of the Los Angeles region. In 1993, for instance, Asians accounted for 32 percent of the undergraduate students at UCLA, 20 percent at USC, and 23 percent at Caltech—rates that pointed to two- to threefold Asian overrepresentation among elite undergraduate ranks.

Several theories have been offered to explain the success of Asians in school. One earlier explanation attributed this success to the Confucian culture that prevails in many Asian societies. This view emphasizes a cultural reverence for learning and scholarly achievements and its role in shaping parental behavior. Parents urge their children to study longer hours, reward them for doing well in school, and emphasize the importance of education for social mobility; consequently, Asian students are motivated or compelled to learn and succeed. A second explanation accentuates the role of stable Asian American families, which provide a good learning environment for educational success. The selectivity of highly educated Asian immigrants is also a factor.[11] Although these explanations have merit, they do not capture all the important determinants. We argue that the social environment in the receiving country is an essential consideration. In a society dominated by whites, where racial minorities often must find their own special channels of social mobility, education has been a primary route for many minority groups. In other words, the reception context in the United States forces Asian immigrants and their native-born children to pursue higher levels of education as a means of upward mobility. It is the combination of culture, family, selectivity of immigration, and the receiving context that determines the remarkable educational achievements of Asian Americans.

The occupational mobility of Asian Americans is another piece of evidence often cited in support of the model minority thesis. Historically, Asians tended to be clustered at physically difficult, low-prestige, and low-paying occupations; Chinese often worked as laundrymen or small restaurateurs, Japanese as gardeners and farmers. But after the Second World War, the occupational status of Asians gradually improved. Previous studies have shown Asians climbing the occupational ladder with such success that the native-born Chinese and Japanese had reached or almost achieved parity with whites.[12] The Los Angeles data shown in table 11.3 demonstrate the significant progress that Asians have made over the past two decades.

Employment in high-skill occupations (HSOs)—here defined as professional, managerial, and technical occupations—went up significantly among native-born Angelenos of all ethnic stripes between 1970 and 1990, reflecting the area's transition to a high-tech, high-information economy. But even within this comparative frame, the performance of native-born

TABLE 11.3 | **Percentage of Selected Ethnic Groups in High-Skill and Low-Skill Occupations, Los Angeles Region, 1970–1990 (Employed Persons Aged 25–64)**

	High-Skill Occupations			Low-Skill Occupations		
	1970 (%)	1980 (%)	1990 (%)	1970 (%)	1980 (%)	1990 (%)
Native-born						
Asians	36	39	50	28	20	14
Chinese	39	58	69	23	11	7
Japanese	36	38	51	29	21	12
Koreans	35	28	50	23	25	14
Filipinos	31	30	39	36	21	20
Asian Indians	N/A	58	50	N/A	21	17
Vietnamese	N/A	N/A	41	N/A	33	39
Other Asians	33	24	29	33	31	25
Whites	34	39	44	23	18	15
Blacks	16	24	31	49	36	28
Hispanics	13	19	25	49	40	31
Foreign-born						
Asians	35	38	39	40	25	22
Chinese	45	47	43	41	27	21
Japanese	22	36	41	56	33	24
Koreans	N/A	29	31	N/A	33	20
Filipinos	26	39	41	34	21	20
Asian Indians	N/A	58	52	N/A	12	13
Vietnamese	N/A	30	32	N/A	36	33
Other Asians	N/A	27	32	N/A	31	25
Hispanics	8	9	10	66	62	59

NOTE: High-skill occupations include managerial, professional, and technical and related workers, while low-skill occupations include private household workers, service workers, operatives, transportation workers, laborers, and farm workers.

Asians remains impressive. Although the then-small population of native-born Asians held a lead over all other groups in 1970, they pulled farther ahead over the next decades until by 1990 almost half the region's Asian Americans had moved into HSOs. As with the other indicators that we examine, the high overall average conceals considerable intra-Asian diversity. The Chinese American lead over whites opened up dramatically after 1970; Japanese American progress, also dramatic, pales only in comparison with the Chinese American record. On the other hand, Filipinos were doing somewhat worse than native whites in 1970 and lagged further behind in 1990, which meant that the intra-Asian disparity in HSO employment had widened still further.

Looking at the bottom of the occupational spectrum shows that the Asian migration to the L.A. region does indeed contain a proletarian component, but one that has diminished in relative terms over time. In 1970, the Asian immigrants of the L.A. region were a good deal more likely than native whites to be employed in low-skill occupations (LSOs, here defined as all blue-collar occupations, craft excepted, as well as service and farm jobs). By 1990, the proportion of Asian immigrants in LSOs was still larger than that of whites, but the massive immigration notwithstanding, the gap was a good deal smaller than it had been two decades before. In fact, in 1990 the immigrant concentration in LSOs was modest not just in comparison with the overwhelmingly blue-collar Latino immigrants but in comparison with native African Americans and Latinos as well.

Still, not every group of Asian immigrants was equally successful in escaping from the region's humbler jobs. As expected, Asian Indians were the least likely to work in LSOs; just as predictably, Vietnamese reported the largest concentration of LSO employment. Nonetheless, Vietnamese had managed to reduce their dependence on LSOs during the 1980s, even though this same period saw a large influx of Vietnamese newcomers who were less well qualified than those who had come before. And the 1990 rate of Vietnamese employment in LSOs made them more or less comparable with native-born Hispanics and African Americans; since Vietnamese were the most disadvantaged of the region's Asian immigrant groups, this fact alone tells us something about how well the others were doing.

In explaining the occupational patterns of Asian Americans, researchers have pointed to cultural factors, such as an ethic of hard work.[13] The current literature is critical of cultural explanations, emphasizing instead structural factors or socioeconomic characteristics of immigrants. More recent research shows that the occupational status of Asian Americans is associated with their human capital (for example, education), physical capital (money brought to the United States by immigrants from abroad) and social capital (such as ethnic networks, occupational niches, and ethnic enclaves). The social origins of contemporary Asian immigrants, most notably their tendency to come from better educated and more urban segments of their home societies, may also contribute to their current occupational status.[14]

The high average income levels of Asian Americans provide the most powerful evidence for the model minority thesis. The past three censuses show that, for the country as a whole, Asians have significantly higher levels of median household income than all other broad ethnic groups. But median household income may be a misleading indicator, since Asian families have more workers per household than white families and since Asians tend to be concentrated in a few large metropolitan areas where incomes, as well as costs of living, are higher than the national average.[15] In an effort to control for regional location, Paul Ong and Suzanne Hee compared the 1989 median incomes of non-Hispanic whites with those of Asian and Pacific

Islanders both nationally and within the combined four metropolitan areas that have the largest Asian Pacific American populations (Los Angeles, San Francisco, Oakland, and New York).[16] Asian Pacific Americans did have a higher average median household income ($36,000) than whites ($31,000) for the county as a whole, but the order was reversed ($40,000 for whites and $37,200 for Asian Pacific Americans) for the four metropolitan areas.[17]

The evidence from Los Angeles—which eliminates the influence of differences in the regional distribution of Asians and whites and therefore makes our contrast groups directly comparable—yields a picture that differs from Ong and Hee's. In 1989, median family income among the native-born Asians ($48,221) put them significantly ahead of native-born whites ($43,220) and even further ahead of other native-born groups (see table 11.4). Disaggregation by ethnicity shows that native-born Japanese, Chinese, and Filipinos, the numerically larger groups, fared much better than their white counterparts, while the much less numerous (and presumably

TABLE 11.4 | Median Household Income, Los Angeles Region, 1979–1989

	1979 ($)	1989 ($)
Foreign-born		
All Asians	33,302	40,449
Chinese	34,466	38,427
Japanese	27,574	38,677
Koreans	29,732	34,382
Filipinos	41,366	50,056
Asian Indians	39,979	48,539
Vietnamese	21,553	35,564
Other Asians	31,546	33,371
Hispanics	23,277	26,494
Native-born		
All Asians	40,350	48,221
Chinese	40,315	49,146
Japanese	43,993	51,067
Koreans	35,451	37,871
Filipinos	33,036	45,082
Asian Indians	N/A	N/A
Vietnamese	N/A	N/A
Other Asians	31,546	40,197
Hispanics	29,576	35,107
Whites	35,000	43,220
Blacks	21,554	26,386

younger) Koreans lagged behind. Asian immigrants as a whole fared much better than Hispanic immigrants and even native-born Hispanics and blacks. Foreign-born Filipinos and Asian Indians especially outperformed other groups, since many of them were highly educated. Similar patterns obtained in 1979.

As we have noted, white/Asian differences in the number of adults working per family help explain why Asians tend to outrank whites in median family income. According to the 1990 census, native-born Asian families contained an average of 1.5 adults who worked, as opposed to 1.2 persons for native-born white families; similarly, foreign-born Asian families had an average of 1.6 working adults, as compared with 1.1 working adults in foreign-born white families.

If the Asian lead in median family income is consistent with the model minority thesis, a look at personal earnings confounds it. Most groups of Asian men do worse than whites, a result consistent with Ong and Hee's. But caution is needed before we decide that Asians have indeed fallen behind on the wage front, since the prevalence of newcomers, who undoubtedly need time to learn the ropes and gain the specific skills needed by the region's employers, may well drag average earnings down. Untangling the question is complicated further by the diverse ethnic and nativity mix of the region's Asian groups, making it difficult to grasp the picture as a whole.

In effect, two competing hypotheses offer interpretations of the Asian wage lag. The discrimination hypothesis suggests that Asians, while often highly skilled, confront a different structure of rewards than do their white counterparts, lagging behind comparable whites because employers treat the two groups differently. In contrast, the immigrant hypothesis suggests that for the foreign-born it is all a matter of adjustment; with time and the acquisition of better English skills and other proficiencies specific to the U.S. labor market, Asian immigrants receive their just desserts.

We attempted to assess these hypotheses by adjusting for the labor market, family, and individual characteristics that affect earnings, giving Asians the average characteristics of native whites, and then seeing how doing so affects the mean earnings of persons who made at least $1,000 in the year prior to the relevant census year. The answer, as one might expect, differs by nativity, ethnicity, and gender. Among men, native-born Asians do worse than native-whites; adjustment has virtually no effect on Asian earnings, since for the most part native-born Asian men possess the characteristics associated with higher earnings. The earnings of native-born Asian women in 1969 and 1979 surpassed those of native-born whites; adjustment brings Asian earnings down to about parity with whites, suggesting some slight advantages of Asians over whites. The Asian advantage diminished over time, however, so that in 1989 the adjusted earnings of Asian women fell largely below those of whites. Thus, the situation among the native-born, men in particular, generally supports the discrimination hypothesis, indicating the handicapped market position of Asians (see figure 11.3).

The immigrant story, however, reads differently and needs to be looked at in a somewhat different manner. Figure 11.4 shows that time, measured as length of settlement in the United States, clearly matters, as can be seen from the raw data for all Asian groups combined. The newest cohorts did

FIGURE 11.3 | **Earnings Gap Between Native-Born Asians and Native-Born Whites, Los Angeles Region, 1969–1989**

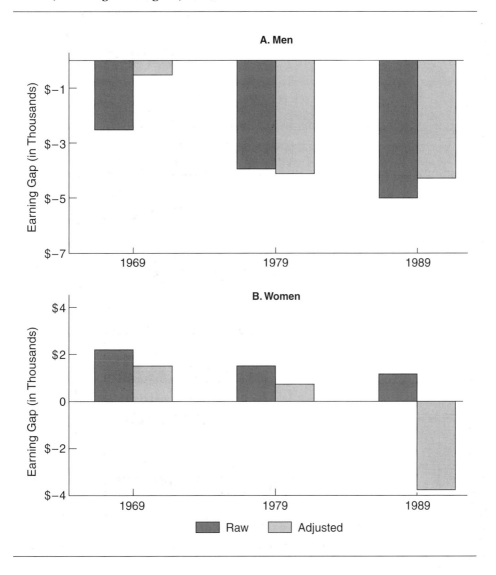

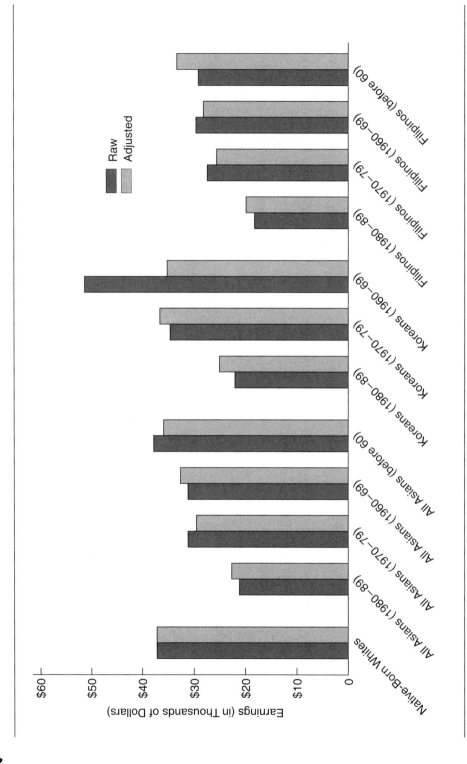

FIGURE 11.4 | Earnings of Native-Born White Males and Selected Groups of Asian Immigrant Males, Los Angeles Region, 1989

much worse than native whites, and the earlier cohorts did better. To be sure, not every individual group experienced the beneficial effect of time in quite the same way; Filipinos, for example, registered modest progress, with men in the cohort of the 1960s still doing worse than whites in 1989, whereas Koreans of the same cohort charged ahead, greatly outdistancing whites in 1989 (see figure 11.4).

But time is not the only attribute that counts; immigrants' labor market and familial characteristics should make them better earners than whites; but giving the older cohorts of immigrants the characteristics of whites pushed immigrant earnings down, indicating that comparable immigrants and whites are not rewarded equally. (For details on the adjustment procedure, see appendix.) Hence, immigrants have a double burden to bear: the time needed to learn the ropes and discriminatory treatment that persists even after they gain the skills and experience that employers want.

A similar view emerges when we trace cohorts over time, though the small size of the populations in place as of the 1960s prevents extensive disaggregations (see figure 11.5). In 1969, men in the 1960s cohort were doing a good deal worse than native whites; the adjustment procedure did little to alter earnings. While earnings for men in the 1960s cohort improved over the next two decades, with the result that Asians had outdistanced whites by 1989, the adjustment yields a continued lag, suggesting that Asian immigrant men were not rewarded for education and experience at the same rate as native whites. By 1989, however, the women of this cohort had surpassed their white counterparts, both before and after any adjustment, evidence of gender differences in the opportunity structures.

Generalizing from older to newer cohorts can be hazardous, since the newer cohorts may not resemble their predecessors and in any case move into a labor market transformed by the increased immigrant presence. The data provide some suggestion of erosion; compared with subsequent cohorts at comparable periods of time, the 1960s cohort seems to have done somewhat better in the first decade of residence, though small numbers make any such conclusion tentative (see figure 11.6). Moreover, the 1980s cohort seems to be doing worse than the 1970s cohort at the end of the first decade of residence—as one might have expected, given the tremendous expansion in immigrant numbers and the immigrant convergence on a limited number of occupations and industries.

It must be noted that reality is more complex than the simplifying metaphors that shape the public discourse about the Asian American experience. The model minority concept is not without its virtues; historically, it helped turn around the negative stereotypes of Asian Americans and enhanced the positive image of Asian Americans, and empirically it is consistent with Asian Americans' advantageous position, relative to other minorities if not always to native whites. On the other hand, discrimination still inhibits Asian American progress. Many Asian Americans could be doing

FIGURE 11.5 | **Earnings Gap Between Asian Immigrants of the 1960s and Native-Born Whites, Los Angeles Region, 1969–1989**

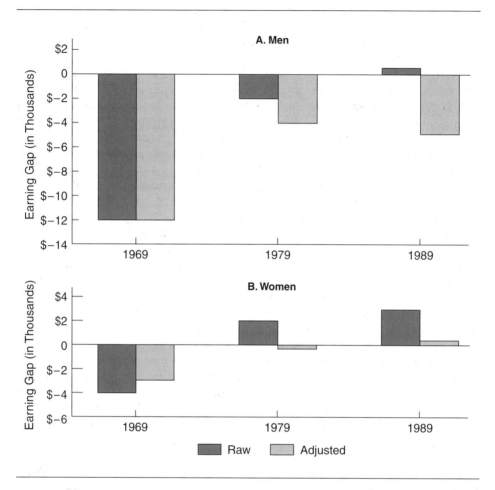

even better, were it not for the persistent effects of discrimination. Diversity further complicates the picture; newcomers abound among today's Asian Angelenos, and these new arrivals are paying a sizable penalty as they struggle to get ahead. But perhaps the most fatal criticism is that the various ethnic groups do not seem to be progressing at comparable rates, no matter how hard they try. The variation suggests that there is no single model minority, but rather an aggregate of groups undergoing very different fates.

TRAJECTORIES OF ADAPTATION

Thus, diversity is the hallmark of Asian American Los Angeles. In this section, we seek to account for that diversity and identify its most important

FIGURE 11.6 | Earnings Gap Between Asian Immigrants in the First Decade of Migration and Native-Born Whites, Los Angeles Region, 1969–1989

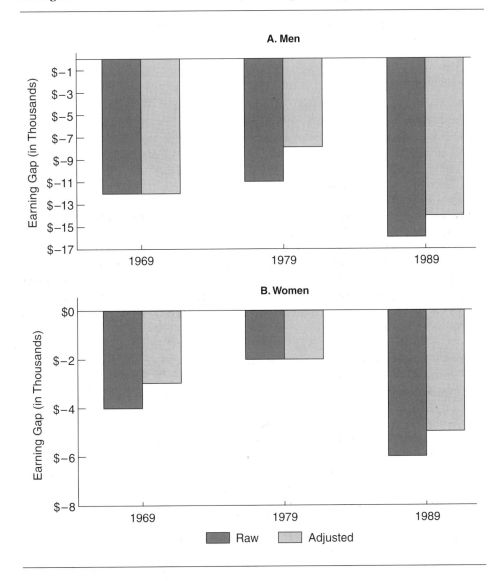

axes. As most Asian Angelenos are immigrants, their origins and the circumstances of their departure from their home countries are likely to explain a large part of the variation in their current status. Asians, especially Asian immigrants, fall into five main categories: professionals, entrepreneurs, capitalists, workers, and refugees. Each type has followed a distinct path of adaptation, and each ethnic group tends toward one or more of these categories. Some groups are relatively successful, while others are not. The varying experiences in initial immigration largely determine the paths and outcomes of adaptation and incorporation; we therefore focus on how Asians have adapted to the social environment under different patterns of initial entry.

Professionals

The large presence of professional workers does much to account for Asians' relative success. Not only do professionals raise the average socio-economic status of their particular ethnic group, but they play an important role in the success of their children and communities as a whole. In 1990, 25 percent of Asians aged 25–64 in the Los Angeles region were professionals, compared with 24 percent of whites, 19 percent of blacks, and 8 percent of Hispanics. Note that the number of Asians with professional training is doubtless even greater, since those who cannot find professional employment in the United States are excluded from the professional category in the census. In particular, professionals were overrepresented among Asian Indians (33.7 percent), Japanese (27.9 percent), Chinese (27.4 percent), and Filipinos (27.5 percent). Although some Asian professionals were native-born (mainly Japanese, and some Chinese and Filipinos), the majority (76.8 percent) immigrated from abroad, primarily from the Philippines, India, mainland China, Taiwan, and Korea.

Studies of the "brain drain" have demonstrated the causal connections between this phenomenon and the differences between sending and receiving countries in terms of living standards, research conditions, and professional employment opportunities. Recent studies further pinpoint the important role of international economic interdependency and articulation of higher education in determining the flows of immigrant professionals.[18] In the context of the immigration of Asian professionals, several factors may be important. The economic involvement of the United States in Asian Pacific countries has created opportunities for Asian professional migration. Furthermore, American influence on the education systems and curricula of Asian countries, along with the exchange of students and scholars, has forged a pool of professionals who are employable in the United States. The so-called educational surplus—that is, the production of college graduates in excess of demand for them—also motivates the migration of higher-skilled persons. The Philippines, for example, produces far more college graduates than its labor market can absorb, and with skills not entirely relevant to the needs of an agricultural economy; the same phenomenon occurs in the Indian subcontinent. In both instances the result is the exodus of professionals. Changes in U.S. immigration policy that favor the immigration of professional and technical workers and allow foreign students to adjust their resident status upon finding a permanent job in the United States have also facilitated the immigration of Asian professionals.

The factors affecting the flow of professionals may not always remain the same, however. Prior to the 1980s, low income and living standards prompted most foreign students from Asia to remain in the United States permanently after the completion of their education. In recent years, economic and political conditions in Taiwan and Korea have greatly improved, leading Taiwanese and Korean graduates of U.S. universities to return to their homelands in increasing numbers.

We detect at least two patterns of adaptation among Asian immigrant professionals in the Los Angeles region. In one pattern, immigrants begin in lower-level slots somehow connected to their original specialization and gradually move up the occupational ladder and back into the profession for which they trained earlier. This tortured road to success reflects immigrant selectivity, since immigrant professionals come from the upper, not the lower, ranks of their peers back home. They immigrate to the United States not to escape unemployment and poverty but to improve their careers and well-being. In the first few years after their arrival, many experience downward occupational mobility, because they lack U.S. labor market experience and English language competence. Scientists or researchers are relegated to jobs as lab technicians or assistants, university faculty become high school or elementary school teachers, and doctors work as nurses or assistants. Their salaries are not commensurate with their human capital. After a sufficient period of time, some Asian professionals gain recognition and get established, while others achieve higher status through additional schooling and extraordinarily hard work.

A second pattern of integration involves a temporary or permanent shift out of the professions. Some professionals move to a new occupation because it is more profitable or enjoyable, but others do so because they cannot find jobs in their field, in some cases finding themselves forced to do menial work. For example, a volleyball coach at the provincial level in China became a cleanup man at the UCLA hospital, a senior doctor was a babysitter, an engineer watched the gate of a swap meet, and a university teacher became a waiter. In time, such downwardly mobile professionals move up, but many never return to their original occupations or positions.

Whether they move right into professions upon arrival in the United States or do so after a detour into more menial jobs, Asian professionals follow the typical immigrant path of moving into ethnic concentrations or clusters. Asian niches abound throughout the region's various professional and semiprofessional occupations, with Asians often constituting a very significant proportion of the entire work force. In their range and type, the Asian professional clusters are no different in terms of immigrant density from the traditional immigrant pursuits, but they are distinctive in the types of work and remuneration they involve. Thus, Asians make up more than one-third of the region's pharmacists and chemists, more than one-quarter of the dentists, and more than one-fifth of the physicians, accountants, computer programmers, electrical engineers, and civil engineers, to cite a few notable examples. Of course, not every Asian group moves into professional niches such as these. Filipinos are much more likely to concentrate in the health care sector and its semiprofessions; 16 percent of the region's nurses are of Filipino origin, as are 18 percent of its lab technicians. Those groups with origins in refugee flows are less likely to move into high-level clusters. Still, Vietnamese immigrants are considerably overrepresented among the ranks of computer programmers and electrical engineers, perhaps a sign of better things to come.

Movement into the professions brings its rewards. In 1989, the average Asian immigrant physician made over $100,000, the average dentist $58,000, and the average electrical engineer $43,000. Some occupations, like dentistry or medicine, allow for self-employment, but most professionals find themselves working as cogs in vast bureaucratic organizations, where they soon encounter the glass ceiling that prevents them from moving to the top rung of the job ladder, especially into management positions. As time passes, these immigrant professionals discover that America seemed to want them for their skills and work ethic as employees but not for their assertiveness and ambition as bosses. The land of opportunity is far more limited than they had expected, and contrary to what they have been taught, meritocracy is not color-blind. Many seek to compensate for their race by outperforming their peers. Working longer hours and carrying out jobs beyond the call of duty, they ironically provide support for the "model minority" stereotype and harden the glass ceiling. In so doing, they alienate their native-born sisters and brothers and drive a wedge between Asians and other minorities.

The problem of the glass ceiling is commonly perceived by Asian professionals. Asian Americans for Community Involvement (AACI) surveyed more than three hundred white-collar Asian American professionals in Silicon Valley and found that 80 percent believed Asian Americans to be underrepresented in upper management and that concerns about the glass ceiling increased with age and experience. The respondents felt that Equal Employment Opportunity (EEO) Programs had very little effect at this level; among those whose employers had EEO programs in place, about two-thirds stated that Asian Americans were underrepresented in middle and upper management. Many respondents felt that their employers perceived them as "modern-day, high-tech coolies"—hardworking, diligent employees but not potential managers. The AACI report concluded, "Regrettably, Asian Americans are still a long way off from adequate management representation in corporate boardrooms and executive suites, in educational institutions, and in government agencies."[19] The analysis of census data discussed in the previous section provides considerable support for this point of view.

Asian Americans still have a long way to go before they reach full socioeconomic, legal, and political equality in this country.

Entrepreneurs

Entrepreneurship, usually measured by self-employment, has been described as a characteristic avenue of adaptation and social mobility of Asian Americans. As figure 11.7 indicates, in the Los Angeles region Asian immigrants are much more likely to be entrepreneurs than their native-born counterparts; for most Asian immigrant groups, the trend in self-employment lies on an upward curve. Not all Asian groups are equally interested in running their own businesses, however. Small business tends not to engage Filipinos, in particular. By contrast, the Koreans' propensity for entrepreneurship is now well known.[20] Almost a quarter of Korean immigrants were working for themselves in 1980 and more than a third in 1990, testifying to the ability of Koreans to expand their economic base through self-employment.

The firms run by Korean immigrant entrepreneurs in Los Angeles tend to be small, to use family members or a few employees, and to be concentrated in retail trade, manufacturing, and services.[21] Like professionals, the self-employed establish niches. The liquor trade is prototypical, a site of extraordinary Korean overrepresentation (by a factor of twenty-three) and for that reason a particularly poignant point in the Koreans' troubled relationship with the blacks. All the leading Korean industrial niches provide extraordinary opportunities for self-employment, from the low point in apparel, where 22 percent of Koreans work for themselves, to the high point in laundering, where 74 percent of Koreans work on their own account. As these business lines would suggest, self-employment is not easy work, and Korean immigrant business owners work long hours indeed. But as chapter 7 has already shown, Koreans earn a significant self-employment bonus; those who work for themselves do much better than their compatriots employed in wage and salary jobs, even after controlling for differences in human capital and hours spent on the job.

The Chinese, especially immigrants, also had relatively higher rates of self-employment than other groups in all three census years shown in figure 11.7. Chinese-owned businesses are concentrated in Chinatown, Monterey Park, and the San Gabriel Valley, though Chinese restaurants are found throughout Los Angeles. Chinese firms vary in size, from husband-wife stores to businesses employing more than a hundred workers. In addition to serving their local communities, Chinese immigrant entrepreneurs also play an active role in bridging the United States, their home countries, and other Pacific Rim countries through import-export trade, remittances, and foreign investment. Although the Chinese persist in some of the traditional ethnic trades such as restaurants, there are new business specializations—

FIGURE 11.7 | **Self-Employment Rates by Nativity and Ethnicity, Los Angeles Region, 1970–1990**

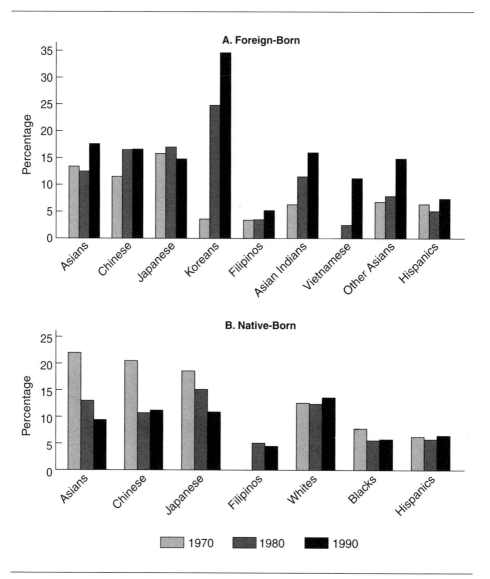

for example, engineering, computers, and data processing—that stand out from the type of businesses that Koreans pursue. Overall, self-employment is a lucrative pursuit, giving Chinese entrepreneurs a substantial earnings advantage over their counterparts still working for others, as chapter 7 has shown.

Capitalists

Capitalists are entrepreneurs with sizable capital. We single them out for analysis because of their growing significance. In the past, Asians seldom immigrated to the United States as investors or capitalists, but as a result of the rapid economic growth in Japan, South Korea, Taiwan, and Hong Kong in the past three decades and most recently in mainland China, along with the passage of the 1990 Immigration Act, a new category of Asian immigrants—capitalists or investors—has emerged. Among this group are Japanese, Koreans, and Taiwanese who want to make a fortune in the United States and Hong Kong Chinese who are fearful of the colony's return to Chinese rule in 1997.

The Immigration Act of 1990 authorized the granting of permanent residency to foreign nationals who make a minimum $1 million investment in a business employing at least ten workers in the United States. In rural or high-unemployment areas, the investment can be as little as $500,000. The act took effect on October 1, 1991. As of September 30, 1992, seventy-three millionaire immigrants had been admitted, among whom fifty-eight, or 80 percent, were Asians, with thirty from Taiwan (the leading country), six from Pakistan, five from India, five from Macau, three from Hong Kong, and one from South Korea, and the rest from other Asian countries. While the number of Asian millionaire immigrants is expected to grow in the foreseeable future, many other wealthy Asians, not quite in the millionaire category, have invested and settled in the Los Angeles region. For instance, Monterey Park, the first suburban Chinatown in the United States, has attracted a significant number of wealthy Chinese immigrants. According to Li-Pei Wu, Chairman of General Bank, it is not unusual for families—mainly those from Taiwan—to bring $200,000 or more to Southern California for investment. Indeed, the 1990 census showed that the Chinese have already established a concentration in security investments—perhaps the first instance of an immigrant niche in finance capitalism.

The adaptation pattern of this category of Asian immigrants is little known, although we may expect it to differ greatly from those of other immigrants. These immigrants are rich, resourceful, and self-employed, but they may still lack knowledge of U.S. laws, market experience, and English ability and therefore may run the risk of losing money, going bankrupt, or becoming involved in legal troubles. An incident reported by the *Los Angeles Times* serves as an example.[22] Taung Ming-Lin abandoned a lucrative career in Taiwan as an importer of U.S.-made products and immigrated with his family to this country in 1990. In addition to investing over $1 million in the United States, he paid $310,000 for 723 acres of land outside Bakersfield, California on which to grow bamboo. Unfortunately, Lin did not know that the land held little agricultural promise, requiring years of irrigation to turn scrubland to farmland; nor did he realize that he had bought property in an area set aside for kangaroo rats and two other animals protected under the Endangered Species Act. In 1994, Lin was charged with three violations of the federal Endangered Species Act. Recently, his bookbinding shop in South El Monte was raided by the INS for allegedly employing undocumented workers from Mexico.

Workers

Workers are defined as persons employed in manual and low-paying jobs, that is, those positions that we earlier classified as low-skill occupations (LSOs). In absolute numbers, the Asian working class is not inconsiderable, but contrary to common perception, currently most Asian Americans in the Los Angeles region are not proletarians. In 1990, for example, 41 percent of employed Asians worked in managerial, professional, and technical jobs and another 39 percent worked in clerical, sales, and craft positions; only 20 percent were engaged in lower-level jobs. Since immigrants predominate among Asians, the class structure of the immigrant population does not differ much from that of the general Asian population. As table 11.3 showed, in 1990 only about 22 percent of Asian immigrants belonged to the worker category, and the percentage of native-born Asian workers was even smaller (14 percent).

Asian workers adapt to the receptive environment via at least two avenues. The majority of Asian workers strive for survival in the secondary labor market, which is characterized by low pay, poor working conditions, high turnover rate, and lack of opportunities for promotion. Most of them do operative and service jobs; for instance, new Asian immigrants, many of them women, have been an important source of the cheap labor that has supported and revived the Los Angeles garment industry. Significant proportions of Chinese and Korean workers, however, work in ethnic enclaves such as Chinatown and Koreatown, where some expect a better chance of upward mobility than in the secondary labor market, although others may suffer exploitation by their coethnic employers.

Refugees

Among Asian immigrants, the Vietnamese, Laotians, and Cambodians are the least successful, because of their refugee experiences. The Vietnamese refugees began pouring into the Los Angeles area in 1975, when U.S. involvement in the Vietnam War ended abruptly. Since then more than 600,000 have settled in the United States, with the heaviest concentration in the Los Angeles region, especially Orange County. The 1978 Indochinese Refugee Act permitted them to become permanent residents. There have been two major waves of Vietnamese immigration to Los Angeles. The first wave, from 1975 to 1980, was made up of South Vietnam's elites, who were evacuated with the U.S. troops and citizens immediately following the collapse of Saigon. Over 166,000 Vietnamese entered the United States as refugees in this period. A later wave consisted of the "boat people" and others who escaped from concentration camps or economic hardship for survival and advancement.

The varying backgrounds of the Vietnamese have determined the heterogeneity of the Vietnamese community and the diverse paths of Vietnamese adaptation in the Los Angeles region. In 1990, for instance, about 49 percent of the Vietnamese in the region had some college or higher education, while about 36 percent had not finished high school, including 7 percent with no formal schooling. Significant proportions were found both in well-paid professional occupations (25 percent) and managerial careers (7 percent) and in low-paid menial or service work (31 percent). Entrepreneurship is also an option for some Vietnamese. In 1990, 11 percent of the Vietnamese were self-employed. The chief Vietnamese occupational niches—as assemblers, hairdressers, electrical technicians, and machinists—reflect the group's overall economic status: not at the very bottom, perhaps, but still several removes from the middle class.

High rates of unemployment are a final distinguishing factor. In 1990, the unemployment rate of Vietnamese was about 7 percent, much higher than the rates for Japanese (1.7 percent), Koreans (2.4 percent), Chinese (3.3 percent), and Filipinos (3.6 percent), and even slightly higher than the rates for Hispanics (5.8 percent) and blacks (5.9 percent). Such high levels of joblessness appear to be linked to the welfare provision of the 1980 Refugee Act, which made it possible for certain unemployed Vietnamese refugees to survive for relatively long periods of time without work. Vietnamese refugees who have little schooling and work skills are most likely to stay unemployed. In short, the Vietnamese are a bifurcated community, and their adaptation patterns are even more diverse than those of other immigrant groups.

CHANGING INTERGROUP RELATIONS AND IDENTITY CONSTRUCTION

Encounters with persistent prejudice and discrimination make Asian solidarity an important issue for all Asian American groups, but the emergence of an increasingly diversified and greatly expanded Asian American population has made solidarity harder to achieve. Asian unity seems all the more urgent in the aftermath of the Los Angeles riots, which heightened black/Korean tensions and demonstrated the vulnerability of all Asians because of the inability of outsiders to distinguish among the different national-origin groups. Many Chinese, Japanese, and Vietnamese reported that their shops were damaged because rioters thought they were Korean. Some Asians accused Korean immigrants of making trouble for all Asian Americans by their insensitivity to blacks. The Chinese complained that they were turned away from a Koreatown relief center, and Chinese Americans in Los Angeles boycotted a dinner with President Bush because he visited Koreatown but not Chinatown after the turmoil. Some Koreans felt deserted by other Asian groups, while others never expected their help. When Korean Americans staged a massive peace rally on the Saturday after the riot, organized Asian American groups were absent.

The riots led to the formation in June 1992 of a broad-based coalition called Asian Pacific Americans for a New Los Angeles, considered an unprecedented event. Asian Americans have lacked a tradition of working together, however, and although there are pressing needs for Pan-Asian coalition, Asian solidarity will not be attained easily.

Economic Differentiation

Solidarity requires a common identity—in this case Asian American—but identity tends to emerge from common interests and experience, and the expansion of L.A.'s Asian population has instead often led to fragmentation. Self-employment, as we have shown, is crucial to the destiny of some groups, such as the Koreans, but matters little to others, like the Filipinos, whose concentration in health care puts them in the hands of large organizations. Looking below the surface, one may find that even the more entrepreneurial groups share less in common than was initially thought; the concerns of Chinese stockbrokers or data processing specialists, for example, are unlikely to coincide with those of Korean launderers or storekeepers. And while Asian immigrant business owners may be indifferent or hostile to government, Japanese and Chinese Americans, among whom almost one in five is working for the state, are unlikely to feel the same way.

Though the various Asian groups often congregate in common occupations or industries, as in the professional examples just cited, the overall level of segregation remains surprisingly high. Occupationally, Chinese and Japanese Americans are more segregated from almost all the foreign-born Asian groups than they are from native whites. The highly entrepreneurial Chinese immigrants are more segregated from the even-more-entrepreneurial Koreans than blacks are from whites. Almost half the Koreans would have to change jobs with the Filipinos for the two groups to share the same occupational distributions.

Residential Segregation

Just as networks have moved the region's various Asian groups into different corners of the occupational world, so too have networks steered them into a fragmented neighborhood and settlement pattern. A close look at Los Angeles County highlights the patterns of intra-Asian separation that have emerged even as the population has grown. As figure 11.8 shows, two broad clusters of Asian settlement had developed in Los Angeles County by 1980. One was found at the center of the county, in and around the old communities of Little Tokyo and Chinatown and the newly emerging Chinese suburb of Monterey Park, which had earlier attracted a sizable Japanese American population. The second was located in the South Bay, just north of Long Beach, and was home to a mixed settlement of Japanese, Filipinos, and Vietnamese.

Ten years later, as figure 11.9 shows, the greatly enlarged Asian population had spread well beyond these earlier concentrations, establishing new Asian neighborhoods in many if not all parts of the county. To some extent, the San Gabriel Valley, east of downtown, had become a broad-based belt of Asian settlement. Even here there was considerable intra-Asian separation, with a clearly demarcated cluster of Chinese living in Monterey Park and adjacent communities and a second, more mixed clump of Filipinos, Chinese, and Koreans in the county's southeast corner. Likewise, the preexisting cluster in the South Bay, attracting many new Asian residents, had spilled over its 1980 boundaries. But relatively few Chinese had gravitated to this part of the county, the affluent communities in Palos Verdes on the southwest coast excepted. Koreans and Filipinos had flocked to the San Fernando Valley, establishing a third Asian concentration here. Living in almost every part of the county, Asian Indians were altogether too dispersed to form clusters of any note.

Thus, even as Asian densities grew, the basic tendency was toward a multinucleated pattern, with different clusters separated by considerable distance. Diffusion and separation characterize the settlement pattern for the broader region as well, as can be seen from the index of dissimilarity (table 11.5). Levels of intra-Asian segregation reach the high moderate level (the upper fifties), which is about where one finds the scores measuring segregation between whites and most Asian groups. By these standard criteria, the Vietnamese are highly segregated from other Asians, a fact that is probably related to their concentration in Orange County. Intra-Asian scores declined little between 1980 and 1990; it appears that initial settlement patterns, once in place, have an inertial effect.

Nonetheless, the growing Asian density within the region does increase the potential for intra-Asian interaction. In 1990, the probability of intra-Asian contact at the small-area level was .2, as measured by the second segregation index, P^*, which shows the probability of contact with other Asian groups ranked well above the likelihood of own-group exposure, and 1990 scores for P^* also represented an increase over 1980 levels. But the contrast to Hispanics, for whom the probability of intragroup exposure stood at .53, puts the Asian situation into perspective; the lower Asian density at the aggregate level, combined with the tendency toward dispersion, is likely to keep interaction possibilities down.

Intermarriage

Ultimately, ethnic identity is shaped in the crucible of the home. While our inability to use the census data to probe the contours of identity is a complaint that resonates throughout this book, the census does allow us to say something about the ethnic characteristics of the home—namely, the degree to which marriages are confined to or cross over ethnic boundaries. As one might expect, the foreign-born women in the region's various Asian groups generally find partners from the same side of the ethnic divide, though some groups of women—Japanese and Filipinas, in particular—are less likely to do so than others. Age often makes a difference in ethnic marital decisions, with younger women less constrained than older women by a preference for coethnics, but not in the immigrant case, since some of the younger women marry prior to migration to the United States and some who marry after migration lack the language proficiencies or interactional opportunities needed to connect with a partner of a different ethnic background.

The experience of other ethnic groups, those of European as well as Latin American extraction, suggests that intermarriage is more likely to occur when the second generation comes of age. As of 1990, that development had not yet taken place for all the groups under discussion here, but what evidence we do have indicates that the second generation brings about fundamental change. In general, as table 11.6 shows, in-marriage rates plummet once we restrict our view to the native-born. Since the internal and external constraints on intermarriage that were operative several decades ago are unlikely to have the same force in these more individualistic times, age has a further, profound effect. Indeed, a comparison between younger and older women shows a dramatic decline in the in-marriage rate, as 86 percent of Asian native-born women aged 55–64 were married to a spouse of some Asian ancestry in 1990, as opposed to 44 percent of women aged 25–34. The change in the odds ratio is even more dramatic. The older women were eighty-one times more likely to marry Asian men than their non-Asian counterparts, but the younger women were only eight times more likely to marry Asian men than non-Asian women. Of course, as chapter 14 will show, even these levels of in-marriage are high relative to the norm for most white ethnic groups. But the trend does appear to be one in which intermarriage is on the rise, a shift hastened by the high educational levels of Asian Americans, the rapid transition to English among the foreign-born, and English monolingualism among the native-born, as described in chapter 5.

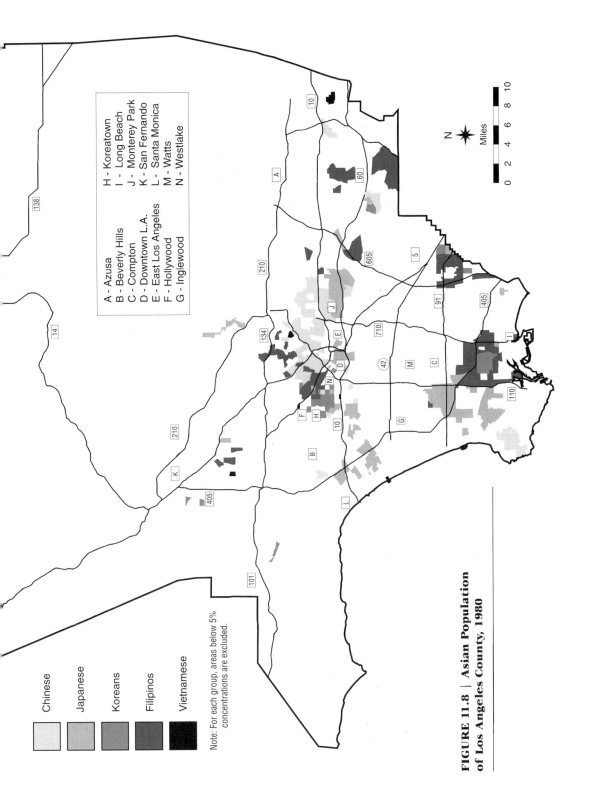

FIGURE 11.8 | Asian Population of Los Angeles County, 1980

Chinese
Japanese
Koreans
Filipinos
Vietnamese

Note: For each group, areas below 5% concentrations are excluded.

A - Azusa
B - Beverly Hills
C - Compton
D - Downtown L.A.
E - East Los Angeles
F - Hollywood
G - Inglewood
H - Koreatown
I - Long Beach
J - Monterey Park
K - San Fernando
L - Santa Monica
M - Watts
N - Westlake

N

Miles

0 2 4 6 8 10

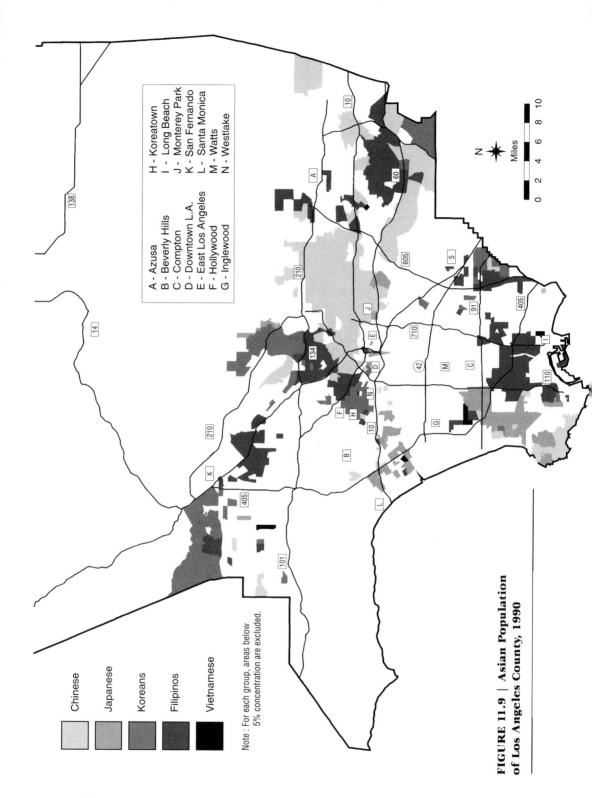

FIGURE 11.9 | Asian Population of Los Angeles County, 1990

Chinese

Japanese

Koreans

Filipinos

Vietnamese

Note : For each group, areas below 5% concentration are excluded.

A - Azusa
B - Beverly Hills
C - Compton
D - Downtown L.A.
E - East Los Angeles
F - Hollywood
G - Inglewood
H - Koreatown
I - Long Beach
J - Monterey Park
K - San Fernando
L - Santa Monica
M - Watts
N - Westlake

TABLE 11.5 | Index of Residential Dissimilarity, Los Angeles Region, 1980–1990

	All Asians	Chinese	Japanese	Koreans	Filipinos	Vietnamese	Whites	Blacks	Hispanics
All Asians		0.38	0.34	0.45	0.39	0.61	0.43	0.73	0.50
Chinese	0.38		0.52	0.60	0.61	0.68	0.57	0.81	0.64
Japanese	0.40	0.51		0.58	0.60	0.75	0.52	0.77	0.62
Koreans	0.41	0.59	0.54		0.59	0.74	0.59	0.84	0.68
Filipinos	0.37	0.60	0.58	0.55		0.73	0.57	0.79	0.57
Vietnamese	0.50	0.62	0.69	0.70	0.66		0.70	0.86	0.68
Whites	0.41	0.57	0.48	0.57	0.49	0.62		0.76	0.46
Blacks	0.66	0.79	0.72	0.77	0.67	0.78	0.64		0.70
Hispanics	0.50	0.66	0.64	0.68	0.52	0.64	0.45	0.56	

NOTE: 1980 above the diagonal; 1990 below the diagonal.

TABLE 11.6 | **Intermarriage Rates of Asian Women, Los Angeles Region, 1990**

	Aged 25–34 Years		Aged 55–64 Years	
	Married Women In-Married (%)	Odds Ratio	Married Women In-Married (%)	Odds Ratio
Native-Born				
All Asians	80	5,293	88	24,990
Chinese	44	33	74	124
Japanese	32	47	89	970
Koreans	29	25	40	57
Filipinos	35	34	59	89
Asian Indians	60	191	N/A	N/A
Vietnamese	67	168	100	N/A
Other Asians	38	61	60	240
Foreign-Born				
Chinese	88	1,618	94	3,872
Japanese	72	338	46	50
Koreans	88	10,483	94	54,065
Filipinos	67	517	90	3,754
Asian Indians	94	10,742	92	25,920
Vietnamese	93	16,585	91	54,740
Other Asians	78	851	88	3,750

Thus, we find evidence of diversity *and* divergence; nonetheless these characteristics do not necessarily negate the possibility of Asian American panethnicity. Common interests do exist, and there is a widely held belief that the small numbers of all Asian groups make some sort of coalition necessary for political, economic, and social advances. Currently, there is only one Asian American in the California legislature, and there are only five members of Asian descent in the U.S. Congress (Senator Daniel Inouye, Representative Patsy Mink of Hawaii, and Representatives Robert Tatsui, Norman Mineta, and Jay Kim of California). In addition, Representative Daniel Akaka (Hawaii) is of Hawaiian descent. Although a solid and enduring Asian identity seems difficult to forge, united fronts that cut across ethnicity, class, and nativity lines have proved viable in particular situations. Perhaps Asian panethnicity, like other ethnic identities, should be seen not as an outcome of primordial sentiments or racial solidarity but rather as a political construct that can be used to the advantage of Asian Americans.

CONCLUSION

Asian Americans in Los Angeles are an increasingly diverse population, differing in ethnic composition, nativity, socioeconomic status, and patterns of adaptation and incorporation. Whether one focuses on demography, culture, or class, treating Asian Americans as a group is likely to conceal more than it reveals.

The term *Asian American* was coined by second- and third-generation Americans of Asian descent during the Civil Rights era for political reasons and was accepted by the larger population for convenience. Throughout the 1960s and 1970s, Americans—Asians and others—de-emphasized the separate identities of Asian groups and together, albeit with different motives, helped solidify an Asian American identity. Since the 1970s, however, the massive new immigration of Asians from diverse backgrounds has challenged the validity of this inclusive concept, and separate ethnic identities have gradually assumed more importance. Recognizing the growing diversity of the population, Asian Americans simultaneously began a process of "deconstruction" and "reconstruction." On the one hand, differences between Asian groups were emphasized and their needs distinguished. The individual group identities under construction today are, however, quite different from those in the past. They are more transnational than national. The Chinese, Vietnamese, and many other Asian groups tend to see themselves not just as Chinese or Vietnamese Americans but as Chinese or Vietnamese transnationals who are not rooted in any specific country. Many immigrant families assume multiple national identities to take full advantage of the global economy and culture. On the other hand, a new Asian American identity dubbed *Pan-Asian ethnicity* came into being and recently has gained more momentum. This new inclusive national identity, like its old counterpart, is more politically than culturally significant.

Using census data for the two decades, we have tried, in these pages, to unravel the demographic, and socioeconomic basis for this identity transformation as it unfolded in Los Angeles. In addition to examining the internal dynamics of the Asian American population, we challenged the commonly held model minority concept of the group and analyzed some key relations between Asian Americans and other populations in the area. In a restricted sense, the model minority image is not farfetched for Asian Americans, if we must lump them together; taken together, they fare much better than other minorities, such as blacks and Hispanics, in terms of the major socioeconomic indicators of education, occupation, and income. The model minority image has been exaggerated and inflated, however; contrary to media reports that Asian Americans have even outperformed whites, we found that in personal income, Asians still lag behind, generally receiving lower earnings returns on their human capital than native-born whites. More importantly, there are considerable differences across Asian American groups in almost every aspect of life. As groups, Japanese and Chinese fare relatively well, but Vietnamese and other Southeast Asians are struggling for survival. Although the majority of Asians in the Los Angeles region are not poverty-stricken, neither have they fully succeeded. Furthermore, even within each Asian group individual diversity is substantial. Given these great diversities, it is dangerous to lump Asians together for statistical convenience and treat them as a monolithic whole in terms of socioeconomic policies. Disregarding the differences among Asian communities will lead to serious neglect of the needs of various segments of the Asian American population.

Massive immigration after 1965 has been the leading force of Asian diversification in the Los Angeles region. The largely different origins and experiences of Asian immigrants have led to diverse paths and outcomes of adaptation and incorporation. For instance, immigrant professionals from India, the Philippines, China, and Taiwan, like their counterparts from other countries, achieve some measure of success after first experiencing downward mobility and then slowly climbing up the occupational ladder; the difference seems to be how far these Asian professionals can go before they reach the glass ceiling. Immigrant entrepreneurs, exemplified by the Koreans and Chinese, manage to survive and with time prosper by running usually small, family-oriented businesses, serving either outsiders or their coethnics while bridging the United States and their native countries in trade. Increasingly, Asian immigrant capitalists come to settle in America, bringing significant investments. There is also the bifurcated refugee population from Vietnam, whose paths of adaptation are just as diverse as those of other immigrants.

Residential and intermarriage patterns indicate that Asians do not necessarily seek out other Asians for close relations. Each Asian ethnic group tends to marry and live in proximity with members of its own group, secondarily with whites. This pattern of association is one more indication of the weak ties that link Asian Americans.

Asian American groups, with their small numbers and their continuing disadvantageous position in American society, recognize the need for Pan-Asian unity. Yet historical enmity, diverse group status and interests, and a lack of intergroup interaction makes unity difficult. Should Asian immigration decline, the barriers to intra-Asian solidarity will gradually diminish. Whether immigrant numbers expand, decline, or remain stable, the ranks of the second generation will inevitably expand, and solidarity is likely to grow when this new generation of U.S.-born Asian Americans comes into its own. In the end, however, the emergence of a new Pan-Asian ethnicity remains uncertain; its prospects hinge on the larger political and economic environment and, perhaps more importantly, on Asian Americans themselves and their conscious efforts at reconstruction.

Notes to Chapter 11

1. Yen Espiritu, *Asian American Panethnicity* (Philadelphia: Temple University Press, 1992).

2. John Liu and Lucie Cheng, "Pacific Rim Development and the Duality of Post-1965 Asian Immigration to the United States," in Paul Ong, Edna Bonacich, and Lucie Cheng, eds., *The New Asian Immigration in Los Angeles and Global Restructuring,* (Philadelphia: Temple University Press, 1994), 74–99.

3. Paul Ong, Lucie Cheng, and Leslie Evans, "Migration of Highly Educated Asians and Global Dynamics," *Asian and Pacific Migration Journal* 1 (1992): 543–67.

4. Ong, Bonacich, and Cheng, *The New Asian Immigration.*

5. Ong, Bonacich, and Cheng, *The New Asian Immigration.*

6. Under IRCA, illegal immigrants who applied for amnesty were eligible for permanent resident status two years after the approval of their amnesty application. Since the INS fiscal year 1989, more than three million illegal immigrants (mainly from Mexico and other Latin American countries) have been granted permanent residency, leading to the relative decline of Asian immigration after 1989. The absolute number of Asian immigrants steadily increased, however, from 236,097 in 1980 to 338,581 in 1990.

7. William Petersen, "Success Story, Japanese-American Style," *New York Times Magazine,* January 9, 1966; "Success Story of One Minority in the U.S.," *U.S. News and World Report,* December 26, 1966.

8. See, for example, "Asian Americans: A 'Model Minority'," *Newsweek,* December 6, 1982, 39, 41–42, 51; David Bell, "The Triumph of Asian Americans," *New Republic,* July 1985, 24–31.

9. See, for instance, Ronald Takaki, "The Myth of the Model Minority," in Ronald Takaki, *Strangers from a Different Shore: A History of Asian Americans* (Boston: Little, Brown and Company, 1987) 474–84; Paul Ong and Suzanne J. Hee, "Economic Diversity," Paul Ong, ed., in *Economic Diversity, Issues and Policies* (Los Angeles: LEAP Asian Pacific American Public Policy Institute and UCLA Asian American Studies Center, 1994), 31–56.

10. Charles Hirschman and Morrison G. Wong, "The Extraordinary Educational Attainment of Asian Americans: A Search for Historical Evidence and Explanations," *Social Forces* 65 (1986): 1–27.

11. Herbert Barringer, Robert W. Gardner, and Michael J. Levin, *Asians and Pacific Islanders in the United States* (New York: Russell Sage Foundation, 1993); Hirschman and Wong, "The Extraordinary Educational Attainment of Asian Americans."

12. Herbert Barringer, David T. Takeuchi, and Peter Xenos, "Education, Occupational Prestige, and Income of Asian Americans," *Sociology of Education* 63 (1990): 27–43.

13. Harry Kitano, *Japanese Americans: The Evolution of a Subculture* (Englewood Cliffs, N.J.: Prentice-Hall, 1988).

14. See, for example, Barringer, Takeuchi, and Xenos, *Education;* Ong, Bonacich, and Cheng, *The New Asian Immigration.*

15. Takaki, *Strangers.*

16. Ong and Hee, "Economic Diversity."

17. Ronald Takaki also showed that in 1980 Asian men generally earned lower personal incomes than white men in California and New York. See Takaki, *Strangers.*

18. Lucie Cheng and Philip Q. Yang, "Global Interaction, Global Inequality, and Professional Migration to the United States" (Paper presented at the American Sociological Association annual meetings, Los Angeles, August 1994); Ong, Cheng, and Evans, "Migration of Highly Educated Asians."

19. Asian Pacific American Coalition U.S.A., *Alert,* "Glass Ceiling Report Published" 13 (September/October 1993): 2–4.

20. Ivan Light and Edna Bonacich, *Immigrant Entrepreneurs* (Berkeley, Calif.: University of California Press, 1988). Pyong Gap Min, *Caught in the Middle: Korean Merchants in Multiethnic America* (Berkeley and Los Angeles: University of California Press, 1996).

21. Light and Bonacich, *Immigrant Entrepreneurs;* Min, *Caught in the Middle.*

22. Mark Arax, "INS Raids Firm of Farmer in Kangaroo Rat Case," *Los Angeles Times,* November 3, 1994.

Middle Easterners: A New Kind of Immigrant

Mehdi Bozorgmehr, Claudia Der-Martirosian,
and Georges Sabagh

IT MAY SEEM odd to open a chapter about Middle Easterners in Los Angeles with the bombing of the federal office
building in Oklahoma City. The reaction of some Americans to the news of the bombing, however, speaks volumes
about the prevailing stereotype of Middle Easterners. As
the worst terrorist act ever recorded in the United States,
the devastating explosion on April 19, 1995 killed many
more innocent people than the bombing of the World
Trade Center in New York City two years before, yet they
shared an eerily common method of destruction; in each
case a vehicle loaded with explosives was parked below the
building and detonated automatically. As several Muslims
of Arab descent were tried and convicted in the World
Trade Center bombing, some U.S. officials and media personalities in a hasty reaction singled out Middle Easterners for blame in the Oklahoma City bombing. Within
days, however, a Newsweek headline read, "Jumping to
Conclusions—Many in the press and public were quick to
assume the crime had Mideast origins. But 'John Doe' is
one of us."[1] Not surprisingly, the news that the terrorists
were homegrown came as a relief to Middle Easterners in
the United States, much as they sympathized with the victims and their families. Yet the stereotype of Middle Easterners as terrorists is too ingrained in the American mind
to disappear even when the facts are known.

Americans were deeply concerned about the Middle
East long before they learned of Middle Easterners in
their midst. Starting with the establishment of the state of
Israel and continuing through the ensuing Arab-Israeli
wars and tortuous peace negotiations, the American media have kept a spotlight on events in the Middle East. De-

velopments in that part of the world came home in 1973 with the Arab oil embargo, which was especially upsetting to Angelenos, who depend heavily on their cars for transportation, as the price of gas skyrocketed. Shortly after the oil crisis came the Iranian revolution, with its vehemently anti-American slogans, culminating in the taking of 52 Americans hostage for 444 days in 1980–81. "Nightline," the nightly television program originally created to keep viewers updated on the "Iranian Hostage Crisis," broadcast images of hostile crowds in Tehran, burning American flags and shouting "Death to America."

Engagement with an enemy thousands of miles away led to preoccupation with the Middle Eastern presence here in the United States. Although a trickle of Middle Easterners had been flowing to the United States for many decades, a new, more sizable wave arrived after 1970. Some intended to stay, but most came as students from oil-exporting countries, seeking a state-of-the-art technical education with the expectation of returning home to their rapidly industrializing economies. For the most part, the students were invisible, and so they remained until the hostage crisis, when Washington decided to police the Iranians living in the United States and discovered it had no idea how many Iranians were actually here.[2] Even years later, an American who had lived nearly a decade in the Middle East observed that "what most LA Iranians did have in common was a wish to be invisible, which may have stemmed from the anti-Iranian feeling during the U.S. hostage episode."[3]

Most Americans, lacking adequate knowledge of the Middle East and unfamiliar with these new immigrants, cannot distinguish Middle Easterners by country of origin and are unaware of the tremendous diversity within this minority group. Much of the public thinks of Middle Easterners as a single nationality (such as Iranian or Israeli) or a single ethnic group (for example, Arab or Armenian). Whenever anti-American sentiments surge in the Middle East, all Middle Easterners in the United States are victimized. During the Iranian hostage crisis, arson of Arab-owned businesses caused Arab shopkeepers to put up signs stating that they were not Iranian. Ironically, similar signs were displayed during the Persian Gulf War, only this time the roles were reversed, with Iranian shopkeepers indicating that they were not Arabs.

Thus, continuing turmoil in the Middle East has cast a long shadow over the growing number of immigrants who over the past thirty years have moved to the United States from that part of the world. Ironically, the same political upheavals that made otherwise invisible immigrants so prominent provided the original spur to migration to the United States. Many of the Middle Eastern immigrants are exiles or refugees who left their homelands because of opposition to government policies and actions or fear of persecution; nonetheless, Middle Easterners have often felt unwelcome in the United States. Even former college students, many of whom have decided against returning to their respective countries, have on occasion felt unwelcome in their newly adopted home. Continuing hostility and rejection trouble Middle Easterners, since by and large they are not a burden socially or economically on the United States.

Given this background and the American media's constant reminder of raging conflicts in the Middle East, Middle Eastern immigrants have received more publicity than is their share. In Los Angeles, Middle Easterners are particularly noticeable. Though more numerous here than anywhere else, the circumstances of their migration have added to the high Middle Eastern profile. Arriving suddenly and converging on just a few places in the L.A. region, the Middle Easterners have quickly gained visibility. Though some of these newcomers have arrived in the traditional refugee way—without a penny to spare—others managed to transfer large sums of money, allowing them to pursue a lifestyle that garners further attention. Middle Easterners, especially Iranians, were among the first immigrants to settle in traditionally affluent white neighborhoods in Beverly Hills, Bel Air, and Brentwood, known in local parlance as "the three Bs." The popular imagination puts the typical Iranian in a Mercedes Benz, shopping on trendy and expensive Rodeo Drive—an exaggerated image,[4] of course, but one that reflects the arrival and settlement of an unusual and different kind of new immigrant. Because of a rich entrepreneurial tradition, and in many cases an availability of capital, Middle Eastern–owned and –operated businesses have sprouted all over Los Angeles County. To cater to a large coethnic clientele, these businesses often have signs in Arabic, Persian, Armenian, or Hebrew script. These signs have become the hallmark of L.A.'s string of mini-malls, further enhancing Middle Eastern presence and visibility.

THE ETHNIC DIVERSITY OF MIDDLE EASTERN IMMIGRANTS

In addition to an outwardly obvious affluence, two less obvious but distinctive features of Middle Easterners are exile status and ethnic diversity. These seemingly unrelated traits are in reality closely tied together. Cataclysmic events in the Middle East have produced a steady flow of refugees or exiles, many of whom were members of religious minority groups who have suffered varying degrees of persecution during periods of rising Muslim militancy and xenophobia. Although non-Muslim minorities make up less than 5 percent of the overall population in the Middle East, they are overrepresented among immigrants from this region to America.

Middle Eastern immigrants originate from over twenty countries in Southwest Asia and North Africa.[5] With the exception of Armenia, Iran, Israel, and Turkey, the countries of the Middle East and North Africa are predominantly Arab. The Middle East is aptly called the cradle of civilization, since Judaism, Christianity, and Islam—three of the world's major religions—originated there. The region still contains Christian, Jewish, and other non-Muslim minorities. The Christian Armenians, even after centuries of residence in various Middle Eastern countries, have maintained their distinctive language and ethnic identity; they are a majority population only in the newly established Independent State of Armenia. Arabs originate from a vast area stretching from Morocco to Iraq and the Gulf states; their native language and culture are Arabic. Most but not all Arabs are Muslims; the group also includes Christians and Jews. Iranians are not Arabs; they come from Iran and speak Persian. Most but not all Israeli-born immigrants are Hebrew-speaking Jews.

Ethnic diversity among Middle Easterners takes many forms, setting them apart from all other ethnic groups in Los Angeles. Like Asians and Hispanics, Middle Easterners come from disparate countries of origin, but unlike Hispanic and Asian nationalities, Middle Eastern nationalities are further divided by religion and ethnicity. For instance, Iranian immigrants include not only Muslims, the overwhelming majority population in Iran, but also Jews, Armenians, and other smaller minorities.[6] Conversely, each ethnic group consists of a multinational population; for example, Arab immigrants mainly come from Lebanon and Egypt, though Arabs from virtually every country in the Middle East and North Africa are now residing in the Los Angeles region.[7]

Whatever their nationality, religion, or ethnicity, Middle Easterners share a common history and geographical origin that has some distinctive features. In the precolonial era, powerful Muslim empires dominated the Middle East and North Africa and challenged European hegemony. The European colonial incursion into the region began in the nineteenth century and continued well after the First World War. During this time the European powers often used the minorities as intermediaries with the local population, and as a result the situation of minorities deteriorated in the postcolonial era. Minorities have become vulnerable in times of crisis and have consequently been overrepresented among the ranks of emigrants from the Middle East. Even though Middle Eastern and North African countries have since gained independence, the region still remains dependent on Europe and the United States. This dependence has not gone unchallenged; often it has resulted in the outbreaks of violence such as the protracted Arab-Israeli conflict and the Palestinian *Intifada* (uprising), the Iranian revolution, the Lebanese civil war, the Gulf War, and acts stemming from religious extremism have produced successive waves of Middle Eastern exiles and refugees to the United States.

Like the other contributors to this book, we rely mainly on data from the Public Use Microdata Samples of the U.S. Census of Population. For all its richness, however, the census is not entirely satisfactory as a source of information about Middle Eastern immigrants, since it contains no information on religion. Another problem has to do with population size; these are relatively new groups, whose numbers grew dramatically during the 1970s and even more during the 1980s. In 1970, relatively few Middle Easterners lived in Los Angeles. The limitations of this population base, combined with the fact that the 1970 microdata set provides a sample of just 5 percent of the total population, means that our numbers for 1970 are too small for meaningful analysis.

A third, more severe problem concerns the proper definition of the relevant groups. The census defines Hispanics, Asians, and African Americans in either racial or ethnic terms, with explicit procedures designed to identify persons falling into any one of these groups. But the census makes no effort to categorize or statistically capture Middle Easterners; in fact, it considers them whites. Thus, non-Hispanic whites include persons of European, Middle Eastern, and North African origin.[8] In 1990, 98 percent of Middle Easterners reported themselves as whites when asked their race. The inclusion of Middle Easterners and North Africans under whites is clearly an instance of arbitrary classification. Middle Easterners should be classified as a separate group, just as Asians and Pacific Islanders are. In any case, classifying Middle Easterners as whites conceals their presence,[9] since they are just as clearly a sociological minority as other, more visible groups in terms of background, regional origin, culture, and ethnoreligious identity.

Of course, foreign-born persons from the Middle East can be identified, since the census does ask about place of birth. But we can also identify native-born persons of Middle Eastern background by using their responses to the open-ended ancestry question, which asked, "What is this person's ancestry or ethnic origin?"[10] Using census data, the only way to identify Middle Eastern groups in Los Angeles is to classify them according to a combination of ancestry and place of birth. Using this procedure, we identified four major groups: Arabs, Armenians, Iranians, and Israelis.

Reporting a first or second Armenian ancestry, the Armenian group includes U.S.-born Armenians as well as Armenian immigrants originating from Turkey, Israel, Iran, various Arab countries, and the former Soviet Union.[11] The Arab group includes all persons who were born in Arab countries of North Africa and Southwest Asia, as well as those who, in response to the ancestry question, stated that they were Arabs or Palestinians. Consequently, the Israeli category excludes all Arabs or Palestinians who may have been born in the state of Israel (or in Palestine, prior to 1948).[12] Defined by Iranian ancestry and place of birth, the Iranian category excludes Armenians and Assyrians who have come from Iran. The residual category "Other Middle Easterners" consists mainly of Turks, Assyrians, Chaldeans, Kurds, and Berbers. "All Middle Easterners" is a combination of the four groups and the residual category. We used the same groups for both the 1980 and the 1990 censuses. In the remainder of this chapter, we will concentrate on the four Middle Eastern groups, leaving out the very heterogeneous group of Other Middle Easterners.

FROM MIDDLE EAST TO AMERICA

The first wave of Middle Eastern immigration lasted from the late nineteenth century until the 1920s, when restrictive legislation assigned very small quotas to Middle Eastern countries. It comprised mainly Armenian refugees fleeing persecutions and massacres in the Ottoman Empire (present-day Turkey) and Syrio-Lebanese whose migration was economically motivated. Like other immigrants at the time, Armenian refugees and Syrio-Lebanese immigrants were of humble origins. These immigrants settled on the East Coast, although some Armenians came to Fresno, California as farmers and landowners. Today, second- and third-generation Armenians and Arabs in America have experienced considerable social and geographical mobility.

The 1965 revision of U.S. immigration laws facilitated a second wave of migration from the Middle East. For these migrants, the impetus to emigration was the cataclysmic events that were occurring there—the 1967 and 1973 Arab-Israeli wars, the Lebanese civil war that began in 1975, the Iranian revolution of 1978–79 and the consolidation of the Islamic Republic of Iran—all of which led some to seek a more secure life in the United States. For the most part, the immigrants in this new wave are far more diverse in terms of national and socioeconomic origins than their predecessors; the new Arab Americans, for example, are more religiously and geographically diverse than the earlier arrivals, who were mostly Christians from today's Syria and Lebanon. Today's population of Middle Eastern immigrants contains groups entirely new to America, of whom the Iranians are the most notable example.

Middle Eastern migration to Los Angeles is a relatively new phenomenon and in this respect differs significantly from the immigration of other groups studied in this book, with the exception of Central Americans. Unlike Asians, earlier groups of Middle Eastern immigrants tended to gravitate to the East Coast. By 1970, however, Los Angeles had a population of 52,400 Middle Easterners, half of whom were native-born. As early as 1965, the small Iranian population in the United States had already established a cluster in California, in Los Angeles County in particular.[13]

In the years since 1970, Los Angeles has become an increasingly important destination for the newcomers from the Middle East. The total number of Middle Easterners in the Los Angeles region nearly tripled during the 1970s, from 52,400 to 144,100; it then doubled again in the following decade, hitting the 300,000 mark by 1990. Behind this increase for the total

FIGURE 12.1 | **Population Growth of Middle Eastern Groups, Los Angeles Region, 1970–1990**

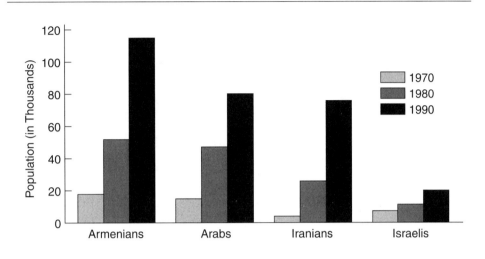

Middle Eastern population lie substantial variations in the rates of growth for particular Middle Eastern groups. The Iranian population grew sixfold in the 1970–80 decade, mainly because of the massive influx of exiles after 1978.[14] Although this rate of growth subsided after 1980, the Iranian group is still increasing faster than all other Middle Eastern groups. In the 1970s, the population of both Arabs and Armenians grew threefold. Although some Arabs joined Armenians in their flight from the Arab-Israeli conflict and Lebanese civil wars, other Arabs, supported by massive oil revenues, came to Los Angeles in pursuit of higher education. The Arab population growth rate dropped off after oil revenues fell in the 1980s, but the Armenian population grew because of the sizable influx of refugees from the former Soviet Union. Israelis increased their numbers slowly but steadily throughout the 1970–90 period, a pattern reflecting their economic migrant status (see figure 12.1).

Migration has utterly transformed the small Middle Eastern community that existed in Los Angeles twenty-five years ago, introducing new ethnic elements and shifting the relative importance of the foreign- and native-born. Iranians not only experienced the highest rate of population growth but, as members of an entirely new group, have the highest proportion who are foreign-born; in 1990, 80 percent of the region's Iranian population was foreign-born (see figure 12.2), and more than 90 percent of these newcomers had arrived in the last fifteen years. To a lesser degree, this dominance of the recently arrived characterizes all Middle Eastern groups in Los Angeles.

FIGURE 12.2 | **Percentage Foreign-Born Among Middle Eastern Groups, Los Angeles Region, 1970–1990**

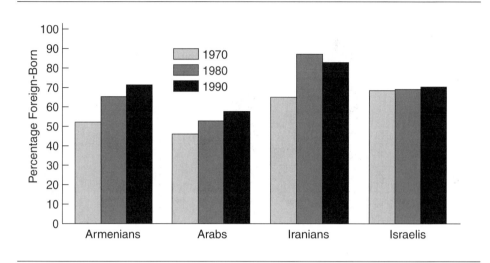

By 1990, Los Angeles had emerged as the largest and most diverse center of Middle Easterners in the United States and in the Western world. Of the 1,731,000 persons of Middle Eastern ancestry in the United States, 300,000 or 17 percent were in the Los Angeles metropolitan region. Not all groups are equally concentrated in L.A. The 1990 census enumerated about 308,000 Armenians, 260,000 Iranians, 921,000 Arabs, and 117,000 Israelis in the United States. Of these, 115,000 Armenians (37 percent), 76,000 Iranians (29 percent), 20,000 Israelis (17 percent), and only 80,000 Arabs (9 percent) were in the Los Angeles region.[15] Although the total population size of 300,000 Middle Easterners is relatively small compared with other minority groups in Los Angeles, it includes a substantial segment of several Middle Eastern immigrant groups, not only in the United States but also worldwide.[16] Los Angeles contains the largest Armenian population outside Armenia,[17] the largest Iranian population in the Western world,[18] the second largest Israeli population in the United States (after New York),[19] and one of the largest Arab populations outside Detroit, Michigan.[20]

PROFESSIONALS AND HIGHLY SKILLED ENTREPRENEURS

Portes and Rumbaut, in *Immigrant America,* have suggested that contemporary immigrant groups can be classified according to their typical mode of adaptation, namely as manual laborers, professionals, or entrepreneurs.

They further argue that "there are two ways to 'make it' in America, at least legally. The first is the salaried professional/managerial route; the other is independent entrepreneurship."[21] From this perspective, Middle Eastern groups generally fall into the entrepreneurial and professional modes, and we would therefore expect them to have made it. Their success, however, is hampered by the simultaneous refugee/asylee status of some groups. This status is more of a handicap for Armenians, who consist of disadvantaged refugees from the former Soviet Union, than it is for the elite exiles from Iran.

Although Portes and Rumbaut's scheme of economic mobility seems to fit Middle Easterners, their ideas about assimilation fit less well. Portes and Rumbaut contend that immigrant professionals experience rapid assimilation because of their occupational success and lack of strong ties with coethnics. While this generalization may apply to geographically dispersed professionals, it is less applicable to a highly concentrated group such as Middle Eastern professionals in Los Angeles. Moreover, according to the sociological literature, immigrant entrepreneurs have a heavy reliance on coethnics that retards their assimilation.[22] The case of Middle Easterners suggests, however, that the lines between entrepreneurial and professional modes of adaptation are often blurred, as many of them are highly skilled entrepreneurs such as doctors or dentists. In fact, a prominent feature of Middle Eastern occupational niches, including professional ones, is their high rate of self-employment. Specifically, over two-thirds of Armenian and over half of Iranian, Israeli, and Arab professionals/managers are self-employed. Working in an ethnic milieu, these professionals are as highly ethnic as other self-employed workers. Economic clustering, whether self-employed or not, in selected niches also increases their likelihood of interacting with coethnics.

Contrary to the existing sociological thinking and conventional wisdom, we argue that economic progress of Middle Eastern immigrants does not necessarily come at the cost of rapid assimilation. In addition to the economic forces mentioned, noneconomic factors such as recency of arrival, refugee/exile status, and previous experience as minorities in the Middle East contribute to the maintenance of their ethnicity and thereby retard assimilation.

Often coming with capital, high levels of education, and experience in the professions and business, Middle Eastern immigrants are unlikely to follow the traditional immigrant pattern of starting out at the bottom of the socioeconomic ladder, and as such are a new kind of immigrant. In 1990, almost half of Middle Eastern men were working in managerial and professional jobs, a proportion comparable to Asians and native whites and over four times higher than Hispanics. Middle Eastern women were less likely to be employed in these higher-level jobs, but they were still doing almost as well as native-born white women (see table 12.1). The indexes of dissimilar-

TABLE 12.1 | Socioeconomic Characteristics of Selected Groups, Aged 25–64, Los Angeles Region, 1990

	Middle Easterners	Non-Hispanic Whites		Asians	Hispanics
	FB	NB	FB	FB	FB
Men					
Four years college or more	43.3%	35.1%	35.1%	44.8%	5.1%
Employed	77.1%	86.6%	85.1%	83.6%	84.6%
Higher white-collar[a]	42.5%	43.6%	45.4%	41.9%	9.0%
Self-employed	31.8%	16.5%	23.9%	18.6%	8.0%
Earnings					
Median	$24,300	$30,223	$30,780	$20,250	$12,150
Mean	$32,149	$36,838	$37,702	$26,720	$15,060
Women					
Four years college or more	24.8%	26.1%	22.5%	35.1%	4.5%
Employed	43.3%	68.8%	62.9%	62.7%	52.8%
Higher white-collar	37.8%	44.1%	39.9%	35.4%	11.4%
Self-employed	14.0%	10.0%	12.5%	11.6%	6.5%
Earnings					
Median	$14,580	$17,820	$16,514	$15,390	$ 8,100
Mean	$17,088	$20,454	$19,754	$18,237	$10,318

[a] Managers and professionals.

ity corroborate these data by showing that Middle Easterners are much more similar to other whites and Asians than they are to blacks and Hispanics in occupational and industrial distribution.[23] Since, on the average, whites and Asians hold better jobs than Hispanics and blacks, the index of occupational dissimilarity is also a crude measure of the economic well-being of Middle Easterners.

Middle Easterners outpace all other major ethnoracial groups by a very considerable extent, as chapter 7 on self-employment has already shown in greater detail. An analysis of the reasons for this unusually high rate of entrepreneurship is beyond the scope of this chapter. Suffice it to say that the presence of former middleman minorities and independent professionals, the availability of both economic and social capital, and a desire to escape discrimination in hiring and promotion are some of the factors that account for this high rate of self-employment. Although self-employment among women in all broad ethnic groups is low, Middle Eastern women still outrank all others, though by a small margin.

The data in table 12.1 indicate that Middle Eastern immigrants have other distinctive socioeconomic characteristics. Although Middle Eastern and Asian men share a high level of education (43 and 45 percent with four or more years of college, respectively), Middle Eastern immigrant women have a much lower educational achievement than Asian women (25 versus 35 percent with four or more years of college, respectively). This disparity reflects the different structures of opportunity for women in the Middle East as opposed to East Asia. In spite of a higher level of education, a much higher rate of self-employment, and a similar occupational profile to the native whites', Middle Easterners' mean earnings are lower than native- or foreign-born whites. We will turn to an explanation of this outcome later in the chapter.

ECONOMIC PROFILES OF MIDDLE EASTERN GROUPS

While highly useful as a typology of contemporary immigration, the typical mode of adaptation does not capture the full range of economic adaptation of individual immigrant groups. Classifying Middle Easterners as professionals and entrepreneurs simplifies the much more varied experiences of specific groups. Although all four groups are highly entrepreneurial, Iranians and Israelis[24] are more likely to be professionals than Armenians and Arabs. In their motivation for emigration, Iranians and Armenians are predominantly exiles and refugees, whereas Israelis and Arabs are economic migrants. Iranians are elite exiles, however, while Armenians include both elite exiles from Lebanon and Iran and refugees from the former Soviet Union. The difference between Armenians and Arabs, on one hand, and Iranians and Israelis, on the other, is partly due to the heterogeneity of the former groups.

Even more basic than the occupational differences are the differences in the rates of labor force participation, which is noticeably lower among both Middle Eastern men and women than among native whites, as well as Asian and Hispanic immigrants. Lack of labor force participation of refugees, most notably Armenians from the former Soviet Union and to a lesser degree from Iran, partly accounts for the lower overall labor force participation of the Middle Eastern men (see table 12.2). Armenian immigrant males have the lowest labor force participation (64 percent). A remarkably high percentage of foreign-born Armenian householders (22 percent) 18 years and over are on welfare, a figure exceeding that of blacks (16 percent). Yet Armenians are not a serious burden on the welfare system because of their small population. Moreover, there is hardly any welfare dependency among the native-born Armenians (1.2 percent).[25]

The traditionally low employment rate of urban women in the Middle East may explain their labor force behavior in the United States. In 1990, in

TABLE 12.2 | Socioeconomic Characteristics of Foreign-Born Middle Eastern Groups, Aged 25–64, Los Angeles Region, 1990

	Armenians	Iranians	Arabs	Israelis
Men				
Four years college or more	23.4%	64.9%	42.4%	39.5%
Employed	63.9%	84.0%	81.8%	87.0%
Higher white-collar[a]	30.6%	51.3%	42.0%	45.1%
Lower white-collar[b]	23.0%	29.1%	29.8%	23.3%
Blue-collar[c]	46.4%	19.6%	28.2%	31.6%
Self-employed	34.8%	33.3%	26.8%	35.0%
Earnings				
Median	$21,475	$27,540	$23,871	$29,484
Mean	$29,120	$34,107	$30,230	$40,250
Women				
Four years college or more	15.4%	33.7%	26.7%	32.3%
Employed	36.4%	47.6%	45.5%	59.7%
Higher white-collar[a]	30.7%	41.7%	36.8%	53.3%
Lower white-collar[b]	48.8%	41.4%	45.7%	31.3%
Blue-collar[c]	20.5%	16.9%	17.5%	15.4%
Self-employed	12.9%	14.4%	15.1%	14.1%
Earnings				
Median	$14,580	$13,770	$14,580	$14,580
Mean	$16,211	$17,441	$17,218	$18,619

[a] Mangers and professionals
[b] Sales and clerical
[c] All other occupations

the Arab states and in Iran, women made up only 13 and 18 percent of the labor force respectively, as compared with 35 percent in Israel and 43 percent in East Asia.[26] Nevertheless, intergroup differences in labor force participation in Los Angeles are even greater among females than they are among males. Proportionately, more Israeli (60 percent) than Armenian (36 percent) women are employed. This difference partly reflects a higher level of female employment in Israel, and the economic migrant status of Israelis in the United States. With the exception of Israelis, Middle Eastern women have the lowest rates of labor force participation of all major groups in Los Angeles, a fact that reflects not only the traditional role of women as homemakers in the Middle East but also the high earnings of their husbands. This pattern, however, is undergoing rapid change. For instance, there was a substantial increase in the labor force participation of Iranian women from 27 percent in 1980 to 48 percent in 1990. Although part of this rapid increase may be attributed to the fact that in 1980 many Iranian exiles from the 1978–79 revolution had just arrived and were not yet in the labor force, as was the case among males, this change suggests that some Iranian women no longer subscribe to their traditional role as housewives. Clearly, Iranian women—and for that matter other Middle Easterners, with the possible exception of Israelis, who already had a high employment level—are increasingly entering the labor force in the United States, a change that has significant ramifications for sex roles and family life.[27]

Differences in the levels of education further account for the economic performance of the four groups. Compared with the other Middle Eastern groups, Armenian immigrant males and females have the lowest educational achievement (23 and 15 percent with four years or more of college, respectively). For the other groups, the variation in educational achievement is much greater for males than for females. Among males, Iranians have a much higher level of education than any other group (65 percent with four years or more of college), while females have only a slightly higher level (34 percent). Interestingly, the male/female gap in education is greatest for Iranians (65 versus 34 percent) and lowest for Israelis (40 versus 32 percent). This marked contrast undoubtedly reflects the greater gender differences in educational opportunities in Iran than in Israel.

Reflecting their higher level of education, the Iranians have more managers and professionals than the three other groups. Conversely, there are more Armenian blue-collar male workers compared with the other Middle Eastern groups. The economic adaptation of Arabs and Israelis is between these two extremes. As expected, the mode of occupational adaptation of females is somewhat different from males', with a greater concentration in the lower white-collar occupations among Armenians, Iranians, and Arabs. Although Israeli females have the same level of education as Iranian females, a larger percentage of Israeli women are professionals and managers; Israeli women even have a higher rate of professional employment than their male counterparts. Many get jobs as Hebrew or Sunday school teachers or work for other Jewish communal services in an effort to strengthen their community in the United States.[28] Regarding male/female differences, Iranian and Arab male immigrants have a higher occupational achievement. The reverse is true for Israelis, and there are no gender differences for Armenians.

The rate of self-employment for all four groups is very high, ranging between 27 and 35 percent, making them similar to Koreans, of whom over one-third are entrepreneurs.[29] The Koreans, however, are an ethnically homogenous group;[30] among Middle Eastern groups, the presence of former middleman minorities accounts for their proclivity for entrepreneurship. Specifically, with the possible exception of Armenians from the former Soviet Union, the Armenian group is entirely made up of these former minorities. Israelis, as defined here, consist only of Jews, a group universally known for its entrepreneurial bent. Jews also make up a substantial segment of the Iranians, thus pushing upward an already high rate of self-employment among this population.[31] Arabs consist of fewer former minorities than the other three groups, Egyptian Copts excepted, a fact that is reflected in their slightly lower rate of entrepreneurship. Nevertheless, the Arab group—and especially its sizable Lebanese subgroup—has a long and well-defined history of commerce, not only in the Middle East but also in the United States.[32] As is usually the case, the rates of self-employment for women in all four Middle Eastern groups are substantially lower than for their male counterparts.

On the whole, Israeli males have the highest earnings and Armenians the lowest. The income distribution of the four groups further reflects the variation in the economic adaptation of each group.[33] Israeli males' earnings, even more than Iranian males', are most concentrated in the highest quintile, whereas Armenian males' earnings are evenly distributed across all five earning categories (see figure 12.3). The even distribution of earning quintiles among Armenians suggests that not all Middle Eastern groups—and more specifically not all members of each group—are high earners. As table 12.2 shows, almost half of Armenian males are blue-collar workers who earn much less than their coethnic professionals and entrepreneurs.

FIGURE 12.3 | Earnings Quintiles of Foreign-Born Middle Eastern Groups, Los Angeles Region, 1990 (Males Aged 25–64)

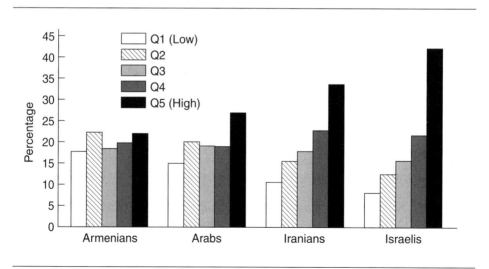

CARVING OUT NICHES

Immigrants usually carve out niches to continue an economic heritage, to have greater opportunities of working with coethnics, to fill a void in the existing economic structure, and to avoid discrimination, among other reasons. A distinctive trait of Middle Eastern immigrant occupations and industries is that they are heavily concentrated in higher-status occupations and in financial and retail services, a pattern that has more or less persisted over time. Moreover, this immigrant trait appears to have carried over to the native-born, although the sample size is too small for a definitive conclusion. Foreign-born Middle Easterners were almost as clustered in occupations and industries (around 40 percent in niches) as the foreign-born Asians in both 1980 and 1990. Yet no occupational niche in Los Angeles is heavily identified with Middle Easterners as a whole or any Middle Eastern group, as are liquor stores with Koreans and hotels with Asian Indians.

Tables 12.3, 12.4, and 12.5 list the top ten occupational and industrial niches for Middle Easterners and for each of the four groups. The top ten list corresponds to the niches with the highest index of representation, and they are ordered according to the number of Middle Easterners in each occupation or industry. Almost all the top ten Middle Eastern niches are managerial, professional, and sales occupations, all highly desirable and lucrative niches. Many self-employed Middle Eastern professionals have incorporated their firms. As chapter 7 described, such entrepreneurs, whose companies are often bigger and more lucrative, are generally better off economically than the unincorporated self-employed. A few low-income niches are distinctively female (for example, hairdressers), but women also make up a sizable proportion of the better-paid accountant and sales niches (see table 12.3).[34] Thus, when Middle Eastern women work, they tend to be highly specialized, a pattern that is more pronounced for Middle Easterners as a whole than for any group within it. In general, Middle Eastern niches are quite lucrative, with average earnings ranging from $30,000 for auto mechanics to $100,000 for physicians. Moreover, there appears to be some upgrading in occupational niches from 1980 to 1990. New niches, such as lawyers, designers, and musicians, appear for the native-born Middle Easterners, reflecting the entry of the Middle Eastern Americans into a wider labor market. For instance, several of the popular new designers in the burgeoning Los Angeles fashion industry are of Middle Eastern origin.

Except for banking and engineering, self-employment among immigrants exceeds 30 percent for the remaining eight industries (see table 12.4). Over half the Middle Eastern jewelers and launderers have their own businesses. Even 20 percent of the engineers are self-employed. As the term *retail* in several of the industries listed in table 12.4 suggests, these niches

TABLE 12.3 | Top Ten Occupational Niches for Middle Eastern Groups, Los Angeles Region, 1990

	Index of Rep.	Self-employed (%)	Female (%)
Foreign-born			
Supervisors in sales	2.5	56	16
Accountants	1.7	14	37
Others in sales	1.9	28	44
Real estate (sales)	1.7	40	37
Managers in food/lodging	2.5	38	21
Physicians	2.8	53	10
Auto mechanics	2.0	27	0
Civil engineers	5.1	10	7
Hairdressers	1.9	31	86
Electrical engineers	2.1	8	4
Native-born			
Managers in administration	1.6	22	29
Secretaries	1.5	9	100
Lawyers	2.7	55	20
Real estate (sales)	1.8	21	52
Others in sales	1.5	17	76
Physicians	2.6	59	3
Designers	1.9	20	84
Managers in real estate	2.1	23	50
Managers in finance	1.6	4	34
Music	5.0	66	22

are characterized by high self-employment rates. Concentration in retail trade reflects a historical continuity in this population, especially for Armenians and Jews. The convergence in real estate is a carryover of the construction boom in the Middle East, of which many immigrants were direct beneficiaries. The Middle Eastern influx also coincided with the construction boom in Los Angeles in the 1980s. Using a combination of skills, capital, opportunity, and experience, Middle Easterners are highly visible in the

TABLE 12.4 | Top Ten Industrial Niches for Middle Eastern Groups, Los Angeles Region, 1990

	Index of Rep.	Self-employed (%)	Female (%)
Foreign-born			
Real estate	1.6	37	31
Banking	1.9	0	70
Retail gas station	10.3	33	4
Engineer service	3.0	20	18
Auto repair	2.3	43	7
Retail apparel	3.4	31	43
Office physician	1.5	53	38
Retail jewelry	8.2	54	17
Laundering	3.5	57	27
Retail furniture	2.8	38	19
Native-born			
Real estate	1.8	21	54
Theaters	2.2	26	47
Legal service	2.2	42	42
Elem. and sec. school	1.5	0	70
Engineer service	2.0	22	41
Security investment	2.3	24	11
Accountant service	1.9	53	41
Misc. prof. specialty	2.8	64	51
Retail drug store	2.2	27	62
Retail furniture	1.8	28	50

construction industry of Los Angeles, itself one of the major industries in the region.

Another striking feature about the Middle Eastern niches is that with the exception of jewelry manufacturing they are entirely service-based; Middle Eastern immigrants have thus made their economic home in growing, not declining, sectors of the L.A. economy. It is worth noting that Los Angeles is a major center of the jewelry industry, which, as an industry that imports its materials and exports many of its products and trades internationally, has been fortified by the arrival of immigrants. Otherwise, this industry was in a state of decline because of the high inflation of the 1970s and 1980s. In contrast to the Asian niches, those in which Middle Eastern immigrants are involved are higher-profit activities that feature specialized services to the general population.

Individually, the four foreign-born Middle Eastern groups are even more heavily concentrated than are all Middle Easterners combined. Iranians and Israelis, the two most recent immigrant groups, had higher levels of concentration in 1980 than Arabs and Armenians. Although percentages in niches have dropped since then, Israelis, with 73 percent, still remained heavily specialized in 1990. Israelis are the most distinctive group in their occupational specialization, partly because they are economic migrants and partly because they are the most homogeneous of all four groups.

Even though the four groups have some similar occupational niches, Iranians and Israelis are overrepresented in professional specialty occupations (see table 12.5). The occupational heterogeneity of Arabs is clearly seen in their overrepresentations on the opposite ends of the occupational spectrum as auto mechanics on one end and civil engineers on the other. Armenians are overrepresented as manufacturers of jewelry using precious stones (index = 35.4). Remarkably, self-employment rates are very high for most of the niches. Self-employment exceeds 30 percent for seven Iranian, six Israeli, four Armenian and four Arab occupational niches. Interestingly, levels of self-employment are high both for high-status occupations (physicians) and for blue-collar workers (hairdressers and auto mechanics). Thus far we have demonstrated that Middle Eastern immigrant groups have carved out niches in managerial and professional occupations, in some of which they opt for establishing their own businesses. Whether these immigrants are successful, however, is more problematic. We turn next to this question.

EARNINGS

Earnings are a widely accepted, although limited, measure of economic success. Native-born whites are the reference group against which the economic performance of all other groups is measured. Thus, economic success usually means parity in earnings with the native-born whites, controlling for such factors as education and job experience.

Given their high socioeconomic profile, we would expect Middle Easterners to earn at least as much as native whites. We compared actual (unadjusted) mean earnings to adjusted mean earnings, which were calculated by giving Middle Easterners the average labor market and household characteristics of the native whites. Since the native-born Iranian and Israeli populations are small, especially after controlling for age and labor force participation, they were excluded from the analysis. Their current high socio-economic status suggests, however, that Iranian and Israeli Americans will fare still better, surpassing even native-born Armenians and Arabs.

Although foreign-born Middle Easterners have relatively high earnings compared with other major foreign-born groups (see table 12.1), they are not earning as much as native whites (see table 12.6). Some may argue that

TABLE 12.5 | **Top Ten Occupational Niches, Foreign-Born Middle Eastern Groups, Aged 25–64, Los Angeles Region, 1990**

	Index of Rep.	Self-employed (%)	Female (%)
Armenians			
Supervisors in sales	2.0	56	20
Accountants	1.7	13	42
Auto mechanics	3.3	22	0
Manufacturers of precious stones	35.4	33	5
Bookkeepers	1.6	12	82
Real estate (sales)	1.5	18	39
Managers in food/lodging	1.7	72	41
Designers	1.7	59	21
Bank tellers	4.8	0	86
Civil engineers	3.5	0	6
Iranians			
Supervisors in sales	3.0	60	15
Accountants	1.9	13	41
Others in sales	2.4	30	48
Wholesale representatives	1.7	52	16
Civil engineers	7.9	13	9
Managers in food/lodging	3.0	30	13
Physicians	3.9	52	14
Real estate (sales)	1.8	62	39
Hairdressers	3.2	32	93
Engineers (not specified)	5.7	0	7
Arabs			
Supervisors in sales	2.7	52	13
Cashiers	3.3	17	28
Accountants	1.7	19	27
Others in sales	2.0	29	41
Managers in food/lodging	2.7	33	16
Physicians	3.5	39	7
Real estate (sales)	1.5	29	36
Insurance sales	2.9	14	6
Auto mechanics	1.9	21	0
Civil engineers	4.6	10	4

TABLE 12.5 | *(Continued)*

	Index of Rep.	Self-employed (%)	Female (%)
Israelis			
Managers in administration	2.0	30	21
Elementary teachers	1.6	0	100
Real estate (sales)	2.9	42	30
Auto mechanics	4.1	43	0
Wholesale representatives	2.0	36	0
Managers in real estate	4.3	32	15
Electrical engineers	4.0	8	0
Nursing aides	1.9	0	72
Computer programmers	2.5	0	0
Lawyers	1.7	39	39

because they are recent immigrants, Middle Easterners would not be expected to do as well as native whites. If so, then the earlier immigrant cohorts should be doing relatively better than the later ones. At first glance, it appears that indeed they are, for their actual (unadjusted) mean earnings are greater than those of the native whites. After adjustment, however, these figures drop substantially, suggesting that even though Middle Easterners have higher labor market skills, they are not given equal treatment with whites despite their racial classification as white. The most recent immigrant cohort (1980–90) is even more disadvantaged than the earlier cohort, because of the influx of less-educated and less-skilled refugees. Among Iranians who immigrated before 1980, for example, 72 percent of males and 42 percent of females aged 25–64 years had four years or more of college. The corresponding rates for the 1980–90 immigrant cohort are 54 percent and 27 percent for males and females, respectively.

Immigrants, especially exiles and refugees, usually experience downward mobility during the initial phase of resettlement; only later, after improving their English and acquiring occupational skills, do they recuperate economically. Iranian exiles who arrived in the late 1970s have experienced some downward social mobility;[35] this has also been the experience of the entire 1970–79 Middle Eastern cohort.

Immigrant status appears to be a handicap, since native-born Armenians and native-born Arabs are more successful than their foreign-born counterparts despite their lower skills. This handicap is not merely in English-language proficiency, the usual immigrant disadvantage; as we will demonstrate later in the chapter, it does not apply to Middle Eastern immi-

TABLE 12.6 | Mean Earnings, Middle Easterners, Los Angeles Region, 1990

	Raw Mean Earnings ($)	Adjusted Mean Earnings ($)	Earnings Gap[a] ($)
Men			
White NB	46,060	46,060	
Middle Easterner NB[b]	52,530	53,455	7,395
Middle Easterner FB			
1980–90 cohort	33,195	37,370	−8,690
1970–79 cohort	41,425	38,715	−7,345
1960–69 cohort	58,520	45,670	−390
Pre-1960 cohort	60,365	46,175	115
Women			
White NB	25,990	25,990	
Middle Easterner NB[b]	28,105	28,170	2,180
Middle Easterner FB			
1980–90 cohort	17,390	19,280	−6,710
1970–79 cohort	23,175	24,210	−1,780
1960–69 cohort	30,020	27,910	1,920
Pre-1960 cohort	28,820	32,160	6,170

[a] Column 2 minus adjusted mean earnings for native whites ($46,060 for males, $25,990 for females).
[b] This category consists of Armenians and Arabs, excluding Iranians and Israelis.

grants, who on the whole have a good command of English.[36] On a positive note, Middle Eastern women who immigrated before 1970 outperform their American counterparts in earnings, a phenomenon attributed to the extreme selectivity of the Middle Eastern female immigrants, especially at that time, when few women emigrated.

If recency of arrival mainly accounted for the earnings gap between Middle Easterners and native whites, then this factor should also hold for each Middle Eastern group. Yet Israelis who arrived between 1980 and 1990 earn even more than the native whites (see table 12.7). Adjustment further increases their earnings, indicating that even though Israelis have lower labor-market skills, they are handsomely rewarded. The Israeli experience is consistent with the sociological research findings that economic migrants experience less downward mobility in their adaptation than do exiles or refugees.[37] Other research has shown, however, that taking advantage of premigration education and skills, Cuban exiles have reversed this trend in the long run and have experienced upward mobility.[38] Thus, exile or immigrant

TABLE 12.7 | Mean Earnings, Middle Eastern Groups, Los Angeles Region, 1990 (Males Aged 25–64)

	Raw Mean Earnings ($)	Adjusted Mean Earnings ($)	Earnings Gap (Col. 2 − $46,060) ($)
Armenian FB			
1980–90 cohort	28,445	32,170	−13,890
1970–79 cohort	38,370	40,600	− 5,460
Iranian FB			
1980–90 cohort	34,600	38,590	− 7,470
1970–79 cohort	44,160	40,465	− 5,595
Arab FB			
1980–90 cohort	31,080	34,560	−11,500
1970–79 cohort	39,520	34,775	−11,285
Israeli FB			
1980–90 cohort	49,045	51,805	5,745
1970–79 cohort	41,860	43,615	− 2,445

status cannot be a full explanation. Unlike Arabs and Iranians, Israelis in the United States have no strong negative stereotypes and therefore are less likely to experience discrimination in the labor market than would either Arabs or Iranians.[39] Moreover, Israelis indirectly benefit from their connection to the established and affluent Jewish community in Los Angeles,[40] which will be discussed further in chapter 14.

RESISTING ASSIMILATION

Given the overall high levels of education, occupation, and English language proficiency of Middle Eastern groups, one would expect these groups to become less ethnic and assimilate rapidly. It is puzzling, therefore, to find that some Middle Eastern groups remain relatively unassimilated. One explanation is the heavy participation of Middle Easterners in ethnic business.[41] Sociologists have argued that the self-employed remain more ethnic than their wage and salaried counterparts, because their co-workers or employees are often coethnics.[42] This explanation, however, does not fully account for the Middle Eastern experience. For one thing, many professionals among Middle Easterners would be expected to assimilate rapidly because of their English proficiency and high levels of education. Although many of them are self-employed and as such often work in an ethnic environment, not all professionals are self-employed, so we would still expect professional status to affect ethnic attachment adversely. There are also several noneco-nomic factors that mitigate—or at least retard—Middle Eastern assimilation, including recency of arrival, exile and refugee status, as well as premigra-tion ethnic solidarity. The variation in ethnic change among the four groups is a function of the extent to which these factors apply to each group, above and beyond economic factors.

As rich as the census data are on economic adaptation, they are rather limited on ethnic change. To address this shortcoming, we supplement the census with our own survey of Iranians in Los Angeles where applicable. To address ethnic change, data are presented for the foreign-born and the 1.5 generation. Given the recent arrival of Middle Easterners, especially Irani-ans and Israelis, it is more fruitful to look at this generation, who arrived as young children instead of the second generation, since it is most applica-ble to all four groups. The following section presents an analysis of the relevant census variables of residential segregation, language use, and inter-marriage.

Living Among Anglos

Concentration in L.A. County, as opposed to the other four counties in the Los Angeles region, is a feature that distinguishes Middle Easterners from Asians and all other broad ethnic groups. Yet even within L.A. County, Mid-dle Easterners are by and large the only recent immigrant group to settle in the few remaining traditionally non-Hispanic white neighborhoods. The indexes of dissimilarity are lower between each of the four Middle Eastern groups and non-Hispanic native-born whites than they are between any other group in Los Angeles.[43] Generally, the less segregated a group is from native whites, the greater its assimilation, but this is not necessarily so for Middle Easterners who are residentially concentrated among whites. For in-stance, although Iranians live in white neighborhoods, they still live in a close proximity to relatives, friends, and other coethnics that retards assimi-lation.[44]

As figure 12.4 shows, Middle Easterners, especially Iranians, have settled among the native whites in the most affluent parts of Los Angeles County. Iranians have concentrated in Beverly Hills and the affluent areas of the Westside (for example, Brentwood, Bel Air, Malibu, and Pacific Palisades), as well as the affluent western parts of the San Fernando Valley such as En-cino, Sherman Oaks, and Woodland Hills. Israelis have settled in areas of Jewish concentration, such as the western San Fernando Valley and the Fairfax district. Iranian Jews also live near Israelis in the San Fernando Valley and Fairfax, reflecting a tendency among Jews to gravitate toward each other regardless of place of origin. Armenians are congregated in Glendale, Pasadena, Hollywood, and Montebello, often initially along na-tional-origin lines (for example, Armenian Iranians in Glendale, Armenians from Syria and Lebanon in Pasadena, Armenians from Armenia in Hollywood and increasingly in Glendale, and native-born Armenians in Montebello).[45] These cities and neighborhoods are so heavily identified with Armenians that when prospective emigrants in Armenia or Iran are asked about their destination, they may answer "Hollywood" or "Glendale," respectively, instead of America. Although Arabs dwell in the same areas of Los Angeles County as the rest of the Middle Easterners, they are much more scattered, because of their tremendous heterogeneity in national origins.

Intermarriage

Intermarriage is traditionally used as the best indicator of assimilation; the higher the rate of intermarriage, the more assimilated the group. Since the number of married female native-born is too small to be meaningful, we focus on the first generation. Middle Eastern immigrant groups are very likely to be in-married—defined as marriage between two members of a group, regardless of place of birth—since many of them had married in their respective countries of origin. In-marriage for females is almost universal among Armenians (94 percent) and very high among Iranians (90 percent). This rate is lower for Arabs (79 percent), and much lower for Israelis (57 percent). The Israeli rate, however, has to be interpreted cautiously, because it is based on only 173 cases.[46] These percentages, however, do not take into account the availability of potential mates. The odds ratios tell similar stories for Armenians and Iranians, but different ones about Arabs and Israelis. The odds ratio for Arabs is the lowest of all four groups, even lower than that for Israelis. Thus, foreign-born Arabs have the highest likelihood of intermarriage among Middle Easterners since they have been in the United States longer, almost 30 percent having arrived before 1975.

The very low rate of intermarriage among Middle Easterners, especially for Armenians and Iranians, can be interpreted in terms of marital norms of Middle Eastern societies. Intermarriage between Muslims and non-Muslims is generally forbidden in the Middle East, unless non-Muslims convert to Islam. Moreover, even the religious minorities are separated from each other, so that intermarriage between them is unlikely. It is expected, therefore, that Armenians will have a low rate of intermarriage. The Iranian case, however, is more complicated. The sizable presence of Jews accounts for the low rate of intermarriage among Iranians. For instance, Iranian Jewish householders not only are very endogamous but prefer their sons and daughters to marry Iranian Jews. Given the changing societal context in Los Angeles, their second choice is any other Jew, and only third an Iranian of a different religious background.[47] The first two choices are also the preferences of sons and daughters in their own mate selection; surprisingly, their third choice is a non-Iranian non-coreligionist over another Iranian.[48]

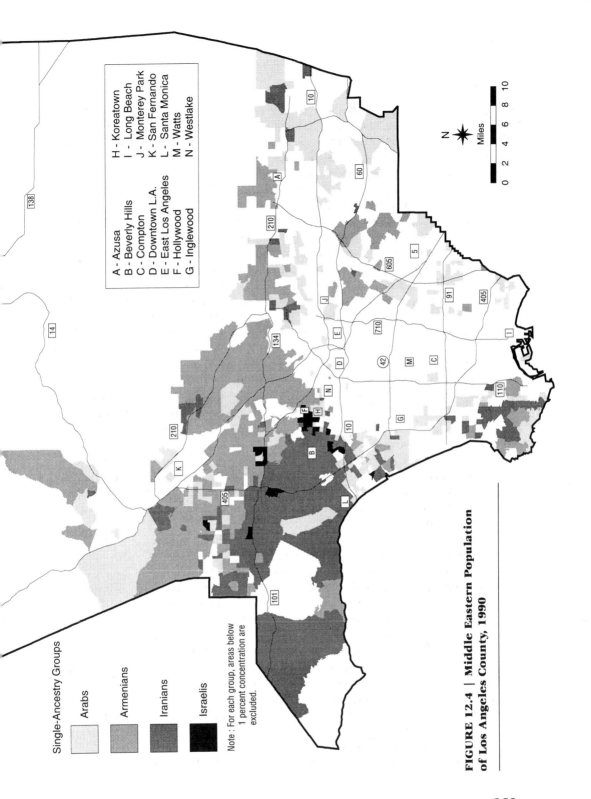

FIGURE 12.4 | Middle Eastern Population of Los Angeles County, 1990

Single-Ancestry Groups

Arabs

Armenians

Iranians

Israelis

Note : For each group, areas below 1 percent concentration are excluded.

A - Azusa
B - Beverly Hills
C - Compton
D - Downtown L.A.
E - East Los Angeles
F - Hollywood
G - Inglewood

H - Koreatown
I - Long Beach
J - Monterey Park
K - San Fernando
L - Santa Monica
M - Watts
N - Westlake

N

Miles

0 2 4 6 8 10

Bilingual Fluency

Language use is a major indicator of ethnicity among immigrants and of ethnic change among their native-born children. As could be expected, ethnic language maintenance and use are particularly high among foreign-born Armenians and Iranians and also substantially high among foreign-born Arabs and Israelis. Fully 92 percent of first-generation Armenians speak Armenian at home; 2 percent speak English, and the remaining 6 percent speak another language at home (see figure 12.5). Of Iranian immigrants, 84 percent speak their mother tongue at home, as do 68 percent of Arabs and 80 percent of Israelis. The Iranian survey provides more detailed data on the social context of language use. According to this survey, Iranian householders speak their ethnic language outside the home with close friends. On the other hand, about half the Iranians speak English to their co-workers, reflecting their participation in ethnically mixed work settings.

Some of the group differences may be attributed to the differences in age distribution, since older immigrants are more likely to retain their mother tongue. There are proportionally more elderly among Armenians than among Iranians and Israelis (15 percent of Armenians are sixty-five or older, as compared with only 6 percent of Iranians and 2 percent of Israelis). Reflecting their higher levels of intermarriage, a higher percentage of foreign-born Arabs (22 percent) spoke a language other than English or Arabic at home (see figure 12.5). While these high levels of ethnic language use are not unusual, loss of ethnic language is very surprising among the native-born Arabs and Armenians. Only 31 percent of native-born Armenians speak Armenian at home, and only 16 percent of native-born Arabs speak Arabic.[49] Clearly, a sizable portion of Armenian and Arab Americans in Los Angeles are not using their mother tongues at home because they are exogamous.

The language use of the 1.5 generation is much closer to that of their parents than to that of the second generation. The 1.5 generation is just as likely as their parents to speak an ethnic language at home, partly because they immigrated with their parents and often live with them. Israelis are an exception. Among them the percentage speaking Hebrew at home has declined from 80 percent for the first generation to about 68 percent for the 1.5 generation. Hardly any of the 1.5 generation Armenians and Iranians speak only English at home (3 percent and 8 percent, respectively); parental pressure for maintaining the mother tongue is clearly effective, at least at home where it can be enforced. By contrast, about 20 percent of both the Arab and Israeli 1.5 generation speak only English at home, twice the rate for the first generation (see figure 12.5). The Arab experience is partly attributed to its multilingual feature; about one-fifth of first-generation Arabs speak a language other than Arabic or English at home. Nevertheless, both the Arab and the Israeli experiences suggest that, at least for some groups,

FIGURE 12.5 | **Language Spoken at Home, Middle Eastern Groups, Los Angeles Region, 1990 (Ages 5 and Over)**

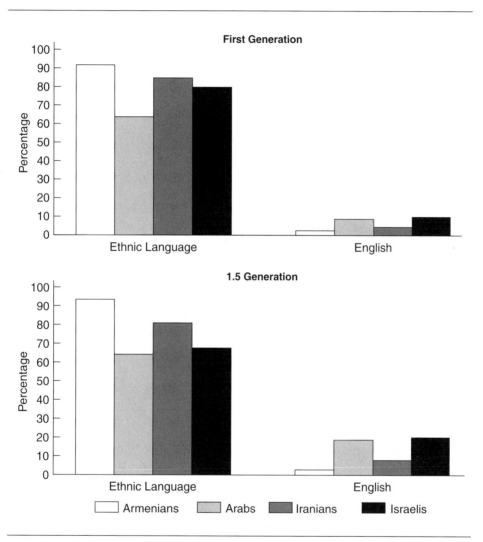

the process of linguistic assimilation starts with those who immigrate as children.

Although Middle Easterners, with the possible exception of Israelis, do not come from countries where English is commonly used, they show a remarkable degree of English proficiency. This language proficiency surely reflects their high levels of education, some of which they obtained in the

United States. Of those who speak a language other than English at home, about 80 percent of Iranians, Arabs, and Israelis claim that they speak English well or very well (see figure 12.6). Less than 60 percent of Armenians claim equal levels of English proficiency. A remarkably low percentage of Israelis (5 percent) do not speak English well or at all. The percentage of those who do not speak English well or at all is negligible among the 1.5 generation of Middle Easterners (see figure 12.6). Although facility with

FIGURE 12.6 | **English Proficiency, Foreign-Born Middle Eastern Groups, Los Angeles Region, 1990 (Ages 18 and Over)**

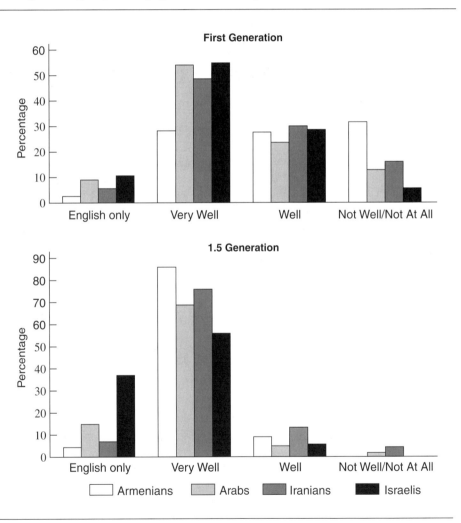

spoken English helps Middle Easterners economically, as we noted earlier in the chapter, it also encourages assimilation.

Using these indicators, one can classify the four groups according to their levels of ethnic attachment. A highly unassimilated ethnic group would have high rates of residential concentration, in-marriage, and use of the ethnic language. Thus, it would score high on all these dimensions, as do Armenians and Iranians. Israelis are the most highly assimilated of the four groups, since they score medium, low, and medium on these dimensions. With a pattern of low, medium, and medium scores, Arabs fall between Israelis and Armenians/Iranians.

Armenians are unassimilated because they arrived in the United States with a highly developed ethnic identity. Although many Armenians are refugees and exiles from the Middle East, they feel a stronger bond to their symbolic homeland, the newly reestablished state of Armenia in the former Soviet Union, than they do to their respective countries of origin. The arrival of new immigrants has led to a resurgence of ethnicity, even among the second and subsequent generations of Armenian Americans in Los Angeles. Iranians have strong ethnic identities since they are recent immigrants and include Jews and other religio-ethnic minorities with long and well-defined histories of minority experiences.[50] Among Iranian subgroups, the Muslims are the most assimilated, but even they are not fully assimilated because of their exile status and strong sense of nationalism.[51] As economic migrants, Israelis are the most assimilated. While Israelis are mostly Jewish, they are the only Jews originating from a country where they constitute a majority population. Unlike Jewish immigrants from other countries who have a developed and strong sense of minority identity, Israeli Jews arrive in the United States with a strong sense of national identity. Arabs fall in between these groups because they are a heterogeneous group consisting of many subgroups such as early and recent immigrants, religious minorities, and the Muslim majority, as well as students, economic migrants, and refugees.

CONCLUSION

Middle Easterners are the newest immigrants in Los Angeles, and one of the most distinctive groups. They are a prime example of a new kind of immigrant to the United States, that is, professionals and highly skilled entrepreneurs. As such, their experience adds to our understanding of the adaptation and assimilation of these increasingly important types of immigrants. Often well endowed with both financial and human capital (high education, professional skills, English proficiency), they are expected to adapt successfully to the American economy and society. Indeed, some Middle Easterners are doing very well, not just the entrepreneurs who, having brought a lot of capital, are expected to be successful but also physicians and engineers, many of whom are U.S.-educated and have done well because of their specialized skills. The small household size of Middle Easterners clearly gives them a further economic advantage. Having the smallest mean household size of all major foreign-born ethnic groups (3.1 persons), Middle Easterners have the highest per capita income of all groups, exceeding even the Asian foreign-born. Nevertheless, using earnings as a measure of success, we have shown that Middle Eastern economic success is mixed at best. Clearly, all Middle Easterners are not affluent, as others generally perceive them. Only recent Israeli immigrants are successful economically; the other three major Middle Eastern immigrant groups—Armenians, Arabs, and Iranians—are disadvantaged economically relative to their high education and labor market skills. The native-born Armenian and Arab Americans, however, fare better than their immigrant predecessors, a fact that attests to discrimination toward immigrants in the labor market. Discrimination is a serious problem, particularly for Arabs and Iranians in light of their negative stereotypes in the United States. But even the native-born have not reaped the benefits of affirmative action that are bestowed upon other minorities, since Middle Easterners, including North Africans, are classified as whites.

In spite of their small population size, Middle Easterners are perhaps the most diverse ethnic group in Los Angeles, consisting of at least four major groups (Arabs, Armenians, Iranians, and Israelis) and many ethnoreligious subgroups within each group (such as Christians, Muslims, Jews). Although lack of information on religion in the census does not allow us to do justice to their full range of ethnoreligious diversity, in this chapter we have explored the patterns of economic adaptation and ethnic change among Middle Easterners as a whole and among Arabs, Armenians, Iranians, and Israelis. Unlike many other immigrants, Middle Easterners, with the exception of Israelis, did not come to Los Angeles for economic reasons. Indeed, Iranians and Armenians are mainly exiles and refugees. These two groups typify family migration, and Iranians and Armenians have come to Los Angeles to be near family members.

Even more than Asian groups, Middle Eastern groups, especially Iranians and Israelis, are predominantly immigrant entrepreneurs and professionals. Since entrepreneurs and professionals are exceptions in American immigration history, this feature adds to the distinctiveness of Middle Easterners. Iranians, Israelis, and Armenians rank among the most entrepreneurial immigrants in Los Angeles, with Arabs trailing only slightly behind. Middle Easterners are also among the best-educated immigrant groups, with a high proportion of professionals. Many Middle Eastern professionals are also entrepreneurs, such as doctors, dentists, and lawyers who own their own practices. Compared with other immigrant groups, there are proportionally more Middle Easterner self-employed professionals. This pattern of self-employment explains, in part, the high ethnic attachment of Middle Eastern professionals; at their workplaces, many interact with coethnic partners, assistants, and even clients or patients.

In terms of assimilation, the patterns are complex and not closely associated with the occupational profiles of the groups. Despite their high human capital, Middle Eastern immigrants on the whole are surprisingly unassimilated. Armenians and Iranians are the least assimilated, Arabs are next, and Israelis the most. Though these levels of ethnicity exceed our expectations of highly educated and professional groups, they are congruent with the experiences of entrepreneurial minorities. Furthermore, the entrepreneurs have created a highly visible Middle Eastern milieu in Los Angeles. Given their small numbers, high educational achievement, and professional occupations, many native-born Middle Easterners were on their way to assimilation until the massive influx of recent immigrants, which in turn created ethnic communities in Los Angeles. These communities attracted Middle Easterners not only from overseas but also from other parts of the United States. Such convergence in a short period has revived ethnicity and retarded assimilation for the time being. As Middle Easterners are painfully aware, however, the 1.5 and second generations are very vulnerable to assimilation. Middle Eastern Americans may shed their cultural ties, but not as long as they continue to live in Los Angeles.

Notes to Chapter 12

1. Jonathan Alter, *Newsweek,* May 1, 1995, 55.

2. Daniel Levine, Kenneth Hill, and Robert Warren, eds., *Immigration Statistics: A Story of Neglect* (Washington, D.C.: National Academy Press, 1985).

3. Peter Theroux, *Translating LA* (New York: W. W. Norton, 1994), 49.

4. Indeed, our 1987–88 survey of Iranians in Los Angeles showed that most do not own a Mercedes Benz.

5. Geographically speaking, Afghanistan, Sudan, Somalia, and Mauritania are marginal cases, as are the newly established Independent States with majority Muslim and Armenian populations in the former Soviet Union.

6. We have used the concept of internal ethnicity to refer to this phenomenon. See Mehdi Bozorgmehr, "Internal Ethnicity: Armenian, Bahai, Jewish, and Muslim Iranians in Los Angeles" (Ph.D. diss., University of California, Los Angeles, 1992).

7. As this phenomenon is analytically distinct from internal ethnicity, we have referred to it as subethnicity. See Claudia Der-Martirosian, Georges Sabagh, and Mehdi Bozorgmehr, "Subethnicity: Armenians in Los Angeles," in Ivan Light and Parminder Bhachu, eds., *Immigration and Entrepreneurship* (New Brunswick, N.J.: Transaction, 1993), 243–58.

8. U.S. Department of Commerce, *Population Projections for States, by Age, Sex, Race, and Hispanic Origin: 1993 to 2020* (Washington, D.C.: U.S. Government Printing Office, 1994), C1.

9. With the exception of Armenians, the first-generation Middle Easterners can be identified by country of birth, but the second and later generations "disappear" in the general white population. The ancestry question, introduced for the first time in the 1980 census, has made it possible to identify Armenians as well as the native-born population of Middle Eastern origin.

10. Since the Census Bureau is legally proscribed from collecting data on religion, it does not code reported ancestries that are religious in character (for example, Jewish).

11. The inclusion of Armenians from the former Soviet Union as Middle Easterners seems appropriate since, when asked about ancestry, they identified themselves as Armenians and *not* Russians.

12. Yinon Cohen and Andrea Tyree follow a similar procedure by using place of birth and ancestry, but they also add language, to distinguish between Israeli-born Jews and Arabs. See "Palestinian and Jewish Israeli-born Immigrants in the U.S.," *International Migration Review* 20 (1994): 243–55.

13. U.S. Immigration and Naturalization Service, *Aliens in the United States* (Washington, D.C.: Government Printing Office, 1965).

14. Mehdi Bozorgmehr and Georges Sabagh, "Iranian Exiles and Immigrants in Los Angeles," in Asghar Fathi, ed., *Iranian Refugees and Exiles Since Khomeini* (Costa Mesa, Calif.: Mazda Publishers, 1991), 121–44.

15. If we include all Iran-born persons, including the sizable Armenian subgroup, the census enumerated 285,000 Iranians in the United States, of whom 100,000 are in the Los Angeles region, and 80,000 in Los Angeles County itself.

16. Paris and Berlin are the only other two Western metropolitan regions which have very large North African and Middle Eastern (Turkish) populations, respectively.

17. Der-Martirosian, Sabagh, and Bozorgmehr, "Subethnicity: Armenians in Los Angeles."

18. Mehdi Bozorgmehr, "Diaspora in the Postrevolutionary Period," *Encyclopedia Iranica* 7 (1995): 380–83.

19. Steven Gold and Bruce Phillips, "Israelis in the United States," *American Jewish Yearbook* (1996).

20. On Detroit see Barbara Aswad, "Arab Americans: Those Who Followed Columbus," *Middle East Studies Association Bulletin* 27 (1993): 5–22. Arabs are so scattered in the United States that they are not concentrated in any one metropolitan area. Consequently, Los Angeles, with only 9 percent of the total U.S. Arab population, has become one of their largest centers.

21. Portes and Rumbaut, *Immigrant America* (Berkeley and Los Angeles: University of California Press, 1990), 83.

22. See Edna Bonacich and John Modell, *The Economic Basis of Ethnic Solidarity* (Berkeley and Los Angeles: University of California Press, 1990); Jeffrey Reitz, *The Survival of Ethnic Groups* (Toronto: McGraw-Hill, 1980).

23. In 1990, the occupational D for foreign-born Middle Easterners was smallest when compared with whites (.24) and Asians (.31) and largest when compared with foreign-born Hispanics (.57) and native-born blacks (.44). Moreover, this pattern persisted from 1980 to 1990 and holds true for industry with minor modifications.

24. See Pini Herman and David LaFontaine, "In Our Footsteps: Israeli Migration to the U.S. and Los Angeles" (Master's thesis, Hebrew Union College, 1983).

25. The other three Middle Eastern immigrant groups in Los Angeles have very low rates of welfare dependency, ranging from 1.6 percent for Israelis to 3.7 percent for Iranians and 4.8 percent for Arabs.

26. United Nations Development Programme, *Human Development Report 1993*, 168, 194, and 214.

27. See Nayereh Tohidi, "Iranian Women and Gender Relations in Los Angeles," in Ron Kelley and Jonathan Friedlander, eds., *Irangeles: Iranians in Los Angeles* (Berkeley and Los Angeles: University of California Press, 1993), 175–215.

28. Steven Gold, "Gender and Social Capital among Israeli Immigrants in Los Angeles," *Diaspora* 4 (1995): 267–301; Steven Gold, *Israelis in Los Angeles*, 41.

29. See further Ivan Light and Edna Bonacich, *Immigrant Entrepreneurs* (Berkeley and Los Angeles: University of California Press, 1988).

30. Pyong Gap Min, *Caught in the Middle: Korean Merchants in Multiethnic America* (Berkeley and Los Angeles: University of California Press, 1996).

31. Ivan Light et al., "Internal Ethnicity in the Ethnic Economy," *Ethnic and Racial Studies* 16 (1993): 581–97.

32. Alixa Naff, *Becoming American: The Early Arab Immigrants' Experience* (Carbondale, Ill.: Southern Illinois University Press, 1985).

33. Earnings include income from wage/salary and self-employment for the employed persons only. Other sources of income are excluded.

34. Arlene Dallalfar, "Iranian Women as Immigrant Entrepreneurs," *Gender and Society* 8 (1994): 541–61; Arlene Dallalfar, "Iranian Immigrant Women in Los Angeles: The Reconstruction of Work, Ethnicity, and Community" (Ph.D. diss., University of California, Los Angeles, 1989).

35. Bozorgmehr and Sabagh, "Iranian Exiles and Immigrants."

36. Compared with the other groups, Armenian immigrants have a poor command of English, a handicap that translates into lower earnings.

37. Israelis are the first Jewish economic migrants to the United States. See Gold and Phillips, "Israelis in the United States."

38. Alejandro Portes and Robert Bach, *Latin Journey* (Berkeley and Los Angeles: University of California Press, 1985).

39. Predominantly Christians, Armenians are less likely than Iranians and Arabs to experience prejudice and discrimination but still more so than Israelis.

40. See Steve Gold, "Patterns of Economic Cooperation Among Israeli Immigrants in Los Angeles," *International Migration Review* 28 (1994): 114–35.

41. Ivan Light et al., "Beyond the Ethnic Enclave Economy," *Social Problems* 41 (1994): 65–80.

42. Bonacich and Modell, *The Economic Basis;* Light and Bonacich, *Immigrant Entrepreneurs.*

43. There are two caveats concerning these data. First, the index of dissimilarity (D) is calculated for the five counties, whereas Middle Easterners are heavily concentrated in L.A. County. Second, the number of observations for Israelis is too small to make the interpretation of the D meaningful.

44. Bozorgmehr, "Internal Ethnicity."

45. After the initial settlement, the trend is toward moving into nationally mixed Armenian neighborhoods (for example, the convergence of Armenians from Lebanon, Iran, and Armenia in Glendale).

46. Since Jews cannot be easily identified in the census, in addition to place of birth we also used ancestry data to define Israelis. Therefore an Israeli who married a non-Israeli Jew is considered intermarried, even though some Jews would not consider it so.

47. Bozorgmehr, "Internal Ethnicity."

48. Shideh Hanassab, "Premarital Attitudes of Young Iranians Regarding Mate-Selection: Arranged Marriage vs. Inter-Marriage" (Ph.D. diss., University of California, Los Angeles, 1993).

49. These figures are not reported for Iranians and Israelis because of small sample sizes.

50. Bozorgmehr, "Internal Ethnicity."

51. Georges Sabagh and Mehdi Bozorgmehr, "Secular Immigrants: Religiosity and Ethnicity among Iranian Muslims in Los Angeles," in Yvonne Haddad and Jane Idleman Smith, eds., *Muslim Communities in North America* (Albany, N.Y.: State University of New York Press, 1994), 445–73; Hamid Naficy, *The Making of Exile Cultures: Iranian Television in Los Angeles* (Minneapolis, Minn.: University of Minnesota Press, 1993).

African Americans: Social and Economic Bifurcation

David M. Grant, Melvin L. Oliver, and Angela D. James

THE MODERN HISTORY of black Los Angeles is bracketed by violence. In August 1965, the Watts district in L.A.'s South Central black ghetto erupted in three days of burning, looting, and altercations that pitted the area's African American residents against the city's largely white police. Even back then, there was controversy over whether the disorder qualified as a riot or a civil uprising. Whatever the verdict on this narrow point, few would quarrel with the Kerner Commission on Civil Disorders in its judgment that the "Los Angeles riot, the worst in the United States since the Detroit riot of 1943, shocked all who had been confident that race relations were improving. . . ."[1] By the early 1990s, few observers were confident about the state of race relations in the United States, let alone Los Angeles, but no one was quite prepared for the outburst that erupted in April 1992, moments after four Los Angeles police officers were acquitted of charges that they had beaten a black motorist, Rodney King, a year before. In three short, action-packed days of violence, Los Angeles exceeded the record for all previous civil disorders, in terms of loss of life, injuries, and property damage.[2]

The events of 1965 and 1992 are inextricably intertwined. Clearly, the more recent outbreak, in its scale, its intensity, its diffusion, and the variegated cast of characters it engaged, is more than an echo of the earlier event. But as the underlying causes seem so much the same—persistent tension between the police and the community, on the one hand, and economic exclusion, on the other—one is tempted to conclude that not much has changed for black L.A. over the past several decades.[3]

This essay takes a different point of view. Focusing on

the years between 1970 and 1990, we argue that African American Angelenos experienced increasing differentiation and bifurcation. By differentiation we mean that African Americans increasingly differ from one another in the kinds of jobs they perform, their educational attainment, and the neighborhoods in which they live. By bifurcation we mean that black L.A. has been increasingly split between those who are well-to-do and those who are faring poorly. Clearly, class distinctions have always existed within the black community; we contend, however, that they have grown over the past two decades and are likely to widen further in the years ahead. In underlining the centrality of bifurcation, we do not dismiss the continuing importance of race but rather seek to identify its meaning and its relationship to the social, economic, and political forces at work in late-twentieth-century L.A. We concur, echoing W. E. B. DuBois, that the "color line" is still the problem of our times.

BLACKS IN LOS ANGELES: A HISTORICAL OVERVIEW

The promise of the West and the early settlement patterns of Los Angeles residents had the potential to develop a racially integrated city. From the time of the 1888 land boom, when African Americans first became a sizable presence in Los Angeles, black homeowners could be found in all areas of the city. The heart of the black community grew along Central Avenue, however, spreading south from Temple Street,[4] as chapter 2 has described. Although some black Angelenos succeeded in moving to mixed neighborhoods, they had a depressingly familiar experience when looking for work. Economically, Los Angeles was a Jim Crow town; its booming oil, film, auto, and rubber industries never opened their doors to blacks, who were forced to find employment in domestic service and transportation. Even so, black Angelenos benefited from the region's rapid economic growth, which pushed wages in Los Angeles to among the highest in the nation, with a trickle-down effect even in the humbler occupations to which blacks were confined.[5]

Once the black population doubled, as it did during the decade of the teens, matters took a turn for the worse. Whites confined blacks to the Central Avenue area through mob intimidation, violence, and restrictive covenants. Restrictive covenants in housing titles—forbidding the sale or lease to persons other than whites—became increasingly common and effective barriers to black residential growth following a 1919 California Supreme Court decision that made such covenants enforceable by law.[6] Later, as the region's population diffused to new areas of growth in the San Fernando and San Gabriel valleys, white homeowners associations pushed covenants to ensure racial homogeneity there.[7] As the labor shortages of the Second

World War attracted new migrants, black Angelenos found themselves sorely overcrowded and facing heightened racial tensions when their growing numbers pushed the ghetto boundaries south and westward. The residential development of the valleys housed both new white migrants to the area and whites fleeing neighborhoods in the basin that were being successfully entered by blacks.

Occupationally, Los Angeles became one of the last cities to integrate blacks into the industrial order. Whereas blacks were increasingly becoming a blue-collar work force in Detroit, Chicago, Cleveland, and New York in the 1920s, blacks in Los Angeles were nearly excluded from such emerging dynamic industries as autos and rubber.[8] Unions in Los Angeles, with the exception of the United Packinghouse Workers, were either hostile or indifferent to blacks. Consequently, domestic service jobs retained their traditional importance, employing over half of Los Angeles' black population as late as the 1930s. Blacks increasingly looked to the public sector for employment, even though racial slights and job segregation prevailed. Clerical jobs and segregated all-black fire, police, and janitorial units provided access to steady, relatively well-paid work. Good jobs in the City Department of Water and Power were closed to African Americans on the grounds that the city "did not have separate camp facilities for whites and nonwhites."[9] Black professionals as well were locked out of opportunities in the public sector; blacks were not allowed to teach in junior or senior high schools until 1936. Nevertheless, the public sector was a major source of African American employment in Los Angeles during the 1930s.

For black Angelenos, the outbreak of the Second World War meant major economic changes on the home front. Primed by millions of federal dollars, prodded by federal mandates and local black political activity, and desperate for workers of any kind, the region's manufacturing employers finally began to hire black labor. The opening of wartime industry gave blacks a foothold in the shipyards and in the steel and aircraft industries. While many of these jobs were lost after the war, the establishment of the African American working class in Los Angeles had begun.

Jobs drew black migrants to Los Angeles at an unparalleled rate. Between 1940 and 1944, the black population grew from 63,774 to 118,888, an increase of 86 percent.[10] But white Angelenos refused to make housing equally available to their new black neighbors. By the time the Supreme Court finally overturned racial covenants in 1948, patterns of racial residential segregation were firmly in place.[11] The building of public housing in Watts further isolated an already congested black community. White flight from the South Central area intensified after the 1965 Watts riot, and by 1970 Los Angeles ranked third, following Chicago and Gary, Indiana, as the nation's most segregated metropolis.[12]

The black Los Angeles of that time was a spatially concentrated and economically marginalized community. The South Central area, home to the majority of the region's black residents, was nearly all black. The movement of blacks into industry was less complete than in other cities where the industrial base was initially larger and blacks had been incorporated at an earlier time, and integration into the industrial order did not necessarily translate into high wages or occupational advancement. Public sector jobs were an important source of economic security for blacks, particularly for the black middle class, but even these jobs typically failed to reward blacks for their educational training; college graduates working in the post office received wages comparable to those of white high school graduates. Thus, the Los Angeles of 1970 had a class structure that found most African Americans at the bottom and only a select few near the top. The remainder of this chapter tells how that community was transformed.

THE INCREASING BIFURCATION OF BLACK LOS ANGELES

To support our claim that black Los Angeles has become increasingly differentiated and bifurcated, we describe the contours of the two black L.A.s by comparing native-born blacks with the other major native-born ethnic groups in the region: whites, Latinos, and Asians. Shifts in the residential distribution of black Los Angeles play a crucial role in our story. By 1970, South Central Los Angeles had reached its full maturation as a black ghetto (see figure 13.1), containing a population that was 80 percent black. At this time, 55 percent of those African Americans who lived in Los Angeles made their home in the South Central area, as did 50 percent of all black residents living in the five-county L.A. region. Twenty years later, South Central was a much different place. Although the majority of South Central's residents in 1990 were black (50.3 percent),[13] the Latino presence had ballooned from 9 percent in 1970 to 44 percent in 1990. The transformation of South Central L.A., with much of the oldest housing stock in the region, from a black ghetto to a Latino barrio is well under way.

At the same time that blacks were becoming less concentrated in South Central L.A., they were experiencing less occupational segregation in the labor market. In 1970, blacks were moderately segregated from whites, Latinos, and Asians. Twenty years later, blacks increasingly overlapped with these groups, as their diminishing scores on the index of occupational dissimilarity indicated.[14] As blacks became less distinctive in the kinds of work they did, their incomes correspondingly increased. Between 1969 and 1989, real earnings, as measured in median annual earnings, increased among men for all the region's native-born ethnic groups; black men, however, had the greatest percentage gain, followed by white, Asian, and Latino men (see table 13.1). The bad news for black men is that even though they narrowed their earnings gap, in 1989 black men still made only 72 cents

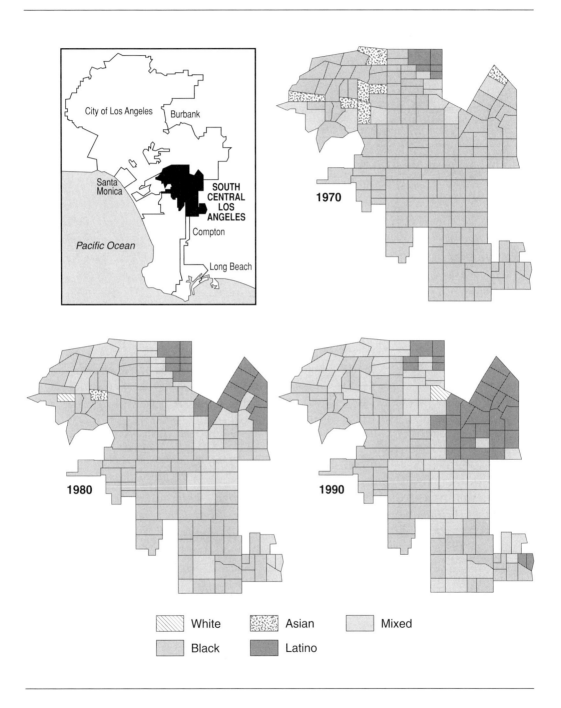

TABLE 13.1 | Median Annual Earnings (in Constant 1989 Dollars), by Racial/Ethnic Group, Los Angeles Region, 1969–1989

	1969 ($)	1979 ($)	1989 ($)	Change 1969 to 1989 (%)
Men				
Blacks	24,025	24,508	27,303	13.6
Latinos	27,436	26,713	28,315	3.2
Whites	34,252	34,689	37,820	10.4
Asians	32,804	32,743	35,393	7.9
Women				
Blacks	13,803	17,237	22,247	61.2
Latinos	13,481	13,841	18,202	35.0
Whites	17,211	17,237	22,247	29.3
Asians	19,085	20,683	25,281	32.5

for every dollar earned by white men, 77 cents on the dollar compared with Asian men, and 96 cents on the dollar compared with Latino men.

The increases for black women's median earnings are even more impressive (see table 13.1). Like black men, black women showed the greatest gain vis-à-vis other women in median earnings over the 1969–89 period, increasing an astounding 61 percent, compared with Asians (33 percent), Latinas (35 percent), and whites (29 percent). More importantly, black women's median earnings reached parity with white women in 1979 and in 1989 exceeded Latinas' earnings by 22 percent while trailing Asian women's by just over 10 percent.

Although these indicators point to growing prosperity for black Angelenos, other measures direct our attention to bleaker trends. While black earnings increased significantly, the percentage of black families living in poverty dropped only slightly, from 22 percent in 1970 to 18 percent in 1990. Moreover, the number of blacks living in concentrated poverty (census tracts with poverty rates of 40 percent and higher) increased by over 15,000 between 1980 and 1990, suggesting a growing geographical divide between the poor and nonpoor black population. Evidence of the economic divide is strengthened when we turn to data on the distribution of earnings and income.[15] Since the earnings and income distributions changed for reasons related to structural and demographic shifts, we have used the 1970 distributions as our baseline figure, showing how the real earnings and income received in 1990 fit into the 1970 distributions. As figure 13.2 shows,

FIGURE 13.2 | **Black Annual Earnings Quintiles, Los Angeles Region, 1970–1990**

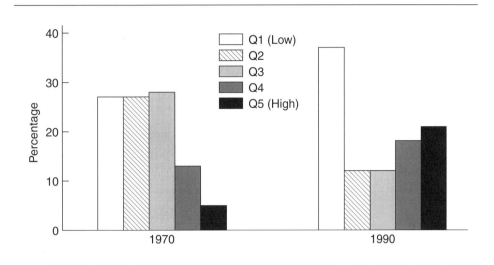

change occurred at the extremes of the earnings distribution; the number of blacks in the poorest quintile soared, and those at the high end increased as well. The middle three quintiles accounted for 70 percent of black earners in 1970 but just over 40 percent in 1990.

Polarization is a major theme in recent writings on income distribution, but among the native-born ethnic groups in the Los Angeles region, polarization applies only to African Americans. Figure 13.3 charts the family incomes of blacks, non-Hispanic whites, Latinos, and Asians in 1970 and 1990, following the adjustment procedure used for the earnings distribution. In 1990, blacks were the only group to exhibit the U-shaped distribution associated with polarization. The U-shaped pattern is not as pronounced for family income as it is for annual earnings, yet it clearly demonstrates a growing bifurcation in the economic status of African Americans in Los Angeles. By contrast, the distribution of family income among whites and Asians shows a strong movement toward the upper-income quintile in 1990. While Latinos, like blacks, show a large increase in the upper-income quintile, they maintain a pattern of strong representation in the middle ranges that differs from the African American trend toward bifurcation.

This quick sketch of residential and economic patterns suggests that growing *internal* divergence best describes the trajectory of black Los Angeles. In the next section, we seek to account for this shift.

FIGURE 13.3 | Family Income Quintiles Among Native-Born Ethnic Groups, Los Angeles Region, 1970–1990

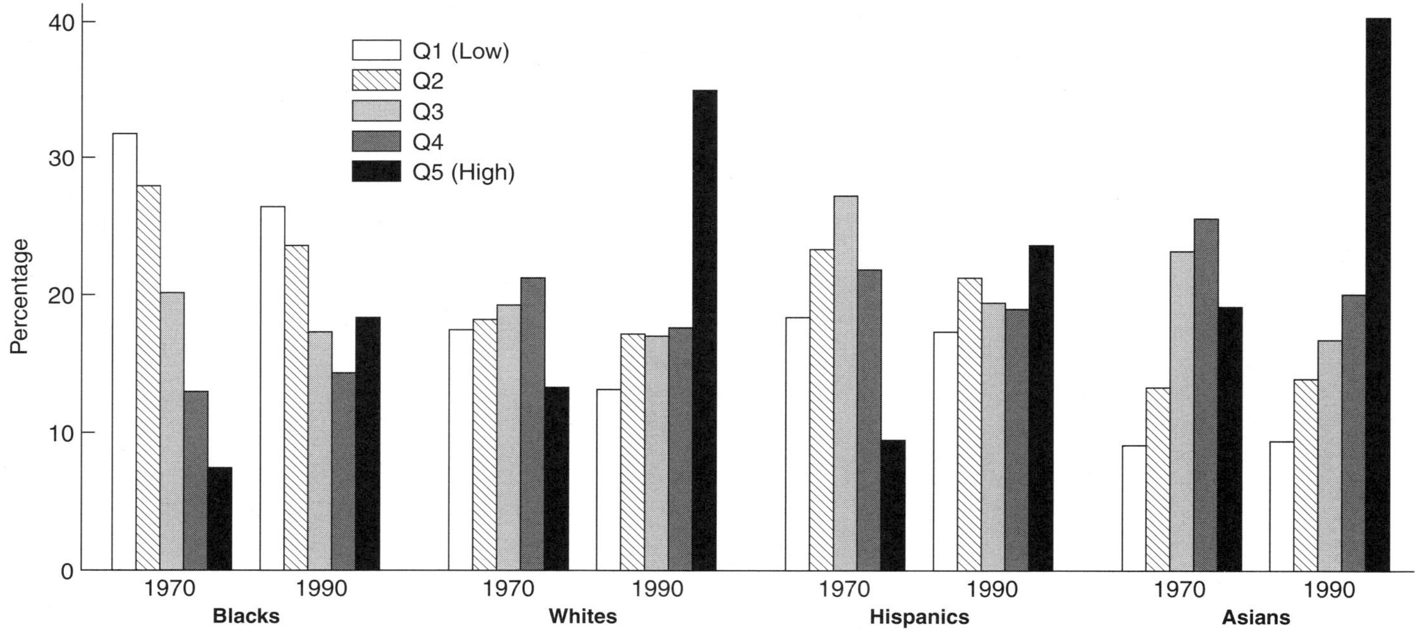

POLARIZATION IN THE LABOR MARKET

While oil shocks, global competition, and the end of U.S. global hegemony sent the smokestack economies of cities like Chicago, Detroit, and Newark into a tailspin, defense contracting allowed the illusion of limitless growth and prosperity in the Los Angeles region to continue.[16] Moreover, Los Angeles produced its own distinctive brand of economic restructuring, characterized by rustbelt deindustrialization alongside sunbelt corporate boom, with high-tech flexible manufacturing co-existing with third-world sweatshops. As the bifurcation of black earnings just reported suggests, the L.A. economy has produced winners and losers, as well as nonplayers, among the region's black population.

Men

A flurry of research over the past decade has addressed the "crisis" of black men in the labor market, so-called because black men have been falling behind other men in terms of their relative earnings and rates of labor force participation.[17] As the preceding section showed, this crisis has no basis in Los Angeles; black men have made considerable progress in terms of earnings. Adjusted earnings relative to those of white, Latino, and Asian men show that black men have closed the gap with each succeeding decade since 1970. Labor force participation, however, is another story. The employment rate of black men (aged 25–64) in Los Angeles fell about nine percentage points between 1970 and 1990, from 78 to 69 percent—a modest drop. Looking at how employment differs over time by age and educational attainment, however, illuminates the bifurcation picture.

Figure 13.4 shows the rate of employment for young black men (aged 25–34) in Los Angeles in 1970, 1980, and 1990 by level of educational attainment.[18] The only group that does not exhibit a steady decline in employment is the most highly educated, men with at least a bachelor's degree. While employment among those with some college education declined in each succeeding decade, the major falloff was among those with a high school education or less. Of the young black male high school dropouts, fully two-thirds worked in 1970. In stark contrast, only one-third of black male high school dropouts worked in 1990. Similarly, the rate of employment among high school graduates fell precipitously. In 1970 almost nine of every ten black male high school graduates were active participants in the labor market; this figure declined to six of every ten in 1990.

To balance this tremendous fallout at the bottom of the labor market for poorly educated black men there is some good news: Educational attainment for black men in the Los Angeles region has increased with each passing decade. The percentage of young men with a high school education or

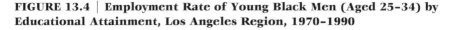

FIGURE 13.4 | Employment Rate of Young Black Men (Aged 25–34) by Educational Attainment, Los Angeles Region, 1970–1990

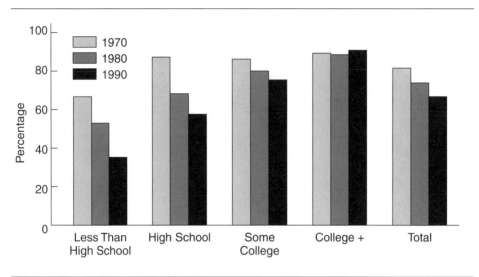

less fell from 70 percent in 1970 to 45 percent in 1990. In terms of educational attainment and employment, the problem for black men, consistent with the notion of increasing bifurcation, is twofold. First, despite significant overall educational improvement, in 1990 nearly half the young black men had a high school education or less, and only about half of them were employed. Second, education, particularly college education, has become an increasingly important asset for young black men for employment alone, leaving aside earnings, mobility, and other labor market outcomes. The employment rate of the highest- and lowest-educated young black men in Los Angeles differed by about twenty-two percentage points in 1970 but had doubled to fifty-five percentage points in 1990. This growing divergence in employment appears to be almost entirely driven by the precipitous decline in employment among less-educated black men, since the growing number of college graduates have had consistently high rates of labor force participation.

Much of the recent literature on black men in the labor market links the decline in labor force participation to the decline of industrial manufacturing in central cities; the employment prospects of low-skilled, poorly educated black men have dwindled as plants have cut back, closed, or moved to the suburbs, the South and Southwest, or overseas.[19] One can tell a similar story for Los Angeles, but with major complications. Durable manufacturing ranked as the second largest sector of employment for black men in each decade from 1970 on. Although slightly underrepresented in goods production overall, blacks had successfully established themselves in a number of pockets within the L.A. manufacturing complex by 1970. In that year, when 41 percent of the region's black workers were employed in industries that could be classified as niches, a quarter of those African Americans employed in black concentrations worked in manufacturing. Ten years later, African American niches retained 32 percent of the region's black labor force, but by that time only 2 percent of the black workers employed in these specializations made a living in manufacturing.

The statistics on black men's declining presence in manufacturing are not surprising; the region's most heavily deindustrialized areas are to be found in South Central Los Angeles and in the surrounding communities immediately to the east. Between 1978 and 1982 alone, L.A.'s industrial corridor lost more than seventy thousand high-wage auto, steel, rubber, and civilian aircraft jobs, and more than two hundred Los Angeles–based firms, including Hughes Aircraft, Northrop, and Rockwell, moved all or part of their operations out of Los Angeles County.[20] Diminishing opportunities for employment in well-paying, largely unionized jobs in Los Angeles suggest that deindustrialization accounts for a significant portion of the drop in black male labor force participation.

Manufacturing decline, however, is far from the entire story. Unlike many other cities with documented mismatches along the dimensions of skills and/or location, Los Angeles witnessed the addition of thousands of low-skill jobs to the area's economy.[21] Many of these jobs, if not most, were located in the city of Los Angeles itself, within easy commuting distance from the core of the black population. Since considerations of availability and proximity suggest that the usual hypotheses of a mismatch between black men's skills and employers' requirements do not apply, shifts on the supply side might provide a better explanation.

As chapters 9 and 10 have described, the advent of immigrants from Mexico and Central America greatly expanded the supply of low-skilled labor during the years after 1970. Why the lion's share of the region's low-skill jobs went to immigrants and not young black men is not quite clear. Some analysts argue that young black males did not want these jobs, particularly those in the highly competitive craft sector, which produces items such as furniture and clothing and demands long hours, often for sub-minimum-wage pay.[22] Roger Waldinger's interviews with employers in L.A.'s hotel and restaurant businesses provide supporting evidence for this view; employers claim that few blacks, if any, apply for the entry-level jobs they have available. As more immigrants move into these jobs, the jobs may be perceived by young black males as undesirable and labeled pejoratively as "immigrant jobs."[23]

Alternatively, employer behavior may explain why Latinos not blacks, filled low-skill jobs in L.A.'s expanding low-skill sector. A survey of employers in Chicago demonstrated that employers had a clear preference for immigrant Mexicans over blacks.[24] Employers often viewed black men as unreliable, dishonest, and lacking the proper "attitude" they sought in employees. Employer interviews in Los Angeles document that local employers hold similarly negative views of black men as potential employees.[25]

Adjudicating among these and other interpretations is beyond the scope of this chapter. Our evidence, however, points to black displacement by immigrants in only a few areas of the economy. While the detrimental labor market position of black males cannot be explained by a few occupations, an examination of a few examples can shed light upon the potentially negative effects that immigrant labor can have on black access to low-skill jobs. Consider the example of janitors, the largest single black occupational niche from 1970 on. In 1970, one in three janitors was black and one in fourteen was foreign-born Latino. The next two decades saw the total number of janitors more than double, yet the number of black janitors fell by more than three thousand, while the number of immigrant Latino janitors rose by more than thirty-nine thousand (see table 13.2). A transformation of this type is difficult to explain. It is unlikely that African Americans simply did not want or were unavailable to fill the growing number of janitorial positions; more likely, however, is the possibility that janitorial jobs became increasingly difficult for blacks to get. The main janitor's union (Service Employees International Union) did little to keep pace with demand. As the size of the union sector diminished, the union and its primarily black workers found it increasingly difficult to protect their position in the Los Angeles market.[26] Moreover, employers were likely to find immigrants an attractive work force, since immigrants made less than blacks in 1970 and their wages underwent further relative erosion over the subsequent twenty years. As the African American janitorial work force shrank, it increasingly shifted to a public sector concentration, which offered fewer contacts with private sector employers, where the great bulk of the foreign-born Latino work force finds work.

Showing a different pattern but a similar result is the construction industry. Construction is an industry from which African American men have long been excluded. With its union hall hiring procedures and on-the-job training apprenticeship programs, which often take several years to complete, opportunity for discrimination and exclusion is rampant.[27] The history of black underrepresentation prompted a number of federal efforts to increase black employment in construction and the skilled trades through contracting requirements in the 1970s.[28] Nonetheless, in 1990 black men in the Los Angeles region continued to be underrepresented in the industry, even though thousands of low-skill, relatively well-paying construction jobs were created during the preceding decade. Foreign-born Latinos, however, made tremendous gains in construction. Blacks and foreign-born Latinos

TABLE 13.2 | Characteristics of Selected Groups Employed as Janitors, Los Angeles, 1970–1990

	1970	1980	1990
Native-born blacks			
Index of representation	4.6	3.1	1.8
Percentage	33.0	23.0	12.0
Number in occupation	14,800	14,160	11,226
Percent male	80	74	74
Mean adjusted earnings	$18,893	$12,376	$18,951
Percent in public sector	36.0	44.0	46.0
Foreign-born Latinos			
Index of representation	1.5	2.1	2.6
Percentage	7.0	23.0	46.0
Number in occupation	3,300	13,820	42,609
Percent male	85	79	66
Mean adjusted earnings	$15,593	$10,156	$13,572
Percent in public sector	12.0	10.0	9.0
Total number in occupation	45,200	60,740	92,369

each made up about 5.5 percent of construction workers in 1970, but in 1990 only 3 percent of construction workers were black, while 25 percent were foreign-born Latinos. It is reasonable to expect that the stimulus of federal contracting requirements would give blacks an edge over foreign-born Latinos in the construction industry and that the discriminatory forces that kept blacks out of construction would keep others out as well, yet clearly this did not happen.

Since young black men with low levels of education are not likely to find jobs as janitors or construction workers, what kinds of employment do they find? Despite declining rates of labor force participation, the fact is that a large majority of young black men with a high school education or less worked in 1990. One important growth sector for low-skilled black men is in transportation, communication, and other public utilities (TCPU) industries.[29] Black men in 1990 were overrepresented in occupations such as bus and truck drivers, freight and baggage handlers, and telephone installers.

A noticeable feature of these growth areas is that they are mainly found among predominately large private and quasi-public firms (for example, airlines and gas, water, and power companies). Large firms are more likely than smaller ones to have affirmative action hiring policies, internal labor markets, and better wages and benefits. To the extent that black males benefit from employment in such firms, trends toward downsizing, subcontracting, and flexible employment are likely to diminish job opportunities.[30] Using census data, we cannot assess the role of firm size and affirmative action on the recent employment trends of black men with low levels of education in Los Angeles, but the growth of employment in transportation, communication, and utilities is consistent with arguments that emphasize these institutional forces in the labor market.

While most low-skilled black men met worsening employment conditions, many other black men, particularly among the college-educated, made large gains in the L.A. area between 1970 and 1990. Many black college graduates found jobs in state, local, and federal government, but the fastest growth occurred in expanding areas of the labor market in which blacks had previously been underrepresented. The two fastest upper-tier growth industries for all men in the Los Angeles area over the two decades were financial–insurance–real estate (FIRE) and Professional Services (see figure 13.5). The growth of black men in these industries outpaced the rapid growth of men in the region as a whole.

Even more impressive gains occurred in the occupational distribution of black men's employment. In 1970, black men were severely underrepresented in the top occupational categories of managerial-administrative, professional-technical, and sales occupations. Again, the gains of black men in these occupations far exceeded those of all men in the region over the 1970–90 period.

Black men's narrowing of the relative wage gap as well as their industrial and occupational gains over this twenty-year period have resulted from a combination of factors. Principal among these forces is education; the percentage of black men graduating from college more than doubled during this period. A college degree is often the first requirement for entry into the corporate sector, and it may also serve as a strong counterweight to the negative stereotypes employers often hold of black men, a symbol that a candidate does not fit the preconceived undesirable mold. Second, black men's gains in Los Angeles are in part a consequence of the extraordinary economic strength of the region. Indeed, Los Angeles may present a best-case scenario nationally for the labor market incorporation of black men during the 1970–90 period. Occupational incorporation and advancement require a healthy economy with growing opportunities; Los Angeles meets this requirement, while most major urban metropolises with large black populations do not. Finally, and especially during the earlier part of our twenty-year period, affirmative action plans in both the private and public sector helped to open new economic opportunities.

Women

In comparison with black men, black women and their labor market experiences have received relatively little research attention, possibly because

FIGURE 13.5 | Net Industrial and Occupational Change for Men, Los Angeles Region, 1970–1990

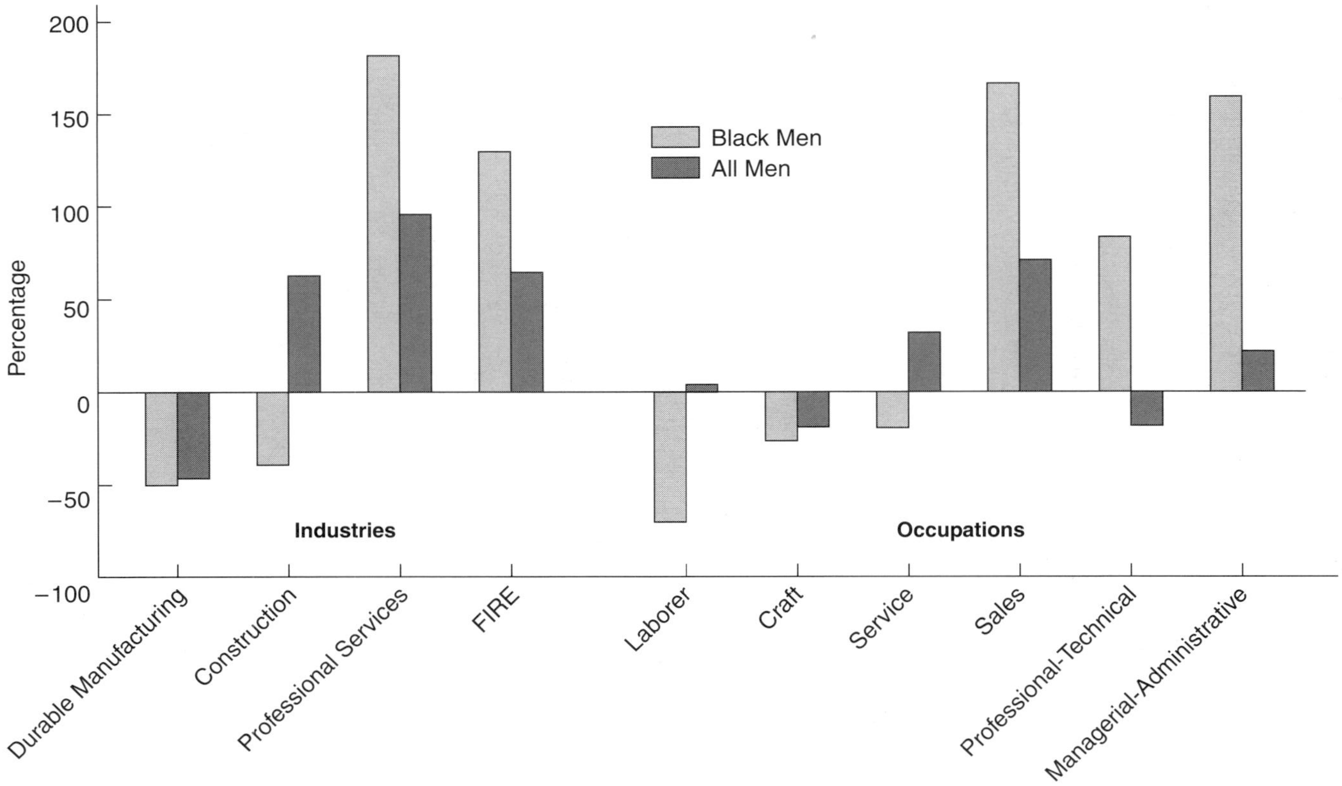

tive light. Nationally, descendants of the "old immigration" from England, Germany, and Ireland remained an overwhelming presence in 1980, accounting for almost 60 percent of the nation's population; African Americans, at 12 percent, were the next largest ethnic group. Furthermore, although African Americans were the largest group in many cities, with Italians, Poles, and French emerging here and there in second, third, fourth, or fifth place, it still held true that "the largest five ethnic groups specified in *every* urbanized area [included] the nation's three largest groups: English, Germans, and Irish."[12]

How present-day Los Angeles stacks up on this count returns us to the question we began to address in the last section: How should we interpret the way in which whites have reported their ancestry? One way is simply to count all persons who specified any given ancestry, so that, for example, all who answered "English" are counted as English, even though some of these same people may have also answered "Irish" or "Croatian" and ultimately get counted under these categories as well. By this measure, the L.A. region appears to have moved some distance, though not that far from the national norm of a decade ago (see table 14.1, column 3). Mexicans rank number one in size, reminding us of L.A.'s uniqueness; African Americans occupy the number five spot. In between these two groups of non-European origin are Germans, English, and Irish, who rank as the second, third, and fourth largest ethnic groups, respectively. They coexist with a large group of whites of other European ancestry, an aggregation of very small ancestry groups that together represent almost half the European-ancestry population. White ethnics in Los Angeles are thus seen as more of a jumble than elsewhere.[13]

But this picture of ethnic composition in L.A. largely results from the procedure of pooling ethnics of each ancestry, counting some respondents more than once. For example, "Irish-German" respondents appear twice, once as Irish and once as Germans. This might not be a major drawback if it were not for the fact that the incidence of multiple ancestry varies systematically among the region's diverse population groups; since those of European background are more likely to report multiple ancestry than persons with origins elsewhere, whites are more likely to be double-counted than others.

For this reason, we have adopted an alternate way of counting white ethnics, one which does not double-count but still gives weight to each ancestry for people reporting multiple ancestries. We have first treated each person reporting multiple ancestries as two people—one with the first ancestry, the other with the second, but otherwise identical—and have then weighted each such "pseudo-person" by half the usual census weight. With this procedure, two English-Irish respondents, for example, are equivalent to one Irish single-ancestry respondent and one English single-ancestry respondent.

Taking multiple ancestry into account by assigning weights in this way

TABLE 14.1 | Ethnic Composition of the Los Angeles Region, 1990

	(1)	(2)	(3)	(4)
	Persons Reporting Ancestry			
	Single (%)	Mixed (%)	Pooled (%)	Weighted Percentage
English	3.3	14.4	17.7	6.9
Germans	4.8	18.4	23.2	9.4
Irish	2.6	13.4	15.9	5.9
Italians	1.8	3.9	5.7	2.8
Polish	0.8	2.5	3.2	1.4
Russians	0.8	1.8	2.7	1.3
Other whites	15.2	22.8	38.0	21.9
Mexicans	24.5	1.2	25.7	25.7
Blacks	7.6	0.3	7.9	7.9
Japanese	1.2	0.1	1.2	1.2
Chinese	2.0	0.1	2.1	2.1
All others	12.2	1.2	13.5	13.5
Total	—	—	—	100.0
Total Population				(14,483,894)

NOTES: Numbers are percentages of all persons in each group, both natives and foreign-born. "Single Ancestry" means that respondent indicated only that ancestry; "Mixed" persons indicated more than one. "Pooled" is the sum of the two. Columns 1–3 do not sum to 100 percent. See explanation of weighted counts in text.

puts L.A.'s ethnic composition in somewhat different light (see table 14.1, column 4). The ranking of groups remains quite similar, especially at the top, but the size of the major European groupings relative to Mexicans, blacks, and the various Asian groups diminishes considerably.

Disaggregating the region's ethnic groups by single and multiple ancestries further slims down the importance of the region's European ancestry groups (table 14.1, columns 1 and 2). Multiple ancestry, as we've noted, is much more common among whites of European origin than among any of the other groups. Indeed, because multiple ancestry is the modal pattern among whites, the size of single ancestry groups tumbles dramatically relative to the weighted counts.

Taking several looks at ethnic composition moves us beyond the conventional views of the Los Angeles region and its ethnic character. It is not simply that Mexicans and, to a much lesser degree, various Asian groups occupy an increasingly dominant demographic role; rather, the ethnic affiliations of the European-origin versus non-European components of the population are of distinctly different types. Whereas ancestral-based identity appears increasingly residual among the former, as once-distinctive groupings shrink and melt into a diffuse white mass, the same type of ethnic slippage is barely in evidence among the latter. And even if the direction of change is the same among both broad groupings—that is, if ethnic mixing is at work among those of non-European origin also—the pace of change is so different that the two groupings are on entirely different trajectories. When one projects these trends into the future, it is not difficult to picture tomorrow's L.A. as home to a smaller "post-ethnic" Anglo population living alongside an ever-larger intensely ethnic group of Angelenos, most with origins south of the border or around the Pacific Rim.

WHITE ETHNICS IN COMPARATIVE PERSPECTIVE

Education

Ethnic differences in educational attainment have attracted considerable scholarly attention, and for a variety of reasons. For one thing, the ancestors of today's ethnics arrived in the United States varying considerably in literacy and other school-learned skills; at the turn of the century, immigrants from southern and eastern Europe, including the relatively literate Jews, ranked well below their counterparts from western and northern Europe in school attainment.[14] Second, while schooling levels moved upward among all groups with the advent of the second generation, the disparities remained striking. Educational gaps were so impressive that many scholars linked them to deep-seated cultural patterns—a connection that, if correct, should still be traceable today. Finally, in today's economy schooling exercises a critical—indeed, ever more critical—influence on employment and opportunities for advancement.

Regardless of any past educational deficiencies, the region's white ethnic groups have evolved into a highly educated population, with levels of schooling that generally put them well above the region's average. But we do find significant differences, as well as lingering traces of the large disparities of the past (see figure 14.1). First, the data highlight the exceptional educational achievement of Russians/Jews, with the proportion reporting completion of at least a college education more than twice the average for the region. Second, there are marked disparities among the remaining groups, with the English well ahead of the Irish and Italians. Third, when compared with nonwhite groups, white ethnic achievements turn out to be less than commanding; though gender differences are not displayed in figure 14.1, white women trail especially far behind native-born Japanese and Chinese women, who outpace Russian/Jewish women as well. In this respect, the Southern California pattern stands at variance with the European-origin lead over the non-European groups described by Lieberson and Waters. In Los Angeles, the traditional racial order gets rearranged. As earlier

FIGURE 14.1 | **Educational Attainment Among Selected Native-Born Groups, Los Angeles Region, 1990 (Men and Women, Aged 25–64)**

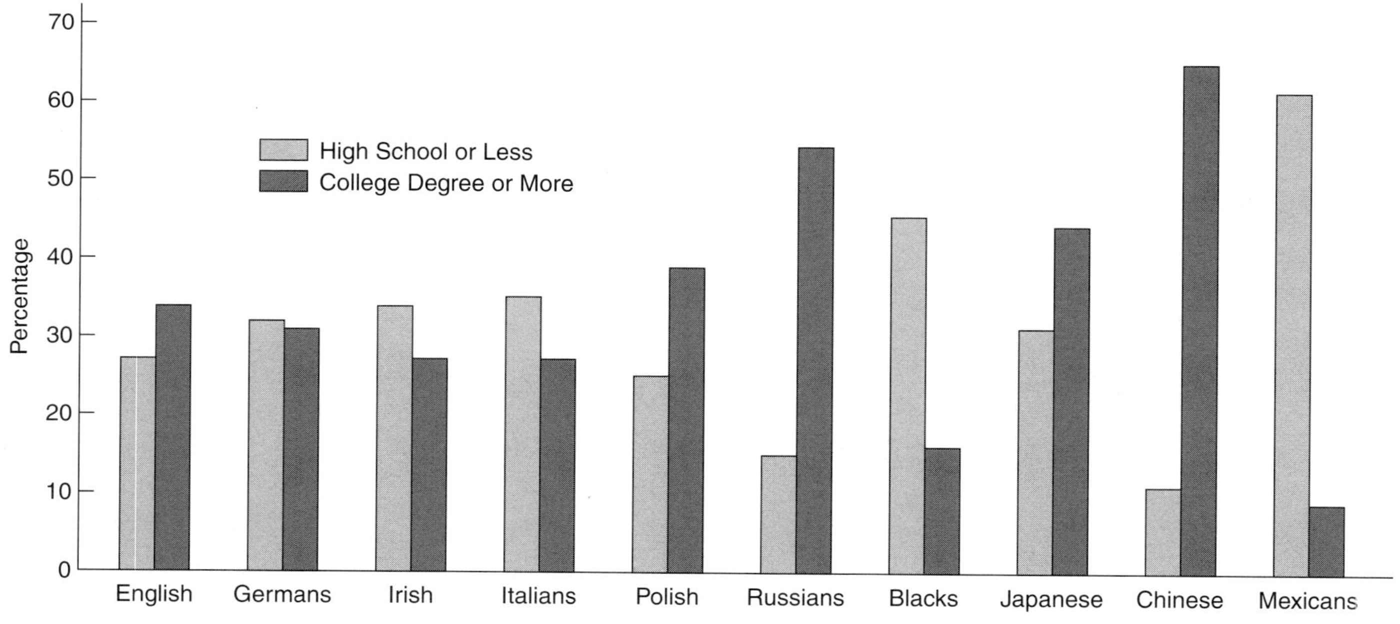

chapters have already shown, education is not the only arena in which the region's whites find themselves lagging behind Asians.

Concentration and Diffusion in the Labor Market

The traditional assimilationist framework began with the assumption that new immigrant groups start at the bottom and move up over time. Although it was not always explicitly acknowledged, the stories of ethnics making the transition from the bottom to middle or higher levels of the social structure seemed inevitably to entail the dissolution of the occupational and residential concentrations in which the immigrants and their immediate descendants had clustered.

This conception seemingly conflicts with scholarly perspectives stimulated by the new immigration, in which ethnic adaptation is seen as a process of collective mobility; groups move up from the bottom by specializing in and dominating a particular branch of economic life. In most studies, attention has focused on the consequences of specialization for the immigrant generation, particularly in ethnic enclaves or more broadly in ethnic economies, as discussed in chapter 7, on self-employment. Some scholars, however, have delved into the implications of continued specialization farther down the generational road. For example, Michael Hout has employed a cognate concept, the notion of an "enclave middle class," to explain patterns of social mobility among U.S. blacks.[15] Similarly, Calvin Goldscheider and Alan Zuckerman have argued that "Jewish exceptionalism in socioeconomic status" continues into the third generation and beyond, maintained in persistently high levels of self-employment and concentration in the professions.[16] In this view, ethnic economic distinctiveness is not necessarily an indicator of backwardness, nor even necessarily a direct product of immigration.

Whatever the pattern in the rest of the nation, the evidence for Los Angeles provides strong support for both the traditional and newer views. While for most groups of white ethnics diffusion out of ethnic niches has been accompanied by movement to the higher reaches of the social order, it has not meant invisibility for the assimilated; the region's post-ethnic group of Anglos continues to occupy a distinctive place, both in the ethnic division of labor and in the occupational hierarchy, relative to the groups of non-European origin. Furthermore, one group, the Russians/Jews, stands apart from the overall white ethnic trend, with intriguing parallels among the native-born Asian groups whose fate we also examine.

At the aggregate level, the major white ethnic groups find themselves distributed among the region's occupations and industries in remarkably similar ways. Using the index of dissimilarity (D) to measure how groups differ from each other, we find that the occupational distributions of the three largest groups—the Germans, Irish, and English—are barely distinguishable, with Ds all around .10 (see table 14.2). The differences in their industrial distributions are even smaller, indicating a highly pronounced pattern of overlapping. The Italians, a relatively small group, show some distinctiveness vis-à-vis the larger groupings, but not much. Only with the Polish and the Russians—both groups, but particularly the latter, reflecting the presence of Jews—do we see sizable differences from the other white ethnic groups, as indicated by larger Ds. In both cases, the higher D holds for both the industrial and the occupational distributions, telling us that these groups have concentrated in segments of the economy in ways that clearly differentiate them from the others.

A sharper view emerges when the frame of comparison is changed. A wider set of comparisons among the native-born brings out more clearly the overlaps among the white ethnics; the occupational and industrial distributions of the Asian groups are markedly dissimilar, more so than is the case among the region's largest white ethnic groups. Though the Japanese and Chinese Americans have moved up the occupational ladder, they have retained a distinct position within the division of labor, relative to all other groups as well as to one another. Enlarging the frame to encompass all the region's groups further highlights the distinctiveness of the major white ethnic groups relative to the non-European-origin population. Differing little from one another (if we except the Russians), the white ethnics work in a mix of occupations and industries quite unlike the complexes among which the other groups are sorted, hence the sharply higher D when any of the white ethnic groups is compared with any of the non-European-origin groups. Finally, looking at the white ethnics in the broadest context brings out the particularities of the Russian/Jewish case. While not the highest among the many sets of Ds reported in this volume, the Ds distinguishing the Russians from the other white ethnics are comparable to what we see when we contrast Japanese Americans against the other white ethnics and not much smaller than the differences between blacks and the other white groups. And one cannot help but notice that the Russians overlap least with native blacks, Hispanics, and Asians, testifying to the distinctive role of the Russians/Jews in L.A.'s ethnic division of labor.

A similar pattern emerges when one looks at the data with a sharper lens, this time searching for loci and degrees of industrial and occupational concentration. In this volume, we do so by using the concept of an ethnic occupational or industrial niche, an occupation or industry in which a group's share is at least 50 percent greater than its share of the total economy.[17] From this perspective, the white ethnics (again excepting the Russians) appear unique in L.A.'s ethnic mix, providing the only instances of either no clustering at all or very low levels of clustering. As figure 14.2 shows, among Germans and Irish—both groups with noted historical tendencies to concentrate in particular branches of economic life—only 1 percent of each group report working in an industry that could be classified as

TABLE 14.2 | Occupational and Industrial Segregation (Index of Dissimilarity) Among Native-Born Ethnic/Racial Groups, Los Angeles Region, 1990

	English	Germans	Irish	Italians	Polish	Russians	Japanese	Chinese	Blacks	Mexicans
English		0.07	0.09	0.12	0.12	0.23	0.24	0.36	0.33	0.32
Germans	0.06		0.06	0.10	0.12	0.26	0.25	0.37	0.29	0.30
Irish	0.07	0.05		0.10	0.13	0.27	0.26	0.39	0.27	0.28
Italians	0.12	0.10	0.09		0.15	0.25	0.27	0.40	0.31	0.29
Polish	0.11	0.13	0.13	0.14		0.21	0.26	0.34	0.34	0.38
Russians	0.24	0.26	0.26	0.25	0.19		0.33	0.37	0.45	0.48
Japanese	0.22	0.23	0.25	0.27	0.27	0.34		0.32	0.38	0.37
Chinese	0.21	0.22	0.24	0.25	0.22	0.30	0.28		0.53	0.54
Blacks	0.30	0.29	0.27	0.31	0.35	0.45	0.28	0.36		0.20
Mexicans	0.22	0.20	0.21	0.23	0.29	0.38	0.26	0.38	0.22	

NOTE: Occupations are shown above the diagonal, industries below the diagonal.

FIGURE 14.2 | Niche Employment, Los Angeles Region, 1990 (Native-Born Employed Persons, Aged 25–64)

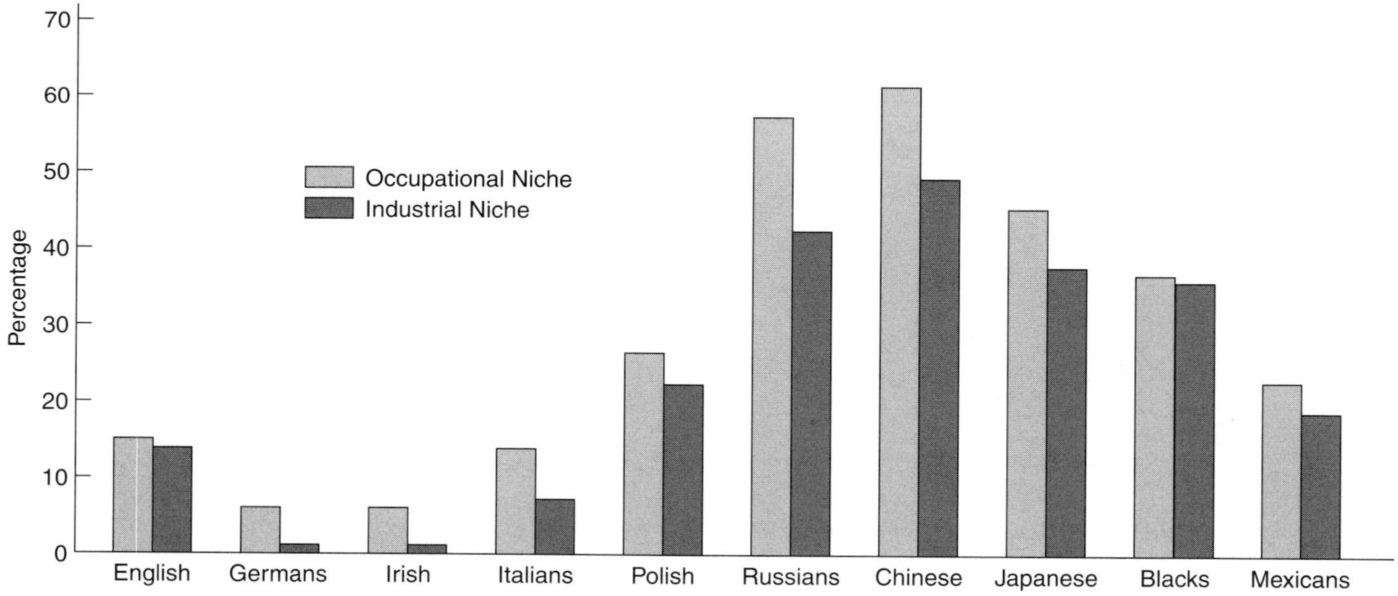

a niche. The proportion working in occupational niches appears to be a little higher, at 6 percent, but this is still not much more than none at all. Among the region's largest white groups, only the English have retained any clusters of note; the defense industry and the elementary/secondary school complex appear to constitute niches of a sort, although these are clusters whose links to the earlier pursuits and concentrations of the English is hard to divine. Still, even the clustering of the English is quite low in comparison with the region's non-European-origin groups.

When we bring the Russians/Jews back into view, however, the picture changes sharply. Once again, they provide a striking contrast to the other white groups, and in doing so they lend support to the newer concept of ethnic adaptation as a process of collective mobility. Several traits stand out from the patterns of economic specialization that the Russians/Jews have established. First, the Russians/Jews have moved into a narrow tier of occupations and industries, in this respect mirroring the experience of immigrants and of African Americans, from whom they otherwise diverge markedly. Forty-two percent of the Russians/Jews work in industries that could be classified as niches. Among occupations, the Russians/Jews show an even higher level of ethnic clustering (57 percent), which makes them more concentrated in the occupations in which they are overrepresented than most of the other ethnic groups with which this volume is concerned. In particular occupations, the concentration of Russians/Jews is even more striking; Russians/Jews are overrepresented by a factor of more than 6.0 among lawyers and psychologists, 5.5 among actors, and 4.0 among physicians.

Second, while there is nothing surprising about many of the individual occupations or industries where notable Russian concentrations appear, the complex of industries and occupations points to a clear break with historical patterns (see tables 14.3 and 14.4). With the possible exception of designers, we find no hint of a linkage to the earlier specialized pursuits of the Jewish immigrant past. And with the exception of teaching, the Russians/Jews of the Los Angeles region seem to have moved beyond the activities that engaged the second generation. Only the extraordinarily high level of self-employment—24 percent for the group overall and 35 percent for those in niche industries—represents continuity over time.

The third distinguishing feature of the Russian/Jewish economic trajectory in the region is that this group appears to have concentrated in a particularly favorable complex of industries and occupations, a *post-industrial ethnic niche*.[18] Mainly working in professional or managerial jobs requiring high levels of education, Russians/Jews enjoy high earnings. In a twist on the usual assumption that links economic status with diffusion out of ethnic economic specializations, Russians/Jews in their niche earn almost 40 percent more than those employed in industries with lower levels of Russian/Jewish concentration.

TABLE 14.3 | Russian/Jewish Industrial Niches, Los Angeles Region, 1990 (Employed Men and Women, Aged 25–64)

	In Public Sector	Index of Rep.	Mean Years Education	Self-employed (%)	Mgr/ Prof/Tech (%)	Mean Earnings ($)
Legal services	No	3.98	16.9	45	82	81,302
Theatres/ movies	No	3.77	15.2	22	79	65,555
Real est	No	1.83	14.9	38	40	52,757
BusServ, NEC[a]	No	1.90	14.4	44	64	43,022
MD offices	No	2.23	17.0	56	90	76,446
Accting svces	No	2.97	15.5	60	81	59,322
Man & PR	No	2.67	15.5	48	85	52,965
Colleges	Yes	1.61	17.8	0	90	45,936
Securities	No	2.22	16.2	10	38	90,892
Radio TV	No	2.94	15.0	7	72	61,514

[a] Percentage female > 50.

While the Russians/Jews are distinctive among the white ethnics, their case has parallels among the region's Asian Americans. Like the Russians/ Jews, earlier generations of Japanese and Chinese Americans tended to cluster in a relatively narrow segment of the economy. Their descendants still maintain distinctive niches, which engage a relatively large share of the native-born Asian American labor force, but now in activities related to business or the professions. As with the Russians/Jews, Japanese and Chinese Americans do better in the industries and occupations in which they

TABLE 14.4 | Russian/Jewish Occupational Niches, Los Angeles Region, 1990 (Employed Men and Women, Aged 25–64)

	Index of Rep.	Mean Years Education	Self-employed (%)	Public Sector (%)	Mean Earnings ($)
Mgrs. admin. NEC	1.52	15.1	24	1	70,155
Lawyers	6.13	18.0	45	13	93,451
Elem. teachers[a]	1.64	16.5	0	87	27,965
Sales reps	2.07	14.3	20	0	61,686
Accountants	1.75	15.9	40	7	60,368
Real estate sales	1.96	14.8	46	2	48,338
Physicians	3.94	18.1	60	15	120,551
Actors	5.51	15.2	29	0	67,591
Psychologists[a]	6.51	18.7	56	12	42,131
Designers[a]	1.66	14.7	46	0	45,069

[a] Percentage female > 50.

have concentrated than they do in other fields. And in one final parallel, niche transformation and persistent concentration have also accompanied a shift to positions high in the occupational structure.

What the Russians/Jews have attained through transformation of their ethnic niche the other white ethnics have achieved in less spectacular fashion through diffusion. All the white ethnic groups rank above the region's average in the percent employed in professional or managerial occupations. At the other end of the occupational spectrum, white ethnic employment in blue-collar jobs falls below average, though for several groups employment in craft jobs comes close to parity. Similarly, white ethnics have gravitated toward the advanced service sectors, all the while maintaining a significant presence in durable manufacturing—the region's key export sector up until the late 1980s—and the public sector. As in education, the Italians seem to lag slightly behind the others, especially in their penetration of higher-level occupations. And though the occupational and industrial data suggest that the white ethnics are better positioned than most of the region's other groups, the native Asian advantage in education seems to be translated into an occupational advantage as well.

Income and Earnings

The case of the Russians/Jews excepted, our view of white ethnics' role in the economic structure confirms the basic assimilation perspective—namely, that diffusion is accompanied by movement upward in the occupational structure. But does this pattern of movement and convergence carry over to earnings, or do we find persistent interethnic earnings differences? Clearly, some disparities should be expected on the basis of education alone; we can anticipate a continued Russian lead and, very possibly, a slight Italian lag. Yet some differences may remain even after taking education into account. Similarly, we should be able to count on large earnings advantages when the white ethnics are compared with the region's non-European-origin population; when we move on to this comparison, however, the question of how well native-born Asians compare in translating their occupational and educational assets takes on considerable importance.

The comparison of men's average earnings in figure 14.3 provides the most stunning confirmation of Russian/Jewish exceptionalism so far; compared with the English, who serve as our reference group, Russians/Jews hold a very substantial advantage. Clearly, some of the differential results from the high levels of Russian/Jewish education, but education explains only part of the disparity; the Russian/Jewish lead shrinks by only a third after we control for differences in background characteristics. In this respect, the Los Angeles pattern hews quite closely to the portrait drawn by Lieberson and Waters a decade ago; so too do the differences among the

FIGURE 14.3 | Earnings Gap Between Selected Ancestry Groups of Native-Born Men and English Native-Born Men, Los Angeles Region, 1989

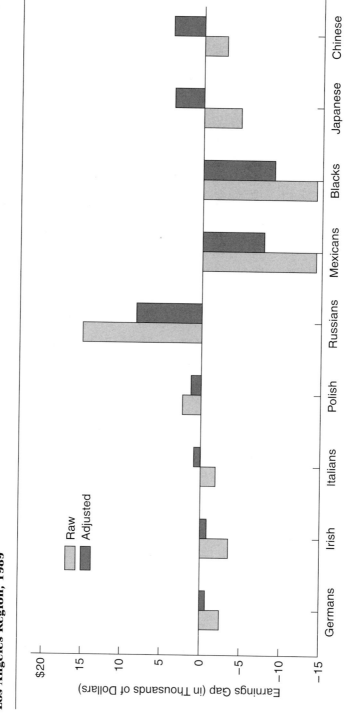

other white ethnic groups, with the English doing better than the others, though by a slight margin and one that gets trimmed—and in the Italian case reversed—after we apply controls for education and other individual characteristics. Taking women (see figure 14.4) into account modifies the picture, since the greatest disparities, both absolute and relative, are to be found among men. Not only are ethnic differences among women relatively slight, but the English advantage relative to Irish and Italian women appears to be entirely due to differences in background characteristics.

But if this sketch of earnings differences is consistent with the view we have gained of white ethnics in the region's economic structure thus far, it presents a different perspective on differences along the European/non-European divide. As other research has shown, the Asian educational advantage is not converted into the earnings advantages that one might expect and that conventional economic and sociological theories predict. (See discussion in chapter 10.) Instead, native-born Chinese and Japanese men in the L.A. region do a good deal worse on average than their white ethnic counterparts. Furthermore, their disadvantage remains after controlling for background characteristics, as one might have predicted, since Chinese and Japanese men are better educated than the white ethnics, the Poles and Russians excepted. African Americans and Mexican Americans lag still further behind white ethnics, though in this case much of the gap reflects skill disparities. Among women, the picture is substantially different, with whites relinquishing the lead to Asians, and with the gap between those two groups and Mexican Americans and African Americans smaller in both absolute and relative terms than among the men.

How well group members do in reaping the rewards of paid labor is only one dimension of the economic distinctiveness of ethnic groups; income, whether earned or otherwise, largely counts for how it affects living standards. From this perspective, the key factor is how income gets packaged in households and then made available to household members; per capita income mainly reflects the combined impact of women's and men's earnings and their interaction with household size, which in turn is linked to fertility and family structure. Applied to households in the Greater Los Angeles area, this indicator provides further confirmation of the reshuffling of L.A.'s ethnic order (see table 14.5), with whites no longer in undisputed control of the economic upper reaches. As we might expect, the Russians/Jews stand at the top in both household and per capita income, but Japanese and Chinese households follow quite closely behind; thus the high earnings and labor force participation of Asian American women compensate for the labor market disadvantages still experienced by Asian American men. Other related household characteristics that also favor the Asians can be seen in table 14.6. In number of earners per household (1.4 and 1.5, respectively), the Chinese and Japanese exceed all but the low-earning Mexicans. The relatively high number of earners among the Asians, coupled

FIGURE 14.4 | Gap Between Selected Ancestry Groups of Native-Born Women and English Native-Born Women, Los Angeles Region, 1989

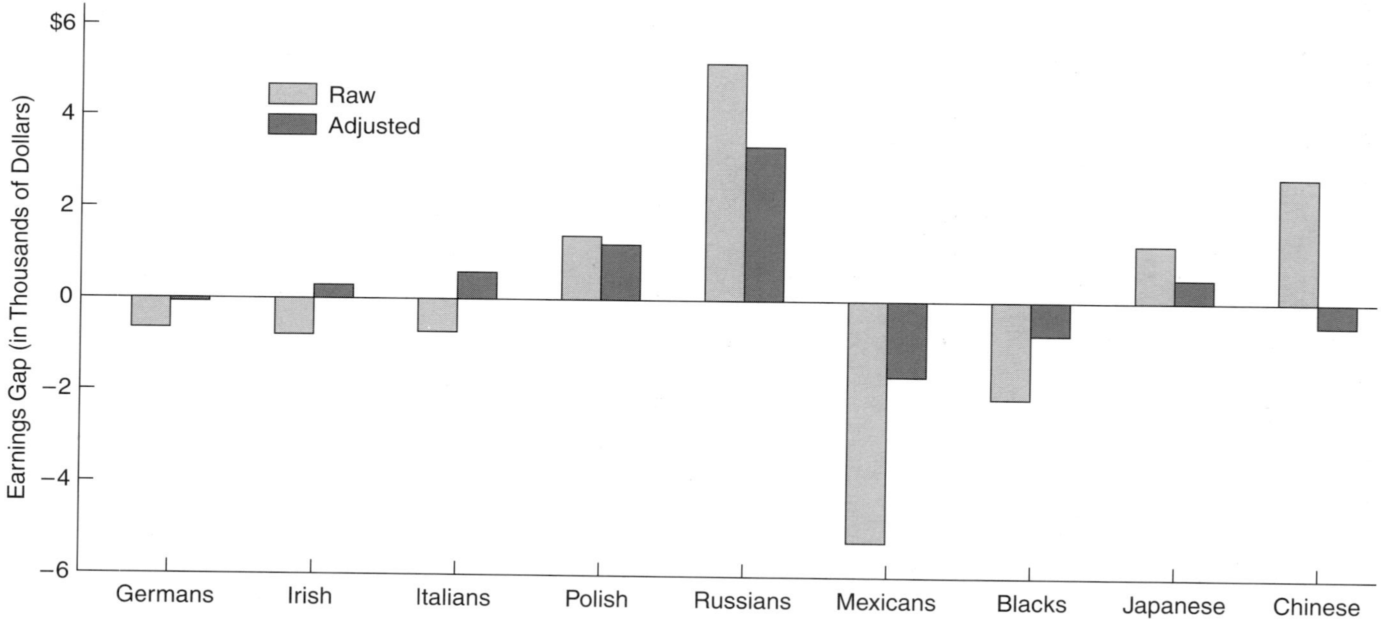

TABLE 14.5 | **Selected Household Economic Characteristics, Los Angeles Region, 1990 (Native-Born Householders, Aged 18+)**

| | Median Household | | Per Capita |
	Size	Income ($)	Income ($)
Russians	2	44,992	22,496
Japanese	2	40,936	20,468
Chinese	2	39,720	19,860
Polish	2	38,880	19,440
English	2	36,448	18,224
Germans	2	36,448	18,224
Italians	2	35,235	17,618
Irish	2	•34,016	17,008
Blacks	2	21,868	10,934
Mexicans	3	28,348	9,449

with small households, results in the lowest *dependency ratio* (defined here as the ratio of non-earners to earners) of all groups. At the very bottom, by contrast, lie Mexican Americans, whose per capita earnings are depressed by low earnings and (in this comparison group) large household size.

SPACE AND SOCIAL STRUCTURE

Residential Concentration and Diffusion

Frederic Barth's seminal book[19] recast the understanding of ethnicity by moving attention away from preoccupations with the content of group culture, toward a focus on intergroup boundaries and the processes that make boundaries persistent or permeable. Though Barth developed his perspective without reference to the tenets of assimilation theories, one can extend his work by simply contending that assimilation involves a process whereby boundaries separating ethnic groups steadily lose salience, so that interaction increasingly occurs across, rather than within, previously existing boundaries. From this perspective, the economic diffusion that we have observed among white ethnics is a reflection of extensive boundary crossing and thus serves as an important indicator of assimilation. Likewise, since personal identities and interpersonal affinities derive, in part, from workplace settings, the kind of industrial and occupational convergence that we have observed can also be a contributor to assimilation.

The local community is perhaps even more important than the work-

**TABLE 14.6 | Selected Household Economic
Characteristics, Los Angeles Region, 1990
(Native-Born Householders, Aged 18+)**

| | Mean Household | | |
	Size	Persons Employed	Dependency Ratio[a]
Blacks	2.7	1.10	1.45
Mexicans	3.4	1.50	1.27
English	2.4	1.16	1.07
Irish	2.4	1.20	1.00
Germans	2.5	1.30	0.92
Polish	2.3	1.20	0.92
Italians	2.4	1.30	0.85
Russians	2.2	1.20	0.83
Chinese	2.4	1.40	0.71
Japanese	2.4	1.50	0.60

[a] Household size (minus number employed, the result divided by number employed)

place in maintaining or rearranging ethnic boundaries. To the extent that residence is a choice—and for most Americans of European descent choice has always dominated locational decisions—patterns of residential segregation serve as indicators of the strength of ethnic affinity, revealing a preference for or against the option of living with others of one's group. The neighborhood context also acts as the crucible of identity, structuring interpersonal relationships in ways that increase or decrease the potential for in-group interaction.

Of course, Los Angeles never boasted classic ethnic neighborhoods of the type found on New York's Lower East Side or in Boston's North or West Ends. But as chapter 2 showed, the years before the Second World War did see segregation processes that bore some relationship to the patterns that characterized older eastern and midwestern cities, with concentrations of Russian Jews, Italians, Mexicans, Chinese, Japanese, and African Americans emerging in the areas adjoining downtown. Prosperity, the massive influx of postwar migrants, and urban renewal broke up these early ethnic clusters, especially those of the whites, while the relentless pace of suburbanization pushed the region's whites ever farther from the center. Most whites now live outside Los Angeles County, where they were a minority of the population in 1990. What is true for the white population overall holds for the largest groups of white ethnics; only among the smaller groups of Italians, Poles, and Russians/Jews does a majority still reside in Los Angeles

County. In the outlying areas that they now prefer, the region's other white ethnics have scattered almost randomly. Applying the index of dissimilarity (D) to residence, we find levels of ethnic integration for whites that rank extremely high by all historical standards. To be sure, the level of integration we observe among whites when looking at the region as a whole is higher than that within Los Angeles County, with its older areas of settlement, but even so the difference is one of degree, not of kind.

But on residence as on other dimensions, the Russians/Jews stand apart from the broader white ethnic pattern. In an area where change appears to be the only constant, the Russian/Jewish case reveals remarkable continuity with the past. Russians/Jews remain uniquely concentrated in Los Angeles County, in this respect bearing more resemblance to immigrants than to other white ethnics. True, some older Jewish ethnic communities such as Boyle Heights now belong to history, having failed to attract the Jewish newcomers who came to L.A. in the immediate postwar years. But as newer Jewish residents settled on the city's Westside and in the San Fernando Valley, old-timers abandoned the Eastside, pushed, in part, by massive highway building that erected several freeways right through the heart of their older neighborhood.[20] Otherwise, the Jews' spatial distribution has changed only gradually, shifting in ways that contrast with the general Anglo trend.

Within the county, Jews have mainly clustered inside the boundaries of the city of Los Angeles; consequently, most of L.A. County is virtually devoid of Jewish clusters of any note. Unlike many of the county's remaining whites, who headed for the county's desert-like northern peripheries in the 1970s and 1980s, the Jews have largely stayed put. Within city boundaries, the Jews have settled in a relatively compact contiguous area that spills over from the Westside of L.A. city (and including the separate municipalities of Beverly Hills, Culver City, and Santa Monica) to the southern portions of the western San Fernando Valley, where they live in neighborhoods of relatively high Jewish density (see figure 14.5).

Of course, residential patterns are in part a function of economics, and one could argue that the Jewish pattern of segregation is just an expression of the Jews' underlying economic differentiation. While it is certainly true that Jews have clustered in the region's wealthier areas, a closer look at some of these communities highlights the ethnic dimension in segregation among whites. Rather than dispersing among the region's more expensive municipalities, Russians/Jews are concentrated in a narrow subset of these more affluent communities. Thus, Jews are heavily overrepresented in Beverly Hills, a separate municipality on L.A.'s Westside, but underrepresented in far more exclusive enclaves, such as San Marino, east of downtown L.A.; Rolling Hills and Palos Verdes, in the southwestern part of L.A. County; and other upscale communities elsewhere in Orange and Los Angeles counties.

Intermarriage

As a force for assimilation, residential mixing is most important for the way it affects the structure of interpersonal life—namely, by increasing opportunities to interact with others, thereby increasing the likelihood that closer relationships will develop across ethnic boundaries. Of course, the statistics on segregation do not tell whether persons living in more integrated settings actually mix, only to what degree they have the opportunity to do so. Although the use of the U.S. census as our primary data source limits our ability to talk about the social and especially the cultural aspects of groups, it does allow us to examine a particularly intimate arena where ethnic boundary-crossing potentially leads to profound changes in ethnic identities: marriage.

A variety of factors, most notably group size, affect the probability that a group member will cross ethnic lines to marry; all things being equal, a member of a large group is a good deal likelier to marry another of his or her own ethnicity than a counterpart from a smaller group. Since our interest lies in the role that ethnicity plays in mate selection, we focus on determining how likely women of each group are to marry members of the same group, after controlling for the number of potential coethnic mates. In table 14.7, we present, for two age cohorts of each native-born group, an in-marriage rate and the ratio of the odds of in-marriage to the odds of out-marriage. The two indicators provide different insights into the dimensions of intermarriage. Only a minority (32 percent) of young married Japanese American women, for example, have Japanese American spouses; given the relatively small size of the pool of Japanese Americans, however, this in-marriage rate means that Japanese American women are still forty-seven

TABLE 14.7 | **In-marriage Among Selected Groups, Los Angeles Region, 1990 (Native-Born Females)**

	Aged 25–34 Years		Aged 55–64 Years	
	In-Married (%)	Odds Ratio	In-Married (%)	Odds Ratio
Japanese	32	47	89	970
Chinese	44	33	74	124
Mexican	66	6	83	66
English	25	6	35	5
German	32	4	36	4
Irish	24	6	24	6
Italian	14	5	35	19
Russian	24	38	48	57
Black	92	993	98	10,635

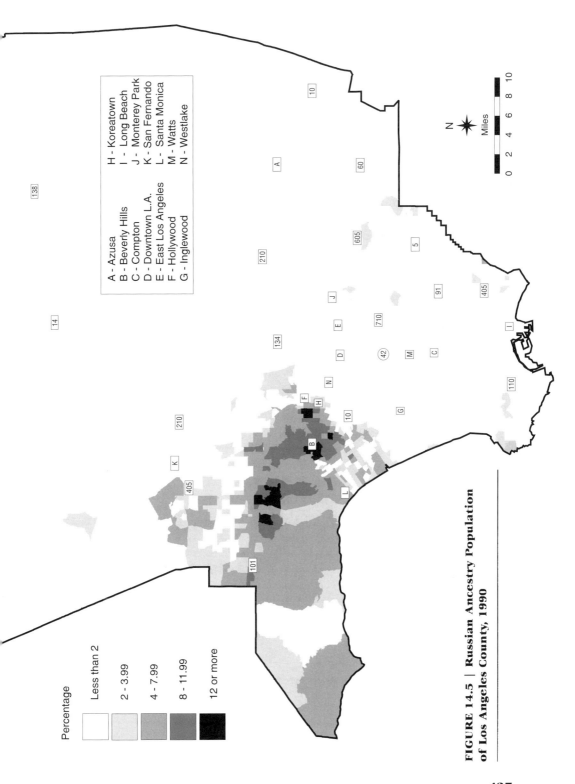

Percentage

Less than 2

2 - 3.99

4 - 7.99

8 - 11.99

12 or more

A - Azusa
B - Beverly Hills
C - Compton
D - Downtown L.A.
E - East Los Angeles
F - Hollywood
G - Inglewood
H - Koreatown
I - Long Beach
J - Monterey Park
K - San Fernando
L - Santa Monica
M - Watts
N - Westlake

N

Miles

0   2   4   6   8   10

FIGURE 14.5 | Russian Ancestry Population of Los Angeles County, 1990

times more likely to marry a Japanese American than an outsider, after controlling for group size.

At first glance, the table suggests that the differences in intermarriage primarily reflect the European/non-European divide, with most white ethnic women marrying outsiders and most women of non-European background marrying coethnics. Once group size is taken into account, however, it can be seen that young Mexican women are not much more likely to marry Mexican men than white ethnic women are to marry within their groups; that the likelihood of in-marriage for most white ethnics is not substantially higher than chance; and that Russian/Jewish women are much more likely than other whites to marry coethnic men. Of course, patterns for all adults reflect the decisions of earlier as well as more recent cohorts, and that conflation may obscure trends toward assimilation among younger persons less attached to ethnic cultures who came of age in a more liberal time. Contrasting older and younger women does indeed alter the picture, though not for the larger white ethnic groups, among whom intermarriage had already become the norm some time ago. Younger Mexicans now appear identical to most white ethnics, generally in-marrying Mexican men but not much more likely to do so than anyone else. In a social refrain to the economic similarities noted through this chapter, younger Chinese and Japanese women look much like their Russian/Jewish counterparts, with dramatic changes between older and younger cohorts suggesting that L.A.'s native Asians are hurtling toward assimilation at an even faster rate than the Russians/Jews.

CONCLUSION

In many respects, this review of ethnics in the L.A. region is consistent with the conclusion reached by Lieberson and Waters a decade ago, that the differences among the descendants of yesteryear's European immigrants have now been largely eclipsed, greatly overshadowed by the disparities between themselves as a group and the increasingly large proportion of the population who trace their origins to Asia, Africa, and Latin America. Still, Los Angeles has its own tale to tell. Its colonial history and its past role as a receiving point for internal rather than international migrants should have flattened ethnic differences among whites well beyond what Lieberson and Waters described, and this is exactly what we have found. Residents of English ancestry do appear to retain a slight economic advantage over the region's other major white ethnic groups, the Russians/Jews aside, but beyond this one distinction, none of the other subtle interethnic contrasts that Lieberson and Waters found noteworthy a decade ago appear relevant to today's L.A. scene.

The great exception, of course, is the Russian/Jewish group, which maintains a singular position in L.A.'s ethnic order. This finding also resonates with Lieberson and Waters, but the specific story told here seems significant in and of its own right. First, we note the simple passage of time; an additional ten years beyond Lieberson and Waters' publication should have been enough to push the Russians/Jews further along the trajectory followed by the other groups, and yet that appears not to have happened. Second, as we have argued, Los Angeles itself should have been the source of change in the same direction. As an environment, L.A. has been far more corrosive of ethnic affiliations than the centers of traditional Jewish concentration. For the postwar Jewish migrants who flocked to L.A., the move simultaneously entailed a rupture with prior affiliations and institutions and settlement into communities where "few distinctive markers set [Jews] apart from their Christian neighbors," as Deborah Dash Moore has argued.[21] The newcomers also adopted a more individualistic, more privatized lifestyle, as noted by the historian Marc Lee Raphael, who writes that "nearly everyone who visits a Jewish community in the West comments on the obsession with self-fulfillment and the informality of Jewish life."[22]

But if L.A.'s Jews seem so different from their Eastern, more traditional counterparts, why have they not been swept along by the tides of assimilation into the larger Anglo pool, where the region's other white ethnics now blend together? One answer may be the recency of the community, largely a product of a postwar migratory boom that increased the area's Jewish population more than threefold. A second answer may lie in the distinctive economic and residential concentrations that these newcomers established; as highly educated professionals and business owners, working in a narrow range of industries and occupations, Jews had more in common with one another than with others and experienced frequent in-group contacts, thus reinforcing ethnic boundaries. While past may not be prologue, Jews' apparent commitment to continued residence in L.A. County—and particularly the city of Los Angeles, where they constitute a growing share of the dwindling white population—together with the greater sensitivity to ethnic identity imposed by increasingly multicultural contexts, suggests a continued Jewish persistence in place for some time to come.

Notes to Chapter 14

1. Michael Novak, *The Rise of the Unmeltable Ethnics: Politics and Culture in the Seventies* (New York: Macmillan, 1972); Nathan Glazer and Daniel Patrick Moynihan, *Beyond the Melting Pot: the Negroes, Puerto Ricans, Jews, Italians, and Irish of New York City* (Cambridge: MIT Press, 1970).

2. Stanley Lieberson and Mary Waters, *From Many Strands* (New York: Russell Sage Foundation, 1988); Richard Alba, *Ethnic Identity: The Emergence of the European Americans* (New Haven: Yale University Press, 1989); Mary Waters, *Ethnic Op-*

tions (Berkeley and Los Angeles: University of California Press, 1990).

3. Arthur Gibben and Marsha Maguire, compilers, *The Irish Cultural Directory for Southern California* (Los Angeles: UCLA Folklore and Mythology Publications, 1985).

4. Raphael Sonenshein, *Politics in Black and White* (Princeton: Princeton University Press, 1993); Mike Davis, *City of Quartz* (London: Verso, 1990).

5. Lieberson and Waters, *From Many Strands,* 21–22; Reynolds Farley, "The New Census Question About Ancestry: What Did It Tell Us?" *Demography* 28 (1991): 411–29.

6. See Lieberson and Waters, *From Many Strands,* 25–27.

7. Elliot Barkan, "Immigration through the Port of Los Angeles," in Mark Stolarik, ed., *Forgotten Doors: The Other Ports of Entry to the United States* (Philadelphia: Balch Institute, 1988), 164.

8. On Boyle Heights and Lincoln Heights, see chapter 2 in this volume and the references cited there; Nicholas Loverich, in *Yugoslavs and Italians in San Pedro: Political Cultural and Civic Involvement* (Palo Alto, Calif.: Ragusan Press, 1977), discusses ethnic patterns in the L.A. port community of San Pedro.

9. Data for Los Angeles County only.

10. Calculated from the *1940 Census of Population, Public Use Sample.*

11. Raymond Breton, "Institutional Completeness of Ethnic Communities and the Personal Relations of Immigrants," *American Journal of Sociology,* 70 (1964): 193–205.

12. Lieberson and Waters, *From Many Strands,* 72; emphasis added.

13. Of the 22 percent of the population who are classified here as "other white," a bit less than one-third gave either no answer or the unclassifiable answers of "American" or "white." The remainder are members of very small groups, all less numerous than the Russians and Poles; the one exception consists of those of French descent, also present in relatively small numbers, whom we have decided not to discuss for a variety of reasons, the most of important of which is that the French have played a minor role in both the history and sociology of American ethnic groups. The "all others" category includes Asians and Hispanic groups not otherwise classified, as well as "others."

14. Stephen Steinberg, *The Academic Melting Pot* (New York: McGraw Hill, 1974); Joel Perlmann, *Ethnic Differences* (Cambridge: Cambridge University Press, 1988).

15. Michael Hout, "Opportunity and the Minority Middle-Class: A Comparison of Blacks in the United States and Catholics in Northern Ireland," *American Sociological Review,* 51 (1986): 214–23.

16. Calvin Goldscheider and Alan Zuckerman, *The Transformation of the Jews* (Chicago: University of Chicago Press, 1984).

17. With total economy defined as all employed persons aged 25–64.

18. While we refer to an individual occupation or industry as a "niche" when mak-

ing detailed comparisons between groups, we also use the term to refer to the entire cluster of industrial and occupational concentrations that characterize a group.

19. Frederic Barth, *Ethnic Groups and Boundaries: The Social Organization of Cultural Difference* (London: Allen and Unwin, 1970).

20. Max Vorspan and Lloyd Gartner, *History of the Jews of Los Angeles* (San Marino: Huntington Library, 1970), 118–19; Deborah Dash Moore, *To the Golden Cities* (New York: Free Press, 1994), 56–59.

21. Moore, *To the Golden Cities,* 264.

22. Marc Lee Raphael, "Beyond New York," in Moses Rischin and John Livingston, eds., *Jews of the American West* (Detroit: Wayne State University Press, 1991), 63.

CONCLUSION

(See photo captions on next page)

(photos on previous page, from top to bottom)
Romanian Baptists run "Kinder Cuts," a children's hair salon, La Habra, 1993; Russian sign at a drug store, West Hollywood, 1994; Little India, Artesia, 1993 (Artesia and neighboring Cerritos are now among the most ethnically diverse communities in the United States); Latino workers salvage bricks from an earthquake-destroyed store, Whittier, 1988; Whittier College graduation, 1993. (Photos copyright Stephen J. Gold.)

Ethnicity and Opportunity in the Plural City

Roger Waldinger

BOOSTERISM HAS NEVER been alien to Los Angeles, but the seemingly boundless prosperity of the 1980s—that last great expansionary wave—pushed it to new heights. "Just as New York, London and Paris stood as symbols of past centuries," proclaimed the Final Report of the Los Angeles 2000 Committee, "Los Angeles will be THE city of the 21st century."[1] Unlike past visions of Los Angeles as the best of all possible worlds, with no place for ethnic outsiders, *LA 2000* saw "a mosaic with every color distinct, vibrant, and essential to the whole" and embraced it. The newcomers transforming Southern California were certainly different, but difference made L.A. not only bigger but better than before. The emerging multi-ethnic Los Angeles, asserted the report's authors with confidence, was a "community that welcomes and encourages diversity and grows stronger by taking the best from it."[2]

So much for prophecy. A few years into the 1990s the optimism that suffused *LA 2000* vanished. The long tide of postwar, Cold War–induced prosperity came to a crashing halt early in the decade, as factories either closed or decamped, retailers and banks showed managers and clerks to the streets, and property values plummeted. Gradually it became clear that Angelenos were witnessing the end not of a boom but of the region's near-continuous history of growth.

With good times gone, the region's hospitality to outsiders disappeared. Never happy about the influx of the foreign-born—though not averse to employing newcomers willing to work at bargain rates—California's badly rattled Anglos decided that it was time to "save our state" by stopping illegal immigration. The occasion for doing so was

445

the election season of 1994; the mechanism was California's plebiscitarian democracy, which allows for referenda on proposed changes to the state constitution.

A motley coalition of right-wingers, environmentalists, and former officials of the Immigration and Naturalization Service launched a campaign to add a constitutional amendment denying illegal immigrants all but the most essential state services. The "save our state" measure, which in due course became Proposition 187, was of dubious legality, shutting illegal immigrant children out of schools when the constitutional right to education for all resident children, legal or otherwise, had been reaffirmed by the Supreme Court just ten years before. And it had little dollar-saving value, since enforcing exclusion carried a significant monetary cost, regardless of legalities or ethics. But the voters had little patience for niceties such as these, and the state's political leadership saw no capital to be gained from persuading them to think otherwise. Indeed, the safe money lay in leading the anti-immigrant charge. No matter that Governor Pete Wilson, as a U.S. senator, had fought hard for a temporary migrant-worker program tailor-made for the needs of the state's growers, nor that he had gladly acquiesced in the special agricultural workers' amnesty, written by two California congressmen and a New York colleague in a way that gave carte blanche to virtually any illegal with sufficient nerve, determination, and the necessary false documents. Now gains were to be made by urging the electorate to vote their fears, and Wilson proved up to the task.

The Proposition 187 campaign and the reactions it evoked exposed the political fault lines dividing Californians of all ethnic hues and stripes. With 187 a surefire winner among white voters, still the dominant bloc in the electorate, few politicians had the stomach for open, high-profile opposition until the election's closing weeks. Latinos, who initially told pollsters that they too favored a halt to illegal immigration, eventually took umbrage; seventy thousand demonstrators, many waving Mexican flags, crowded downtown L.A. in October 1994 to rally against 187. The following weeks saw high school students, the next generation of voters, take their protests to the streets. Toward the end of the campaign, right-thinking Anglos also found the courage of their convictions and led a chorus of criticism against 187 and its deficiencies on both constitutional and moral grounds. As editorialists fulminated and national leaders from both parties joined in the attack, 187 began losing stock in the opinion polls.

Californians talked differently in the privacy of the voting booth; Proposition 187 won handily, with over 59 percent of the vote. Though 187 did best among Anglos, it had broad appeal. Half the black and Asian voters and more than one quarter of the Latino voters also voted yes. Legal action stopped enforcement within a week of 187's passage, and as of this writing the amendment's practical future remains uncertain. But there can be little doubt that California, with its fifty-two electoral votes, sent Washington a message that will not be ignored.

Behind the passage of 187 lies another story, the one that we have tried to tell in this book: There is trouble in the suburban paradise that was once L.A., trouble connected to the sudden and deep ethnic shifts that have transformed the region over the past two decades. Immigration, of both the illegal and, more importantly, legal variety, has been the driving force of change; since 1965, more immigrants have flocked to the Los Angeles region than to anywhere else in the United States. In retrospect, the timing of the immigrant influx could not have been worse. Though the immediate roots of today's immigration stretch back to the 1960s, the immigrants came in dizzying numbers in the very late 1980s, just when the supernova of L.A.'s economy was about to explode. And the choice of destination may not have been the wisest; Los Angeles had grown through migration, but it had historically preferred migrants of the midwestern, white, Protestant type. Of course, African Americans, Mexicans, and Asians had also headed for L.A. in the past, but they had rarely been treated with much kindness, nor had they enjoyed the full fruits of the region's bounteous economy. Never having fully accepted the minority residents who had previously made L.A. their home, the region was poorly prepared for the avalanche of immigrants who arrived after 1965.

But all that is history; Los Angeles is now profoundly, irremediably ethnic. The issue confronting the region is whether this newly polyglot metropolis can work. And that is not a question for the region alone. In L.A., late twentieth-century America finds a mirror to itself. Los Angeles, after all, is not an old, decaying inner city. Instead, it is America's quintessential suburb, the dynamic product of postwar U.S. capitalism at its most robust, and for that reason, as the writer David Reid noted, "the American city the world watches for signs and portents."[3] If residents and prognosticators are right in their sense of foreboding and gloom, then the rest of the country is unlikely to do better than L.A. in its adjustment to the new demographic reality and its implications. But L.A.'s popular transformation from dreamland to dystopia can also be read as a sign of the anxiety aroused by the rapid, unexpected ethnic shifts of the last decade. Before we write its obituary, there is still time for a realistic assessment of L.A.'s encounter with ethnic change. As will be seen in the pages to follow, the lessons learned from this book about ethnic Los Angeles provide reason for trepidation, but also for hope.

OPPORTUNITY AND DISADVANTAGE IN THE PLURAL CITY

If Angelenos have lost heart over the region's changing fortunes and new demographics, they should be excused; social scientists tell them two conflicting stories about the relationship between the modern American urban economy and its increasingly multicultural population base, and the news from both stories is bad. The received academic wisdom emphasizes the passing of the city of production and its baneful consequences for the urban, largely minority poor. In this view, the advent of the postindustrial urban economy of producer services and knowledge-intensive jobs has been good for the well-schooled but leaves out the largely nonwhite unlettered, no matter how willing they may be. The rival interpretation tells a tale of occupational polarization amidst industrial transformation; urban high-tech postindustrial development comes at a price, measured in the decline of the well-paying factory sector and its replacement by proliferating low-skill, low-income jobs. In the new polarized metropolis, minorities serve as the new drawers of water and hewers of wood and have little chance of making small steps toward the middle class.

Notwithstanding the contrast, the two stories accent similar themes. Each account forecasts an increasingly divided—indeed dual—metropolis. At the top stands a growing cadre of well-paid, highly educated labor; depending on one's point of view, the bottom is either taken up by an underclass excluded from employment or else an increasingly impoverished working class. Either way, the new urban industrial order creates an increasingly isolated mass of poor people with ever-slimmer chances of getting ahead. These denizens of the metropolitan lower world come from socially stigmatized, visibly identifiable groups: African Americans, on the one hand, and Third World immigrants, on the other. As a growing minority population finds itself blocked from moving up in the pecking order, widening class differences accompany hardening ethnic boundaries.

Both stories convey a compelling message but prove inadequate to the reality they seek to describe and explain. In Los Angeles, the demographic transformations of recent decades have created a new ethnic order, one far too complex for the binary oppositions of any dualistic scheme. At the end of the twentieth century, Los Angeles is not so much a dual as a plural city, in which the myriad new ethnic groups have created a segmented system, where each group largely lives and works in its own distinctive social world. From this point of view, conventional accounts that emphasize an ever-more-radical separation of majority and minority miss the main drift. There are now too many distinctive groups for the old undifferentiated category of "minority" to make much sense. And with increased ethnic diversity, the divisions among the various Angelenos of non-European origin constitute the salient ethnic differences of today.

The material in this volume accents the interplay between ethnicity and economics and the role that ethnicity plays in organizing economic life. The majority of jobs in the region are held by the increasingly scrambled non-European-origin population, and those positions are not simply divided up at random or by the conventional mechanisms of skill or longevity. Because getting a job remains very much a matter of whom one knows, ethnics get hired through networks; the repeated action of network recruitment leads to ethnic employment concentrations, or "ethnic niches," as we have called them in this book.

In the conventional view, concentration is a newcomers' phenomenon, waning quickly as numbers grow and later arrivals spill over into the broader economy. But in Los Angeles, ethnic clusters have hardly diminished, despite the large and rapid immigrant infusion of recent years. In 1970, just over half the region's relatively small Mexican immigrant population worked in industries that could be classified as Mexican niches. Twenty years later, a vastly expanded Mexican immigrant population was just as concentrated in niches as it had been two decades before. And to a surprising extent, some of the very same specializations in which Mexicans had originally clustered—domestic work, apparel and furniture manufacturing, gardening, and agriculture—retained their importance, providing entry-level jobs for thousands of new arrivals.

Numbers make the Mexican story supremely important, and the very particular niche that Mexicans have established renders their story distinctive. But as an instance of concentration, the Mexican story exemplifies the ethnic economic experience in L.A. In 1990, just about half of every major immigrant group worked in industries that could be classified as niches (see table 15.1). Thus the clusters established by each one of the major groups have turned out to provide very significant absorptive capacity.

Moreover, the immigrant pattern finds its parallel among the native-born. Here the tendency toward concentration is not quite so strong (note the Mexican American difference, a matter to which we shall shortly return); nor is it quite so certain, as some of the native-born populations are still quite small. But these caveats aside, the striking fact is the persistent role of ethnicity in economic sorting. And the situation of the region's longer-established ethnics—Jews, Japanese Americans, and African Americans, who have carved out very distinctive specializations—points to the trajectory that the descendants of the newer arrivals are likely to follow.

The ethnic ordering of L.A.'s economy can be characterized along the horizontal and vertical dimensions of specialization and rank, as table 15.1 shows. On the horizontal dimension, Mexican immigrants, Korean immigrants, and African Americans define three basic modal types, with Mexicans ensconced in manufacturing, Koreans in self-employment, and African Americans in the public sector and few points of niche intersection among them. For all practical purposes, the region contains no black concentrations in manufacturing, nor does it contain Korean and Mexican niches in the public sector. Other groups are also clustered, but none in equally specialized roles.

The region's pattern of ethnic specialization also constitutes a system of inequality. Even the most fortunate of the newer Angelenos are some distance from the top of the hierarchy, as can be seen from a comparison

TABLE 15.1 | Niche Employment, Los Angeles Region, 1990

	Industrial Niches				Employment in Specific Niches, as Percentage of Niche Employment				
	As Percentage of Group's Employment	Mean Years Education	Self-Empt (%)	PubSec (%)	Mfg. (%)	Mgr/Prof (%)	Mean Earnings ($)
Israeli FB	64	14	31	6	18	44	47,678
Mexican FB	55	7	6	0	50	4	16,589
Salvadoran FB	53	8	8	0	37	4	12,748
Guatemalan FB	52	8	7	0	32	3	12,805
Chinese NB	51	16	9	16	24	78	51,060
Filipino FB	47	15	3	20	9	50	34,568
Iranian FB	47	15	35	3	4	41	34,278
Korean FB	46	13	47	0	13	18	28,618
Vietnamese FB	45	13	7	9	73	27	26,839
Chinese FB	44	13	17	5	21	38	31,481
Arab FB	44	14	23	7	4	35	35,307
Russian NB	42	16	35	5	0	68	75,513
Armenian FB	40	12	28	2	12	21	25,395
Armenian NB	38	15	24	6	8	55	38,319
Japanese NB	37	15	10	36	18	58	45,036
African American	36	13	1	57	1	33	31,900
Mexican NB	18	13	3	52	11	18	34,813

with native-born Russians/Jews, the one persistently ethnic European-origin group. Still, as figure 15.1 shows, Chinese and Japanese Americans have moved into advantageous specializations, where they find ample opportunities to work in high-paying white-collar jobs and do better than in industries of lower ethnic density. Other groups—African and Mexican Americans, as well as Korean, Filipino, and Vietnamese immigrants, for example—occupy the middle ranges of the continuum, sometimes doing better in industries of high ethnic density, sometimes doing worse. Mexican, Salvadoran, and Guatemalan immigrants—the most concentrated of all—do the very worst, crowding into menial employment where the wage ceiling is extremely low.

Niching is pervasive, but not every niche proves rewarding. Some do, notably those concentrations that provide opportunities for self-employment; ethnic Angelenos who work on their own earn a considerable self-employment bonus, which holds even after taking human capital factors into account. One could add a public-sector difference comparable to the self-employment bonus; for African Americans, government is an advantageous niche because it reduces exposure to employers who might discriminate as well as to immigrants who might compete for jobs that blacks have until recently held. By contrast, Mexicans and Central Americans seem to have been herded into niches that constitute mobility traps; in these cases, concentration in an ethnic specialization saturates supply and thus increases the potential for competition with one's own kind.

Thus, the economic complexities of L.A.'s ethnic order cannot be reduced to the antinomies of conventional academic views. While the region's ethnic transformation has been accompanied by a growing gap between rich and poor, that division does not organize the ethnic map of contemporary L.A. The march toward greater social distinction has occurred most rapidly *within* the region's African American population; whether one looks at earnings, family patterns, or residence, better-educated African Americans are far more distant from their less-fortunate brethren today than they were in 1970. And while keeping in mind the defects of the model minority view, it is worth noting that native-born Asian families do better than native whites on not one but several significant indicators.

Not only do the new Angelenos span the entire social spectrum from metropolitan heaven to inner-city hell, the purgatories to which the region's poor have been confined clearly are different social worlds. The term *underclass* has gained international fame and notoriety as the master concept for identifying the distinctive characteristics of today's poor, but it is a chaotic concept, referring both to those excluded from the labor market and to those confined to the least secure, most marginal positions that the economy provides. In Los Angeles, these distinct relationships to the labor market define two very different groups.

If we think of the underclass as a relational concept—the most downtrodden of a series of connected groupings—then L.A.'s underclass consists

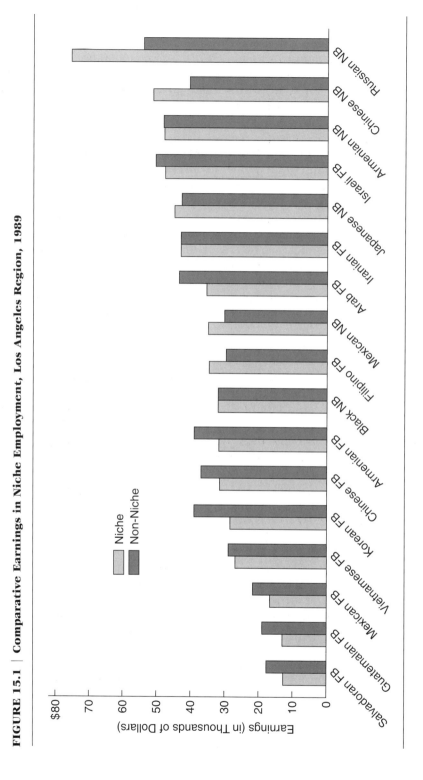

FIGURE 15.1 | Comparative Earnings in Niche Employment, Los Angeles Region, 1989

of those groups whose jobs are at the very bottom of the totem pole. *That* underclass consists of immigrants from Mexico and Central America who have been stuffed into the very lowest-level jobs, where they work in isolation from the rest of the region's ethnic groups.

But in established academic parlance, L.A.'s impoverished immigrants are not an underclass. For conservatives like Charles Murray and Lawrence Mead, the newcomers provide a remembrance of things gone by; they are a collection of hardworking folk always willing to toil, no matter how pitiful the remuneration may be. And for more liberal analysts, such as William J. Wilson, the immigrants laboring in L.A.'s industrial belt hark back to the urban proletariat of yore. As economic restructuring has relegated the traditional working class to the museum, the underclass is the term used to refer to "the groups . . . left behind"—that is to say, impoverished black Angelenos.[4]

The region's poor African Americans can be seen only as an *out*class, however, not as an *under*class, as the comparison with their impoverished immigrant brethren makes clear; the former face a penury of jobs and the latter an abundance, albeit at pitifully low wages. Modifying the concept to refer to the "ghetto poor" will not do; the traditional African American ghetto is shared with Mexicans and Central Americans, who enjoy good connections to the employers of low-level help. And the Mexican residents of east Los Angeles—the region's "purest" ghetto for its high degree of ethnic homogeneity—have no difficulty finding work, though securing good jobs is quite another story.

Poverty has increased among black Angelenos, but not because the openings for unskilled work have become scarcer. In contrast to other urban areas, L.A.'s low-skill sector remains alive and, if anything, all too well; such lower-level jobs as domestics, janitor, or sewing machine operator, which African Americans formerly held, not only remain abundant but have increased enormously. But the pool of those seeking low-level jobs has also expanded as foreign-born newcomers have poured into the region over the last two decades: Mexican and Central American immigrants have largely taken over the easy-entry positions once filled by less-educated black Angelenos. The dynamics of competition are complex and go beyond the scope of this book. Part of the story involves the prevalence of network recruitment, which brings immigrant communities into the workplace, detaching vacancies from the open market and thus diminishing opportunities for blacks. Another part has to do with the choices of employers, who expect that immigrants will be the more productive workers and also see immigrants as more tractable labor than blacks. Together, the inexhaustible supply of immigrants and employer preferences for manageable recruits with connections to incumbent workers have produced industries like furniture manufacturing and apparel in which African Americans are not just a sociological but a quantitative—often very small—minority, vulnerable to the pressure from an immigrant work force. Consequently, immigration has made younger and less-educated blacks more likely to be unemployed in Los Angeles than in other metropolitan areas, all other factors controlled.

The fact that low-skilled whites have been relatively unaffected by the immigrant influx suggests that more is involved here than the simple substitution of one low-skilled group for just any other. To be sure, low-skilled whites have been leaving the region more quickly than comparable African Americans, which may mean that whites who experience an adverse immigrant impact respond by moving away. Nonetheless, migration disparities are unlikely to explain why the jobless gap between low-skilled blacks and low-skilled whites *increased* during the 1980s. The persistent legacy of racism makes African Americans more vulnerable to immigration's displacing effect; never having attained their fair share of the region's most stable, best-paying manual jobs, blacks were also the most vulnerable when changes on both the supply *and* the demand side took a turn for the worse.

Ironically, the African American concentration in government work, while it shelters black Angelenos from the full force of immigrant competition, also presents relatively high hurdles, especially for men with troubled employment and personal pasts. Up to now, at least, government has been relatively immune to changes in the pay schedule for comparable jobs in the private sector. Hence L.A.'s black janitors, half of whom work on the public's payroll, make several thousand dollars more than their immigrant counterparts. But if the public sector pays its janitors well, it also scrutinizes them a good deal more carefully than a hotel or factory would; the average educational level of black janitors is just shy of a high school degree. As a whole, the contemporary black niche provides no replacements for the easy-entry jobs of the vanished past, since educational requirements for government employment are generally quite high.

Consequently, poverty takes a different face among the region's African American poor than it does among its immigrant working class. Blacks do considerably better than Latino immigrants in the earnings distribution, but *not* in the distribution of family earnings, mainly because the typical African American household contains only one earner. Since relatively fewer African Americans hold jobs, poverty rates approach immigrant levels and might well exceed them, were it not for the smaller size of black households. By contrast, Mexican and Central American immigrant households package income by bundling several paychecks earned from factory, service, or household work. Unfortunately, these types of jobs provide meager recompense; while the typical Mexican immigrant household boasts two earners, 22 percent of Mexican immigrant households endure under the poverty level, with close to another fifth just one notch above.

In the end, the demographic transformations of the past twenty years have created a new ethnic division of labor in which ethnicity intersects with class. The region's Chinese and Japanese Americans make up a professional middle class integrated into the region's core industries in manufacturing and professional services. Koreans, Iranians, and Chinese immigrants make up a diversified business grouping, with Koreans struggling as an embattled *petite bourgeoisie* and Iranians and Chinese on the road to high-tech, high-skill entrepreneurship. African Americans divide into two groupings, an emergent middle-class component linked to government and other large employers and an impoverished lower-skilled segment increasingly extruded from the employment system itself. Mexicans are likewise divided into a native-born, working/lower-middle class of skilled laborers and lower-level bureaucrats that overlaps little with foreign-born ranks and an isolated immigrant proletariat confined to the bottom tiers of the region's economy where they are joined by Central Americans, the latest additions to the region's low-wage labor pool.

IMMIGRANTS' PROGRESS

One is often tempted to argue that immigrant Los Angeles has returned to the world of Jacob Riis's *How The Other Half Lives;* like their turn-of-the-century predecessors, the immigrants of the latest wave are learning, sometimes to their sorrow, that the streets are not paved with gold. Of course, even the garment sweatshops of downtown Los Angeles and the dilapidated Victorian rooming houses of the Westlake district compare favorably with conditions that prevailed on the old Lower East Side of New York. And while outsiders may be struck by the gap between immigrant and native standards and compensations, the immigrants keep coming; *for them,* settlement in Los Angeles must represent a change for the better.

From a historical perspective, starting out at the bottom is the American way, as long as the newcomers and their descendants can gradually climb or even claw their way out of the socioeconomic cellar. In this respect, our reports on Los Angeles and its newcomers provide occasion for both congratulation and concern. Substantial numbers of immigrants are clearly making it and doing so more rapidly than immigrants have ever done in the past. For the most part, these newcomers, coming from South and East Asia and from the Middle East, arrive with skills and other assets that ease their entry into American society and hasten their move up the totem pole. Clearly, care needs to be exercised when generalizing about Asian and Middle Eastern immigrants and their success; some groups—for example, Vietnamese, Cambodians, and Armenians from the former Soviet Union—are doing notably worse than others. In most cases, the newest arrivals start quite far down the scale. All groups contain substantial numbers that are not faring particularly well; however glorious the earnings of Korean physicians and Chinese engineers, Korean cooks and Chinese sewing machine operators bring home considerably smaller checks, although one must note that they do a good deal better than their Mexican or Central American counterparts. While poverty rates tend to be lower than the region's average—again with national group exceptions—the proportion of Asian immigrant children living in poverty is disturbingly high, the combination of large family size and reduced earnings associated with recent arrivals depressing per capita income.

But if today's snapshot contains more than a few somber patches, the bigger—and more importantly the moving—picture looks a good deal brighter. Migrations generally become less selective over time, and the advent of large refugee populations has worked against immigrant selectivity for both Asians and Middle Easterners; nonetheless, each decade has consistently brought a cohort of highly skilled newcomers. Not all the immigrants manage to take advantage of the proficiencies they bring with them, one reason why so many get drawn into occupational and industrial niches. While the various Asian and Middle Eastern niches contain their share of less-desirable jobs, they range widely over the job spectrum; hence, average earnings in the ethnic concentrations have gone up, in real terms, over time. On the whole, many of the problems experienced by the region's Asian and Middle Eastern immigrants seem to be associated with the travails of initial adjustment. The foreign-born disadvantage fades as the immigrants gain the skills, experience, and familiarity with local employers needed to compete favorably with native-born white workers. Catching up is not simply an experience associated with a highly selective cohort of early arrivals; the Asian immigrants of the 1970s appear to have progressed faster than did their predecessors who came during the 1960s. Since Asian immigrant women make faster progress toward closing the gap with native white women and are also more likely to be employed, the prospects for improving family incomes are rosier still.

The true test of immigrant adaptation lies in the future, and it is too early to tell how the children of the newcomers will fare; however, the experience of native-born Asians is instructive. While discrimination against Asians persists, it takes the form of preventing male engineers or pharmacists from earning quite as much as comparable white males. This outcome is hardly satisfactory, but it has not barred progress into the middle class. On most indicators of family well-being, native-born Asians do better, on average, than the region's native whites. Of course, today's population of native-born adults is a numerically small group; the pessimist might argue that conditions will change for the worse once the large cohort of immigrant children enters the labor market, a movement that has already begun. There is no gainsaying that scenario, but what we know of the immigrant children suggests that they will begin well positioned to move ahead. Fewer Asian teenagers than whites drop out of high school, and the rate plummets further for children who arrived in the United States under the age of ten— that is, the 1.5 generation. Moreover, 18-to-24-year-olds in every Asian group attend college at rates that exceed that of whites, with the native-born leagues ahead of whites on this count. Forecasts as to how well employers will treat these students when they graduate from college are risky, but it seems reasonable to predict that their educational attainments will steadily lift the Asian economic boat in an economy that increasingly values high-level skills.

The trajectory followed by the newcomers from Mexico and Central America, however, is quite another matter. Clearly, some of the region's residents—mainly Anglos, but not Anglos alone—are unhappy about the massive flow from south of the border. But for now, living the good life in Southern California has much to do with immigration—as suggested by the fact that the region employed twice as many gardeners and servants in 1990 as it did ten years before. There can be little question that L.A. needs the large Mexican and Central American population that it has acquired over the past few decades. It is not just anecdotal evidence that suggests that there would be no gardeners, no baby-sitters, no garment workers, no hotel housekeepers without the Mexican and Central American newcomers. The census data tell the same story; the bottom tier of L.A.'s manufacturing and service sectors rests on a labor force that disproportionately comes from Latino immigrant ranks.

Thus, while some segments of the region's population may dream of "sending them home," the reality is that L.A.'s Mexican and Central American immigrants are here to stay, largely because the economy has learned to make good use of them. But it is not clear that the move to Los Angeles has been all that good for the immigrants. And even if it is judged relatively satisfactory for now—a minimum wage job in the garment center is better than an unyielding plot of land in Mexico's central plateau, not to speak of a visit from a Salvadoran death squad—the terms of comparison might shift drastically in the future, once the immigrants compare their conditions against the standards enjoyed by other Angelenos.

A search for immigrant progress will find few glimmers of hope in the record of the past two decades. The route into the region's economy has been through a relatively small tier of low-paying occupations and industries, as can best be seen by focusing on Mexicans, the very largest group. The chief Mexican concentrations of 1970 had extraordinary absorptive power—not a particularly fortunate characteristic, since these were low-wage, competitive industries to begin with and the expansion of the labor supply had the predictably depressing effect on paychecks. Of course, Mexican employment spilled over into a broader set of industries as the labor force expanded. But while the Mexican industrial and occupational base diversified, it paradoxically became more distinct from that of the rest of the labor force. Already very segregated from other groups in 1970, Mexicans became more and more so, in occupational and industrial terms, over time. As their numbers increased, Mexican immigrants found themselves crowding into a narrow set of industries in the secondary labor market that proved highly responsive—as theory would suggest—to shifts in supply. Employers adapted to the increased availability of greenhorns by expanding employment, but as the newcomers headed for the same industries and occupations in which their kin and friends were already employed, they unwittingly depressed wages for all. Between 1970 and 1990, real earnings in the Mexican immigrant industrial niches declined by over $6,000 a year. The downturn is not simply a matter of exchanging bad jobs for worse; real earnings declined in all of the industries that served as Mexican niches in 1970, before the massive immigration truly began.

But a picture like this, which paints the portrait in aggregate terms, could be misleading. With half the Mexican immigrant population having arrived in the 1980s, it might be thought that their problems had pushed the average down, obscuring the progress that earlier arrivals had made and that, by inference, the newcomers would be likely to repeat. Again, however, the data dash brighter hopes. Comparisons with earlier cohorts at a comparable stage show that the low earnings of recent immigrants are not simply a correlate of recent arrival and the associated pains of adjustment but rather something new, reflecting the increasingly adverse labor market environment of the 1980s. That environment does not work well for the earlier arrivals either, who have seen the gap separating them from natives grow.

So there is substantial evidence to indicate that the newcomers from Mexico (and Central America as well) find themselves not only at the bottom but at a bottom that is increasingly removed from the top and from which exit is hard to find. The immigrants' low skill levels lend further credence to this point of view. The massive absorption of a barely schooled—in some cases, utterly unschooled—population provides the ironic side to L.A.'s march into postindustrialism. Of course, the fact that the immigrants are so extensively employed suggests that these exiles from the fields and factories of Mexico and Central America do indeed arrive with skills that employers want, in contrast to black or Chicano high school graduates or dropouts whose training consists of whatever can be learned in the region's troubled schools. But if immigrants' manual, home-grown proficiencies fit nicely with the wants of employers in the secondary sector, employers at a higher level are looking for skills that schools do—or at any rate should—teach. And these types of skills are precisely what the immigrants lack.

For a decade now, the immigration literature has been embroiled in a debate over charges that America's immigrants are of "declining quality." Specifically, the question concerns the skill levels of the latest newcomers, compared with those of their predecessors. In absolute terms, the educational levels of the region's immigrants from Mexico and Central America have actually gone up over the past two decades. Since that climb was relatively modest, took off from a low base, and left the great majority of the most recent cohort with less than a high school education, it probably means little to prospective employers. Moreover, the disparity between immigrants and natives, and more importantly those natives with jobs (a proxy for skill requirements) has grown to a yawning divide, making it doubtful that the immigrants can find better-paying jobs of the sort that require some level of literacy and numeracy.

But if the future lies with the children, as we have argued, then the immigrants and their problems of today may all be beside the point. Indeed, considerable solace is to be gained from a look at the children of the foreign-born, but not quite enough to convince that the newer generation is moving ahead as it should. The region's age structure has a distinctive ethnic twist, with Hispanics greatly overrepresented among the young. What that means is that Mexican immigrant households contain lots of children; the result is the lowest per capita earnings of all ethnic groups and a very high proportion of children living in poverty. History suggests that those children will grow up with greater expectations than their parents had, but an impoverished family background will make it harder to realize those dreams. Moving beyond the world of cleaning and factory work will require the literacy, numeracy, and interpersonal competencies learned in school; the schooling data, such as they are, suggest that immigrants' children are indeed acquiring those skills, but not at an adequate rate.

A slightly cynical realist, however, one attentive to the immigrant trajectories of the past, would find grounds for satisfaction—although not complacency—in a future of a Polish or Italian American type. From this point of view, what counts *for now* are the prospects that go along with truck driving—the well-paying blue-collar occupation that happens to be the single largest Mexican American occupational niche. Rising college attendance and graduation rates are important, to be sure, but if one can forecast entry into the lower-middle and skilled working classes, a good deal of solace can be found in successful pursuit of the traditional path of immigrant progress.

Strictly speaking, it is too early to tell; only the oldest children born to the relatively small cohort of immigrants who arrived in the 1960s had entered the labor market in any significant numbers by 1990. And with most of the Latino immigration compressed into the 1980s, the full arrival of the second generation will be delayed for another decade or two. Still, the experience of the region's Mexican American population has lessons to offer, provided we recognize that this group is only a crude proxy, and therefore uncertain predictor, for the second generation yet to come.

In many respects, the Mexican American story in Los Angeles bears more than a passing resemblance to the experience of white ethnics of the Northeast and Midwest circa 1930–60. Though certainly not at the top of the region's pecking order, Mexican Americans are not at the bottom either, finding themselves at midpoint on most indicators, which puts them slightly ahead of African Americans. Median household income is up compared with 1970 and per capita income more so, thanks to reduced household size. Real earnings have also increased, for men and for women, although relative to native whites men have fallen further behind. As Mexican Americans have diversified economically, shifting from a position of high to low concentration in niches, their employment profile has increasingly converged with the pattern of whites. Occupational integration has brought upgrading; the proportion with professional and managerial jobs almost doubled between 1970 and 1990. And unlike African Americans, the region's Mexican Americans have a solid base in skilled blue-collar jobs.

On balance, one can detect a passage from humble to modest status for Mexican Americans. Not all signs point in the same direction, however. Male job-holding slipped considerably after 1970. High school graduation rates, as we have noted, also leave much to be desired. More importantly, one wonders whether one could not have asked for more. L.A. boomed during the past two decades, and not much had to be done to absorb the relatively small Mexican American cohorts that entered the labor market during these years. With a return to prosperity still far off on the horizon and a massive second generation ready to hunt for jobs, the region will be hard-pressed to do as well.

And that might not be good enough. Unlike the children of the Italian and Polish immigrants who began with little, ended up with more, but never expected a lot, today's second-generation Mexican Americans experience rampant consumerism and relentless media exposure to the standards of upper-middle-class life. One doubts, therefore, that a truck-driving future will satisfy the children of today's servants and assemblers. And the scenario gets a good deal more pessimistic if the region's next economy fails to deliver or simply throws up more bad jobs.

ASSIMILATION REVISITED

Thus far, we have focused on how well or how poorly groups fare in their climb up the greasy pole. But there is more to ethnic change than dollars and cents. In the past, at any rate, the ethnic experience also involved shifts in self-concept and social worlds. Unfortunately, census data do not provide a window for observing how Angelenos think of themselves ethnically and with what intensity, but they do shed considerable light on the social structures—households, neighborhoods, and speech communities—within which ethnicity is lived.

The problem is how to talk about those social structures and their evolution. Assimilation provides the convenient term at hand, but it has come under severe attack, and not only for the reasons that we advanced in the introduction to this book. As a concept, assimilation is not quite neutral; it asserts not only that outsiders *will* change but also that they *should* change and how, namely by shedding their original group preferences and affiliations. That teleology sits uneasily with a society more accepting of ethnic difference than in the past and less certain as to who or what constitutes the mainstream. Moreover, assimilation takes groupness for granted, when it is precisely the nature of ethnic aggregates that stands in flux. Not every set of outsiders constitutes an ethnic collectivity in any meaningful sense. While those collectivities are likely to evolve into something else, they need not change in the direction that assimilation implies, that is, by merging into some broader American mainstream. And whatever that mainstream might be, its own response to the infusion of new groups plays a crucial role. The Proposition 187 scenario, in which the Anglo campaign to "save our state" led Latinos to demonstrate amidst Mexican flags, further polarizing Anglo opinion, nicely demonstrates the reactive process that transforms an aggregate of ethnic outsiders into a true collectivity. Since aversion can take the form of both conflict and withdrawal, Anglos' continuing out-migration may set a natural limit on the possibilities for the increased intergroup contact entailed in assimilation.

From this perspective, the chapters in this book tell us that the ethnics of Los Angeles are set on trajectories of very different types. One is the two-step path followed by the massive and rapidly growing population of Mexican and Central American origin. The first step is the formation of a new collectivity. In 1970, the Mexican immigrant population was just beginning the transition from the circular migration of bracero days, when immigrants would move back and forth in response to the needs of the harvest and other seasonal industries, to the one-way movement that migration studies have universally shown to be inevitable. Settlement and its imprint show up in the transformation of household structures. In 1970, Mexican immigrant households were only slightly larger than white households; more importantly, 35 percent contained only one or two people and only 23 percent had six or more. By 1990, the median Mexican immigrant household contained five people, more than twice the number in households headed by native whites. Single- and even dual-person households, previously common, were now rarities, and more than a third of the population lived in households of six or more.

If settlement is the first step, the second is the development of a large, distinctive social world encompassing the broader Latino immigrant population. Here, numbers play a crucial role. With so many new arrivals, Latino densities are high in both residential and economic contexts, so that opportunities for interpersonal contacts of all types tend to involve others of the same kind. Although many Latino immigrants live in diverse settings, as in the areas surrounding the ethnically homogeneous core, transition from either black or white to Latino is rapidly underway. Latinos were already more segregated in 1990 than they were ten or twenty years before, and there is every reason to think that the shocks of the last few years—social, economic, and seismic—have only accelerated that trend.

In this light our data on economic segregation and niching take on new significance; ethnic isolation in the neighborhood context has its parallel in the environments where people work. For all practical purposes, the Mexican (and indeed, Central American) niches at the bottom of the labor market are predominately Latino worlds. Granted some of the supervisors and certainly the bigger bosses are likely to be of another kind—very possibly Asians in the clothing shops, Anglos in furniture factories or hotels. But the direction of ethnic change across these occupational divides is more likely to involve employer adaptation to the immigrants than the other way around; the path of least resistance leads employers to hire foremen and other intermediaries who come from the immigrant communities and to work out managerial and supervisory routines that make Spanish the lingua franca.

But there is a certain slippage in our argument for a bigger, more distinctive, more separated immigrant world; we began by talking about Mexicans and ended up discussing Latinos. Clearly, L.A.'s immigrant Latinos are more diverse than ever before, mainly because the large Central American influx of the 1980s added a significant non-Mexican component where none had been before. The Central Americans differ from their Mexican brethren on several counts, including economic and residential factors, but these are differences in degree, not in kind. There is more overlapping than separation; the circles of Mexican and Central American occupational concentration coincide, and there is not a single Central American niche in which one does not find a sizable Mexican cluster. The same holds true on the residential scene, and not only because segregation between the two groups is relatively low. Central American neighborhoods there may be, but none that is exclusively so. L.A.'s Central Americans live in predominately Mexican communities where the common language that brings them together effectively bridges the other barriers that divide them.

Of course, neighbors, whether at work or at home, do not always become friends. The same can be said for ethnic groups. Niche overlap can, and does, lead to conflict; we also know from field research that relations among the members of L.A.'s diverse Latino population are not always of the warmest kind. Still, the structure of interaction counts, especially when reinforced by cultural and linguistic affinities. The region's Latino subgroups are essentially the same in their use of Spanish and fluency in English. At the social level, the differences between recent immigrants from Mexico and their Central American counterparts are slight, especially in light of the disparities that separate both groups from Anglos. The probabilities of contact, at work and at home, are also high although not symmetric, since

Central Americans are more likely to encounter Mexicans than the other way around.

Consequently, we forecast the emergence of a pan-ethnic Latino group, in which Central Americans will be gradually assimilated into a larger and slowly changing Mexican-origin world, before either group is assimilated into the mainstream. Should we be right, this merging of smaller units into a much larger aggregate will mean greater ethnic persistence among the region's Latino immigrants and their descendants. Numbers will be a crucial if not decisive factor, increasing the probability that Latinos, whether at work, in the neighborhood, or in more intimate circles, will interact with others of the same kind.

To this shift we also detect a countertendency, one in which the native-born descendants of earlier Mexican arrivals are increasingly distanced from their immigrant cousins. Adaptation has just begun among the newcomers and will take place more slowly than in the past, for the reasons just advanced. Moreover, the changes in the region's social, economic, and legal environment have made Mexican Americans less like the foreign-born than before. As we have noted earlier, Mexican Americans have diffused over an increasingly wide occupational and industrial spectrum in the last two decades. Although there are certainly instances where the immigrant and Mexican American niches overlap, these are becoming less common. More importantly, perhaps, the Mexican American economic specializations involve contact with the full range of L.A.'s ethnic mosaic. The modest movement into the lower reaches of the middle-class is bringing about related changes in the more intimate structures of life. The native Latino population has begun to move out toward the outer counties, whereas the immigrants remain overwhelmingly concentrated in the Los Angeles County core. Mexican American households are now a good deal smaller than immigrant households, reversing the pattern of two decades ago. And those households are increasingly likely to be an ethnic blend of some sort; young Mexican American women are far more likely to marry outsiders than are women of their mothers' age.

This projection of immigrant/native fragmentation, like all other predictions, is a risky affair. Anglo reaction to immigration may ironically help Latinos build bridges of ethnic solidarity that cross the foreign-born native divide. Mexican American social mobility could well yield the same effect, producing a college-educated elite more open to the politics of identity and sensitive to its appeal. Still, differences in everyday life and work will remain, with consequences for politics and identity. There is considerable anti-immigrant sentiment among the region's Latinos, as shown not just in public opinion studies but by the not-inconsiderable support that Proposition 187 garnered from L.A.'s Hispanic voters.

In the end, the pattern of Latino ethnic adaptation looks distinctive, but not because change is occurring more slowly than it did in years gone by. Nostalgia colors the way in which that earlier experience is seen; the historical literature shows that earlier immigrants often opposed Americanization, making concerted efforts to retain their language and culture. But in the past, the halt in large-scale migration rapidly accelerated the shift from old-country habits and affiliations. As of this writing, a change of that sort is nowhere in sight.

The story is quite different for the region's largely middle-class immigrants from Asia and the Middle East. It would be wrong to say that these newcomers do not have strong ethnic attachments. The more intimate structures of everyday life are defined largely in ethnic terms; witness the prevalence of in-marriages among almost all of the Middle Eastern and Asian groups. And as with other immigrants, these newcomers have a preference for living with their own kind, as can best be seen in Monterey Park, now famous as the nation's first suburban Chinatown, or in Orange County's Little Saigon.

But the broader structures of ethnicity are not nearly as encompassing as in the Latino case and are more likely, therefore, to speed the process of change among immigrants and, more importantly, among their descendants. Once again, compositional factors play a crucial role. Massive immigration has led to a burgeoning Asian population; however, "Asian" as a category has limited sociological content as chapter 11 has shown. The immigrants who have flocked to Los Angeles from Asia are a diverse lot, with little in the way of culture, language, or religion to connect Indians to Filipinos to Chinese at the very outset. Education and skill are unifying elements, but the importance of networks and personal contacts in the search for jobs and homes means that each group of higher-skilled immigrants enters the region in its own way. Consequently, economic specialization may be typical of each of the Asian groups, but these specializations tend to be particular to each group—nursing for the Filipinos, and storekeeping for the Koreans. Occupationally and industrially, the various Asian groups are as segregated from one another as they are from whites.

The same pattern applies on the residential front. Not only have the region's various Asian groups settled along different paths, producing the relatively high levels of intra-Asian segregation noted in chapter 11, but they have also moved into the newer areas in the region's outer ring. There, mixing is more prevalent and the massive Asian migration has therefore yielded declining segregation levels, quite in contrast to the Latino pattern.

Intra-Asian differentiation matters because it increases the likelihood of contacts across ethnic lines. The various individual Asian groups are small; although distinctive in their residential and economic patterns, they are too few in number to dominate an occupation, industry, or even more than a cluster of residential areas. And because Asians are spread out unevenly, their numbers do not add up to the critical mass that would keep contacts within a broader Asian ambit. At the residential level, Asians from one group are more likely to interact with whites than with Asians from some other group. The same is true in industries and occupations, where Asian penetration never comes close to the levels recorded by Latinos, even in such Asian specializations as accounting, nursing, and engineering.

Since the Middle Eastern story reads much the same and is propelled by similar factors, it need not be reviewed here. But in both the Asian and Middle Eastern cases, the newcomers' middle-class—in some cases, higher-class—background helps account for the distinctive pattern of ethnic adaptation. Clearly, personal ties matter for the job search of immigrant professionals or managers, almost as much as they do at the labor market's bottom tier. And there is reason to think that the movement into upper-tier jobs furthers the process of assimilation and acculturation. The nature of work and training at the upper level reduces, if it does not eliminate, the potential for immigrant/native competition. Since whites remained ensconced in occupations like engineering and nursing that have become high-level immigrant niches, these fields become arenas for immigrant/Anglo interaction, which presumably yields changes in friendship, language use, and cultural patterns on both sides of the immigrant/native divide. Higher earnings, greater English-language proficiency, and the enhanced ease in navigating the Anglo world provided by extended schooling also enlarge residential options. Consequently, the move to the suburbs of the peripheral counties is a realistic possibility for many Asians and Middle Easterners. That, in turn, means a shift to neighborhoods of lower immigrant density, where the newcomers have higher levels of exposure to Anglos. Since their children also find better schools, the circle (virtuous or vicious, depending on one's view of ethnic persistence) comes to a close; the combination of class, culture, and context brings the Asian and Middle Eastern second generation into a social environment that both promotes mobility and corrodes ethnic attachments.

As always there are countervailing trends. Generalization is hazardous; the foregoing one clearly fits awkwardly with the experience of refugees from Southeast Asia. Rather than hastening diffusion, the rapid advance up the social scale may create new concentrations that enhance the potential for intra-Asian interaction; note the situation at the region's major universities, where a minimum of one out every four students is of Asian descent. Ironically these settings represent greater Asian density than the suburban communities from which many Asian students come. Intra-Asian national differences may not matter much to students of the 1.5 or second generation who have lost facility in the mother tongue and contact with their ethnic cultural institutions but find virtue in Asian panethnicity.

But no discussion of the prospects for assimilation can conclude without consideration of the region's major native-born groups, namely Anglos and African Americans. Mention of the latter group lays bare the ideological underpinnings to assimilation. On the one hand, the notion that ethnic change occurs through a natural process of generational adjustment shifts the burden of explanation away from whites and their resistance to black progress; and on the other hand, the normative implication, that African Americans *should* change by abandoning their group affiliations, appears inherently and unacceptably ethnocentric. Still, there are intellectual parallels to pursue, most notably the question of whether the region's African Americans remain as confined to occupational and residential ghettos as before. The best answer is that there is greater mixing, although in such areas as Watts and South Central, which have received sizable immigrant inflows, not necessarily because of diffusion. Demographic transition in these historically black neighborhoods helps explain the recent substantial declines in residential segregation; equally important is the fact that African Americans have at last been able to join the outward flow to new suburbs on the periphery that, so far, reflect the region's new-found diversity. The occupational scene is somewhat different, given the persisting importance of a clearly defined black niche in the public sector. But here, composition comes back into play; however overrepresented blacks may be in any industry or occupation, they still find themselves in a minority, which means interaction with and exposure to others.

Since assimilation is a two-way process, one also has to factor in African Americans' reactions to the newcomers from abroad. That response has often been less than favorable, as Korean storekeepers discovered to their distress during the civil unrest of 1992. It is clear that the residential transitions underway in South Central and Watts are also the cause of considerable unhappiness among black residents. And the fire next time may well occur in the black concentrations in government, pitting African Americans against Latinos, who see government as a lever of ethnic mobility and are well aware that blacks have gotten more than their share of public jobs. Any such combustion seems likely to lead to a hardening of ethnic boundaries on both sides.

In the end, however, the region's Anglos may turn out to be the great wild card. As usual a historical perspective helps. The white Anglo-Saxon Protestants of an earlier day were less than overjoyed when the Irish, Italians, Poles, and Jews came searching for opportunity in the promised land. It took a long time for the established groups to accommodate themselves to those newcomers and their descendants. Signs and ads reading "Irish or Jews need not apply" may belong to the past, but their memory has not yet been extinguished.

Anglos' discontent with immigration inhibits contact and for that reason alone retards tendencies among the immigrants to assimilate. But the options available to the diminishing Anglos of the L.A. region (no longer just Protestant and Anglo-Saxon) are not the same as before; restrictive covenants and ethnically discriminatory hiring practices are no longer the order of the day. Flight remains a possibility, however, and one should not forget that many of the region's Anglos are themselves migrants or the children of migrants, with weaker roots to the area than might be found in older parts of the country. To put it bluntly, the entire region might follow the path of the San Fernando Valley, from orange groves to "Leave It to Beaver" to the growing impoverished Latino barrio of today, ringed by prosperous, nervous whites on the hillsides, wondering whether they will be next to leave. And all that in the space of fifty years.

THE LESSONS OF LOS ANGELES

Congress revised the U.S. immigration laws in 1965 having little inkling of the consequences that would flow from this act. It certainly had good intentions, although the Congressional mindset was more on the past and its injustices than on the factors that would influence future flows to the United States. As the legislative history shows, Congress was conservative, indeed far too much so, in its assumptions about how immigration would unfold in years to come. What no one in Washington expected—and in fact what no one there wanted—was a flood of newcomers from the countries that have sent the great majority of immigrants who have arrived over the past thirty years.

But those immigrants had good reason to come to the United States, namely, jobs and the possibility of doing better than they could at home. If the immigrants sought to move to the United States, employers were also looking to fill their bottom level jobs at low rates; the best available candidates turned out to be foreign-born. In the Los Angeles region, farmers in the still-verdant outlying areas found a growing immigrant labor force to be particularly handy; so did hospitals, hotels, restaurants, manufacturers, and also the region's good burghers, who came to enjoy the convenience of an expanding servant and gardening class.

The fit between the desires of immigrants and those of the region's established inhabitants goes far to explain L.A.'s continuing attraction for the foreign-born. History is important, too, most notably the eight-decade-long tradition of recruitment in Mexico's Central Plateau for work in California's fields and farms. Geography also comes into play, in L.A.'s proximity to Mexico and location on the Pacific Rim, which makes the region a natural reception point for newcomers from Mexico and Asia. The postwar economic boom, once seemingly endless, added to the magnetic force, ensuring that there was always room—indeed, usually need—for an extra hand.

But once a nucleus of newcomers had been put in place, immigration became a self-feeding mechanism, with a momentum all its own. The more immigrants who moved to Los Angeles, the easier it was for the next batch to follow behind. Settlers were able to help with jobs, housing, and the money to come to L.A. Employers became accustomed to recruiting and hiring newcomers, all the more so once there was a cadre of experienced hands who not only furnished a continuing supply of applicants from back home but vouched for them, trained them, and made sure that they fulfilled the boss's basic expectations. Entrepreneurs gravitated to Los Angeles in much the same fashion; seedbed immigrants established business concentrations in specialized lines like apparel, construction, or import/export trade. Once in place, those clusters sent a signal to prospective immigrants about the commercial opportunities to be found in L.A. The contacts between veterans and newcomers as well as the institutions they founded (such as newspapers and churches) further lubricated the movement into business.

These mechanisms made for a steadily expanding immigrant economic base, in part through their effects on natives. With immigrant recruitment networks keeping job information from leaking out into the broader labor market, natives found it harder to get jobs in industries and occupations that became immigrant-dependent. They also found those jobs less desirable, especially as the immigrant influx made it easy for employers to push the wage level down. And as the region's core manufacturing sector eroded, replaced by labor-intensive industries that could make good use of the growing immigrant work force, restructuring further weakened the region's hold on its native workers, Anglo and African American workers alike. Once an importer, L.A. became an exporter of less-skilled Anglos, who left for better opportunities in neighboring states. African Americans also joined the outward flow, although with fewer resources, not as many could do so; proportionately more dropped out of the labor force altogether. As the supply of natives dwindled, options for immigrants correspondingly increased.

And so Los Angeles became an intensely immigrant region, receiving a disproportionate share of the immigrant inflow that began to grow in the 1970s and then burgeoned in the following decades. Native Angelenos found the sudden, massive ethnic transformation unsettling, but the boom times of the 1980s had a soothing effect on their nerves. The region's elite, sensitive to the downside of immigration, nonetheless accepted it as the price for catapulting the region into the ranks of the world's global cities. Thanks to understanding administrations in Sacramento and Washington, there was never any reason to worry about policies that might have curbed the region's hunger for cheap, immigrant labor, such as more vigorous protection of labor standards, a more permissive environment for union organizing, enforcement of the penalties against hiring undocumented immigrants (enacted as part of the Immigration Reform and Control Act of 1986), not to speak of a stiff hike in the minimum wage. And the immigrant advocates played their role in the process as well, assuring those members of the public who cared to listen that the newcomers had come here only to work at jobs that no one else wanted to fill.

The good times eventually ended, however, and once they did the politics and perceptions of immigration changed as well. Thinking that they had imported workers, the region's Anglos were aghast to find that they had gotten mothers and fathers equipped with children, instead. True, the newcomers had been willing to do the region's dirty jobs, as the immigrant advocates had noted, and at bargain basement wages. But in a state where the tax system retained some progressivity, low earners made relatively slight contributions to the public's till. Moreover, the arrival of the newcomers' children—and there were many of them relative to the number of immigrant earners—meant that immigration eventually produced claims on the state's services. As some observers worried that the immigrants' children would be less eager than their parents to take on the region's undesirable jobs but not equipped with the skills to do much better, one began to sense that the bill for immigration had finally come due.

Unfortunately, Californians had grown accustomed to hearing their political leaders tell them that something could be had for nothing, and when it came to immigration matters, the state's political class was not about to change its tune. Hence, the electorate succumbed to the sirens of Proposition 187—and who could blame them, since few political figures of any prominence had dared to tell them the unpalatable truth that immigration was now part and parcel of the good Southern California life. And it was not simply that the region's economy had learned to accommodate to the immigrant presence; more importantly, its adaptation to immigration was so deep and pervasive that any shift in the abundant flow of newcomers would come at a fairly stiff price. One could reduce the supply of immigrant cooks and maids, but hotel and restaurant prices would then go up, with less than salutary effects on the region's crucial tourist trades. One could curb the inflow of foreign-born garment workers, but that would simply transform what had been a growth industry into another one of the region's declining sectors. And one could encourage the legions of foreign-born laborers and construction workers to go home, but their departure would not help the region's hard-pressed builders nor do anything to contain home prices that were already far too high.

All this is not to say that one should not strive to reduce immigration, in my mind the very direction to which the evidence from this book points, but one still must note that there is no free lunch. The effects of curtailing immigration will be felt far beyond L.A.'s foreign-born communities. And the costs of yesterday's search for cheap immigrant labor will be paid tomorrow and the day after, in the form of educating the children of poorly schooled immigrants and making sure that they have the tools needed to do well in the next century.

While Washington can do more to curtail immigration than it has in the past, its hands are far from free. Scaling back drastically, as the nation did in the 1920s, is not on the agenda, especially now when international flows of goods, services, and people are accelerating and the United States is moving toward greater economic integration with its neighbors. Since the same changes in communication and technology that lubricate trade also facilitate migration, the ties between immigrant communities and their home societies will be harder to disrupt now than they were earlier in the century. And one should not forget that the regime of restricted immigration lasted barely two decades, with modest upward flows beginning shortly after the Second World War. As the forces pushing people to move across national boundaries are both strong and worldwide, they seem unlikely to decline.

Thus, even if Washington makes some move toward restrictionism, the United States is likely to remain an immigration country, allowing five or six hundred thousand persons to enter the country each year, rather than the eight or nine hundred thousand of the recent past. At that level, Los Angeles can expect to receive a large and disproportionate share of the country's immigrants for the foreseeable future; the networks that link newcomers to settlers and connect immigrants to the region's employers will exercise a long-lasting inertial effect. Similarly, attempts to alter the skill composition of the migration flows, even if successful, will yield results only gradually, and with further delay in Los Angeles, where the history of low-skilled immigration will mean more of the same.

Consequently, ethnic Los Angeles is here to stay, whether the region's political class and its largely Anglo electorate wish it or not. Immigrant adaptation takes time, even under the best of circumstances, and for Los Angeles and its troubled economy these are not the best of times. The first step is to recognize the permanence of the region's ethnic transformation, admit that it results from the actions of both immigrants and established residents, and make the necessary adjustments in policies and programs. But the prospects for realism in immigration matters are poor, since fantasy flourishes in L.A. Unfortunately, continuing controversy can be expected as the region seeks to turn the clock back in its search for a homogeneous Anglo world that is no more.

Notes to Chapter 15

1. *LA 2000: Final Report of the Los Angeles 2000 Committee* (Los Angeles: 2000 Committee, 1988), 59.

2. *LA 2000,* 51.

3. David Reid, ed., *Sex, Death, and God in L.A.* (New York: Pantheon, 1992), xxxi.

4. William J. Wilson, *The Truly Disadvantaged* (Chicago: University of Chicago Press, 1987), 41.

Sources of Data, Group Definitions, and Measures

THIS APPENDIX describes the sources of the data that appear in this book, the definitions used in identifying the various racial/ethnic groups, and some of the measures that appear in the group chapters.

THE DATA SOURCES

The Bureau of the Census has produced publicly available computer datasets based on several of the census counts conducted during this century. Datasets are currently available for 1910, 1940, 1950, 1960, 1970, 1980, and 1990, and other census years may be available soon. For most of these years, only individual-level data are available, and these include characteristics of individuals and the households in which they live. Because of concerns about privacy, these Public Use Samples (or PUS, for years 1910–70) and Public Use Microdata Samples (PUMS, for years 1980–90) have very limited geographical information, allowing analysts to determine the location of persons only down to the level of the city or county in which they live, and then only if the city or county has a large enough population. The exceptions are 1960, when no cities or counties were identified, and 1980–90, when some smaller geographical units were introduced, although these were still quite large in terms of area and population. Unless otherwise mentioned, the data appearing in all tables and figures derive from PUMS.

To compensate for the lack of geographical information in the individual-level data, the Census Bureau has also released datasets that contain selected pieces of information about the residents of moderately large areas called *census tracts* and somewhat smaller areas called *census blocks*. We use data from these Summary Tape Files (STF) for 1980 and 1990 to compute the indices of residential segregation.

Although chapter 2 draws on the 1940 and 1950 PUS data, and chapter 8 on the 1950 PUS, statistics we primarily use data from the 1970 PUS and 1980–90 PUMS. There are some differences in the way the data were collected and processed that affect the comparability of statistics computed from these three years, and these are worth noting.

First, although the Census Bureau attempted to count the members of each and every household in each census year, it also asked additional questions of selected households. In 1970, there were two additional questionnaires, one administered to 15 percent of households and another administered to 5 percent of households. When releasing the data to the public, the Census Bureau subsampled from each of these two independent samples, so that there were two datasets, each representing roughly 1 percent of the total population. The 15 percent sample included information about parentage and language, while the 5 percent sample had a detailed self-identified Spanish-origin question and no information about parentage and language. This procedure presented us with a dilemma.

This dilemma was accentuated by the fact that in 1980 and 1990, the Census Bureau ceased to ask about parentage and instead asked about ancestry (see chapter 14). How we identify the ethnic groups we are concerned with here is the largest problem we face in comparability across the years, but there are others. The 1980 and 1990 PUMS datasets are 5 percent samples, as opposed to the two 1970 1 percent samples. All else being equal, this means that 1980 and 1990 counts, especially of subgroups and their characteristics, are likely to be more accurate. Also, in the 1980 and 1990 PUMS, the Census Bureau was much more ambitious than they had been in the past in imputing answers to questions that respondents did not answer or answered incorrectly. This change is reflected, for instance, in the fact that the "manufacturing, not specified" industry category is large in 1970 but does not exist in 1980 or 1990.

Despite these differences, the Census Bureau did take care to make data comparable across census years wherever possible. We believe that the incompatibilities across the years, major and minor, are not serious enough to preclude analysis over time.

GROUP DEFINITIONS

Exploring the ethnic diversity of the Los Angeles region requires that we be able to distinguish between members of the groups with which we are concerned. Especially given the Census Bureau's longstanding policy against identifying people by religious affiliation (preventing, for instance, the straightforward identification of Jews), this task is more complicated than it may seem on the surface. It is further complicated by the fact that our three main census years—1970, 1980, and 1990—differ from each other in the information they provide that might allow us to perform our classification.

Still, there are a number of commonalities across years. For all years, we used a "place of birth" variable to distinguish between persons born in the United States and those born abroad, and a "citizenship" variable to further distinguish between foreign-born persons born to U.S. parents (and who were then reclassified as native-born) and foreign-born persons born to foreign-born parents. Our next task was to identify five broad groups: Hispanics, Asians, Blacks (non-Hispanic), Whites (non-Hispanic), and Native Americans. Among the Hispanics, we distinguished five subgroups: Mexicans, Salvadorans, Guatemalans, other Central Americans, and other Hispanics. We divided Asians into the six largest groups—Japanese, Chinese, Vietnamese, Filipinos, Koreans, and Asian Indians—and disaggregated non-Hispanic whites into Middle Easterners and other whites. The latter group was broken down into English, Germans, Irish, Italians, Polish, and Russians. We subdivided Middle Easterners into the four largest groups: Armenians, Iranians, Arabs, and Israelis.

The most serious difference between 1970 and the later years lay in the variables used to classify groups. The 5 percent sample, which is what we have primarily relied upon in this book, has a race variable, a Spanish-origin self-identification variable, and a place-of-birth variable. Because Hispanics potentially span all of the racial and place-of-origin categories, we identified them first using Spanish origin.[1] We also used Spanish origin to identify Mexicans and Other Hispanics but could identify Central Americans only by their place of birth; we were therefore unable to identify U.S.-born persons of Central American ancestry. We identified whites, blacks, and several Asian groups using the race variable and identified additional foreign-born Asians on the basis of their place of birth. We likewise identified subgroups among the white foreign-born on the basis of place of birth but were unable to identify the native-born in this fashion, for reasons already mentioned.

Because of the inability to identify white ethnics in the 5 percent sample, we also used the 15 percent sample. The 15 percent sample includes a parentage variable, recording father's place of birth if foreign-born and mother's place of birth if father is native-born. The parentage variable allowed us to classify some white (and other) ethnics, but unfortunately for the purposes of ethnic identification most native whites in L.A. come from families who have been in the United States three or more generations. Another drawback of the 15 percent sample is that it does not include the Spanish-origin variable, and so Hispanics were identified using the less reliable Spanish-surname and Spanish-mother-tongue variables. Otherwise, procedures were the same as with the 5 percent sample.

Unlike the 1970 census, with its two incompatible samples, the 1980 and 1990 censuses included variables that were broadly similar. We were able to use these variables in consistent ways across the two years so that our classifications were highly comparable.

We used the race variable to identify blacks. We used the place-of-birth and the Spanish-origin variables for Mexicans. Unlike the 1990 data, the 1980 Spanish-origin variable does not differentiate Central Americans from other Hispanic groups; therefore, for both years, in addition to the place of birth we used the first- and second-ancestry data to identify Central Americans. For Middle Easterners and Anglo whites we used the same variables as for Central Americans. In order to identify the six major Asian groups, we used the race and the place-of-birth data.

INTERMARRIAGE RATES

Raw rates of intermarriage do not tell the whole story of intermarriage, since those rates do not take into account the relative size of the available pool of same-group versus other-group mates. To compensate, we adopted—with some minor modifications—the approach used by Lieberson and Waters.[2] We computed the following figures:

- Women In-married: Percentage of native-born or foreign-born married women in a particular group married to males of the same group.

- All group husbands: Percentage of all married men who are of the same group.

- In:Out odds—group: The ratio of in-marriages to out-marriages among women of the same group.

$$\text{In:Out odds–group} = \frac{\text{\# group females married in}}{\text{\# group females married out}}$$

- In:Out odds—others: The ratio of nongroup females married to group versus nongroup males.

$$\text{In:Out odds–others} = \frac{\text{\# nongroup females married to group males}}{\text{\# nongroup females married to nongroup males}}$$

- $\text{Odds ratio} = \dfrac{\text{Odds of a group female marrying a group male}}{\text{Odds of a nongroup female marrying a group male}}$

The odds ratio is the final result and the most important number in the table. If females choose marriage partners randomly with respect to group composition, then the ratio between these odds will be 1.0. The more the ratio exceeds (or is less than) 1.0, the greater (or smaller) the relative propensity of group members to in-marry.

Our departures from Lieberson and Waters are as follows. First, they report intermarriage rates for first marriages, whereas we report for the currently married, regardless of number of marriages. Second, in order to capture differences in intermarriage rates among the native-born and the foreign-born, we conducted separate analyses for native-born and foreign-born women but included in each analysis all married men, regardless of their nativity. In keeping with this procedure, we counted a marriage to a foreign-born male of the same group as an in-marriage.

INDEX OF DISSIMILARITY (D)

The index of dissimilarity (D) is most commonly used in studies of residential segregation, but we also use it to describe the degree of difference between the occupational and industrial distributions of the groups we study. First, we must note that D is a dyadic index; that is, it compares only two groups at a time, such as whites versus blacks or Chinese versus Koreans. Second, in order to calculate D, we must first divide the population up into a set of meaningful units, whether those be occupations or industries, census tracts (encompassing thousands of people), or census blocks (including hundreds of people). Let us assume we are talking about census tracts, for the moment. The index is calculated by comparing the group composition of each tract against the composition of the region as a whole. If the composition of each tract is identical to that of the region, then D will equal 0, its minimum value. If each tract includes members of only one or another group, then the region is completely segregated, and D will equal 1, its maximum value. If D takes on an intermediate value, say 0.55, this tells us that 55 percent of the two groups would need to exchange places across the tracts in order to make their distributions identical and bring D down to zero.

How we go about choosing our unit of analysis makes a big difference in the calculated value of D. Since residential segregation generally takes place at the neighborhood level, we might like to use neighborhoods as our unit of analysis. Unfortunately, census tracts are usually bigger than neighborhoods, and it is often the case that neighborhoods are split between two or more tracts. If a black and a white neighborhood, each of them completely segregated, are included in a single tract, the composition of the whole tract will falsely tell us that this area is well integrated. Alternatively, we can use the smaller census block as our unit of analysis. In this case, each block of each of these segregated neighborhoods will be counted as segregated. Using these smaller units means that we are unlikely to understate segregation, but relative to the composition of the entire neighborhood, we may overstate it instead. In this book, we use tract-level statistics, since these are the most commonly used elsewhere.

Our use of D to compare occupational and industrial distributions parallels Lieberson's.[3] It is worth noting that because of the tendency for ethnic groups to cluster in specific industries and occupations, smaller groups tend to be represented in fewer industries than larger groups. This means that smaller groups will normally be less like each other than larger groups will. Also, it is generally understood that women are confined to many fewer occupations than men and that the occupational distributions of men versus women within the same group are likely to be more different from each other than from other groups' men or women, respectively. We decided, however, that treating men and women together within each group better suited our purposes than disaggregating them would have.

EXPOSURE/ISOLATION INDEX (P*)

The exposure index (P*) measures how likely members of a subject group are to be exposed to members of a target group. It can be used anywhere D is used, but in this book we use it only to describe the likelihood of residential contact. This measure, like D, is dyadic and varies between 0—no likelihood of contact—and 1—certainty of contact. Unlike D, P* depends on the relative numbers of each group. As a result, P* is not symmetrical. It is easy to see that if the subject group is 35 percent of the population and the target group is 65 percent, subject group members are more likely to encounter target group members than vice versa. P* looks at the composition of each census tract and weights the likelihood of subject group exposure to the target group by the proportion of the subject group living in that tract. Thus, for example, if some subject group members live in areas where they have a high degree of contact with the target group but most live in areas where they have a low degree of contact, P* is going to be relatively low.

INDUSTRIAL AND OCCUPATIONAL NICHES

An industrial (or occupational) ethnic niche is an industry (or an occupation) in which members of an ethnic group are concentrated. For each ethnic group in each industry (or occupation), we calculated an index of representation (RI), which is simply a group's proportion of industry employment divided by group's proportion of total employment. An RI of 1.0 means that the group is "at parity," an RI of less than 1.0 means that they are underrepresented, and an RI of greater than 1.0 indicates overrepresentation. We operationalized ethnic niches as industries in which the

RI is at least 1.5 (that is, industries in which the group is overrepresented by 50 percent or more). If an industry has both public and private components, we treated each component separately. Furthermore, no industries employing fewer than one thousand persons are regarded as niches, since a niche in a very small industry is unlikely to have a large impact on a group, and proportions in very small industries are not likely to be reliable.

Mathematically the index of representation is written as:

RI = (EthInd/IndCnt) / (EthCnt/TotCnt), where:

RI = Index of representation
EthInd = # group in industry
IndCnt = # all in industry
EthCnt = # group employed
TotCnt = # all employed

These ratios were computed for all employed individuals, aged 25–64 years.

EARNINGS REGRESSIONS

In order to assess how groups differ in their levels of and returns to human capital, we used earnings regressions to compare the actual and adjusted earnings of ethnic groups to native whites—the reference group—in 1980 and 1990.[4] We conducted separate regressions for 25–64-year-old employed males and females, native-born and foreign-born. For foreign-born, in order to minimize cohort effects and avoid some of the complications of treating period of arrival as an independent variable, we conducted separate regression analyses for each period (1980–90, 1970–79, 1960–69, and before 1960). In our regressions we controlled for the following variables:

Education in years (YRSED)
Experience = AGE – YRSED – 6
Experience squared
English Ability, dummy coded:
    ENGGOOD = 1, if native speaker or speaks English very well
    ENGFAIR = 1, if speaks English well
    REFERENCE CATEGORY = speaks English poorly or not at all
Married (versus not) = married and spouse present
Healthy (versus not) = no disability limiting the ability to work
Child (for females only) = number of children ever born
Full Time = worked at least 35 hours during the previous week

Weeks Worked = number of weeks worked during the previous year
Sector, dummy coded:
  PRIVATE = 1, if currently works in the private sector
  PUBLIC = 1, if currently works in the public sector
  REFERENCE CATEGORY = self-employed workers.

INCOME AND EARNINGS DISTRIBUTION

Sometimes we would like to use a single statistic in comparing groups, such as when we talk about how the average income of white families is lower than that of Asian families and both are higher than the average for black or Latino families. Single statistics, however, especially averages, can be very misleading; they tell us nothing about the range of (in this example) incomes within the group, nor about how equal or even the distribution of income is.

In order to look at how income is distributed within groups, how that distribution changes over time, and how distributions differ between groups, we have created a set of tables in which we divide the distribution of group income into five rank-ordered parts. We started by taking the distribution of income among all families in the region in 1970 and dividing it into five equal parts, or quintiles. In other words, we divided the distribution up so that the 20 percent of families with the lowest incomes were placed in the bottom quintile, the 20 percent with the highest incomes were placed in the top quintile, and so on.

Rather than calculating quintiles for each group and each year, we took the dollar cutoffs between quintiles for the entire population in 1970 and applied them across groups and (after adjusting for inflation) across years. Having this single set of cutoffs, we can easily compare the distribution of incomes across groups or within a group over time. Most interesting are the top, bottom, and middle quintiles; the percentage of group families at the top is a measure of group well-being, the percentage of families at the bottom is a measure of deprivation, and the percentage in the middle is a guide to the degree of within-group income polarization. Tables for individual earnings were created in precisely the same way as for family income.

Notes to Appendix

1. For some of the difficulties in classifying Hispanics, see José Hernández, Leo Estrada, and David Alvírez, "Census Data and the Problem of Conceptually Defining the Mexican American Population," *Social Science Quarterly* 53 (1973): 671–87.

2. Stanley Lieberson and Mary C. Waters, *From Many Strands* (New York: Russell Sage Foundation, 1988), table 6.1.

3. Stanley Lieberson, *A Piece of the Pie* (Berkeley and Los Angeles: University of California Press, 1980).

4. "Actual earnings" refers merely to the group mean. The "adjusted earnings" figure is an estimate of how much a group member would earn if he or she had the characteristics of the average male or female reference group member. This was calculated by regressing earnings on measurable characteristics of the group, such as age, educational attainment, and disability status, multiplying the group's regression coefficients by the independent variable means for the reference group.

Index